"I have observed from a distance my friends Joe and Cindi Ferrini as they have embraced with grace, wisdom and even with joy the challenges of caring for a son with special needs, and aging parents needing care. I have no doubt that others facing the same kinds of challenges will learn much from what Joe and Cindi share in this book."

Bob Lepine
Co-Host of FamilyLife Today

"Joe and Cindi Ferrini show us how to face life's Unexpected Journeys with grace and strength. The story of their own journey is refreshingly honest and the lessons they share with us are both practical and profound. This book is indispensable for anyone caring for a loved one with special needs."

Tim and Joy Downs
Authors of *Fight Fair* and *The Seven Conflicts*

"In their book, *Unexpected Journey*, you are convinced that Joe and Cindi are among God's choice servants entrusted with a special life assignment, caregivers to their beloved special needs son and their parents through illness and aging. Their story, and the stories of others, permits us to peek into the highs and lows of the marathon journey of love and care they embrace."

Crawford and Karen Loritts
Senior Pastor/FamilyLife Conference Speakers

"We loved this wonderful book! Joe and Cindi have opened up their hearts and lives by sharing their journey of weathering the storms of life as a special needs family and how they overcame the statistics of isolation by being undergirded by extreme FAITH, HOPE and LOVE! Your life will be changed from hearing from a family that is living-proof that with the right LIFE-CHANGING perspective and a plan, you too can defeat the odds!"

Dr. Gary and Barbara Rosberg
America's Family Coaches, Award winning Authors,
National Syndicated Radio Co-Hosts, and writers of *The Great Marriage Experience*

"It is an unexpected journey filled with laughter and tears, joy and heartache, promise and discouragement. If we met I could listen to you, love you and pray for you but I really wouldn't understand because I have never been where you are at. Joe and Cindi Ferrini have been there and this book will encourage, inspire, enlighten and help you to take the next step. The Ferrini's would like to walk with you on your unexpected journey. This book will help you and I am happy to recommend it."

Greg Speck
Yr   University,
Author of *Sex, It's Worth Waitin*'   itual High

Unexpected Journey

When Special Needs Change Our Course

◆

Joe and Cindi Ferrini

◆

© 2009

Editor: Linda Meixner, Cleveland, OH
Cover Design: Premier Designs, Cleveland, OH
Page Composition: Premier Designs, Cleveland, OH
Cover Photo: Courtesy of www.istockphoto.com

Scripture quotations taken from the New American Standard Bible®, unless otherwise noted.
Copyright © 1960, 1962, 1963, 1968, 1971, 1972, 1973, 1975, 1977, 1995
by The Lockman Foundation (www.Lockman.org)
Used by permission.

Library of Congress Control Number: 2008911322

ISBN: 978-0-9677612-2-0

Joe and Cindi Ferrini
Unexpected Journey: When Special Needs Change Our Course
PO Box 360279
Cleveland, OH 44136-0005
www.joeferrini.com
www.cindiferrini.com

Printed in the United States by
Morris Publishing
3212 E. Highway 30
Kearney, NE 68847
1-800-650-7888

We dedicate this book to those who have accepted the challenges of their special journey, who have weathered the storms when life got tough-er, who have taken the detours and changes life gave them, and through it have loved all-ways.

Preface

Writing this book was not necessarily something we thought we'd do. After all, we've lived it once; we didn't want to go through it all again. The first time was hard enough!

We saw a need for a book "out there" to address the needs of those caring for anyone with special needs. As we speak around the country and share parts of our story, people tell us they've been looking for help and hope in the midst of a situation that is never-ending and always demanding. People we meet express the frustration that other people in their lives (family, friends, coworkers) simply don't "get" what they are dealing with. We've been there and certainly understand.

While on the phone with a long-time friend and in the midst of getting our special needs son ready for his shower, our friend said, "Oh, you have to help Joey shower?" This friend of over twenty-five years was surprised at our role and responsibilities. It wasn't her fault. We seldom talked about it because most people (and I'm not saying this of our friend) don't care. They see us do what we do and figure it's really no big deal because we "make it look easy." The truth is that it's not easy; it takes every ounce of energy, patience, and endurance we are given. It's demanding and grueling and often thankless. But our friend asked the right question to get us rolling on this book.

Sharing with others what we are going through is like visiting the Grand Canyon. We've been there, and we can tell others what we saw, the vastness of the expanse, the beauty of the colors in the rock formations, fabulous sunrises or sunsets, and the grandeur. But unless others experience it as we have, they will likely never quite get the view. A photo gives an idea of what the Grand Canyon looks like, but unless they've walked in our shoes, stood on the edge of the wide-open space, and taken in how "big" it is, they can't experience it. Neither a picture nor conversation can capture the ten-mile width, 277-mile length or one-mile depth. Only experiencing the adventure will allow others to know what it's really like. If they were to say to us, "So, what's the big deal? It's just a big hole in the ground!" that would be insulting. We've just experienced a place that is like no other, and to summarize it away in a simple statement does it no justice.

We hope to give the reader a glimpse into the lives of those who give full-time care to others who need special care and attention. We hope to give the full-time caregiver some hope for the long journey. We are talking about those who sacrifice their lives to care for others, the self-sacrificing caregiver, not getting paid to do this job. And, we appreciate the hardworking caregivers who are paid for doing this difficult work, making our load lighter.

We all face daily challenges: Some people are challenged by algebra, some by finances, and others by relationship issues to name a few. But all caregivers face similar challenges. This book addresses the challenges they encounter every day (yes, every day) as they give up their dreams, their free time, and sometimes relationships and careers in order to care for another.

This book is not something younger caregivers could write. They've not put in the kind of hours in this type of life experience to see the results of their labor of love, and they are simply too much in the thick of it (and sick of it) to be able to find the time to do so. So that is why we're doing it. We've run the course of caring for a son with special needs who is now an adult, cared for parents with special needs in their elder years, and we're here to say, "You *can* make it!"

Having read reviews of other books written within the special needs community, we found that readers had difficulty finding a book that had "the answers." It's true that *one* book won't give everyone all the answers. It's also true that no book will give any one of us what we want—a cure so that the person we are caring for can live a healthy, happy life. No single book will work for each of us because every special needs person is different from the next, and every caregiver, family, school, medical facility, community, church, and circle of friends and support is as different as the one being cared for.

One commentary we read summarized a book on special needs by saying that the best the author had to offer was that people with disabilities are just like anyone else and caring for them involves the same challenges we all have. Ouch! If you are a full-time caregiver, you know your life is different from everyone else's simply because the loved one you care for is so different from everyone else in your life. In addition, trying to "do it all" can put the caregiver at great risk for health problems, compromising the level of care she or he can then provide. We hope the author and reviewer reads *this* book.

For that reason, we have chosen not to write a technical work but to touch the heart with hope, not to give medical or legal advice but to help shape the thinking process when it comes to various issues and to be informative, practical, helpful, and hopeful by reaching all readers right where they stand.

If you are looking for a cure or an answer to change everything at once (or at all), this book isn't for you. If you need to be encouraged for today and to make it until tomorrow and maybe get a few ideas to help lighten your load for the long haul of the journey, then this will be just what you need. If you've been wishing you could share what you deal with on a day-to-day basis with others, then this is the book you'll want them to read. We want to help you gain a healthy perspective that will allow you to go the distance when the distance cannot be marked or calculated. It's not a sprint but a marathon with no end and no medal. We hope you'll share it with others when you feel you can't articulate what you are going through. We know we couldn't verbalize some things to family or friends, but we have said them here, so others will, we hope, understand the frustrations as well as the joys of caring for people with special needs.

Each chapter begins with several scenarios to start you thinking, followed by our story, and ending with raw, real-life examples that wonderful people shared from their hearts. All names have been changed (except for the members of our immediate family) to protect the identities of the contributors who shared comments of a very personal nature. We thank all who contributed to the section **Others' Stories** (round bullet points), sharing their pain, joy, struggles, frustrations, and triumphs with honesty and transparency. We know each comment will help others in their own personal journey.

If you are one who has never cared for someone with special needs, you might be challenged to offer help occasionally. Be careful. This could be dangerous reading. We might see some changed lives along the way! (When you see check marks, those are ideas for you to think about.)

We've written in small segments because they were often all we had—and it's the only way someone caring full time for another person will be able to read it—in small segments.

At the risk of overlooking even one person who has meant so much to our family, we have shared examples where you might find yourself unnamed. You know who you are, and you are very special to us! Each of you has been the how when we've asked why.

We've come to realize that normal or typical simply does not exist for us. Our specific journey has taken on many facets of color and design in order for us to experience all there is to this life. Normal is only a matter of perspective, and when caring for someone with special needs, our normal looks different from other people's normal. Once we get into our normal, well, it becomes normal to us! May we all be patient until we find what normal looks like in our individual lives.

Table of Contents

Introduction

When the bright ten-year-old little girl came in for her piano lesson, the teacher wondered why she wasn't able to master the skill of playing. Months into lessons, the teacher realized the little girl had been practicing on a stiff cardboard facsimile of piano keys.

Without hearing the sound of real music and without feeling the pressure of her fingers on the keys as the sounds were made, she was unable to understand and comprehend fully what it would take to master the skill of playing even the simplest pieces. No matter how much she loved music, she would not be able to play it without the basic instrument.

With like frustration, we were given a child with special needs to care for, and we love him immensely; but we did not know the first thing about mastering the skill of caring for him in a way that would allow him to flourish. We didn't know what he needed or what we needed. It took us some time to wake up to the needs we had, and we had many! We began the long search for the right individuals (and many were needed) to teach us and help us in our journey. We needed people who had studied for years in helping and teaching others to come alongside us and teach us what they knew. Like going from a cardboard template to a real piano, we were in unfamiliar territory.

According to familycaregiving101.org some fifty million people in the United States care for loved ones over eighteen with special needs, and approximately ten million more do the same for those under eighteen. Some have Alzheimer's disease (two of our parents did), some Parkinson's. Some are in state facilities because they cannot be cared for at home, some have muscular dystrophy. Some can't talk, can't hear, or can't walk. Some have a mental illness, but each reflects a situation that interferes with their ability to participate intellectually in comprehension and communication or in relationships. Sometimes you can see it - sometimes it's hidden.

We have met many caregivers. One of them might be you. As we have spoken around the country for a variety of different ministries, we have shared **Our Story** of our special needs son and our caring for our parents before their deaths. We have listened and learned from **Others' Stories**. For those from whom we've not had the privilege of hearing and learning, we hope you'll have a chance to tell **Your Story** and sometime share it with us. We've chosen to write thirteen chapters so this book can be studied in an Adult Bible Study (set for a quarter-13 week study) or in a group study with others with whom you identify. Use the questions at the end of each chapter to conduct your self-examination and group discussion.

This book is about the stories we all have to share with hope that others will want to listen and learn, too. If you don't have a story to share now, hold on! You will, and maybe someone's story from this writing will help prepare you! We've had the opportunity to air our frustrations, share our hearts, open people's eyes, share our hopes, victories, and failures, express unfulfilled dreams, encourage others, and recognize the value and worth of each person's life. Maybe along the way the hearts of some will be touched to pray, offer to help, console, ease someone through final days, learn to understand what our days and lives really look like, become a good listener when our hearts are breaking and we are at wits end, go into a caregiving profession to make a difference in the lives of others, or someday care for their own loved ones with hope from those who have shared their experiences here, and for the glory of God.

We appreciate each contributor, reader, caregiver and friend, knowing that you are special to Him and special to us. May we all share together in the joy of the journey.

Starting Out

"SPECIAL NEEDS" are two words that conjure up countless thoughts and emotions.

Webster defines *special* as "uncommon, noteworthy, particularly favored, individual, unique, extra, additional, confined to or designated for a definite field of action, purpose, or occasion." He defines *needs* as "obligation, a lack of something requisite, desirable, or useful; a condition requiring supply or relief; to be in want or under obligation." One step further requires us to find out what Mr. Webster defines as *disabled* because some challenge whether particular *factors* render a person disabled. So for the sake of discussion, and all being on the same page, we'll go with Webster's definition, "incapacitated by illness, injury, or wounds; physically or mentally impaired."

We invite you to visit *Joni and Friends*, a website sharing a Disability Information and Statistics page, defining *a person with a disability* as "an individual who has a physical or mental impairment that substantially limits one or more major life activities, a record of such an impairment, or is regarded as having such an impairment." The population of the USA includes 54 million people (20.6%) living with some level of disability and 26 million with a severe disability. Some 9 million are disabled to the point of needing personal assistance for everyday activities; 1.6 million use wheelchairs, 4.8 million use canes, 1.8 million use walkers, 4.2 million use hearing aides, and 1.7 million use back braces. Of those with disabilities 6.1% are under 18, 6.9% are between the ages of 18 and 24, 14.1% are between ages 25 and 54, 28.4% between 55 and 64. The likelihood of experiencing a disability increases with age - 38% over 65, and 56% over 85. Some 19 million people who were defined as severely disabled do not use a wheelchair, cane, crutches, or walkers. In other words, 73% of Americans with severe disabilities do not use such devices; therefore, a disability cannot be determined solely on whether or not a person uses visible assistive equipment. (Resources on our website will link you to other sites for statistics as well as varying disabilities, mentioned below or not.)

These special needs include those factors that challenge people in their ability to communicate, to think, to move, hindering them from being able to participate normally in learning, basic day-to-day life, and relationship skills. Some special needs are noticeable at birth, some come as a result of a tragic accident, others take time to come into view, and still others in later years result in decreasing reasoning skills accompanying disease and illness. Each disability is different, yet many manifest themselves in like behaviors and mannerisms. The list is long: attention deficit disorder (ADD), attention deficit/hyperactivity disorder (ADHA), dementia, developmental delays, severe allergies, Alzheimer's disease, amyotrophic lateral sclerosis (ALS), asthma, autism, behavioral issues related to brain injury or birth defects (brain and spinal injury, brain malformations, brain damage, brain disease), BPD (borderline personality disorder now called emotional-impulse regulation disorder or ERD), cerebral palsy, fine motor skills, learning disabilities, premature birth, eating disorders, epileptic seizures, language and speech disorders, mental illnesses, mental retardation, obsessive–compulsive disorder (OCD), oppositional defiant disorder (ODD), oral motor/feeding problems, orthopedic disabilities, sensory integration and motor impairments, speech impairments, spinal cord injuries, spina bifida, traumatic brain injury/head trauma, vision and hearing impairments, including total blindness and deafness, chromosomal abnormalities, birth defects, and cleft palate are only a few off the top of our heads. The list goes on and on and on. The various levels and degrees of each disability or serious health issues with long-term repercussions make the list even longer. Some have several of the listed disabilities, yet the people represented in the previous list (and the disabilities not mentioned) all look for hope and healing in the midst of how each special need reveals itself.

List below those issues that are a part of your life right now or in the past—in your own life or the life of another with whom you are close:

_____

_____

_____

Special needs, as Webster defines them, can be caused by a difficult birth, illness, injury, or wounds. Based upon what you listed above, what caused the situation or issue that challenges you in your life or in the life of someone you have observed:

_____

_____

_____

So Who Needs The Attention?

Special needs—these words have been spoken over and over in our home. Although our son has special needs that have required most of our attention in a "special" way since 1981, we have also added to that loving responsibility our parents (yes, all four of them), whose health issues required special care for varying periods of time. Those needs included caring for them through cancer and all its disabling affects, Alzheimer's, dementia, mini-strokes, brain aneurysm, massive heart attack, and the therapies necessary to help them regain whatever function was possible. For those counting ailments, we really did have just four parents between us. But in the process, guess what!? We discovered we had some special needs, too!

If you are a caregiver, we hope you are smiling. That means there is hope! You may have even read that opening paragraph saying, "What about me? I have special needs, too!!!" Go ahead. Be honest because if you aren't, this book won't really be of any help or value to you. You see, we need to be honest. We need to say, "I'm losing it" or "I can't take it any more" or "I'm so tired, frustrated, and weary, I don't know if I can say I LOVE my loved one anymore (at least today)!" OK, do you feel better now? Did you say, "YES! That's EXACTLY how I feel"? And did you say it in your heart for only God to hear or did you yell it out loud? The answer is important. After all, we wouldn't want anyone to think we couldn't handle the heavy load. The less said the better then, right?

Sure, I can handle it. Sign me up!

As Christians whose child has special needs, parents with Alzheimer's or other challenges, we wanted others to see that God chose the right people for the job because we have a good attitude and right heart. But the facade of the positive attitude and the look that says we "have it all together" or comments like "You sure handle everything so well" and other countless misapplied phrases of which we've lost count set us up for total failure. The best one—we can't resist—is "God must have thought you were very special to handle this challenge because I just couldn't handle it." If you haven't screamed yet, you probably did JUST NOW! We'll address that one later, but for now—

If you're tired, frustrated, and weary, you probably said faintly through tears, "Yes, that's it. I'm at the end of my rope." Well, my friend, we've been there. And unfortunately, we know we'll be there again. We are here to share with you our challenges, struggles, and joys in the midst of some thoughts and ideas that have helped us not GET OVER IT but GET THROUGH IT!

If you knew how long it took for us to get to the writing of this book, you'd know how much we truly understand that **you'll** have trouble getting to read it!

We've kept it in short segments because we know that's how you'll have to read it. We know—we **really** know! We've been there, oh, by the way—we're still there! So get ready for the ride! Here we go!

OUR STORY

We were married in 1979 with the hopes that we would someday have children. We had hopes and dreams of what our children might do, vacation and travel thoughts, retirement wishes. The initial plan was for Cindi to leave teaching high school home economics after five years, which is when our first child Joey was born. Joe had just set up his solo practice in general dentistry, and after a few years business was looking as if it could make us a one-income family. We were on target! We had no debt except for a home and the remainder of his practice. We were paying bills, serving in the church, mentoring and discipling people, enjoying lots of free time with family and friends. Life was good. Actually, life was great.

Then—life happened. And as we have come to find out, when "life" happens, it usually has a twin. That twin is the "opportunity" to look up. After all, when you're as low as you can be, there is no place else to look but up to God. Each of us will experience our share of hardship, crisis, and disappointment in this life. Many of us will experience more of these "opportunities" than we had hoped! But we have to recognize that each of those experiences is relative to other experiences. Some people, even in similar situations, will have it easier than we do. Some will have it harder. No matter where we find ourselves, we know this: God's hand has a purpose in every situation—and ours was no mistake. Neither was yours. In Psalm 138:8, the Scripture says, "The Lord will accomplish

God uses our lack of faith to expose our weaknesses and deficiencies. We show our greatest strength in the way we trust in the One who sends the trials to our lives.

what concerns me." This passage has been our anthem. We know He loves us so much that nothing will come into our lives without His wanting us to have it, endure it, live in it, and love through it. And when times get rough, we remember Psalm 57:2—"I will cry to God Most High, to God who accomplishes all things for me." God has given us what we need. When we are done questioning Him, questioning ourselves, and crying out to Him, we can rest in knowing that He has a purpose in everything that comes into our lives. And we will likely question more. We think doing so is helpful. When we question and He answers, we draw closer to the One who loves us dearly. God uses our lack of faith to expose our weaknesses and deficiencies. We show our greatest strength in the way we trust in the One who sends the trials to our lives.

We will interweave our story throughout the book, but we give others the opportunity to share their stories as well, and YOU will have an opportunity to share your story, too.

OTHERS' STORIES

- I often feel at the end of my rope at the end of the day. I would love a resource that could help me see that what I'm feeling is normal and yet give me hope for the future. Caring full time for another person, doing the same thing for them that I do for myself (and more sometimes) is draining.

- I sometimes wonder whether there is a purpose in my day-to-day life of caring for another person. Some days I think, "Wow, I really had it together today." And other times I want to scream and run away from it all.

- Watching my sister and her family take care of an adult with special needs is inspiring to me. I see what they do as the ultimate sacrifice of loving another person.

- For some years I've watched from a distance a family care for someone in a wheelchair. I don't know what the disability is, but he is always well cared for and the family never seems to get frustrated or upset. It is amazing to me.

- My survey sat dutifully in my "to do" folder for about five months. Had I known what these months were going to be like (lots of doctors visits and challenges) I would have simply smiled, sincerely apologized, and not accepted it. Finally, here it is!

YOUR STORY

When was the beginning of the challenge that you are presently experiencing or watching someone else experience?

_____

_____

_____

How are you feeling right now? Are you in a nice place of calm, having weathered some of the storm, or are you in the midst of that storm? Describe it.

_____

_____

_____

If you are an "on-looker" to someone who is experiencing the frustration and heartache of caring for someone with special needs, what are you seeing in that person? Do you see their frustration or do they look as if they have it all together?

_____

_____

_____

_____

Are they carrying on "just fine" (or so you think) or do they look as if they are ready to explode with all the responsibility!?

_____

_____

_____

Are you carrying any of the burden? If so, how? If not, are you willing?

_____

_____

_____

_____

HIGHWAY
101

CHAPTER ONE

The Journey Begins with Great Expectations

Matthew and Melissa eagerly awaited the birth of their first child. After thirty-five hours of labor and complications to Mom and baby, the future of this child was very uncertain. What they knew and what was stated in medical records is that brain damage to the child had occurred at birth. They would realize the extent only much later down the road.

....

Sal and Ginny were married many years and looked forward to retirement, when the devastating diagnosis hit Ginny. Life took them down a different road.

....

Single all her life, Katherine had many wonderful friends. She knew her elder years might be difficult with no "certain someone" to help care for her. As the years unfolded, so did many uncertainties, and many hopes and dreams vanished as did friends and family along the way. What was she to do when she was diagnosed with multiple sclerosis?

....

First Experiences

Cindi:

As a teenager my first experience meeting a person with special needs made me a bit uncomfortable. She was lovable and loving and a child in every way. This young gal, just a few years younger than me, wanted to sit by me and stroke my hair. Down syndrome was evident in her features and behavior, but for someone who had never been around anyone with special needs, I didn't always know what to do, how to act, or what to say. I was always kind to her but uncomfortable. I never asked her to move or go away, and because of that I think she liked being around me. I experienced her in different situations, watching her express different moods as quickly as a tornado touches down. She was very strong and nothing could stop her when she was angry, and it was frightening to me! She'd do her emotional or physical damage then return to life as "normal," ending the whirlwind as quickly as it started; but is life ever "normal" after the damage of a tornado? Doesn't something happen that changes things? Aren't there pieces to pick up, damage to repair, and things to change?

Joe:

Having finished my requirements for graduation early in my senior year at the Ohio State University School of Dentistry, I was given a menu of options and opportunities regarding where I could spend my discretionary free time. From that menu, I chose to work at University Hospital in Columbus, Ohio, doing dentistry for children with special needs.

We were taught in dental school to look into the eyes of our patients to be sure that they were experiencing no discomfort (okay, PAIN) as a result of the procedure. Providing dental care for children with special needs at University Hospital, I practiced looking into their eyes, making sure I caused no discomfort. As I looked into their eyes, I saw that those eyes were absolutely beautiful, even captivating. It wasn't just the color of their eyes, or the fact that some of them couldn't even focus their attention on something. It was just "that look." For most of them, the only communicating they could do was with their eyes. It was fascinating to me to watch their eyes while they were in my dental chair.

In my early years of dentistry, I worked at several nursing homes whose residents were children with special needs. Dealing with drooling patients with flailing arms, squealing with uncontrolled emotion, was very sobering. It was not only challenging from a dental perspective but emotionally as well. From the dental perspective, providing care was difficult, but even more difficult was dealing with their overall needs from an emotional perspective. Talking about my daily experiences at these nursing homes with Cindi was difficult; I choked up at the very thought that I really could not help these children. Sure, I could clean their teeth, but these children could not take care of themselves, let alone ask for a need to be met. Sadly, even the well-intentioned caregivers could not care for the patients' dental needs adequately. I was always thankful to be able to come home where things were calm and "normal."

Great Expectations

Dreams, hopes for the future—we all have them and anticipate with great expectations that those words will be fulfilled in a positive way. Sometimes we even put down on paper what we think the future will look like. Goals, dreams, aspirations, things we want, and even things we don't want, things we will take the time to invest in, and things we won't, dreams of the person we hope to marry, hopes of a family and retirement. We all have our list.

OUR STORY

Our world celebrates those who are bright, capable, able, beautiful, charming, and contributing members of society. And why wouldn't we all want that for our very own children?

Cindi:

In a journal I started for our firstborn, I wrote:

> **December 24, 1980:** *Our little Ferrini is already receiving gifts. Dad has plans for a boy, I can tell. Baseball, bat, mitt—but they all squeak! For Dad's sake, I hope it's a boy!*

> **January 1, 1981:** *It's a joy to know that I am carrying a child that is a gift from God. (Ps. 127:3-5)*

> *Ps. 119:73 says, "Thy hands made me and fashioned me; give me understanding, that I may learn Thy commandments." To begin to think that our lives will be used in God's plan for bringing lives to Him eternally is a wonderfully awesome role. As our baby is developing emotionally and physically, I pray we are consistent in our efforts to help him or her develop spiritually.*

> **February 7, 1981:** *The first visit to the doctor was a good one. He said all seems to be just fine.*

> **April 5, 1981:** *I keep praying that our little Ferrini will be as healthy as it appears to be now.*

Although I never wrote it in the journal, I had secretly hoped for a girl. When people would say, "Do you hope for a boy or a girl?" I would say, "I will be happy with whatever God gives us." And you know the next question others would ask, "Well, as long as it's healthy, right?" Now, I ask you, how is a pregnant mother or anyone supposed to respond to that question or comment?

"Right, of course, I mean if the child isn't healthy, I'll just turn it in for a better model. One that's not broken. If the child is defective I'll offer it to someone in the hospital nursery as a trade-in. I don't care—I'm up for an unhealthy child that I can take care of for the rest of my life." Or how about this one, "Oh, I can handle an unhealthy child. God will give me what I need and I'll do fine."

We'll stop here! And later, we'll have responses for, "You must be a very special person for God to give you this challenge."

April 13, 1981: We haven't figured out if it will be a boxer or gymnast! Joe was delighted to feel the baby move so strongly!

But somewhere in the midst of doctor appointments, helping Joe at the office, taking some little vacations, having fun with family and friends, setting up a nursery, and teaching my fifth and final year at the high school, one tenth-grade student posed this question, "Mrs. Ferrini, if you KNEW your baby was going to have problems, wouldn't you have an abortion?"

I was stunned. Not at the question, but at what went through my mind. A strong impression came upon me that said, "Be careful how you answer, because there is a problem with the baby." I promptly dismissed that thought as one of my own fleeting thoughts, and answered as my heart believed, "No, I would not have an abortion. As a Christian (one of the many wonderful opportunities I had to share my faith with the kids I loved!), I believe all life is valuable. The Bible says in Psalm 139:13-15, 'For Thou didst form my inward parts; Thou didst weave me in my mother's womb; I will give thanks to Thee, for I am fearfully and wonderfully made; Wonderful are Thy works, and my soul knows it very well. My frame was not hidden from Thee, when I was made in secret.'" That prompted much discussion, much of which I don't remember, but I'm pretty sure I've lived it out over the years.

My pregnancy continued without complication. At some point between April and July, I sensed the Lord preparing me: "You are having a boy." I was very happy, not at all disappointed, having at first hoped for a girl. My thoughts turned from pink to blue, from ballet to sports. I was in good health with the exception of nausea those first three months. I continued to exercise, ate well, and did everything expected of me. I had no ultrasounds (they were not routine in the early 80s), no additional tests like the ones they do these days, the ones that put fear in most every "mom-to-be," indicating the chance their child will have _____ (you fill in the blank with the many stories you've been told or heard!). Based on my monthly check-ups, everything was going as hoped and right on schedule.

July 27, 1981: Today is the due date, but no signs as to the arrival.

A call from [my girlfriend] Bernie to check up on me [about 9:30 p.m.] was welcomed. Shortly after that, I thought I might have a bit of bloody show.

11:11 p.m., just before I could read through Philippians 4:13, the verse that claimed, "I can do all things through Christ who strengthens me," it happened! My water broke! (It was everywhere. How could I have ever wondered if I would know when or if that happened!?)

11:43 p.m. – first apparent contraction. It's funny to me now, but I remem-

ber asking people, "How will I know I'm in labor?"

11:54 p.m. – 1:41 a.m. contractions every 10 minutes

1:47– 1:59 a.m. contractions every 5 minutes

2:02 – 2:35 a.m. contractions every 3 minutes—going to hospital!

It was becoming a very long day. Many times I had quietly quoted the Scripture verse from Philippians 4:13, "I can do all things through Christ who strengthens me." He gave me strength to be a good patient. I didn't yell or scream or misbehave in any way. Except for nearly breaking Joe's fingers as I clutched his hand during one of the many very strong contractions, I was a good patient. (And believe me you know when you're in labor! That death grip is not an act of the will!) I was kind to the doctor, to the aides who were "learning" how to draw blood and took multiple tries, to the nurse who literally stabbed me with her needle when I finally asked for a pain reliever twelve plus hours into labor, to all the many nurses (as shifts changed) who had to examine me, to anyone who came into our room.

Joe:

Cindi was amazing throughout the entire birthing process. She was strong, and always kind to all who attended to her needs, even to the nurse who stabbed her with the needle. I have given thousands of injections to patients and that injection given to Cindi was unnecessarily brutal. But even so, Cindi said, "Thank you" just the same.

Having experienced firsthand the birthing process with Cindi, leading up to the emergency C-section required because Joey was "stuck" in the birth canal for many hours, I realized more than ever that I was married to an incredible and amazing woman. As a dentist I've had patients say to me that they would rather have a baby than come to the dentist, and some of these patients were men!! After observing the birthing process that Cindi went through, I can confidently say to these patients, "I DON'T THINK SO!!"

July 28, 1981:

2:30 p.m. – going for X-rays after some 14 hours of labor, we met one of Joe's patients in the elevator, a doctor on staff at the hospital. That was an awkward moment!

3:30 p.m. – My OB-GYN suggests a C-section to avoid possible serious damage to the baby. (I had been a great patient, but now knowing surgery was inevitable, I just wanted it over with!) The baby is in the anterior position.

4:51 p.m. – Joseph Philip Ferrini, Jr., was born after 18 hours of labor; scoring a 10 on the APCAR test. I think we have a genius!

Cindi:

I might not have said it aloud and didn't write it out as my heart was wishing it, but I hoped for a healthy, smart, strong baby. Simple. Oh, and if it was a boy, may he be athletic like his dad had been! Not a request out of the ordinary. OK, maybe genius was over the top, but if you've had children, I'll bet you prayed that, too!

For anyone who has experienced the birth of a child, having your own or watching childbirth on the Discovery Channel, you can't help but wonder, "How does any child escape injury coming through that birth canal or via surgery, without having some kind of special needs?" Many have said, "Watching the birth of a child is evidence there is a Creator!"

"For in Him all things were created, both in the heavens and on earth, visible and invisible, whether thrones or dominions or rulers or authorities—all things have been created through Him and for Him," Colossians 1:16.

The sheet covering me during surgery obstructed my view of everything taking place. As soon as I heard he was born, I asked the usual, "Does he have ten fingers and ten toes, and everything else he's supposed to have?" He did! Joey was beautiful and looked absolutely perfect. This is not just a new mother of her first child talking. He really was. Having been born via Caesarian section, his features were well in tact with the exception that his head was elongated. I assumed that was due to the many hours of labor and his efforts to come into this world naturally. The mop of gorgeous black hair, normal cry, good color, and not one blemish anywhere on his body, seemed to point toward a normal healthy baby. Later when I could hold him, he nursed well. He seemed to be all we had hoped for—or was he? It was just the shape of his head.

Joe:

As the doctor was removing Joey during the C-section procedure, the nurses in the room raised their eyes and stepped back when they saw Joey; almost as if they saw something they didn't want to see. I didn't think much about it at the time. Later, from the nursery, Joey was brought into the hospital room for Cindi to nurse him. A very sweet nurse caring for Joey wrapped him tightly in a blanket and placed him in his basinet. After she did that, she touched my arm and looked me straight in the eye with almost tears in her eyes and said, "God bless you as you care for this child." I thought at the time, "Well, that was a very nice thing to say to me!" But as I watched other dads come for their babies, those words were not shared with them. And I never heard those words when we had our daughters (even one who had a tough two weeks in NICU). Clearly, there was a stirring in my heart that something was not right. I never said anything to Cindi, writing my thoughts off as those of a new paranoid father who wanted only the very best for his son. Other than these two incidents, initial tests on Joey seemed fine, including his Apgar score of ten! (Given twice to a newborn—at one minute and five minutes after birth—**APGAR** stands for: Activity (activity and muscle tone), Pulse (heart rate), Grimace Response (reflex), Appearance (skin color), and Respiration (breathing rate and effort). A third test may be taken at ten minutes if there are concerns.)

I made sure Joey came home from the hospital wearing a Cleveland Indians baseball cap, a sleeper from the Ohio State University, and I placed a Cleveland Browns autographed football in the corner of his crib. As you can imagine, I had some pretty big dreams for my son. Playing catch with him someday was on the top of my wish list!

Where Expectations, Hopes, and Dreams Collide with Real LIFE!

All was not well. Things didn't go as planned. We didn't understand why Joey wasn't doing things the other kids were doing. We didn't understand why his head circumference was way over the top of the chart compared to others his age. He couldn't roll over or sit up when others his age were. No problem—he's like his dad, laid back, seldom in a hurry, well paced.

We didn't get it. Maybe we didn't want to. Maybe whatever was wrong would go away. It seemed that every moment held the anticipation that he'd do something, anything, yet nothing was happening.

Things weren't right. By three months of age, children should be able to lift their head and chest when lying on their stomach. Joey still couldn't lift his head or hold it up. The pediatrician expressed some concern but said we'd watch and see how he'd do over the next few appointments.

Joe:

About this time, I was becoming much more concerned about Joey. One night, about 3:00 a.m., Joey woke up. I told Cindi that I would get him and that she should just try to get some much needed sleep. I scooped him out of his crib as if I'd just made a great catch in football and brought him into the family room to play on the floor for a while. Hoping to tire him out, I rolled him gently

All was not well. Things didn't go as planned. We didn't understand why Joey wasn't doing things the other kids were doing.

back and forth, even gently rolling a ball to him, attempting "catch" with my infant son! As he began to open his eyes, I saw something that took me back to my experience at University Hospital with the special needs children in dental school. I knew that look. I picked Joey up and held him in my arms and said, "Oh God, not my son!"

I cried myself to sleep that night, not sharing my concerns with Cindi or anyone. I figured if what I saw was true, Cindi would eventually find out.

At ten months Joey was still not making normal developmental progress, so our pediatrician suggested we see a pediatric neurologist. He did the usual tapping of muscle reflex areas, measuring of his head, looking into his eyes, having Joey try to follow with his eyes as the doctor moved an object in his hand. That was hard for Joey. If he were "normal," it shouldn't have been. Children developing normally should do that at three months. Joey seemed to look around the room fine and even found places of interest to focus his attention, but following a moving object was tough. He could not roll over, sit up even with support, and crawling wasn't yet on his radar screen. Anyone who held him commented he was "loose" like a Raggedy Ann doll.

"Special"-ists

The neurologist said something about being "developmentally delayed, but he should be able to catch up to others down the road." He was diagnosed as hypotonic, meaning a lack of muscle tone. That diagnosis led us to believe the doctor was thinking maybe a few exercises and this therapy will get him where he needs to be to catch up. A little delay and playing some catch up seemed fine with us. Although we pushed him for more of a diagnosis, he remained pretty vague, so we did not panic. We were not seeing first words, first crawling steps, or any other milestones we should have been seeing. In the back of our minds—we were wondering.

"Special" Friends

Cindi:

Around that time Joey was turning one, I invited some friends, all of whom had children around Joey's age, to meet at my parents' place. We enjoyed a hot summer day, letting the kids run around their two acres of property and throw stones in the pond before settling down with a typical hot-dog kid-friendly lunch!

Well, it was a shocker to me. *All* of the other kids were running around, but Joey could barely sit up. Mom or I had to carry him wherever he needed to go. The other kids were easily picking up stones and tossing them through the air into the water. They could pick up their own hot dogs and feed themselves. Something wasn't right here. Joey couldn't do any of what I was observing. He could barely grasp the tiny stones. Mom or I handed the stones to him. He could toss the stones, but he didn't have the "form" of the other kids. We were still cutting up his hot dog into little pieces so he wouldn't choke on it. He seemed to move around fairly well in the walker, slouched against the back of the seat, moving his feet to get places; yet at twelve months, he was not doing what even a five-month-old usually does. He responded to his name and seemed to recognize those who were around him most, but he lacked in other areas, and the gap was growing bigger and bigger between what he should be able to do and what he could do, and this day made it much more obvious to me.

Sometime during that day, one dear friend, Betsy, whose son was actually younger than Joey but running circles around him, made it a point to quietly and privately "chat" with my mom. I don't know all that they discussed, but I know that she expressed her concern regarding Joey to my mom. I was very grateful for her concern and her prayers and took her and my mom's suggestion to get further help.

The doctor ordered a CAT scan. Joey was medicated and fell asleep in order to remain still enough for the image to be scanned clearly. It was found that Joey's brain was large, but there were no growths to cause any alarm. He then suggested therapy at a city hospital where Joey would get physical, occupational, and speech therapy.

We began learning things we were never trained to do. We never knew how many steps there were to learning how to crawl. We learned each step, one by one, and invested many hours teaching Joey these steps over and over and over and over and over and over until they were etched in that large brain and he could do it himself. Over and over meant not days but months. Many times we felt like the Wallendas, the great tight-rope walkers, trying to balance therapies, work, ministry, and life walking along a fine line, teetering from side to side, hoping not to tilt too much in one direction and fall off.

Cindi wrote in Joey's journal:

April, 1983 (20 months):

We pray for you every night (and a lot throughout the day). Although your skills are not where they could or should be, we know God is going to work in a very special way through you. We pray that you will let the Lord control and direct your every step, thought, word, etc., and that you'll be open to His will for you. He's going to use you to accomplish wonderful things for His glory.

The biggest thrill for Dad and me was that you stood up in the middle of the kitchen from a crawling position for the first time on the 25th. You kept doing it–about fifteen times. You were so pleased with your accomplishments!

May 1983 (21 months):

While Dad was downstairs praying with a friend about your motor development, my friend and I watched you stand up and take two steps. We were all praising the Lord! Then several days later you took eight steps, then nineteen, then twenty-nine steps in a row! (But who's counting?!) You're on your way!

"Special" Attention

One problem in the midst of learning how to walk was that Joey did not know how to catch himself when he fell. He could not comprehend that action. Walking behind him ready to catch him so he wouldn't topple over like a pillar was exhausting, requiring our attention most of our day because he could not be left unattended at any time. The exhaustion was coupled with the frustration of comments made by well-meaning people who intended to be helpful and instructive, comments such as "Just let him go. He'll learn how to fall" or "Quit babying him. He needs to learn by himself" or "If you keep doing **that** (babying him), you're not going to help him." Biting our lips to be gracious was often a challenge, knowing in our hearts that it **was** our desire for him to learn these things, but his brain was not letting him!

He began making sounds like "mama" and "papa" but were they words or only sounds? Did we really hear him say "Jesus" when we'd sing "Jesus Loves Me"? Whatever we really heard didn't matter; we were encouraged that he seemed to comprehend even though he could not properly respond!

Little did we know that becoming educated in various therapies to help our son would not be the full scope of our learning curve! We were beginning to understand Philippians 4:13 more than we had ever considered.

"Special" Plans

No matter what the speed or lack of his progress from the very beginning, no matter what our hopes and expectations were, this is what we both knew based upon our faith:

God knows each of us and He has a plan for us.

Psalm 127:3, "Behold, children are a gift of the Lord; the fruit of the womb is a reward."

Proverb 16:9a, "The mind of a man plans his way, but the Lord directs his steps."

Isaiah 44:24, "Thus says the Lord, your Redeemer, and the One who formed you from the womb, 'I the Lord, am the maker of all things.'"

OTHERS' STORIES

- We were excited to be called to serve as missionaries. Those plans quickly changed when we could not serve with our child, who is autistic. We had to come home, get him therapies, and hope someday to go back, but it doesn't look likely. If it doesn't happen, we will be at square one all over again pursuing what God has in store for us.

- We had a high-risk pregnancy for a multiple birth. One of the children suffered a brain hemorrhage at birth and had seventeen surgeries within the first two years of life.

- We wondered whether she would live a normal life, make it on her own, or marry.

- I need a resource that would help me understand if what I think and feel is normal in caring for my child with special needs.

I don't think he meant to be mean, but I cried all the way home, feeling the first rejection my child faced.

- (A doctor) A resource for parents that has practical advice about providing day to day care, and keeping their heads above water is so needed. They need to know it's OK to be angry, sad, disappointed, and all the other emotions that come, and then learning that God is big enough to handle their doubts and emotions. Someone who has gone this way before needs to help those who are just beginning the journey that is life-long.

- Getting the news that our life was changing forever, we felt like we were hit by a truck and things were not going to change.

- Having a special child brought a new normalcy in our family. If you didn't already know, "no one is really normal."

- My friend's parents were told that her sister might have Down syndrome and they could abort; but they chose not to. Her sister was born healthy and "normal."

- I question what "could have been."

- After an ultrasound, my doctor said, "You're gonna have a *special needs kid.*" I'm sure he just felt bad for what we or our child would go through—emotionally or even financially (prosthesis), but I felt as if he were saying, "Yuck or eww!" I don't think he meant to be mean, but I cried all the way home, feeling the first rejection my child faced.

- I've watched so many of my friends' children effortlessly develop, turning over on time, sitting up without months of therapy to do so, saying words early and conversing at three. I struggle when I see other moms with healthy babies after the months and months of therapy that yields results but ever so slowly.

YOUR STORY

At some point of every person's life, there will likely emerge a challenge/change/crisis—some special need that will require an adjustment in thinking and action. What are some situations that you might consider special needs? To help you out, here are some thoughts to get you started: Unborn child's health issues, autism, mental retardation, mental illness, debilitating arthritis, attention deficit disorder, attention deficit/hyperactivity disorder, Alzheimer's, long term illness, disabled war veteran, dementia, diabetes, chronic illness (chronic fatigue, Epstein-Barr), blindness, deafness, progressive or degenerative illnesses, etc. Please add to the list as many things as you can think of:

What would you consider a major challenge/change/crisis point in your life or in the life of someone you know and love (present, past or future)?

_____

_____

_____

_____

If you have experienced a major challenge/change/crisis, please share your initial great expectations of "life" and how they played out for you (your dreams, hopes, desires, etc.).

_____

_____

_____

If you are presently in a major challenge/change/crisis, please describe where you are in the midst of it right now.

_____

_____

_____

Has a previous challenge/change/crisis prepared you to deal with a current one?

_____

_____

_____

If you are going through a challenge/change/crisis, how can you describe the "pain" of this challenge/change/crisis that you are going through? Or that a loved one is going through?

_____

_____

_____

_____

What things are you noticing about yourself and how you are dealing with it?

_____

_____

_____

Have others offered to help?

_____

_____

_____

Are you willing to accept help if it were offered to you?

_____

_____

_____

Do you take the time to seek people who will listen to your heart when you are having a hard time?

_____

_____

_____

During this time, what questions are you asking yourself?

_____

_____

_____

What are you asking others? What are you asking God?

_____

_____

_____

If you haven't experienced a major challenge/change/crisis in life, do you think you're prepared for what might lay ahead?

_____

_____

_____

_____

CHAPTER TWO

Under Construction: Disappointment, Discouragement, and Death of a Vision

In 2007 the Alzheimer's Association (www.alzheimers.org) stated that five million people suffered from Alzheimer's with some ten million helping take care of them. A ten percent increase is estimated by 2012. With longer life expectancies, the Alzheimer's Association has estimated that by 2030 some 7.7 million will have the dreaded disease. The statistics also convey the burden that Alzheimer's imposes on individuals, families, state and federal governments, businesses, and the nation's healthcare system. Imagine the initial individual disappointment, the discouragement of family and friends as they witness changes and the inevitable death of what each person had hoped for in their future.

Many children with special needs could have been born "normal" but because of malpractice or unfortunate circumstances even under the care of the best doctors can have severe problems later on. In addition, consider the many children whose lives are affected because they have been in a car accident, fallen off their bike and received traumatic brain injury, or had a severe virus or high fever resulting in permanent change.

Life Changing

Ours is but one life-changing issue. We can't tackle them all as we write, but what is yours? Just for a moment we'd like you to put yourself in the place of someone who has just been diagnosed with Alzheimer's. What questions would you ask yourself before your mind is overtaken by the ravages of this disease? What would you ask yourself if you were going to be the caregiver to one who has just received this news? What dreams are changed for you? Is there disappointment? Is there frustration? Think about it for longer than a minute or two.

Close your eyes and the pages of this book and linger there. Only when you feel as if you might even have a *glimpse* of what that might look and feel like and what changes it will make in your everyday life can you open your eyes. OK, go for it!

Take a moment and write down your thoughts:

_____

_____

_____

_____

OUR STORY

Feeling discouraged about Joey's slow progress and the failure of the pediatric neurologist to attach a specific name to what was wrong, we decided to do a little research on our own. Because we didn't have the Internet to locate a diagnosis (which can be as helpful as it is dangerous), we checked out a book from the library, hiding it from the view of others as though we shouldn't be allowed to check it out. Based upon what we read in our research and comparing Joey's lack of development to what we read, we both suspected that Joey was mentally retarded with a degree of cerebral palsy. We didn't want to say "it" out loud so that others would hear us, but we wondered how many people in our lives could see "it" but were afraid to say "it" out loud to us. Betsy was the only one with the loving courage to challenge us to check things out further. So we did. Far less was available about the topic than we thought there would be; the book was actually from the 1950s! That was the most current information on what we suspected.

Reading the book, we saw Joey throughout the pages as a toddler to young adult. Of course, we wanted to deny "it," and we were angry that the neurologist had not told us the truth. We made an appointment to talk with our regular pediatrician because he had known Joey since birth and was helping us get the answers we were looking for. We sat down and told him we were not happy with the neurologist's vague diagnosis and wanted to "hear it like it was," asking him for his professional thoughts.

> *It was like being punched in the stomach. We were stunned, but we didn't cry. We were probably in shock because we didn't feel anything for a while.*

That is exactly what he did. He told us straight up, "I believe he has cerebral palsy, possibly with mental retardation." Before we could say the words, he said them. We had hoped not to hear "it," and "it" took our breath away. It was like being punched in the stomach. We were stunned, but we didn't cry. We were probably in shock because we didn't feel anything for a while.

We Were Hurting

We were numb and in great emotional pain. We were disappointed. We felt like we hit a dead end. Sometimes we were angry. There we were with a love so strong for each other and together for our son, yet we could not help each other, trying to tread water way over our heads in the sea of deep disappointment, the intense pain of raw emotions and the onset of discouragement with things not yet on our horizon. We suffered from the shock of what we had heard; it's called the "death of a vision." Our great expectations were not going to happen. Granted, maybe some of our expectations were a bit unrealistic, but we *never* thought "it" would happen to us; we never dreamed it could be true. Looking at Joey, we wondered but never thought it could happen to us this way.

We didn't wake up from some weird dream. It was "real life," and all of a sudden our world came crashing down. What happened to that "he'll catch up" phrase we heard? This is looking quite different! Instantly, life changed. Forever. Not just for the day or a week but for the rest of our lives. So many thoughts swirled around in our heads. So many questions surfaced. And so many emotions—anger, fear, worry, anger, doubt, questions, anger, more questions. It went on and on! But the bottom line was this: We wanted to be loved in our pain.

Are We Allowed to Doubt? Ask Questions?

In our state of numbness, we had so many unanswered questions. Each question eventually helped us work through our denial, anger, suspicions, the deals we'd make with God if He'd heal Joey, the "why's of our parents illnesses", the discouragement, and finally the acceptance. We suspect in whatever place you find yourself, if you have a challenge in your life, you will have asked or are asking the same questions we did and will answer throughout this work. Here is a "short list" of questions we asked:

- ✓ What was the cause? What went wrong?
- ✓ Was it something in the pregnancy?
- ✓ Was it the difficult and long labor? When did it happen?
- ✓ Did we cause it? Did God cause it? Or did He allow it?
- ✓ Were we being punished? Did we sin?
- ✓ Why me? Why us? Why Joey/our parents?

✓ Was Joey/were our parents being punished?

✓ Was this really, possibly God's will? How could it be?

✓ What does God say about the value/importance of life?

✓ If we pray hard and often enough will Joey/our parents be healed?

✓ If we go to more doctors will someone have a way to fix the problems?

✓ Can we have other healthy children?

✓ What will happen to Joey someday—when we die?

✓ Will we be able to afford all the care he'll need for now and the future?

✓ Will he be able to go to school?

✓ Did God know what He was doing sending Joey to us?

✓ Will these feelings of great loss, pain, sadness and grief ever subside? Will it ever lift and go away? How long are we allowed to grieve?

✓ What will this do to our marriage (caring for Joey/our parents)?

✓ What is Joey's potential? Will he able to be on his own or always with us?

✓ Why do we feel helpless when we are walking with and know the Lord?

✓ Can we trust Him for what we'll need? What will Joey need?

✓ Will our faith be shattered or grow deeper?

✓ Will we be able to run the race set before us, or crumble under the weight of this responsibility for a lifetime?

✓ Can we pray and make this problem go away?

✓ Will prayer be my last resort, like I feel it is now, or will I make it my first response?

✓ Will we be able to protect our son? Will we have help? Will we need help? Will there be people, organizations, schools, etc. to help or do it ourselves? Will there be the same helps for our parents when we have need to help them?

✓ Will we surrender THIS part of our lives or hold on to it in desperation?

✓ Will we be able to deal with guilty thoughts or relinquish those thoughts to the Lord?

✓ Will the frustration of caring of our child with his many needs go away, subside, or always remain?

The Roller Coaster Ride

Some people like roller coasters, but not everyone enjoys the ride! Some actually find it terrifying. We were on our own roller coaster, "hanging on" for dear life! And if you're in this place, you will likely feel the sting of trying to come to grips with these questions, too. Perhaps you have a few questions of your own to add to the list!

The dreams for the future—of enjoying sports or playing catch with Joey—those visions down the road we had anticipated faded into disappointment and grief. We were mourning, experiencing the death of a vision. We wanted to deny the reality of Joey's mental retardation and cerebral palsy, but he was always before us. There was no denying "it."

We went through, and to some extent, continue to go through the same grieving process people go through when a loved one dies. The difference is that with time, the memory and the sting of the death of that loved one continue to fade away by God's grace, and the memories of good times and positive thoughts replace the sting of death. But when you have the responsibility for the *daily* care of a person

> *We look at our child and face the reality of the responsibility we have that will never get better and likely, short of death (another grieving process), never change.*

with special needs, the sorrow remains with you every single day. What happens as time goes on when caring for another is that mourning is suppressed in light of the daily responsibilities that go along with caring for your special needs loved one. We find that those feelings of sorrow come to our mind in the middle of the night when all is quiet or when there is a peace or calmness in the home, and we look at our child and face the reality of the responsibility we have that will *never* get better and likely, short of death (another grieving process), never change.

Joe:

Clearly the greatest frustration and hurt that I have over Joey's condition is that it doesn't make any difference how much money I make, how many doctors we see or how far we travel trying to give Joey the best care possible, I am forced to come back to the reality that *I cannot help my son get better.* All parents desire to give and do the best for their child. Cindi and I did absolutely everything we could to help Joey, but we could not take away his cerebral palsy, mental retardation, seizures, allergies, etc. **WE COULD NOT HELP OUR SON GET BETTER!** We knew that we needed to change our goals and expectations for Joey because he was not going to change. *We were going to be the ones needing to change.*

What made everything more difficult and discouraging at times were the well-meaning people who'd say, "If he could just talk, he'd be normal." "If he could just walk, he'd be fine." "At least you still have him." We just didn't see it that simply. After paying thousands of dollars in doctor bills (the specialty list goes on and on) and tests (CAT scans, MRIs, EKGs, EEGs, etc.), spending countless hours with doctors and therapists yet reading Joey's ultimate diagnosis in an outdated library book, you can imagine how devastated we were that people would blow this off as "just" anything. Our life was and is *just changed* forever!

Cindi:

In case Joey would some day be able to read and comprehend what I was writing in his journal, I was very careful to remain positive, pointing out what he could do and whatever progress he made instead of all he couldn't do. I always expressed our love for him. No one would ever love him the way we do, but in my "real world" I was panicking. I was afraid. I doubted my ability to go the distance with a son who was retarded, mentally handicapped, or developmentally disabled—whatever word was currently in vogue. I was wondering *how* it happened. I searched mentally through my entire pregnancy, trying to find something that may have caused his disabilities. What I was really doing was fishing for an answer (any answer) so we could "fix" what was broken.

So why are the disappointments, discouragement, and death of a vision (what life would have been like) so challenging for those of us going through them? These pose challenges because they show us our selfishness as vividly as if we looked at ourselves in the mirror. They show us that we want control, a life of ease, and a life free from pain and suffering. We want our way, and we don't want it interrupted or inconvenienced.

Realization

Coming to grips with what the future would hold was devastating, but the first step to defining the problem was realizing one existed. No matter how many times someone said he'd soon catch up, no matter who said everything was going to be fine, we had to come to the realization that our life was not going to be normal and he was not going to catch up to others his age. He was not going to have the same abilities, and he was not going to be like everyone else. In addition, people unintentionally added to the confusion and frustration by suggesting our struggle (anyone's struggle) was caused by a lack of faith or insufficient prayer. Sometimes those biblical solutions are true and helpful, but sometimes we err by treating a physical illness/disease/heredity issue/disability as simply a spiritual condition. This balance may be difficult to grasp.

We needed to make initial adjustments. And in time, we had to settle into the idea that these adjustments were just the beginning, and they would be ongoing. We needed a clear understanding of our overall purpose in this as well as the knowledge that our purpose had to dictate our overall lifestyle, not our circumstances dictating our lifestyle. We don't mean *lifestyle* as in what cars we drove or how we'd vacation. We mean *lifestyle* as in how we will walk with the Lord through this. How will we depend on Him for our needs and for direction in a situation where we were clueless and untrained and initially unwilling? We mean, how will our life look to others who are watching us go through day-to-day struggles that would last year after year after year, crisis after crisis, and struggle after struggle? And yes, how would our life look in times of joy and rejoicing?

Pain and Promise

Proverbs 14:13, "Even in laughter the heart may be in pain and the end of joy may be grief."

In the meantime, the panic was temporarily overridden by joy accompanied by a different kind of panic—the news that I would have another child. Although we had moments of question and doubt, we never sensed that this child would have special needs like Joey.

Cindi:

August, 1983 (2 years old):

You are gaining such confidence in your walking! Sometimes you try to run, but you're not ready for that yet!

We found out that next April you will have a little brother or sister. It's going to be wonderful to have a big brother like you.

We started you on occupational therapy for your arms, hands, and fingers and look forward to your doing as well at that as you are with your walking.

I took Joey every month to a hospital in downtown Cleveland for all his therapies (physical, occupational and speech) and to learn how to teach him to crawl, turn over, walk, pick things up, move his lips to try to form words, learn to lick his lips when there was food on them, in other words the fine motor skills. But it was becoming harder and harder. Sometimes my mom went with me. She was so helpful, but when she wasn't able to accompany me, I'd have Joey, a growing belly, and some type of equipment to haul home like a huge exercise ball the same size as my belly! Joey in the stroller, diaper bag, ball, purse, therapy equipment… I looked as if I had packed to leave home!

November, 1983: You are trying to say "Daddy" and "Jesus." You're using both hands together more.

December, 1983: You are learning a few motions to some songs – about Jesus – and I want to teach you a little sign language since you aren't talking yet... and you seem to enjoy it.

February 13, 1984 (2 ½): You said, "Mama" and "Dada" when we asked you. It was the first time you purposely said it (to our knowledge). It was a thrill for us to hear! We hope this is the beginning of your speech!

April 21, 1984: You came today (to the hospital) to see your new little sister. You kept blowing kisses through the window of the nursery to Kristina (born the 18th). You knew her right away. When we asked "where's baby Kristina?" you didn't point at my belly anymore, but right at Kristina!

The Learning Curve

Life has a way of moving on in the midst of the best or worst of what happens in it! Sure, we are always learning some concept or another, but little did we know that our education in various therapies to help our son would not be the full scope of our learning curve!

We had no idea that we would have new great expectations to learn how to deal with behavior, pain, emotions, seizures, allergies (some severe that could be fatal), asthma issues, insurance companies, pharmacists, more doctors, more tests, sorrow, grief, financial concerns, fears, worries, complications of medications, future children, (some) family members who didn't understand, (some) friends who didn't know what to say, sleepless nights (for years, not months), schooling, meetings (one after another after another after another), school assessments, more doctor visits, job searches (one after another after another after another), doctors' appointments, more tests, caring for all personal needs all his life, caring for aging and ill parents while raising two daughters, running a dental practice, serving in ministry—but that's for another chapter. Without going into every detail of every challenge, suffice it to say we had many; and we learned to deal with each one as it came our way.

Surely God *could* change our situation. He performed many healings. He has the authority (Mark 11:33, 7:37, 9:25-27; Matt. 9:35; Luke 7:22). He healed the blind man in Mark 10:46-52 and Luke 18:35-43 and others with blindness (Matt. 20:30-34; John 9:1-12), healed the leper (Luke 5:12-16), the paralytic (Matthew 4:24; Luke: 17-26), a deformity (Luke 6:6-11), an epileptic (Luke 9:37-43; Matthew 4:24; 17:15), a woman sick for eighteen years (Luke 13:11-13), a woman hemorrhaging for twelve years, (Matt. 9:20-25), a leper and the deaf (Matt. 11:5). They all certainly had special needs that He addressed. So, yes, *He very well could* change our situation and heal Joey.

"This Is a Test"

Somewhere in the midst of all of the emotion, the changes, the challenges, the sleepless nights, anger, worry, sadness, grief, joy, fun, tough times, hope for a healing, we heard something like this, "BEEP, BEEP, BEEP, BEEP. This is a test. This is a test of the emergency broadcast system. This is only a test. Had it been a real emergency, you would have been instructed what to do."

When the shrieking beep on the radio or TV gets our attention, we stop for a moment, making sure it's *only* a test, and then go about our usual course of business. But what happens if it's *not* a test? We'd better be listening! We stop, look, and listen for what to do next!

Like the shrieking noise of the public address system, God got our attention. Instead of a weather crisis or national security issue, He sent us Joey. He reminded us, like unpredictable weather, such is life. And life is not always fair. God clearly had our attention! We couldn't ignore, neglect, negate, delete, or otherwise change that Joey was in our life and that God was clearly challenging us to respond to Him.

Tested, Tried, True

God gave us biblical examples from which to learn. For instance, Job was a godly man (according to Job 1:1 he was a blameless, upright, God-fearing man, who turned away from evil). He honored God in all ways, yet God allowed Satan to test him to see how faithful he would really be when life didn't go his way (Job 1:1-22).

What happened to him was tragic. According to the world's standards Job "had it all," then lost all his children, his health, his fortune, dealt with a less than helpful wife and friends who were not as supportive as they could have been. Our circumstances were different, but somehow I think we could have related a bit with one another. He experienced losses, and so did we. As he fell to the ground and worshipped in the midst of all this tragedy, he said in Job 1:21, "The Lord gave and the Lord has taken away. Blessed be the name of the Lord." Job continued to be faithful to God but he lost everything. God later blessed his faithfulness by restoring what had been taken away, yet life would never be the same as it had been before.

Could we respond as Job did? Could we take it by faith that this was the work of the Lord?

Another biblical example occurred when God asked Abraham to sacrifice his son Isaac in Genesis 22. That couldn't have been easy! Was God testing Abraham's faith? Sure, He was! Besides, the events would make a good lesson for many future Sunday school classes! How would Abraham respond to this request of the Lord? Who did He love more, God or Isaac? In an act of obedience, Abraham showed his love and devotion to God and walked his son to the place where he would be sacrificed. At precisely the correct time, God provided *exactly what* was needed just at the *moment* it was needed, so his son did not have to be sacrificed. A ram appeared "and Abraham went and took the ram and offered 'the ram' up for a burnt offering in the place of his son. And Abraham called the name of that place "The Lord Will Provide" (Gen. 22:13, 14).

When one of us was ready to quit, the other had just the right thing to say or enough energy to "see it through," which was an encouragement to persevere.

By God's grace we were never placed in a situation like Abraham, but we found ourselves at various crossroads in life when Joey was very young. On numerous occasions we thought we could not get through another night of seizures, but the Lord always provided for our needs. When Joey was sick for days at a time with complete loss of his ability to control his emotions, his faculties, etc., the Lord would give us the physical strength we needed to get through those days and nights of caregiving. When one of us was ready to quit, the other had just the right thing to say or enough energy to "see it through," which was an encouragement to persevere. We've been tried and tested over and over. We realize that all parents need to work through challenging times when raising their children. That is just a normal part of parenting.

Joe:

When there were times we would sense the opportunity to open up to some family members and friends regarding the challenges that we face everyday, the comeback we would get was something like, "Oh, when my child had a fever, or when my child had bad allergies." Of course, the insinuation is that "we all have problems and issues that we need to work through in our lives." Granted, that is true. But on one occasion while Joey was in the hospital because of days of seizures and a possible diagnosis of spinal meningitis followed by a spinal tab to rule out meningitis, someone said to me (while in Joey's hospital room) something like, "Hey listen these things (sicknesses) happen to all kids. So shape up, man, and get it together." Well this person caught me on a bad day. I was tired and hungry, and I said, "Really!? Well that's wonderful that your child got better after his bad cold or asthma attack, but after this hospital stay my child is STILL going to be retarded and have cerebral palsy, and he's still going to have epilepsy. So don't try to cheer me up with something overly spiritual like 'This (sickness) too will pass.' Joey's condition is NOT going to pass. Why don't you see that?"

State of Crisis: Not Why but How

Like Job and Abraham, we were in a state of crisis. Any state of crisis will cause us to think differently. Great fear can occur in a state of crisis. What if we can't handle this? Will this fear paralyze us? We doubted, we cried, and had bouts of deep discouragement as we begged the Lord through prayer for a healing. Broken bones can be set and healed, severe cuts can be stitched and mended, but would He choose to heal Joey in that way, or would He choose something else for us? We wondered how He would lead us. Then *slowly*, when no healing was coming, when only slow progress was made, we began to think differently. What if this is where God has called us to serve for a time or for the rest of our lives? In times of crisis, we find out who we are, who our close family and friends are, and how we're going to make it through whatever the difficulty. We looked to our past to do some evaluating. We looked to God to comfort us and asked Him for explanation. We looked to our future and had to adjust our thinking. We thought about our purpose in the midst of raising a son who had so many special needs. Our thoughts began to change. It changed from "Why did this happen to *us*" to "Why did this happen to *him*?" to "How will we honor the Lord through caring for Joey?" We asked the questions posed at the beginning of this chapter once again but this time in a different light. We were going to experience *real* purpose in life in "serving Christ" to glorify Him and make Him known through caring for our son, whose disabilities might never be healed. Our life was going to require that we remain flexible in *everything* we'd do as we'd learn *how* to deal with life. Some would say it was just what two people who are pretty structured and organized needed, and there is much truth to that. Adjusting to this type of challenge is difficult for anyone facing it. We had no choice but to be flexible because doing so was necessary in every facet of our life.

State of Trust

We went before the church and asked the leaders of the church to pray over Joey for healing. We prayed for our parents during their challenges, trusting God to heal. Sometimes healing is heaven. No leader, counselor, or doctor can replace the kind of trust we must have in God. And none can take the place of those who can spiritually lead us to a stronger relationship with the One who can—and sometimes does—choose to heal.

We trusted Him for what was needed, accepting His plan and adjusting the right set of lenses to set our sights on the vision He had for us. Ps. 138:8; 57:2 clearly tells us that God will accomplish in our individual lives what His plan is for that life! In order to accept the "test," we needed to deal with the initial shock and challenges we faced and put on those special lenses that would allow us to have His perspective. Proverbs 16:11 says, "Where there is no vision, the people perish." What did He want us to see? We were about to find out! We were about to catch His vision for what testing our faith might look like. God has made promises throughout His book—the Bible—and we were about to find out how true and accurate they were!

The Process

In *On Death and Dying* Elizabeth Kubler-Ross outlined her five stages of grief, which we experienced:

Denial – "This isn't happening to me!"

Anger – "Why is this happening to me?"

Bargaining – "I promise I'll be a better person if _____."

Depression – "I don't care anymore."

Acceptance – "I'm ready for what ever comes."

The only step we slid through was the depression stage. We spent moments, not weeks, there, and we'll share many of them with you; but we simply didn't have the time to *dwell* there! As we learned about developmental milestones Joey was missing, we asked those "what if" questions, but staying in that place would have had us missing the needs he had and the many ways we could help him. We had a child to care for, doctors to see, and ground to cover if we wanted to help him achieve his greatest potential. We realized dwelling there would not only hinder him, but us as well.

We found something very interesting about the process. Early on we couldn't believe that our son had so many needs and might never develop the ability to be on his own. Sometimes we'd experience happiness, frustration, joy, guilt, and jealousy all at the same time. We couldn't anticipate what would happen down the road. We couldn't see clearly in the fog of the day when we were going through some very difficult stages; but somewhere down the road around the bend and a few miles ahead, we found joy. We don't know the date. We just know the journey finally led us there. Someone has said, "It's not about waiting for the storm to pass but about learning to dance in the rain." Someone else has said, "When life gives you a lemon, you make lemonade." Those are great thoughts, and we can certainly learn from them; but the process is different for everyone. Some people may need weeks; others, years. Getting through the grief process is difficult because we live in a society that tells us to move on quickly! We're all on our own timetable, and we just have to be careful not to dwell in a ditch of self-pity for too long.

OTHERS' STORIES

- We knew shortly after our son's birth that he was going to have severe special needs. Here I was with my firstborn, dealing with the recovery from major surgery (having had a C-section), getting no rest, and learning how to deal with feeding tubes and seizures in our newborn. Add to that the calls to the hospital to retrieve records because it was so blatantly a malpractice suit, lawyers, papers, documents, phone calls, multiple doctor visits for my newborn and me, continuing education on his multiple medical issues, and then early intervention therapies. I was simply exhausted. I had help, but honestly, it was just not enough. Life might have been different if it had been full of fun and excitement, but it was filled with much sadness, few answers, and cover-ups, one on top of another. My discouragement and disappointment was that it was a never-ending trial of unanswered questions.

- I had no idea how sacrificial caring for my parents was going to be when dementia struck. Cutting up their food and getting them to doctors' appointments was an unending chapter in my book of life. There came a time I just couldn't wait until they could go to a nursing home, but it wasn't an option yet. I felt guilty wanting some free time, but there seemed to be few options.

  After two years of doctors' visits, I couldn't believe hearing the neurologist flippantly say, "I thought you knew she was retarded."

- In 2008, Olympic weightlifter Melanie Roach told an interviewer that not making the 2000 Olympic team was devastating but nothing compared to having her child diagnosed with autism.

- Our initial challenge was finding the "blessing" in having a child with special needs and dealing with the emotional heartbreak and loss of the "dreams" we had for him, and us.

- When I would see special needs kids, I never thought the parents did something to cause it; yet everyone questions us in ways that make us feel as if we did something wrong.

- I'm tired of hearing all the doctors and professionals say, "Time will tell."

They are professionals and I feel they know more than they are telling.

- After two years of doctors' visits, I couldn't believe hearing the neurologist flippantly say, "I thought you knew she was retarded."

- Knowing several people with special needs (young and old) makes me very thankful for the abilities I have.

- I feel personal frustration because I can do nothing to change things.

- Our oldest was not diagnosed with multiple learning disabilities until age nine. The younger siblings' abilities caused the oldest to struggle with envy and discouragement.

- As a social worker I saw many families in distress. The entire family can fall apart as a result of caring for one with special needs of any age.

- My greatest challenge is trying to figure out how much am I supposed to accept two children with special needs; how much am I supposed/allowed to feel disappointment, hurt, anger, and bitterness that comes with this situation. It's hard to be strong and say this is what God has given us to bring Him glory, which I know is true, but I still cry in my pain and struggle.

- We all learn our best lessons in the school of pain, loss, trial, and grief.

- When I learned my child had Down syndrome, I was filled with anxiety, worry, and even a bit of anger at God. We already had four healthy children aged three to nine. Caring for a new baby with special needs seemed like a daunting task. Both my parents were deceased, and I wondered how I was going to manage this without help.

- One great challenge for me is realizing the broken dream that my child will not follow the normal sequence of life. It breaks my heart to think of this sweet child being an outcast, or weird, as the disability becomes more obvious.

- I struggle, unable to forgive the doctors who allowed this to happen. If they had given me a C-section a few hours before my child was born, he would be completely healthy today.

- In the shock over what we were learning and discovering regarding our special needs situation, I was disappointed at the complacency of others to our challenge. Not until some of my friends have gone through similar struggles did they ever care to ask us how we were doing. And complacency was one thing, but sometimes people were actually critical. Please walk a mile in my shoes before you criticize the very difficult walk (or wheelchair ride) I have.

YOUR STORY

Depending on the place/stage you find yourself, you may have your own questions to add to those we were asking ourselves. What are they?

What dreams have we had to let go?

Describe the series of events leading to this "death of a vision":

Can you relate to Job? Abraham?

What testing(s) have you had to deal with? Do you feel your faith is being tested?

To whom/where did you go for answers?

CHAPTER THREE

Detours and Interruptions in Life

A television ad for an arthritis medication says, "You're not the person you were before you had rheumatoid arthritis."

"My memory is shot. My legs feel like lead, every muscle in my body is screaming, so why do people think the problem's all in my head?" asks a magazine ad for chronic fatigue syndrome (CFS).

The small print in an ad about fibromyalgia reads, "People don't understand."

Journalist Bob Woodruff, co-anchor of ABC News and World Report, was wounded (nearly fatally) by a roadside bomb in Iraq while covering the war. He spent thirty-six days in a coma with his wife, family, and friends at his side. When his wife Lee first saw him, his brain was protruding from his skull "like a second head." Lee said something to this effect: "My world just stopped. I had to concentrate on the tiniest thing to figure out what I had to do to make it." In February 2007 the couple shared Bob's road to miraculous recovery in a memoir called **In an Instant***.*

On the way to Jericho the Samaritan in Luke 10:30-37 came upon a man who had been robbed, beaten, and left for dead. The scripture reports two men who had passed by this man. The Samaritan bandaged the injured man, took him to an inn, stayed with him until the next day, and paid the innkeeper for the expense of his care, promising to cover any additional expense on his return trip. Likely, this was a bit of an interruption to what both the Samaritan and the injured man had planned for the day!

Did I Ask for This? Did I Sign up for This Committee?

No matter what trial, health issue, or challenge we experience, the likelihood is that we did not plan for it! When we participated in sports and cheerleading in high school, we never imagined that we'd have the aches and pains we do now! Neither did we think that some of life's challenges would come wrapped in the packages they did. But here we are, serving on a committee for which we never signed up! We have a lot of challenges going on and they are ongoing! We know that everyone has tough challenges in life, but often they are temporary. Caring for individuals with special needs is demanding, ongoing, and seemingly never-ending. At that point, we realized that life just got tougher!

OUR STORY

The Blame Game

Winning a substantial settlement for spilling hot coffee on oneself may seem silly to some of us. But why not? The person (or establishment) who brewed and served it *should* be responsible for what the customer ordered at the drive-through. Right? Sure! That makes sense. And the server (or establishment) should also be responsible for how the customer took off the lid, as well as how the customer put it on their lap. Sorry—some things *really* don't make sense. Sometimes things are just accidents.

Our basic, sinful, selfish human nature makes us think that life should be convenient, comfortable, easy, and fun. A friend Mick Yoder, who lost a son in a plane crash, profoundly said, "Life is so hard because we think it should be so easy." At least it should be that way for *us*. We're *naturally the exception*. Right? That same human nature naturally wants to find someone to blame. We hurt so bad that we don't want to own up to the fact that life as we knew it will never be the same. Because of this challenge our dreams will never come true. We want someone to own up to what happened. We want to point to someone and say, "They did it. It's not my fault." Remember our ancestors—Adam and Eve (Genesis 3:11-13)? When conversing with God, after eating of the fruit, Adam blamed Eve and Eve blamed the serpent. And of course, the serpent didn't have a leg to stand on at that point. However, we doubt that God was amused. Blame shifting never solves anything.

Like Adam and Eve, the coffee spiller, and us in our own situations, sometimes we just have to say, "I own up to and admit to my own foolishness, mistake, or sin, and as best as I can, I'll move on." And sometimes we simply have no one to blame. God intended whatever happened, and from there we must learn to move on. We've heard that blaming finds no fault in self, no good in others, and no strength in God. We had to stop wasting our time looking to blame others and ourselves, and start relying on God in the process. Psalm 119:71, "It is good for me that I was afflicted, that I may learn Thy statutes."

Move On?

We struggled with and contemplated that "short list" of questions in our minds. What was the cause? What went wrong? Was it something in the pregnancy? Was it the difficult and long labor? When did it happen? Did we cause it? How did I get here and when can I leave?

Of course, we quickly searched our pasts, the pregnancy, the birth, the early days of Joey's life. We couldn't think of anything that *might* have been harmful, but try as we might, we could not get it out of our minds that something or someone had to be the cause of this. We will always wonder. Was the fifteen minutes in a hot tub during the pregnancy the cause? Was Cindi's continued exercise an issue? Was the C-section done quickly enough? Was the doctor negligent? Not one of these questions was ever answered. No one was ever found to be at fault. Despite the recommendation of some people to sue the doctor for malpractice, we resolutely chose not to travel that route.

We certainly could have *tried* to make a case, but how do you put a value on a broken heart and broken dreams? Nothing we could have won would have given us what we wanted.

Sure, we wanted resolution but not by pointing a finger in the wrong direction. Doctors are sued every day but not always with good reason. Sometimes life just happens. We wanted to move on with resolve in our hearts and in a helpful and constructive way.

So much of this battle was waged in our thoughts. If we allow those thoughts to consume us, we wind up on the "self" path: self-absorbed, self-conscious, self-gratifying. We have to deal with our struggles where they begin, and this is the place. We need to defeat selfishness or we will be set up for defeat.

When Sin Is Involved

Are we being punished? Did we sin? Why me? Why us? Why our child? Why our health? Because we are sinful creatures, we will sometimes do things that are wrong and sinful. We won't hang up the laundry list, but if the challenging situation has found us dealing with sins of our past, in order to move on, we must do as David did. We must understand that there will be consequences for our sin. God will not allow us to sin and bless us for it. When a particular situation is a result of sin, the Bible gives guidance as to what to do. In Psalm 32:3-5, David expressed his heart regarding his own sin. He said, "When I kept silent about my sin, my body wasted away through my groaning all day long. For day and night Thy hand was heavy upon me; my vitality was drained away as with the fever-heat of summer. I acknowledged my sin to Thee, and my iniquity I did not hide; I said, 'I will confess my transgressions to the Lord' and Thou didst forgive the guilt of my sin." That is what we must do if we have sinned. If we want to move on from where we are, confess the sin (tell God we know that He knows it was sin), repent (turn away from that sin, discontinuing it), ask for forgiveness (of God and anyone it involved), ask God for the strength to release it to Him, and move on. No, it's not easy. It's not easy because we realize we are to blame. If this doesn't make sense to you, we'll be discussing more about this in the next chapter. If you feel you need to know more now, we discuss it in Chapter 4. Come back here when you're finished there.

If Not Sin, If Not Us, Who or What?

Did God cause it? Or did He allow it? Why me? Why us? Why my child, my health? Jesus was in the process of healing a blind man. His disciples asked Him in John 9:1-12, "Rabbi, who sinned? This man or his parents, that he should be born blind?" Jesus answered, "It was neither that this man sinned, nor his parents; but it was in order that the works of God might be displayed in him." In our hearts, in some vague way, we understood that God's will may have been the cause. Now what? Fight God?

Accidents happen and people make mistakes. Poor healthcare issues and the abuse of drugs and alcohol—all these are possible causes of disabling. But what about those situations where none of these things can be the cause? And for whatever reason, we realize that God permitted it.

Deal With It—Simple But True

If we sinned and we asked forgiveness, we are forgiven. We have dealt with the situation at the most basic and important level. If we recognize that sin was not involved, then we realize that every question is not yet answered. Many never will be answered in this life, but we're all on the same level playing field. So where do we go from here? Let's explore together!

We must first realize that there will be a consequence to our sin. We may not have intended for those consequences, but God says in Galatians 6:7, "Whatever a man sows, that he will also reap." His word is to be taken seriously. That is why Achan (Joshua 7:19-26) died after he stole booty and lied about hiding it. That is why King David, after committing adultery and murder, encountered many family problems (II Samuel 15-18). God is serious and wants us to take His word seriously. All our actions, good or bad, bring consequences.

In addition as with Job, God does not always explain what He is doing, nor does He give Job all the answers to his questions, but He can be trusted to do what is right, and He does so with grace. (Job, Chapters 38-42). "Shall we indeed accept good from God, and shall we not accept adversity?" (Job 2:10). This is the place we find ourselves learning to trust in God!

When we talked about learning to *trust*, we discussed the need to see things through new lenses. That's where we are. We need to make the necessary adjustments in our lenses so that we can move on. We can't get stuck in the past with our feet in cement. That mindset won't allow us to move forward, and we steal from the future the great things God has for us to learn! We will learn to trust Him, not other people, not money, not gadgets, not medicine, not doctors. Nothing. Only Him!

Some of us have made the choice to care for someone with special needs. For others, the choice was not really theirs. This was not on our planned itinerary of life. We must take a detour, and the road ahead will be bumpy. Life got tougher and now we have choices to make. Our choice is how we'll deal with it. Life is full of crises, and we might even be living from one crisis to another. But now we find ourselves wrapped up in caring for another. We can't easily separate what we do from who we are. We have a new identity. We are all thrust into the learning process, and what we learn will change from day to day. So let's consider some things we'll probably struggle with and have to deal with—if not for today, for tomorrow!

Joy and Happiness

On our journey we have noticed people's amazement when they observe someone experiencing joy during what may be a prolonged challenge in life. Let us say that it often takes time to get to a point when the toughest and roughest challenges can be experienced with true joy. The Bible teaches in Psalm 118:24 that "This is the day which the Lord has made; let us rejoice and be glad in it." A simple truth, but sometimes hard to apply! When life is tough, finding the joy and happiness in the midst of it is difficult but possible.

To us *happiness* is a word that the world knows as an outward expression, a natural response to a good situation, even a pretense that everything is fine when it is not. It's related to the immediate. For instance, a person might experience happiness when purchasing a new car, meeting a new friend, or having fun at an event.

To us *joy* is a word that a believer in Christ (a Christian) knows. Joy is an inward response to God in the midst of both good and bad situations. It's a way of relating the present to the future because of a perspective that is gained by knowing that God has a plan and a purpose for each of us. While joy has an outward expression, which might present itself to others as happiness, it is actually an inward response that is a deeper, longer lasting emotion.

God captures our attention through interruptions. These interruptions cause us to examine ourselves and our priorities, and we will then respond accordingly. Any interruptions to my ideal are God's best blessings in disguise. People around us watch how we respond to these interruptions and trials to see whether the God we believe in and follow is real. We become a real and living example of what He can accomplish in each person's life, provided we do not let the root of bitterness take hold in our hearts. We must forgive ourselves and others if there is need, and we must give thanks daily for what we have, not dwell on what we don't have. The interruption becomes an opportunity.

Giving Thanks

When trials interrupt our life, and we still thank the Lord, we have another opportunity to praise Him. I Thessalonians 5:18 says, "In everything give thanks; for this is God's will for you in Christ Jesus." It doesn't say we have to be thankful for the situation but to give thanks. For example, we aren't daily saying, "Dear God, we are so happy you chose to give us a son with special needs. Wow, what a great idea that was!" We aren't saying that because the daily challenges are such that most days we'd gladly trade them in for something more fun and easier! But He's not asking for that kind of attitude. He wants us to give thanks *in* the situation He has allowed, recognizing what we are learning and growing and that our dependency is in Him.

When we choose not to give thanks, we choose to become a bitter, prideful, grumbler who criticizes others, finding no fault in self, no good in others, and no strength from God. Who wants to be that person? Who wants to be with that person? Could that person possibly have any happiness in life? Will this person ever experience true and lasting joy? Will this person ever have the confidence to put trust in God? It boils down to a choice we make.

Trust in the Lord

Again we return to trust. Probably one of the most difficult steps yet greatest blessing was relinquishing "everything" to the Lord. We surrendered. We surrendered all the questions we had. We surrendered control. While we might *try* to do things that would appear as though we had it all together, we would only be fooling ourselves for a time. When we realize we can't try but must trust, we can truly learn to trust in the Lord. We had to stop blaming ourselves, God, doctors, and anyone else who might have had the smallest part in our present struggle.

By doing so, we also surrendered worry, giving us the opportunity to practice putting our trust and faith in Him, to pray for others and ourselves during hardship and trials, to identify with Him, and to realize that through this situation, we would be able to serve Him. As we surrendered to Him, He empowered us to be all we could be for His glory. That's what it's all about—doing everything so that we can point to Him and thus glorifies Him because He is everything! (Colossians 1:17-18 says, "And He is before all things, and in Him all things hold together. He is also head of the body, the church; and He is the beginning, the first-born from the dead; so that He Himself might come to have first place in everything.") Perhaps He has allowed us to go through this situation in life to nudge us with the question, "How much do you *really* trust Me?"

Trust doesn't always come all at once. It comes through obeying, submitting, and surrendering our wills and itineraries to Him. It comes from practicing and eventually achieving all that He has for us—joy and trust. It's called growing! As we grow, we are in the process of serving Him. He begins to work in and through us so that we can point others to Him. It all works together nicely! (Philippians 1:6, "For I am confident of this very thing, that He who began a good work in you will perfect it until the day of Christ Jesus.")

Prayer

If we pray hard and often enough will Joey be healed? When our parents dealt with their disabilities, did we pray and trust as we should? Will our faith be shattered or grow deeper? How can we best pray for him and others?

We pray daily and often throughout the day for all of our children and for those we love and for requests from others. When we realized the extent of Joey's challenges, we were quite persistent in our prayers—like no other prayers we had ever prayed. We followed Jesus' example to find a solitary place to pray (Mark 1:35), sometimes together, sometimes alone. As Christians we know that He is always with us and longs to hear from us. He heard from us a lot!

We were honest with Him about our struggles, our many inadequacies, our frustrations, our doubts, and among other things, our feelings of desperation. We felt like the passengers on the bobbling ship in Psalm 107:23-31. They reeled and staggered as drunken men because of the stormy seas. They panicked, and as aptly worded in scripture, were at "wit's end"! *Then* they began to pray! While we had been prayerful all along, we realized that perhaps we had gotten into the habit of praying at the tail end of challenges rather than at the beginning. So we began to pray proactively and even preventatively, expecting God to show Himself through Joey with a miracle. But the question remained: Would He heal Joey or have another plan?

We could relate to this group of people in Psalm 107 at their wit's end! This was certainly an interruption to their otherwise pleasant trip. A terrific storm changed everything. God didn't promise them—nor did He promise us—that we wouldn't have any storms but that He would help us through whatever difficult times would come our way. This was our opportunity to learn this lesson. What can appear to be a human disappointment or interruption is often the very thing used to show a divine victory. He wanted us to learn to cast our cares upon Him (I Peter 5:6-7), to see things from His perspective instead of our own, and to experience joy in the journey! He wanted us to learn to come to Him for answers to our questions when we were troubled. By learning to communicate with the Lord through prayer, He taught us not to ask for patience, but for wisdom and understanding (James 1:5). What a difference that made! Praying for patience opens us up for more trials and tribulations because those trials and tribulations require us to learn patience. It was a vicious circle. We now pray for wisdom and understanding to gain His perspective, which allows us to have patience because we are seeing the whole picture more clearly.

Scripture teaches us to *ask* for what we want. With scriptures like John 15:7, "If you abide in Me, and My words abide in you, 'ask whatever you wish, and it shall be done for you,'" and I John 3:22, "and whatever we ask we receive from Him, because we keep His commandments and do the things that are pleasing in His sight." I John 5:14-15 tells us, "And this is the confidence which we have before Him, that, if we ask anything according to His will, He hears us, and if we know that He hears us in whatever we ask, we know that we have the requests which we have asked from Him" and Matt. 18:19, "Again I say to you, that if two of you agree on earth about anything that they may ask, it shall be done for them by My Father who is in heaven." We were armed with the Word of God in our hearts, ready to watch and wait for the way He would answer.

Isolation

Do you feel isolated? We often found ourselves isolated and unable to describe where we were. Isolation is like a home without landscaping—something is just missing. We felt abandoned when people stopped asking questions because there are no answers. There was often little to no conversation about what touched us deeply. Had we experienced a broken leg or cancer, we may have experienced love and support from all directions; instead, for a long time people

Had we experienced a broken leg or cancer, we may have experienced love and support from all directions; instead, for a long time people kept their distance.

kept their distance. They likely didn't know what to ask or say, and neither did we, so we were left to try to figure things out alone. Sometimes we even felt that sharing too much might make others feel an obligation to offer to help or do something they might not have wanted to do. We learned that God often teaches us deeper lessons in the quiet, lonely, and even desperate places of our lives, than in the busy-ness of a crowded place. We often asked each other, "What do you think the Lord is trying to teach us here?" Answers varied as much as the difficulty of the day but ranged from "perseverance, faith, endurance, hope, patience, and unconditional love."

And Frustration

Cindi:

Joey was almost three, and Kristina was a newborn; my post-partum hormones were out of kilter. We had just learned the extent of Joey's diagnosis, and feeling very much alone, I remember spending the better part of two weeks crying. I was saddened that he might never walk, talk, or be able to learn—and longed for *someone* to listen, give hope, and not give the "pat" answer that was easy to say but hard to hear.

We have found that when things are at their lowest, God sends relief in ways that we were not counting on. He said in His word, "Come to Me, all who are weary and heavy-laden, and I will give you rest. Take My yoke upon you, and learn from Me, for I am gentle and humble in heart; and you shall find rest for your souls. For My yoke is easy, and My load is light" (Matthew 11:28-30). Sweeping my garage to let off some steam and expend some energy from my frustration, I sobbed. The future was bleak. How was I going to handle this for the rest of my life? Who in my *close* family and group of friends even gets what I'm going through? Why I bothered to answer the phone in the condition I was in, unable to talk and sobbing, I'll never know. But I do know that the person who called had perfect timing. Betsy's loving and quiet voice, tender merciful heart, and listening ear were just what I needed. She was able to help me sort some things by listening to my despair. Life didn't change, but my frustration level lowered. When we are at the point we know something is "wrong" with our child, we need someone to be there when we find out for sure. God sent someone for me. Someone cared. Someone listened.

Isolated But Not Alone

We also learned to recognize that God was indeed with us through these times of isolation. We based our recognition on the *fact* of His word, not the feelings we were experiencing. We know He is always with us: He said, "I will not fail you or forsake you" (Joshua 1:5b). And we reply, "Do not forsake me, O Lord; O my God, do not be far from me!" (Ps. 38:21). We had to cling to the *knowing*, not the *feeling*.

Struggles

When Cindi's mom suffered a brain aneurysm, we struggled to find the place where we could make sense of why it was happening to someone who didn't seem old enough to have this kind of health issue, and we questioned why she was chosen to go through the difficult surgery and long recovery. We struggled with questions. When two of our parents traveled the rocky road of Alzheimer's, we asked, "Why them?" With Joey, we initially asked, "Why?" Then we asked, "For how long"? Today we ask, "What do we do with each day to make a difference somewhere?" Sometimes the difference is in our hearts. Sometimes the difference is in the heart of someone we speak to. We never know. We walk through the struggle knowing it will challenge our marriage, family, job, other relationships, free time, sleep, social life, daily coping skills, emotions, ministry, finances, our ability to understand the special needs person in our life, vacation, time away, retirement, embracing special moments, priorities, loneliness, our routines, setting boundaries, school, work—and that is just the tip of the iceberg!

We learned that life isn't fair. Proverbs 16:11 says, "A just balance and scales belong to the Lord; all the weights of the bag are His concern." He balances our life the way He sees fit and necessary. He knows what we need and distributes as needed. Psalm 138:8 says, "The Lord will accomplish what concern me; Thy loving-kindness, O Lord, is everlasting; do not forsake the works of Thy hands." He cares, is concerned, and does His work for our good. We just might not see it the way He does right away! The challenges and impossibilities we are presented cause us to run to and rely on God, the One who balances our life. Honest talks with Him will allow us to find the peace of mind He wants us to find. We soon learn that telling God what His will should be for us is dangerous. (Read I Chronicles 28:9—don't miss this lesson!)

How do you package that to share with someone else? Read this book and then share it with others!

Still in the Learning Process

You'll never hear us say, "We've arrived! We finally have the answers, and we've got it all together!" You might hear us share victories—the little battles won in the course of the big war; but you will also hear us share our struggles and some of the battles we lost along the way. This book isn't all positive because if it were, you wouldn't want to read it. You wouldn't believe us, and it wouldn't be true. So, like it or not, here is what we are in the process of learning.

We Learned That We Aren't in Control

We can say this *now*—we are glad we began the learning process of who was in control of our lives early in our marriage! So many issues arise in life, and this was going to be just one of them. Unfortunately, our issue was a big and long-lasting one, but really, it prepared us for many things to come and helped us to be able to see these many challenges through the eyes of the Lord instead of through the constant frustration of the finger printed lenses we were wearing. Our observation of others, whose early years seemed less challenging than ours, has shown that when their struggles, the strain of challenges from illness, caring for elderly parents, and deaths, finally occurred later in their lives, the devastation was traumatic. Many don't have the skills to "deal with it" because they weren't able to develop those skills over the years. The bodybuilder doesn't start lifting 200 pounds at a time but skillfully practices and builds up muscle, stamina, and endurance to work up to lifting those heavy weights. If we don't experience our first very difficult challenge in life until we're 40 or 50 years old, we may not have the ability or skills to know how to handle it.

Although we sometimes wonder what life would have been like had we been dealt an easier hand, we know that our son's disability and continued challenges have allowed us to see things and respond to them differently than we might have. We learned back then that no matter how tight a grip we had, being in *control* was not enough.

We Learned to Trust in God's Sovereignty

Sovereignty refers to one who has supreme power and authority. Believers in God agree that He alone possesses both of these characteristics. The problem arises when that power and authority clash with our desires, expectations, and wishes. Wanting our own way, whether we are willing to admit it or not, is simply part of human nature.

To see if that's true, answer the following questions. Would you rather be chosen to go to Disney World, all expenses paid for as long as you'd like or care for someone who has a debilitating disease for an unknown length of time? Would you prefer to have someone mow and fertilize your lawn for the next thirty years or care for a child who will require all of your time, energy, and resources for the next thirty, forty, or more years? Would you like to have a three-months' paid vacation every year with the financial ability to travel anywhere you'd like or would you prefer to find the resources to remodel your entire home making it wheelchair accessible so you can accommodate a family member while you take early retirement and stay home and take care of her or him? Now, if you answered the second part to each question, we'd like to meet you! So would every person who is caring for someone and has given up time, treasures, energy, and dreams. But life is seldom this cut and dry. If you thought these questions were just a bit weighted, here are a few more to make us think a bit further. Would you rather care for a child from birth who will be completely disabled or care for a spouse wounded in war for the rest of her or his life? Would you prefer to retire early and care for your parent whose health is rapidly declining, arrange their meds, their nursing home assignment, visit them daily (or weekly), for the next ten years or find out that a disease you have will soon cause you to stop walking and talking? Would you rather yourself or your loved one suffer in pain indefinitely? OK, these aren't fair either, are they? And maybe that's why our sovereign Lord, who has all authority and power, is better able to make those decisions for us.

Let's revisit the verse we read a bit ago. Proverbs 16:11, "A just balance and scales belong to the Lord; all the weights of the bag are His concern." If we trust Him, we trust that He will give us what we need when we need it. We will trust that He will keep from us what we don't need. And we trust that whatever He gives or allows, that He has made it His concern, and will weight the balance accordingly. We can't know how it might look from His perspective because he sees the entire picture, but perhaps someday He will show us. What we need to know this day is that He is here for us.

His being here for us is what we know as the exchanged life. We exchange our trials for His triumphs. We exchange our dreams for His desires for our life. And we grow through these exchanges. But in the midst of growing in the ways of the Lord, we often find—if we are honest—that we just wish growth wouldn't be so difficult. Yet without hardship, the victory isn't so sweet. Few people say they have grown during times of prosperity and ease. Inquire of others and ask them how they grew and what they've learned about life in the midst of challenge versus ease.

Much of scripture speaks to the different ways we see things, express things, and react or respond to things. Reading and rereading the Book of Job is always helpful for us. Job's life was pretty rough, yet he allowed the suffering and struggle he endured to give him a different perspective, all while maintaining a close relationship with God. Others may have crumbled beneath the pressure into the rubble of bitterness and despair. He did not. We can learn from his attitude and dependence on the Lord. We cannot forget the *bigger* picture, and if we use those special lenses, we might just get a glimpse of it! God never interrupts—His timing is always perfect!

God Is With Us and We Can Learn to Lean on Him

Our Lord is always with us. He knows suffering (death on the cross in Matt. 27:46) and the pain of the world's sin on Him, so if anyone **understands** our pain, He does. (Rom. 5:1-5; I Peter 1:6-8; James 1:2-5; II Cor. 12:9-10; I Peter 2:21; I Peter 3:17-18.)

Because He is always with us, we can ask Him anything anytime. We might start by asking Him questions that refer directly to our hardship like "Why me?" But as we grow, we will begin asking questions like "What can I learn from this? How can I gain wisdom? Who can I help?" And because He loves us so much, He will use these challenging situations to refine us, to strengthen us, to help us be more loving and compassionate, and to use us to point others to Him.

We knew that choosing "God's will" or "our will" would be an ongoing process! We learn early that life isn't fair. But if we believe Proverbs 16:11 ("A just balance and scales belong to the Lord; all the weights of the bag are His concern") and Psalms 138:8 ("The Lord will accomplish what concerns me; Thy loving kindness, O Lord, is everlasting; Do not forsake the works of Thy hands"), then we have to trust that God knew what He was doing, had a purpose for us, and is with us through it all. Deuteronomy 31:6, 8 tells us, "Be strong and courageous, do not be afraid or tremble at them, for the Lord your God is the One who goes with you. He will not fail you or forsake you. And the Lord is the one who goes ahead of you; He will be with you. He will not fail you nor forsake you. Do not fear, or be dismayed."

When we have physical pain, we call on the doctor to treat us. When we are tired, we rest. When we can't do it anymore, God is there for us. He's always with us even *before* we can't go on anymore. We simply need to include Him. A friend once said to us, "If life gets any harder than this, I don't want to be refined as gold. I'll settle for silver." We know the feeling but also know that because we are in a relationship with Him—if we are believers in Christ—He wants only the best for us. He allows trials and hardships for us to be drawn to Him and to learn to lean upon Him. If He wants to refine us like gold, the fire might get hot, but we will be a valuable instrument for Him to use.

We need Jesus every step of the way if we really want to experience joy in the journey. Knowing that joy is not *just* about getting to the destination; it's also about the ride, the view, the experiences, the detours, the forks in the road, and the story we have the privilege of sharing with others. II Corinthians 1:3-4, "Blessed be the God and Father of our Lord Jesus Christ, the Father of mercies and God of all comfort; who comforts us in all our affliction so that we may be able to comfort those who are in any affliction with the comfort with which we ourselves are comforted by God." The grass isn't always greener on the other side, but how would we know that if we haven't checked it out? The world looks different to us now. Experiences, people we've met, obstacles we've overcome or have yet to overcome, seeing through our new lenses—all these are legs on our joyful journey.

We need Him, but we also need the loving hands of friends and family around us in this special journey. We can't make the journey alone.

We Learned That We Need One Another and Others Need Us

In Matthew 5:13, we are told, "You are the salt of the earth; but if the salt has become tasteless, how will it be made salty again? It is good for nothing any more, except to be thrown out and trampled under foot by man." What does that mean for us? What does God expect of us?

Salt is used for different purposes. If you add it to a dish of food, in the right amount it adds a pleasing flavor. It can be used to tenderize food, softening and breaking it down so it's easier to chew. And it's also used for preserving food. Salt keeps food from spoiling when the right amount is used.

A soufflé recipe calls for a small amount of salt. The ¼ teaspoon needed will be sufficient to flavor it perfectly. But suppose you pour ¼ cup of salt into the bowl? What do you think will happen? Of course, the soufflé will be ruined. Even though it will look just fine, you won't want to eat it!

Using salt can be tricky. We need to give a "dash" here and there. Too little and the dish is bland. Too much and it's unpleasant! Salt is used according to its purpose. And when it comes to our trials, they are given to us by an all-knowing Heavenly Father according to the purpose He has for us and given in just the right amount. That is how we are each used by God to fulfill His purposes. When we're refined and strengthened, we're able to help others see His purposes. As they see us being refined and watch God strengthen us, we begin to have the credentials to be used by Him. He has reasons for everything. We just need to be attentive as we look for them like we do when reading road signs on a highway.

Certainly, as we are looking for what God is doing in our life, others are watching us. How are we responding to these trials? How is God *real* in our life? Do we show others that we rely on Him, or do we crumble under the obvious daily pressures? Often, our difficulties and hardships *are* our ministry (II Corinthians 1:3-4).

When Joey was in his mid-teens, we gave a presentation to a group of ministry leaders who had children with special needs. At the conclusion, a young couple approached us to spend some time with them. With blonde hair the basic difference, their two-year-old child looked and acted just like Joey did at that age. We're not sure if they could relate to what life would look like for them in ten or fifteen years, but it was right in front of them like a mirror. We shared the blessings and the struggles and prayed together. God had guided and comforted us over the years, allowing us the privilege of sharing that guidance, comfort, and encouragement with that younger couple and with many other similar couples since.

We have also had to learn to accept help and support from others, which wasn't and isn't always easy. Reluctance to bother others, pride, and the ability to do things on our own caused us to exclude others at times. We clearly missed out on some blessings, but we have learned and recognize the importance of having in our lives others who can support us spiritually, emotionally, and practically! We'll share more in Chapter 10.

If we are depleted, we can't give to others, let alone each other and the family. When we are energized, we are filled and able to give from our abundance. That is the beauty of the true Christian support system if it operates properly. We learn to accept help and support when we need it so that when we are strong and able, we will be able to extend and offer the same to others.

We Learned That We Have Choices

Just like Adam and Eve (Gen. 2:15-17), we have choices—usually between our selfish and sinful ways or obedience to the will of God. The choices we make often show the condition of our heart. Do we choose love over hate, show compassion over impatience, express pride over humility? (Rom. 5:3-5, I Peter 1: 6-8). When everything goes our way, we don't need to make so many choices, but then we don't have the same kinds of opportunity to show how the Lord is working in our life either. Our challenges and struggles have given us the opportunity to show our faithfulness to Him and gratefulness for Him!

OTHERS' STORIES

- Because of drugs in my past and other lifestyle issues, I had to own up to the fact that some of what I was dealing with in my son's special needs was a result of my sin. It was hard to admit, but when I did, I was finally able to move on, get him the kind of help he needed, and deal with my own issues. The consequences of life are often difficult but change seldom happens without ownership of our part in those consequences.

- I was very frustrated trying to live amidst other families with children who are doing the fun and normal things while we are in therapy for our child. Trying to live in both worlds can be stressful and often frustrating. Sometimes secluding ourselves in the world of doctors and therapists is easier because others don't seem to understand the constant emotional drain and lack of energy we experience. If that wasn't sad enough, they don't really seem to care to understand.

- I have bargained many times for God to have someone else do this instead of me. Someone else could do better. I'm beginning to think He thinks I can do it.

- The most difficult challenge is facing each day positively. I have a tendency to pretend everything is OK, but I'm really shutting down.

- As an observer, I see that Christians *do* suffer, sometimes greatly, yet by God's grace they *can* survive and so can the couples' marriage.

- The hardest thing in trying to deal with what we've been dealt is that I always have to be "on." There is no down time. I lack sleep, rarely go out, and have constant concerns over medical issues.

- Since the death of my husband and in the caring for my children (one with special needs), I often wonder where God is. Hiking one day, I saw rays of sun from behind a beautiful tree. I said to myself, "That is how God is; you can't see Him but He is there doing things you'll notice later."

- I'm upset when people say things like, "You are so lucky to have a special needs child who walks and talks, instead of one like 'Johnny' who can't."

- My greatest daily challenge was keeping my daughter safe during seizures, finding doctors and educational programs and eventually a good work environment. We had to be advocates for our child beyond what others need to do for "normal" children. I know. I had more than one.

- I can't believe all I have to do for the person I take care of. I have completely lost my own identity. Sometimes I'm glad I don't have time to think. Then I don't have to think about what happened to put me where I am.

- I never expected to have to care for someone like I do—a lifetime of supervision and care. I'm overwhelmed sometimes. There is a constant source of frustration as well as flow of prayer.

- We can't change insurances because of all the preexisting conditions our child has. This one situation is something we never expected. Life is tough enough without having to deal with insurance companies and high fees.

- Sometimes I wish there were someone to blame, to pay bills, redo all the paper work, and help take care of my child, so my husband and I could have some time together. This is much harder than others have made it look.

- I did a lot of reading about Down syndrome, but it made me even more depressed because the available information *at that time* was pretty pessimistic.

- Keeping my home in order in the way my obsessive-compulsive child needs is difficult, especially before bedtime. This and other issues have caused such stress on our whole family. I feel as if our whole family has OCD, and our extended family has no clue! They try to listen but have become very judgmental saying, "I would never let that happen. I would not let my child do that."

- I wish people knew that caregivers can't turn off the special needs issue that they deal with, and it's not their fault. A child "acting out" is not necessarily undisciplined. It's the way their brain works or doesn't. More grace, less accusation is needed.

- Depending on the needs, very few resources and little support may be available. Caregivers are often on their own to find services, support, and help.

- My parents thought they might need to put my sibling in an institution, but what they saw was horrible—people lying in feces and urine, blank stares on patients' faces, and poor living conditions. They couldn't do it. They had so much love to dedicate their lives to caring for the needs before them.

- The cost of equipment, therapy, hospitalizations, medication, filling our forms, dealing with insurance, dealing with feeding tubes, and making sure proper nutrition is given, physically lifting (the wheelchair, the person from tub to toilet, etc.), can be overwhelming and never ending and gets more challenging as the person grows and develops. A feeding chair to seat my child at a proper angle is over $4,000 and will need to be updated at different growth periods.

- I have a hard time trusting in God when I can't see Him intervening and when watching my child experience pain.

- I knew this special needs world existed, but I never knew how involved I would be in it. (Child diagnosed with 11 disabilities!)

YOUR STORY

Did you, at some point, feel as if life for you should be convenient, comfortable, fun, and easy?

When did you realize life wouldn't be? How did you react/respond?

What stood in the way of your ability to accept this initial challenge? Pride? Frustration? Other?

_____

What are or were your greatest challenges when you initially recognized your life just got tougher?

_____

_____

_____

What is this struggle doing to you?

_____

_____

_____

Did you ever blame someone for your challenge? If so who? Is the blame valid? If not, what should you do? What can you do?

_____

_____

_____

_____

What are some of life's interruptions that have kept you from listening to Him, from obeying Him, from serving Him? Have you been able to find the opportunity?

_____

_____

_____

What does/would "move on" look like for you? Is it healthy?

_____

Is there anything you feel you need to confess? Write out the issues from your heart.

_____

_____

_____

In what ways have you struggled or seen others struggle?

_____

_____

_____

How have you learned that you aren't in control? Has that been a painful lesson?

_____

_____

_____

What does putting trust in a sovereign God mean to you?

_____

_____

_____

What are some choices you may need to make in your heart?

_____

_____

_____

What do you see as initial steps you can take to handle these hardships, discouragements, frustrations, and interruptions, that have made life tougher?

_____

_____

_____

CHAPTER FOUR

Rough Roads Ahead:
Accepting the Change of Course

Remember the Good Samaritan mentioned at the beginning of Chapter 3? When his journey was interrupted, he and the others who passed by the injured man left for dead in the road had to make a choice, filtering all that was happening at that given moment.

....

Just when Steve and Carol were about to retire, they were told that Carol's mom needed more assistance in her daily life. When the diagnosis of dementia came their way, Steve and Carol realized retirement wasn't likely to follow the plan they had mapped out, and they knew they would have to make adjustments.

....

*Brad and Shirley had two children with special needs. The first had mild autism; the second, ADHD. Expecting their third, they were hopeful that another "special needs" diagnosis **just couldn't** happen again. It did. Hopes dashed, they needed to make some decisions.*

....

OUR STORY

Cindi:

A turning point for us occurred while we were on the road home after visiting a couple whose past had included drugs, alcohol, and other life choices that could have easily caused their children to have developmental or long-term problems. They had a very challenging marriage even in the best of times. On the otherwise quiet trip home, I remember saying to Joe, "They have beautiful, healthy, intelligent children. We never did drugs, abused alcohol, or made poor choices that might have affected our children, and here we are with a son who has special needs. It just doesn't seem fair." It really upset me.

But in Joe's calm and quiet manner, he brought to light something I had not been able to see with my limited vision. He said, "Cindi, can you imagine what life would be for Joey if he were in that family? God has given us a good marriage and an uneventful past, so we could better take care of Joey, and we don't have the guilt that we were the cause of his limitations. What would happen to Joey if he were placed in that home?"

Joe was wearing the glasses with God's lenses. He saw that God allowed us to have Joey because we worked to have a strong marriage and because we functioned as a team to help him and our other children.

I saw myself at a fork in the road. I had some choices to make. Would I become bitter because we had to deal with this challenge the rest of our lives, or would I become a better person? Would I choose to respond to our challenges with love and kindness or react to them in ways that would possibly harm or hurt myself and others? Would I allow myself to be indifferent, or would I choose to be compassionate and caring? What we are to become we are becoming right now.

> *He saw that God allowed us to have Joey because we worked to have a strong marriage and because we functioned as a team to help him and our other children.*

The Challenges

With just one child, our initial challenges were mostly physical and emotional. Caring for Joey required a lot of time and effort, but the C-section and recovery that accompanied Kristina's arrival complicated the daily requirements of caring for Joey. With little sleep I (Cindi) still had to deal with Joey's illnesses, allergies requiring hospital visits, seizures that we were yet to recognize as such, multiple therapies, trips downtown, never-ending questions, and life with a toddler who couldn't walk and could not make his needs known. We continued to feed him because he did not yet have the skills to do so himself; he still had diapers that needed changing and behavior issues to deal with.

Much of the time we felt alone. We were physically worn out, emotionally isolated, and spiritually depleted at times. We had great help from Joey's grandparents, who loved him deeply and accepted him fully, but in other circles we often felt people didn't know what to do or say. Occasionally, people asked, "How's Joey?" but they seldom, if ever, asked what life was like for him or us. We were rarely asked to others' homes. Joey was never asked to come to someone's home to play. He didn't fit in with others his age, and we sensed that kept us from being included in some social gatherings. We wondered whether others thought they'd have to "get involved" if they got too close to us. Others watched our girls at various times easily enough, but such was not the case with

Joey. Other than the grandparents and Cindi's sisters, few people in those early days ever offered or took Joey along with his sisters. In fact, we remember only one time we were all invited to someone's house for visiting and dinner. We were so excited!

When Joey was young, we lacked the freedom to do some of the things our friends and their families did. Now that he is an adult, we still cannot simply pick up with our "empty nester" friends for dinner together or accept other impromptu invitations. We've never been able to go out unless we had someone we trusted to come and care for Joey. His care is different from what our girls ever needed. Sometime we felt trapped. We didn't feel the freedom to talk about it either because we didn't want to hurt others' feelings. We didn't want others to feel obligated to invite us over or to include us, knowing we would likely have Joey with us. The bottom line was we didn't really know how to handle some things, and probably hurt some feelings and made some errors along the way. We had so many challenges and didn't want to add more!

We also faced a challenge to our faith. We asked "Why?" We asked a lot of questions and sometime felt as if no answers were forthcoming. We believed God tested us as He did Job, saying to us, "OK, let's see how much you really love Me. Even if I challenge you to the extreme, will you still follow Me? If I never make things better, will you still love Me? No matter how discouraged you become, will you still tell others about Me?" We saw that He might not answer our questions directly but instead showed us "how" He was going to guide us and help us.

It would have been easy to let these challenges churn and poison—

Our Thoughts

Cindi:

I grew weary of hearing so-called words of encouragement. People told me what a great job I was doing. I was tired and uncertain and didn't really want to hear it! In my thoughts I wanted to quit! Once when Joey was about four years old and Kristina under two, I remember a very frustrating day, which ended with me sobbing in bed. I said to the Lord, "I can't take it any more. I'm ready for you to take me home with You. It won't be hard for Joe to remarry, so why don't you just send him a new wife—and SHE can deal with all of this!" Clearly, He had another plan, and although I was disappointed to wake up the next morning, I knew I had to think differently.

My mother-in-law told us "everything would be fine if Joey could just talk." In my thoughts I'd say, "NO! He'd still be retarded! If he could talk, he still couldn't make all his wishes and thoughts clearly known! Talking wouldn't get him to understand that 2+2 = 4, and he'd still need our help showering, dressing, and getting places. He still couldn't walk right and he'd still act like himself—and probably say things that people would make fun of or laugh at!" I wanted to share my thoughts, but they were negative, so I kept quiet.

This wasn't the way to do it. I thought no one wanted to hear my troubles. That is where trouble starts—in our thoughts—but it doesn't have to end there. Today, when we meet younger couples with special needs children or parents with needs, we encourage them to share their thoughts with someone who will listen and let them work things out verbally. If we develop a healthy thought process, we can grow and develop in positive and healthy ways. We can harvest happiness instead of bitterness, but doing so requires practice and renewal of our mind with scripture and setting our thoughts on what is true, honorable, right, pure, lovely, good, excellent, and worthy of praise according to Philippians 4:8.

Isaiah 55:8-9 says, "'For My thoughts are not your thoughts, neither are your ways My ways,' declares the Lord. 'For as the heavens are higher that the earth, so are My ways higher than your ways, and My thoughts than your thoughts.'" When we realize that He is mighty, that He is sovereign, omnipotent, omniscient, and merciful, we will learn to think differently.

Having a husband, a friend, or even a counselor to talk to is vital to our own personal health. What a blessing to have someone willing to listen through the tough times, and there are many!

As we surrender our lives to the will of God, we will begin to adjust our thinking, knowing our thoughts would give birth to—

Our Attitudes

In the book of Genesis (Chapters 37-50) Joseph is left for dead by his brothers, sold into slavery, wrongly accused of adultery with Potiphar's wife, thrown into prison, and elevated to a position of power in Egypt. What allowed him in the end to extend kindness to his brothers when they came asking for favor? He suffered years of unfair treatment, years of questioning when those "good" dreams he was given would amount to something, and yet he was still waiting! Genesis 50:20 provides the answer. Joseph said to the brothers who had caused much of his bad fortune, "And as for you, you meant evil against me, but God meant it for good in order to bring about this present result, to preserve many people alive."

He could have mumbled and grumbled and kept it all in. He did not allow his thought life to take him in a wrong direction, down the wrong road, but developed the right attitude. Instead of thinking "the world" was against him, he saw that God had a far-reaching plan.

That car ride home and the conversation we had about God graciously giving us Joey was *one* of our turning points. Joe also had said, during that car ride, "God tells us to give thanks *in* all things (Eph. 5:20, Philippians 4:6-7). He didn't say we should be thankful *for* everything. So we need to give thanks for Joey even though we might not be thankful for his retardation, his seizures, his health problems, his lack of development, and all the rest of it. We will give thanks in all those things." We saw that life would be only as good as we could make it. Sure, it wasn't easy, and we still had many more years to care for him, but our perspective changed. It wouldn't always be convenient, comfortable, fun, and easy, but a right attitude would help us to respond properly, and thus, we could choose to do what was right. Choosing what we felt was right would ultimately show—

What We Value

Choosing what we feel is right means choosing what we value. It's that simple and it's that complicated. In our society we want to "fix" things so that life is not interrupted or inconvenienced. If we could take a pill to look the right way, to weigh the right amount, or to change our challenging circumstance, we'd pay the price to pop that pill. Because no pill can cure us from challenges and struggles, we have to decide what we value because that's how we'll decide what we'll do.

Even though we never considered terminating a pregnancy, when the young student asked the question, "If you KNEW your baby was going to have problems, wouldn't you have an abortion?" The answer itself was simple. "No." That answer stated what we valued. We valued life. That was complicated.

Many things go through our minds when it comes to what we value, especially life. No matter on what side of the fence we put ourselves in the "valuing life" debate, we all ask questions that help us define the values we hold. "If I keep this baby and whatever problems it brings, am I ever going to have a life?" "I can't permit this parent/child/friend to remain in a vegetative state. Quality of life isn't good. But is this fair to the individual and me?" "My loved one has lost the ability to reason. Is it fair for her or him to continue living?" Those who ask questions like these may think they lead to rational conclusions—but do they? In the end is the conclusion reasonable or selfish?

What is the problem? We fail to think of the other person, yet we can convince others and ourselves that we have. Consider the parents who terminate a pregnancy because they do not want a child with a disability even though they cannot confirm its severity. We are really thinking about ourselves. We tell ourselves, "I want what is convenient, comfortable, fun and easy for *me*" and in the process delude ourselves into thinking our decision will benefit the other person. (We had been asked to pray for a couple in the process of deciding whether or not to terminate a pregnancy because doctors had determined their child would be born with a cleft palate. Knowing how "fixable" that deformity can be, we were saddened when we learned that they decided to terminate the pregnancy. Granted, surgeries would be required, some extensive, but a full and joyful life is possible with a lip and palate that are imperfectly formed.)

In debating taking the life of the unborn or a newborn with obvious or possible limitations or the elderly or those who can't care for themselves, we can take personal inventory on where we stand in valuing of life. The DVD and accompanying book from National Geographic called *In the Womb* show a heart cell jolting to life on day twenty-two, arm buds developing in week four, glassy eyes forming in week six. Taste buds and separate digits on hands and feet appear by week eight along with purposeful movement, followed in the next four weeks by kicking, covering the face with the arms, facial expressions like squinting and frowning, and response to touch. Statistics show that 88% of clinical abortions happen during these stages, before the twelfth week of pregnancy. Four out of ten women who discover an unplanned pregnancy will choose to abort. More can be found on the website by Prison Fellowship (Mark Early, 1/22/2007) titled "A Visual Apologetic for Life."

Taken a step further, some choose to abort because they have been told that their child has a particular abnormality or disability. The degree isn't always known, yet a decision must be made. Preserving the lives of the challenged says something else about where we stand in valuing life. Psalm 10:2 says, "In his arrogance the wicked man hunts down the weak, who are caught in the schemes he devises." The individual is left with emotional issues and guilt to be dealt with in the future if not in the present.

What does God say about the value of life? Does He specify a certain quality of life? Is it acceptable to take a life that isn't normal or the life of a person who can't make decisions, reason, or take care of himself or herself? And how do we know where the dividing line is? And who wants to be responsible for answering that question when standing before God, the giver of life?

Genesis 1:26, "Then God said, 'Let Us make man in our own image, according to Our likeness.'" We are made after His image and thus we are of great value to Him.

Ephesians 2:10, "For we are His workmanship, created in Christ Jesus for good works, which God prepared beforehand, that we should walk in them." He created us with a purpose.

Psalm 119:73, "Thy hands made me and fashioned me; give me understanding that I may learn Thy commandments." In Psalm 139:1-24, we read that God is "intimately acquainted with all my ways" that He "form(ed) my inward parts; Thou didst weave me in my mother's womb. I will give thanks to Thee, for I am fearfully and wonderfully made; wonderful are Thy works, and my soul knows it very well. My frame was not hidden from Thee when I was made in secret and skillfully wrought in the depths of the earth. Thine eyes have seen my unformed substance. And in Thy book they were all written, the days that were ordained for me when as yet there was not one of them." He knew us from the beginning of our tiny life.

Exodus 4:11, "And the Lord said to him, 'Who has made man's mouth? Or who makes him dumb or deaf or seeing or blind? Is it not I, the Lord?'" He makes no mistakes.

Colossians 1:16, "For in Him all things were created, both in the heavens and on earth, visible and invisible, whether thrones or dominions or rulers or authorities—all things have been created through Him and for Him." He creates that which He loves and for which He has use.

Isaiah 45:9 says, "Woe to the one who quarrels with his Maker—an earthenware vessel among the vessels of the earth! Will the clay say to the potter, 'What are you doing?' Or the thing you are making say, 'He has no hands?' Woe to him who says to a father, 'What are you begetting?' Or to a woman, 'To what are you 'giving birth?' Thus says the Lord, the Holy One of Israel, and his Maker: 'Ask Me about the things to come concerning My sons, and you shall commit to Me the work of My hands. It is I who made the earth, and created man upon it. I stretched out the heavens with My hands, and I ordained all their host.'" Do we think we have the right to argue with the One who has created everything?

Jeremiah 29:11, "For I know the plans that I have for you, declares the Lord, plans for welfare and not for calamity to give you a future and a hope." He thought about His plan before He brought it forward.

Jeremiah 17:7-10, "Blessed is the man who trusts in the Lord and whose trust is the Lord. For he will be like a tree planted by the water, that extends its roots by a stream and will not fear when the heat comes; but its leaves will be green, and it will not be anxious in a year of drought nor cease to yield fruit. The heart is more deceitful than all else and is desperately sick; who can understand it? I, the Lord, search the heart, I test the mind, even to give to each man according to his ways, according to the results of his deeds." We will be accountable for what we do with what the Lord gives us.

Take a moment to reread the scriptures we just shared, and ask yourself what these verses say to you. No matter what we or any other writer, friend, or family member will share with you, what does God's Word say to you? Do you respect life? Do you trust that God has a better plan? If God has allowed it, who are we to terminate it? We realized caring for Joey was going to be our opportunity to model what we valued.

We were never scheduled for an ultrasound with Joey. At the time of his birth in 1981, they were optional. Today, every pregnant woman can have an ultrasound done, and they are so clear you can almost tell whom the baby looks like! It has become a window to the womb, pointing out potential problems. We wonder what our ultrasound might have shown. We believe that it is wrong to *take* a life, but we were now faced with what to do with this precious life we had been given. We wondered "why" it happened to us. We knew we would have to face many challenging years. Our thinking became more complicated as we analyzed what the future would hold. As Christians, we knew and trusted in God, but this challenge would be a test in learning to trust God in a whole new way. We'd have to rely on Him to answer "how" we were going to make it through this journey. We could see the present, but couldn't see that the future would hold—

The Reality

Mom Ferrini needed heart surgery. I (Cindi) went with her to the doctor to make sure all her questions were answered. We wanted to know why she needed the surgery and how it would affect her afterwards. We wanted Mom to know exactly what to expect from start to finish. The doctor described everything to her and said, "When you wake up, you'll feel like a truck hit you, but each day you'll do better and better and heal well. After surgery, I asked mom how she felt and she replied, "The doctor said I'd wake up and feel like I was hit by a truck. That's true, I do, but we failed to ask what size truck it would be!"

That is reality! Reality is sometimes a shock.

Sometimes we just don't know what hit us, and we can't anticipate what the outcome will be when we don't know what is then ahead of us. In her case, healing took time, but eventually she experienced better health and better quality of life.

When caring for someone with special needs, operations and medications will often improve health or quality of life but not cure the individual or change the course of that person's life to make her or him what we'd call "normal." The reality in this case is summarized in this question: Will we be able to run the race set before us or crumble under the weight of this responsibility for a lifetime?

God is not a respecter of men. There is no partiality (Romans 2:11) with Him. It doesn't matter who we are—rich or poor, healthy or unhealthy, good looking or not, well-dressed or shabby, happy or sad, motivated or unmotivated, talented or untalented. When He wants to do something in and through our life, look out! That's when reality hits!

The reality is the day-to-day grind of life and the realization that we have no control over it, and that nothing will ever be the same. That part of life we didn't see coming our way. That part of life, when it hits, we wish hadn't—if we're truly honest. If we are open to learning, it's in that reality where He will give us new vision. He gives us the bigger picture as He walks us through the tests and the storms that challenge us. Until we are willing to become active learning participants, we flounder, trying to figure out

> *It doesn't matter who we are—rich or poor, healthy or unhealthy, good looking or not, well-dressed or shabby, happy or sad, motivated or unmotivated, talented or untalented. When He wants to do something in and through our life, look out!*

what's going on. When we see that He has a plan and that He cared enough for us to entrust His plan to us, we can see the reality and live for Him through it.

For us the reality was caring for our son, and the knowledge that doing so would last a lifetime—either his or ours! When our parents were ill, we knew some illnesses would take a few weeks to recover, but then we faced the reality that more serious health issues might take years of caring before their deaths. A different window of time accompanies every reality. It's never what we expect. No matter what the reality looks like, it is likely a surprise. And what one of us would have chosen it?

But God has a way of comforting us through scripture, telling us the plan He has for us.

Psalm 138:8 comforts us with these words: "The Lord will accomplish what concerns me." He's the God who is acquainted with all our ways, and He will never leave us, no matter what we do or go through according to Psalm 139:1, 3, 8 and Deuteronomy 31:6. And He will give us the strength and the courage to accept the trial or challenge. In addition to knowing that God will accomplish what concerns us, we can be assured that it will also be done so that in the end, it will bring glory to Him and His ultimate purposes. John 9:2-3 says, "And His disciples asked Him, saying, 'Rabbi, who sinned, this man or his parents, that he should be born blind?' Jesus answered, 'It was neither that this man sinned, nor his parents; but it was in order that the works of God might be displayed in him'"—great words from scripture to help us sort out what is real and necessary as well as what our options and values are.

We will find as we learn to listen to what God says to us that He never pushes us or makes us do things. He allows us time to learn, time to figure out where we are straying, how He can help if we allow Him, and yes, He'll even help us sort out—

Our Options

We picture, we plan, we work out details, we discuss, we contemplate, we might even try to manipulate, but sometimes not everything goes as planned. In our case, the disabilities of our son dictated our options. Might the Lord have a different plan—a different vision of the road on which he had placed us? Will we surrender THIS part of our lives or hold onto it in desperation? Will we be able to deal with guilty thoughts or relinquish those thoughts to the Lord? We have choices in how we will answer those questions in our everyday living. We are learning to be aware of and available to the change of course He has planned for us, and when the reality of that happens, we can find joy in the journey because our hearts are prepared and willing to do what He asks. Isaiah 45:9 says, "Woe to the one who quarrels with his Maker." Who are we to say what is best for us?

A defining moment occurred when an elder from our church talked to us about Joey. After hearing us share a few things, he said to us, regarding Joey's condition, "God made Joey just the way He wanted Joey to be made." The shock of that statement took our breath away like a blow to the stomach. Although the statement was true, we were in the early years of caring for Joey and it wasn't until he was much older and we'd experienced years of observing, caring for, and being with him, that we both came to the same conclusion that the elder shared. Yes, Joey was indeed created to have special needs for specific reasons and specifically for us and for reasons only God knew but would slowly reveal to us.

In the first chapter we talked about Proverbs 16:9a, which says, "The mind of a man plans his way, but the Lord directs his steps." No matter what choices we make in life, and there are many, we say we know what we want or think we do! Perhaps because the Lord knows our human nature so well and loves us so much, He is willing to come alongside us and gently direct our steps. This, too, becomes an option.

I Chronicles 28:9, "As for you my son, Solomon, know the God of your father, and serve Him with a whole heart and a willing mind; for the Lord searches all hearts, and understands every intent of the thoughts. If you seek Him, He will let you find Him; but if you forsake Him, He will reject you forever."

God does not force Himself on anyone. He's always there, but we need to ask

Him for His guidance. How about you? Have you ever asked Him? Do you know how? You may already know God intimately. You might say you know who He is, and others may be wondering just what we are trying to say. As we contemplate the options we have before us, what we allow our thought life to be, what we will choose our attitude to reflect, what we truly value, and of course the reality of all we experience, we have another wonderful option, and that is the option of—

Knowing Christ

All the things we've discussed are individually and collectively great things to do, but in and of themselves (attitudes, values, and options) they will likely fail us at times. We can't do any of those things alone. We might have a good attitude for a while, but at some point, we will probably lose it. How can we make it real and permanent? Our position is that we need the Lord in our life guiding us to make right choices, and helping us to behave properly with the right attitude.

Most of us have heard about Jesus Christ, know of His name, and maybe a little about Him. Perhaps you know Him as a prophet or the one who died on a cross and was raised from the dead or one who performed miracles. Perhaps you are just learning about Him for the first time as you read through this book. Maybe you only know His name as Jesus, Christ, God, but know little else about Him. If you know His name, we hope you will be curious to get to know Him personally and seek after Him. If you already know Jesus as your Lord and Savior, we hope you will see changes in your heart that will result in living for and serving Him and develop an intimate relationship with Him.

Like any other relationship, the way to get to know Him is to spend time with Him. When we spend time with others, we learn who they are, what makes them tick, what ticks them off, what makes them happy and sad, and how they will respond in different situations. The way we can get to know the Lord and His truth is through reading the Bible. To learn those very important truths, we need to be in the scripture. The best way to do that is to read the Bible daily and learn how to pray. The Bible is like a compass that will always point us in the right direction on the road ahead, and prayer is the way we will communicate with a loving God.

Joe:

Cindi and I are confident saying that if it weren't for our relationship with the Lord and knowing Christ as our personal Lord and Savior, our life would be much different. While statistics vary, we have read that up to 85% of marriages with a handicapped child or other person with special needs in the home will end in divorce. We look back over the years of our marriage and know our relationship with the Lord has sustained us through difficult times. He is the foundation upon which we have continued to build our personal lives and marriage. Because He is the foundation, we know how we've made it through difficult times. For those who don't understand *how* anyone can have that sure foundation and relationship with the Lord, we want to share with you how you *can* have it.

It is comforting for us to know that there is a God and that this God loves us and cares for us. In John 3:16 we read, "For God so loved the world, that He gave His only begotten Son, that whoever believes in Him should not perish, but have eternal life." This is probably the most familiar verse in the Bible. It's the verse that folks write on signs and then hold up in the end zones at football games during extra points and field goals.

Yet for some of you, hearing that God loves you may be a foreign concept. You may have believed all your life that God was not approachable and that He was somewhere "over the rainbow." That was my concept of God for the first twenty-two years of my life, but the Bible very clearly makes the claim that He loves us. In fact the Bible also claims that God wants us to know Him and have a relationship with Him. John 17:3 says, "And this is eternal life, that they may know Thee, the only true God, and Jesus Christ whom Thou hast sent." Knowing God and being known by Him is what makes life worth living. And this knowledge gets us over all the bumps in the road.

What prevents people from accepting what scripture has to say about the love of God and His desire for us to have a relationship with Him is something called sin. Scripture tells us that people feel isolated from God and all alone in this world because we are separated or isolated from Him. The beginning of the Bible clearly shows that people were created to have fellowship with God, but they chose to go their own independent way; and fellowship with God was broken. Humans' continued pursuit of independence from God, even to this day, can be characterized at one extreme as an attitude of hostile and active rebellion against Him and at the other extreme as passive indifference to Him. Both ends of this behavioral spectrum encompass what is characterized as sin. The Old Testament prophet Isaiah wrote, "All we like sheep have gone astray; we have turned, everyone, to his own way" (Is. 53:6a). In Romans 3:23 in the New Testament, the Apostle Paul wrote, "For all have sinned and have fallen short of the glory of God." Sin created the gap of separation between God and us keeping us isolated from Him and preventing us from having a healthy relationship with Him.

Yet many individuals say something inside of all of us longs to be right with God. Many men and women have spent their entire lives trying to get right with God in order to make it into heaven. Most people are under the impression that God uses some type of magical scale in heaven to weigh our good and bad deeds for that ticket into heaven. They believe whichever way that balance tips when they die determines our eternal destiny.

Of course, the basis for saying that they will make it to heaven is their comparison of their behavior with someone worse than them. They think to themselves, "At least I'm not a serial killer," "I go to church. Well, at least I go to church on Christmas and Easter" (we call these people CEOs, Christmas and Easter Only people). "I don't cheat on my taxes," "I'm a good mom," "I'm a good dad," "I brake for animals." People have endless lists of qualities they think will earn them a place in heaven.

Because they've been a "nice person" all of their life (at least in their mind) and because they heard somewhere that God is a loving God, they believe God will say, when they die, "Oh yeah, you're the nice person. Come on into my heaven!" What we need to keep in mind is that no where in the Bible does it say that God 'grades on a curve'.

Yes, God is a loving God. But He is also a Holy God and a Righteous God. And it is His holiness and righteousness that will not allow any sin to come into His presence. Unfortunately, the fact that God is a Holy God doesn't stop people from thinking that they can get to heaven or, at least get closer to God because they're good people. We need to understand that "closeness" counts in horseshoes and hand grenades, but when it comes to trying to get right with a Holy God, closeness doesn't count. Sin has separated man from God and until the issue of sin is dealt with on an individual basis, people will remain isolated from God. So what is the solution?

Because of God's great love for us, He provided the solution. Romans 5:8 says, "But God demonstrates His own love toward us, in that while we were yet sinners [that is, while we were isolated from God], Christ died for us." This passage makes it clear that Jesus is the solution! Jesus Christ is God's only provision for our sin. Through Jesus alone, we can know God personally and experience His love.

Christians hold the unique belief that God became a man in the person of Jesus Christ. In other words, God stepped over from His side to our side and bridged that gap between God and man. One of the primary purposes of Jesus' ministry was to restore our relationship with God and bridge the gap between humans and God that was created by sin.

To really begin to understand what Romans 5:8 is stating requires understanding God's grace. That is a topic for another time, but here's a helpful acronym to keep in mind when thinking about God's grace:

G – God's

R – Riches

A – At

C – Christ's

E – Expense

To put it another way, we experience God's love and blessings throughout our lives even in the midst of raising and caring for individuals with special needs as a result of what Christ did for us on the cross.

It is important to keep in mind that not only did Jesus die for us, but He also rose from the dead. In I Corinthians 15:3 we read, "Christ died for our sins... He was buried... He was raised on the third day according to the Scriptures... He appeared to Peter, then to the twelve. After that He appeared to more than five hundred."

It wasn't enough for Jesus just to die on the cross. The only way that Jesus could verify that He was who He said He was and that He could do what He said He could do, He had to do something different. He rose from the dead.

Historically, evidence is available that can prove beyond a shadow of doubt that Jesus indeed rose from the dead. (The following references, *The Resurrection Factor* and *The New Evidence That Demands a Verdict* are excellent reading for additional support for this claim.) People have tried for 2000 years to disprove the resurrection but have been unable to do so. More than anything else, it is the resurrection that validates the deity and the claims of Jesus Christ. And one of the most profound claims of Jesus appears in John 14:6. Jesus said, "I am the way, and the truth, and the life. No one comes to the Father except through me."

Please note the use of the definite article *the*. Jesus is not a way to heaven. Jesus makes a very exclusive statement in John 14:6. He is saying no one—absolutely no one—gets into heaven except through Jesus.

Sincerity, church membership, and being a nice person are not the criteria for salvation. God does not grade on a curve. Jesus' statement in John 14:6 is a pretty bold statement, but He makes it very clear that He is not just another way to God. He is not just another option to obtain salvation. No! Jesus is very clearly stating that He, because He is God, is the only way to heaven. Many people do not like to hear statements like that, but we all need to understand that Jesus first made that statement. The choice is a matter of believing what Jesus said or not, and that choice is ours. Jesus will never force us to believe in Him. The evidence and reliability of Jesus' resurrection demands a decision from everyone.

Because of Jesus' death, burial, and resurrection anyone can have the free gift of complete assurance of eternal life in heaven. The next step is to make the choice by faith to accept and receive this free gift of eternal life from Jesus or to reject His claims.

Ephesians 2:8, 9 says, "For by grace [there's that word again] you have been saved through faith. And this is not your own doing; it is the gift of God, not a result of works, so that no one may boast." When we choose to receive this free gift of eternal life, we receive many blessings, one of which is found in John 1:12, "But as many as received Him, to them He gave the right to become children of God, even to those who believe in His name." By receiving Jesus as our Lord and Savior, we become children of God. By faith we agree with God that we are separated from Him because of sin. And by faith we turn from our sin and embrace God's forgiveness. And by faith we receive Christ as our Lord and Savior and receive the assurance of eternal life.

Receiving Christ as Lord and Savior does not provide us personal happiness, but we believe that all Christians have the best opportunity to experience true happiness in this life because of their relationship with Christ. On one hand receiving Christ does not give us any assurance that we will have a trouble-free life. But on the other hand receiving Christ guarantees us the assurance that God will never forsake us even during our darkest times; Hebrews 13:5.

If this makes sense to you, then we ask that you take the time right now and receive Jesus as your Lord and Savior. The following is just a suggested prayer that you can pray. Please keep in mind that God is not concerned with the words as much as He is concerned about the sincerity of your heart.

> *"Lord Jesus, I need you. Thank you for dying on the cross for my sins. I recognize that I am sinner and separated from you. Please forgive me. By faith, I receive You as my Lord and Savior. Thank you for forgiving my sins and giving me eternal life. Make me the kind of person You want me to be. Amen."*

We cannot deny, conceal, excuse, rationalize, or minimize our sins when we approach our God. But thankfully, we can rest assured that when we confess our sins before Him, He will forgive them. Proverbs 28:13 promises, "He who conceals his sins does not prosper, but whoever confesses and renounces them finds mercy."

If you have just asked Jesus into your heart and have done so, you have become His child. If you are not ready, you can ask Him any time. He is always there, ready to hear from you. He will not pressure or push you. He will wait patiently for you to come to Him.

If you feel you can't ask Him into your heart because you have questions or concerns that are not yet addressed, then you will want to spend more time reading the Bible. By doing so, you will be able to get to know more about Him. The Gospel of John in the New Testament is a great place to start. Follow with the reading of the other three gospels, Matthew, Mark, and Luke, which are also in the New Testament. You will begin to see who this Jesus really is.

Others might not be ready to make that commitment because they think they need to *know* more. Let us assure you, if that were the case, we'd still be reading and learning and would not have made that decision to trust in Christ. Both of us received Christ in 1976 and realize that we will never arrive at a place where we *know enough or know it all*. With that thought in mind, let us take you back to a time and place that will likely surprise you.

From the time they were born, we prayed and sang with each of our three children every night before tucking them into bed. At the end of our routine, we always said, "If ever you want to ask Jesus into your heart, let us know and we'll pray with you." We would never force them, but they would know the option was always available. We went to church, so they were regularly exposed to Christ. We talked openly about our faith at home and led Bible studies, and the children were always surrounded with "Christianity." They had the privilege of hearing about the Lord from birth, but we let them know it was their own decision, not ours, that would secure their souls with God. Christianity is not hereditary! Being born into a Christian church or denomination does NOT make you a Christian or give you assurance of eternal life in heaven.

Cindi:

One night, as I was tucking three-year-old Joey into bed, he pointed vigorously to his chest. Because Joey did not yet have the ability to talk, and the only sound he made at that time was "ahhhh." I was concerned that he might have pain in his chest. I tried not to overreact, but I wanted to get to the bottom of whatever his issue was before I left his room for the night. I asked him whether he was OK. He pointed again to his chest. I asked him if he was hurting. He shook his head no. Often, he seemed removed and easily distracted, but this time he was very much intent on getting his point across to me. He kept pointing to his chest, a little harder this time. I asked him if something felt funny inside. He shook his head no and again and a little harder pointed to his chest. It finally occurred to me, he was pointing to his *heart* and maybe he wanted to ask Jesus into it! I asked, him, "Joey, do you want to ask Jesus into your heart?" He smiled, and I could tell, at that moment, he was as lucid, coherent, undistracted, and on target, as I have ever seen. His eyes were bright, and focused directly and intently on me as he nodded, "Yes!" I believe he understood simple "faith"– the active trust of accepting Jesus.

So I bowed my head, taking his little hands in mine. I peeked. He had his eyes closed. I closed my eyes and prayed a similar prayer to the one we shared with you above. With the short prayer finished, we opened our eyes, and I asked Joey, "If you prayed that prayer, where is Jesus right now?" With a huge smile, he pointed to his heart.

We share this simple story to show that no one must have all the answers. Salvation is so simple, but we tend to complicate it. We must simply come to Him as little children and put our trust in Him. Mark 10:15, "Truly I say to you, whoever does not receive the kingdom of God like a child shall not enter it at all." I can assure you that Joey was not a Bible scholar when he professed his faith in Jesus, and he is not a Bible scholar today. He has never read through the whole Bible, but he hears it taught at home and at church and can read portions of it in his children's Bible. He does not have the answer to why bad things happen to good people. He does not even ask why God, if He was such a good God, allows children in third-world countries to die of starvation. He isn't concerned about who gets into heaven and who doesn't. He doesn't seem to wonder why he was created the way he was. He may have had questions, but from the looks of things, God answered them satisfactorily for Joey to want Jesus in his heart.

Since that time Joey has been very aware of good and evil, right and wrong. He knows what is not good on television, and he knows when he is misbehaving. He has learned to apologize when he is wrong, and he often suggests we pray about things, simply by touching us and making us look at his folded hands.

It's so simple. Please don't try to complicate it. You can come to Him whenever you are ready. He's always ready and waiting to hear from you. Without Him, you will do fine for a while, but with Him, you will do fine for the long haul! Salvation occurs at a point in time, but the process of growth is a lifetime. He'll give you the right perspective to run the course of endurance with excellence!

You can pray silently, out loud, in a group, or alone. Practice praying. Luke 11:10-13 tells us, "For everyone who asks, receives; and he who seeks, finds, and to him who knocks, it shall be opened. Now suppose one of you fathers is asked by his son for a fish. He will not give him a snake instead of a fish, will he? Or if he is asked for an egg, he will not give him a scorpion, will he? If you then, being evil, know how to give good gifts to your children, how much more shall your heavenly Father give the Holy Spirit to those who ask Him?" As you learn more about Him, He will then help when it comes to—

Getting the Right Perspective

"You deserve a break today." "You're number one." "You deserve better than this." We've all heard these phrases and have probably bought into them from time to time. The phrases actually make a lot of sense when you're in the midst of sorrow and sadness and feeling as if you'll never experience joy again; however, if we have become children of God, we know that sometimes He allows things to happen in our life that provide us with a new perspective.

We might not make the volleyball team or get that part we wanted in the play. We might be overlooked for a promotion or be talked about unkindly without merit. It's disappointing, but we know we'll live through it and grow from it. But there are times we wonder, "How much more can I take?" in a situation where no change for the better will occur any time soon. We want a break. We want something better than what we are going through. How do we start to get the right perspective in times like those?

It's easy and it's hard. It's easy because scripture tells us *how* gaining the right perspective can be accomplished; it's hard because we have to be *willing* to do it! We started this section by giving people's responses to rough times—take a break because you are number one and you don't deserve this! But God always has a plan different from our own. When we take the time to investigate what He's trying to teach, we find His way is always best. We may have been too self-focused to recognize what was best for us. He wants us to learn to trust Him. Proverbs 16:20, "He who gives attention to the word shall find good, and blessed is he who trusts in the Lord."

Trust takes time to build. We learned to trust our parents as they held the seat of our bike until we were ready to take off on our own. They didn't want us to fall, so they kept us secure until they felt we were confident and ready to go off by ourselves; then they let go. Before we knew it, we were pedaling on our own.

Trusting God is similar. It takes time to watch how He has worked in our life, how He's held us securely even when we didn't know His hand was upon us. Then, when the timing was right, He allowed us to take a step of faith. Yet He stayed right there in case we bobbled and fell. We may think we're the ones who take those steps all on our own, but based upon what scripture says, He's right beside us all along, allowing us to take those steps of faith. The better we know the Bible, the more we will understand what is ours to claim! Here are some scripture verses to ponder as you learn to put your trust in Him.

Psalm 46:10, "Be still and know that I am God." He wants us to come to Him.

I Peter 5:7, "Cast all your care upon Him, for He cares for you." He wants to take our burdens.

Joshua 1:5, "I will be with you; I will not fail you or forsake you." He is always with us.

Proverbs 16:20, "He who gives attention to the word shall find good, and blessed is he who trusts in the Lord." If we do our part, He always does His.

Psalm 146:5, "How blessed is he whose help is the God of Jacob, whose hope is in the Lord his God." We can trust Him with everything, even our hopes and dreams.

Isaiah 43:7-8, "Every one who is called by My name, and whom I have created for My glory, whom I have formed even whom I have made." Whatever He has created has a bigger purpose than we can know or see, and whatever it is, it will honor and glorify Him in the end.

As we learn to trust Him, we learn and desire to obey Him. As we obey Him, taking those steps of faith becomes easier. That faith leads to trusting Him again for the next thing that comes our way. When we walk closely with Him, we don't always know whether it was our idea or His, our plan or His, our course of action or His. He leads, we listen; He guides, and we go. We must simply be careful not to take the credit for what He gives as if it were all our idea. Proverbs 27:1 says, "Do not boast about tomorrow, for you do not know what a day may bring forth." And Proverbs 16:18 reminds us, "Pride goes before destruction and a haughty spirit before stumbling." The Lord encourages us in II Corinthians 12:9, "My grace is sufficient for you, for power is perfected in weakness." Paul continues, "Most gladly, therefore, I will rather boast about my weaknesses, that the power of Christ may dwell in me." It is always about Him, never about us. He controls. He comforts. He heals. He strengthens. He disciplines. He loves. He will never disappoint us, so can we accept what He has given. And if we always got what we thought we wanted, would we really have come to know Him?

"And we know that God causes all things to work together for good to those who love God, to those who are called according to His purpose. For whom He foreknew, He also predestined to become conformed to the image of His Son." (Rom. 8:28-29) Remember, that Christ has the bigger picture in mind, and that our—

Acceptance Is Seeing the Big Picture

It's hard for us to see the big picture. We say we "get it," but God must chuckle hearing those words! We all want the fairytale ending to our lives, but that's only in fairytales. Perhaps God wants us to live in a real world where we learn to trust Him for the ending. He doesn't just *look over* what is going on, He is *involved* in what's going on. We need to include Him, and if we ask, He's there to help.

Cindi:

I remember my mom saying to me, "When I see God, I'm going to ask him why He allowed Joey to be the way he is." And for quite a while, I admit, I felt the same way. We all have that *one* question we think we'll blurt out when we first see God! But the longer that I have known Jesus as my Savior and watched how

He works in every situation, I sense I won't be asking *any* questions! Because of who He is I believe we will have nothing to question, only to thank and worship. Isaiah 55:9 helps us to understand a little about who God is by what He says about Himself: "For as the heavens are higher than the earth, so are My ways higher than your ways, and My thoughts than your thoughts." I believe instead of even considering asking a question, I will likely fall flat on my face in awe and in tears, say to the Lord, "Oh, that little thing! How silly of me to be concerned about that *now*! I see your plan, and what a beautiful one it was!"

Joe:

Coming to the realization that Joey would never be an athlete and that I would never be able to play catch with him or be able to help him make career decisions was not an easy process. My life, our lives, our blueprints for our life as a family, the way life was going to be for us—none of it was happening the way I had hoped it would. I distinctly remember standing at a crossroads when thinking about Joey and our life in general. I could either shake my fist at God and say, "How dare you!" or face the reality and say, "Okay, God, I see the situation before us. I don't understand it, but I see where we are." My next decision would influence everything from that moment on.

Believe me, I agonized at this crossroad. I would like to say, "Ah, it was a piece of cake!" "No problem, God, bring it on. I'll be fine. Let's move on." But I struggled. I hated the idea of having a handicapped son. I knew I was going through the steps of grieving, and I hated it. But it was through much prayer support and by God's grace (there's that word again) that I was finally able to say, "Thank you for my son being just the way he is." From that point forward, my entire perspective changed. Don't get me wrong. Life didn't get easier. It fact it got tougher as we mentioned earlier. Only now, I took God's perspective on our situation. Once I surrendered my will to His will, I loved my son at a whole new level in a way I could not prior to making my decision to receive Joey just as he was and is.

It's often hard to say when those actual moments are when we move from wanting, demanding, and expecting our own way to full acceptance of the situation. For us it began with recognizing that God had a plan just for us and that we had no control in this situation. It didn't always feel good because we all want that life of ease, but remember what the scripture says in Psalm 138:8, "The Lord will accomplish what concerns me." We never had control, nor will we ever. When we accepted that fact, we could move on and learn what God had in store for us as a family and for our son as an individual. As we have yielded our wills to His will, our desires to His desires for us, we have learned how to walk in obedience to God, loving and trusting Him first, and then seeing what He can accomplish when we allow Him control of our lives.

But can we trust Him for what we need? For what our son will need? Why do we feel helpless when we are walking with and know the Lord?

Hopeless to Hopeful

These are all very real questions that everyone must answer. We can experience the power of God in different ways, including reading the Bible, hearing the Bible taught, meditating on the Word and memorizing scripture. I am convinced that if we faithfully study the Word of God, we will ultimately achieve intimacy with the God of the Word. In addition, praying to God and making prayer a regular part of our lifestyle are essential to drawing closer to Him.

Another way to learn about God and increase our level of trust in Him is to seek fellowship in a Bible-believing church with others who love the Lord. As church members learn about our challenges and situations, we hope they are willing to listen to our concerns and may even offer help when they can. Still another way to experience the presence of God is to tell others about Him, that is, what Jesus did for us and continues to do in our life. This encourages us as we share with others the hope that we have because of our relationship with God.

All these spiritual disciplines are absolutely essential in drawing closer to God, but as we review our life and try to identify one essential discipline that kept us on track with God, it would be acknowledging the importance of being filled with the Holy Spirit. To begin to understand the filling with the Holy Spirit, we need to start with a basic explanation of the Holy Spirit.

To eliminate confusion, let's answer this question: "Who is the Holy Spirit?" Please notice we did not ask, "What is the Holy Spirit?" The Holy Spirit represents a person but can also be understood as the Spirit of God or the Spirit of Jesus. These are all synonymous terms. The Holy Spirit is God. He is third person of what is called the Trinity. The Holy Spirit is coequal with the God the Father and God the Son. As Christians we believe in only one true God, but this one God has seen fit to manifest Himself in three persons. Now you may be saying, "I don't understand this Trinity thing completely." And we would say to you, "You're not alone!" Someone has once said, "He who denies the Trinity loses his soul, but he who tries to explain the Trinity loses his mind." But as you study the scriptures, the evidence is overwhelming that indeed the Holy Spirit is God, the third person of the Trinity.

The Holy Spirit plays many different roles in a Christian's life. For example, the Holy Spirit teaches us how to live by guiding us to truth. In John 14:26, Jesus said, "But the Helper, the Holy Spirit, whom the Father will send in My name, He will teach you all things, and will bring to your remembrance all that I said to you." In the original Koine Greek, the language in which the New Testament was first written down, the word translated as *helper* in our modern English version came from two Greek words—*para* and *kletos*, para meaning "alongside" and kletos meaning "invited, or one called". (Joseph Henry Thayer's <u>A Greek-English lexicon of the New Testament</u>). Combining these words conveys the idea that the Holy Spirit comes alongside of us, attaching Himself to us, strengthening us, comforting us and giving us life. Parakletos is just the opposite of a parasite, which also comes alongside of us and attaches to us and takes life away from us. The Parakletos, the Holy Spirit, gives us life.

The Holy Spirit also convicts us of the presence of sin in our lives. Again Jesus, referring to the Holy Spirit in John 16:8, said, "And He [the Holy Spirit], when He comes, will convict the world concerning sin, and righteousness and judgment." The conviction of the Holy Spirit helps us to better understand how we are to be living out our lives before God. In this case, the Holy Spirit helps people to recognize their state of sin and the need for a savior—Jesus.

As was mentioned earlier, the role of the Holy Spirit that has been most instrumental for us in dealing with the daily issues of life in general and definitely with the issues of raising our son is the role of being under the control of the Holy Spirit. The Bible describes this control as "being filled with the Spirit." In Ephesians 5:18 it says, "And do not get drunk with wine, for that is dissipation, but be filled with the Spirit." Please understand that the issue in Ephesians 5:18 is not drinking. The issue in this passage is one of control. When you're drunk with wine, you are not under control; that's what dissipation is.

If we go back to the original Greek from which our English translation has been derived, we know four things about Ephesians 5:18.

1. It is an imperative statement. This means that to be filled with the Holy Spirit is a command of God. This is not a suggestion.

2. It is written in the present tense. This means that being filled with the Holy Spirit is to be a continuous action. One can be filled today and at the same time realize that tomorrow he or she will need to be filled again, hence continuously.

3. It is written in second person plural. This means it is for all who have the Holy Spirit dwelling in them. Individuals filled with the Holy Spirit have received Jesus as their Savior. When someone receives Jesus, he or she receives God; that is, the individual receives the Godhead—God the Father, God the Son, and God the Holy Spirit—at the same time.

4. The verb "be filled" is what we call passive voice. When a sentence is written in passive voice, the subject, in this case the person desiring to be filled with the Holy Spirit, is acted upon by an outside force, in this case, God the Holy Spirit.

In essence when someone is filled with the Holy Spirit, she or he doesn't get more of God. God gets more of that person. Here is an example, suppose you are driving down a long road and you see a hitchhiker ahead of you. You decide to stop and pick up the hitchhiker. When you stop, you recognize that it is Jesus. So you say to Jesus, "Okay, hop in the back seat." And Jesus responds, "No, you hop in the back seat and I'll drive." You now have to make a decision. Who is going to be in control? You or God? The point of Ephesians 5:18 is that God wants to be in control of your life, but you have to let Him be in control. That is your decision alone. When we ask God the Holy Spirit to fill us, we are asking Him to take control of our lives as we surrender our lives to Him. We are giving Him complete control of our life. By faith, when we ask God to fill us with His Holy Spirit, we are allowing the Holy Spirit to direct and empower our life. It's a choice that only the individual can make.

All who are filled with the Spirit benefit from the "fruit of the Spirit." Galatians 5:22-23 says, "The fruit of the Spirit is love, joy, peace, patience, kindness, goodness, faithfulness, gentleness, self-control; against such things there is no law."

If we are regularly filled with the Holy Spirit, we will begin to experience and manifest the fruit of the Spirit in our life. Once the fruit of the Spirit is regularly being manifested in our life, there will be a character transformation in our life. This takes place as we learn to surrender our life continuously to the control of the Holy Spirit.

For example, it was the Holy Spirit that helped us to have self-control and peace in the midst of Joey's second or third grand mal seizure in an hour. It was the fruit of the Holy Spirit called patience that helped us to watch and stand-by an elderly parent undergoing rehabilitation for the third time. By being filled with the Holy Spirit, we can deal with the daily trials of raising a special needs child or caring for someone handicapped. Knowing that God is faithful and that He will never leave us alone during these trials gives great assurance and confidence to get through these difficult times.

The question is "How can I be filled with the Holy Spirit?" Even though God commands it, we still have a conscious choice to make. We must choose who will be in the driver's seat of our life, that is, we need to decide who will be in control of our lives moment by moment, ourselves or God.

The first step in being filled with the Holy Spirit is to have the desire to be filled with the Holy Spirit. Secondly, we must confess any known sin and repent of those sins. And then, by faith we ask God to fill us with His Holy Spirit.

We know that being filled with the Holy Spirit is a command of God, and we know that He hears our prayers. That's a great combination to give us assurance that we will be filled with the Holy Spirit when we ask.

We can ask simply, "Heavenly Father, please fill me with Your Holy Spirit. Take control of my life and help me to be the kind of person You want me to be. I'm tired of trying to control things over which I have no control. As an act of my will and by faith, I ask you to control, direct, and empower my life by filling me with your Holy Spirit. In Jesus' name I pray. Amen."

If you just prayed that prayer, God has filled you with His Holy Spirit, and isolation and loneliness will fade away in the presence of the author of intimacy! As you allow God to control your life, you gain the renewed hope that you will be able to face another day.

When we choose to submit our wills, our desires, and our thoughts to God every day, we ask Him to give us His strength to live out that day for others, ourselves, and ultimately for His glory. As He works in and through us, we will grow in grace, act justly, and show kindness and mercy in that process. (Micah 6:8.)

We remember a woman a few steps ahead of us in life and with very similar life issues. She said, "Oh, I cried for about two weeks when I learned my son was retarded. Then I was fine with everything." We were glad it worked out that way for her, but it didn't happen that way for us. It took time to see God work and realize He was in control. We have learned a lot and grown in ways we didn't think possible. It took longer than two weeks. For some people it may take years. Some handle the initial news well and then fall apart, never to recover. Others fall apart upon hearing the news and then with help from God and others are able to move on to be productive, helpful, caring individuals. Whatever time frame God has for you, try to understand that it may take time for you to come to a place where you fully accept what He intends for you. In the meantime, know that these trials will produce—

Endurance

We all want to be happy, and those of us who are Christians want to be joyful representatives of the Lord; but when adversity and challenge strike, how can we be happy and joyful?

I Peter 4:19, "Let those also who suffer according to the will of God entrust their souls to a faithful Creator in doing what is right." That's a tough verse to swallow when you're caring for people day and night with little or no help or compassion from others. Yet it is still true. When we do what is *right*, we entrust our souls to *God*! We rely on Him to care for us.

What discourages, delays, or defeats us in our journey can be turned to good. We have often said, "We can't 'figure it out.'" If it's His will and His plan and His way, it's not worth figuring out. We must simply accept what God has for us. Acceptance is a daily process. I Peter 4:12-13, "Beloved, do not be surprised at the fiery ordeal among you, which comes upon you for your testing as though some strange thing were happening to you; but to the degree that you share the sufferings of Christ, keep on rejoicing; so that also at the revelation of His glory, you may rejoice with exultation." Lamentations in the Old Testament gives us further encouragement. Chapter 3:22-24 says, "The Lord's loving-kindnesses indeed never cease for His compassions never fail. They are new every morning; great is Thy faithfulness. 'The Lord is my portion,' says my soul, 'therefore I have hope in Him.'" As we trust and obey Him, we will see Him daily in His fullness in our lives. We build up endurance to get through this day and tomorrow by trusting His faithfulness. In times of greatest challenge, we have prayed out of desperation and come away knowing we have been heard by a God who listens and cares. He delivers His faithfulness when we don't even know we need it.

If we do all this, does it mean we'll never struggle, be disappointed, discouraged, have grief or sorrow? NO! It means we'll know how to deal with it better. Ps. 37:24, "Though he fall, he shall not be utterly cast down; for the Lord upholds him."

When babies initially learn to walk, they fall more often than take steps. Parents and loved ones encourage them! What joy we share as we watch that little one learn what it feels like to stand up and take steps. As we discover what it takes to walk closely with God, taking baby steps to trusting in Him and learning the meaning of confidence in Him and the plans He has for us, we will then in turn be an—

Encouragement to Others

How we respond to our trials is simply a strong reminder to ourselves and to those watching, an example of *how* to trust God. As the Israelites wandered in the desert for 40 years, they faced hardships and challenges. When they came to the Red Sea, God didn't take them away from it or out of it, nor did He have them go around it. God parted the Red Sea so they could go through it on dry land. At times we must admit our failures and at times share our successes. If we desire to glorify the Lord in all we do, we will be an encouragement to others as we live honest and transparent lives. II Corinthians 3:3 says, "You are a letter of Christ, cared for by us, written not with ink, but with the Spirit of the living God, not on tablets of stone, but on tablets of human hearts." As we walk with God, He writes on our hearts His message, which others will read. Are we that letter others will read to know who our Lord is?

Cindi:

Joe's mom used to say to me, "By nature you are an oak, but God sent you Joey and He's making you more like a willow." She was right. I share this often. God creates us and molds us in ways that will make us more like Him. II Corinthians 5:17 says, "If any man is in Christ, he is a new creature; the old things passed away; behold, new thing have come." He changes us to be an encouragement to others.

So, how do we bend and not break? We bend at the knees and come to the Lord in—

Prayer and God's Word

Can we simply pray and make problems, our troubles, and challenges disappear?

We should pray for many reasons. **Prayer is our communication with God.** He says "yes," "no," or "not yet" to our requests. He will indeed answer, but we must be prepared to take whatever answer He gives—and it isn't always what we want to hear. That makes praying hard. Our human nature wants its own way, so when He doesn't give us our way, we are disappointed; but we can learn by listening and waiting to discover His bigger picture.

God speaks to us through the scripture we read daily. It is a source of great strength, which encourages, guides, teaches, reproofs, and holds us up to a standard. We want to live in such a way that others see what He is to us and what He does for us. He tells us in James 1:5-8, "If any of you lacks wisdom, let him ask of God who gives to all men generously and without reproach, and it will be given to him. But let him ask in faith without any doubting, for the one who doubts is like the surf of the sea driven and tossed by the wind. For let not that man expect that he will receive anything from the Lord, being a double-minded man, unstable in all his ways." We read in Matthew 6:33-34, "But seek first His kingdom and His righteousness, and all these things shall be added unto you. Therefore do not be anxious for tomorrow; for tomorrow will care for itself. Each day has enough trouble of its own." We prayed for a healing of our son, but God had other plans.

When the healing didn't happen, we struggled with doubt, wondering whether we really had the faith needed to see a miracle occur. As we searched the scripture, we realized that our plan might differ from what He wanted to accomplish. John 14:13 says, "Whatever you ask in My name, that I will do, that the Father may be glorified in the Son." If we asked "big" we might receive "big." If we prayed more, perhaps we'd see more of God's power. It's so easy to play mind games with ourselves when we think we know what we want! We certainly had a lot to learn, and we could not presume to know what God thought would be best for Joey and for us. Were we more concerned with inner substance or outer appearances?

As prayers were answered, we saw that opening our minds and hearts to God's intention was what He wanted and that He is creative, honest, true, just, and always provides something to learn! We knew that we had to make prayer meaningful. Will prayer be our last resort, or will we make it our first response? It was and continues to be one of the more important lessons He teaches us. He simply wants us to come to Him in prayer, humbly, honestly, often, and first. Before talking to others, before seeking counseling, before asking a friend, He wants us to come to Himself first. We read Jeremiah 29:11 earlier, but let's read on to verses 12-13. "Then you will call upon Me and come and pray to Me and I will listen to you. And you will seek Me and find Me, when you search Me with all your heart." He provides and we must trust that He will.

> *Will prayer be our last resort, or will we make it our first response?*

Prayer helps us to see His perspective. When we travel down a long, hazardous road and seek God along the way, He meets us there. He teaches us specific lessons that are meant for us and no other.

Prayer can help us to turn the burden over to God. Even as the Lord will accomplish *what* concerns me, there is another verse in Psalm 57:2, "I will cry to God Most High, to God who accomplishes all things for me," which helps me understand that He actually takes care of those concerns for me. While we are in the process of struggling, discouraged, discontented, and whatever else we're enduring, we know that He will accomplish in, through, and for us whatever is needed. We don't need to worry (but we sometimes do); we don't need to be anxious about the results (but we sometimes are); and we don't have to be concerned about the future (but we sometimes go there). No matter where we are, we can cry out to Him, and He will not only hear us but also answer us.

Will we hear His voice? We might! We know He speaks to our hearts, and He reassures us time after time that He is in control by faithfully accomplishing what we didn't think could be possible. As we see Him work, our faith is strengthened. As our faith is strengthened, our love for Him grows deeper and we are encouraged. As we are encouraged, we find the strength to endure whatever comes our way.

Prayer will help us to know Him better. God is our greatest source of strength. Through prayer we will get to know Him more personally. Pray to know Him, His ways, and His ways for you. Luke 11:9-10, "And I say to you, ask, and it shall be given to you; seek and you shall find; knock and it shall be opened to you. For everyone who asks, receives; and he who seeks, finds; and to him who knocks, it shall be opened."

Prayer may change how I see the situation and may help me to respond properly to it. We will either become bitter or better as a result of our response to what God has given. We stand at a crossroads when we realize God has not answered our prayer as we thought He would.

When Joey was about 5 years old, after years of praying every night together and often individually, asking the Lord to heal Joey and make him whole, I (Cindi) felt very strongly that God had answered our prayer. I approached Joey's room in the morning with excitement and anticipation as I *knew* he would sit up in bed and speak audibly to me. As Joey looked at me with his big, bright green eyes, I knew it was coming—our first conversation—and he opened his mouth and said, "Ahhhhhh, ahhhhh, ahhh, ahhhh." For a few seconds I sat there as on a frozen movie screen. Nothing. Nothing changed. Then I came to the realization that nothing was going to change.

I had to decide, right there, how I was going to respond. Not to Joey, but to God. At that moment I was crushed that He denied me the answer to the prayer we had been praying. I realized I had a choice to make, and I believe He let me in on a little secret. He does not give everyone a child with special needs. He wanted to give us something so special that for whatever reason He chose us. In a wave of understanding, I realized that God would sustain our compassion for our son, helping us through sleepless nights, behavioral challenges, and health issues. As I shared what happened with Joe, we began to see our challenges in a new and different way. We cherished this secret gift He gave us, realizing that when we share eternity with Joey, we will have the awesome privilege of seeing him whole. Joey is as whole as God wants him right now. God's plan for Joey is perfect for now. Someday he will walk and talk and sing and run, and do all the things that did not come easy for him here on earth. He may even understand math if he even needs it! He will probably be in charge of something in heaven someday. Don't be surprised if he is in charge of a lot of things. Even though we can't see it the way it will be, we think it will be very special!

When God let us in on the little secret plan He had for our life, we chose the way we would respond. For us, it was a point of decision. We loved Joey the way he was, and we love him the way he is, so we had to move on from there in order to get the best care we could for him. We decided that no further testing regarding his retardation and cerebral palsy would be done on Joey unless there was a possibility of a cure or healing. We would be content with God's plan for Joey and love him unconditionally regardless of a label that might be imposed on him. The doctors didn't do that for us. God did. We were no longer interested in what the doctors were thinking in order to put words on paper for some study. Our hearts were healed, and that was probably the only healing that God wanted to take place in the first place. We were just too human to admit it or see it. It took time.

In II Corinthians 12:7-10 Paul asked the Lord three times to take some illness or issue from him. The Lord did not do as Paul asked. Paul shares with us the lesson he learned: "And He [God] said to me, 'My grace is sufficient for you, for power is perfected in weakness.' Most gladly, therefore, I will rather boast about my weaknesses, that the power of Christ may dwell in me. Therefore I am well content with weaknesses, with insults, with distresses, with persecutions, with difficulties, for Christ's sake; for when I am weak, then I am strong." He learned that Christ was his strength and all he needed. We must do the same. Face the issue, meet it head on, get help, pray, move forward, don't dwell on the unchangeable, and seek His strength to get through every day. God doesn't ask us to understand it, He asks us to accept it. He wants us to go with His plan instead of ours.

God doesn't ask us to understand it, He asks us to accept it. He wants us to go with His plan instead of ours.

Prayer can help us connect to others in their time of need. We need to observe when others are going through a tough time; otherwise we risk missing a golden opportunity. Prayer is sometimes the last thing we think about in a crisis, but it should be our first line of defense. For those in crisis, someone uninvolved in it may more easily see the immediate need to pray. Be gentle. Be ready. Be willing. Don't miss an opportunity to connect with someone who is in need.

Mom Ferrini repeatedly told us she never slept, yet whenever we'd check on her, we'd find her snoring and sound asleep, not moving or waking when we'd cover her up. She was very discouraged and shared some things that made us think maybe she was afraid to go to bed alone and maybe even afraid of dying. We were frustrated by her frequent refrain: "I can't ever sleep." After numerous failed attempts to get her from the couch to the bed, we decided to tuck her in bed every night and pray with or for her through Philippians 4:8, "Finally, brethren, whatever is true, whatever is honorable, whatever is right, whatever is pure, whatever is lovely, whatever is of good repute, if there is any excellence and if anything worthy of praise, let your mind dwell on these things." Often, we'd ask her to try to think of something in her day that fit one of the categories, something true from God's word or something for which she could praise God. Usually by the end of the prayer, she was asleep.

When we travel a rough road, are detoured by discouragement, or simply run out of gas, we long for someone to notice and understand. We may not be strong enough to set off a flare that says, "Here I am! I need help!" Those with health issues might not even know what is discouraging them or how to express it. Anyone who takes notice can simply say, "I will pray for you," or if they are open to it, pray *with* them. If we ignore those opportunities, we miss supporting someone (whether patient or caregiver) who is driving on empty.

Prayer helps us to understand the needs others have. If we want someone to "walk a mile in our shoes," we have to be willing to walk a mile in theirs. Have we done so? A good start is to pray for others. Get to know them, their needs, their struggles, and then pray. At that point, you can move to a place where you might walk with them in those struggles. It takes time and commitment and love. We might even learn to enjoy the journey with them.

Whether or not we have the support of fellow Christians, family, or friends, in word and action, we must do what God expects of us. Psalm 73:26 tells us how to respond: "My flesh and my heart fail; but God is the strength of my heart, and my portion forever." What others do or don't do, does not change God's desire that we approach every situation by yielding to Him and by—

Giving Thanks

A dear friend was taught to look intentionally for the "blessing of the day." We often look for the blessing as well. It's catchy. In the midst of otherwise uneventful, bad, long, challenging days, we can usually come up with at least one.

As Mom Ferrini progressed in her dementia, her previously fun personality began to change. The upbeat and positive person was no longer, and her illness took a toll on our household. We decided we had to initiate sharing our blessing of the day when we met as a family for dinner around the table. It was funny at first. Mom had a hard time finding something she could consider a blessing. Dementia had made her negative and self-centered, unlike the way we had always known her. During the first round of sharing blessings, Mom talked about herself and her ailments. We daily talked her through the "blessing" exercise.

Cindi:

Sometimes this exercise took us two steps forward and three back. Mom complained about her physical ailments. One Sunday we all tried to get out the door for church, but we could not convince her to go. Because she often confused the phone with the remote and could never remember how to use the microwave, I decided it would be best to stay home with her. She went on and on for quite some time, repeating herself to a point that I entered into a "brisk" discussion with her. I told her she needed to get her eyes off all her negativity and onto the Lord. I'm not sure whether she was more surprised at my words to her or if I was more surprised at what she shared at dinner as the blessing of her day. "My blessing of the day was the conversation Cindi and I had, and I do need to think differently and thank the Lord. I thank the Lord for our talk." Knowing how "brisk" the discussion had been, I was shocked that she counted it a blessing; but I was also thankful that she said so. It was certainly my blessing of the day, too!

Finding the blessing in every day trials is shown by being able to give thanks. Psalm 100:4-5 says, "Enter His gates with thanksgiving and His courts with praise. Give thanks to Him; bless His name. For the Lord is good. His loving kindness is everlasting, and His faithfulness to all generations." As we practice thanksgiving, it comes easier to us, and we learn that through it all, He is—

Building Character in Us

Our very human nature rebels against pain or crisis in our life, yet it can and often does yield beautiful results if we let it. Crisis builds character. If you don't believe so, you've never had crisis. If you think you'll just skip over this section because you've never experienced crisis, please don't. The fact is you *will* experience some crisis at some point of your life. It's just a matter of time. And when that happens, will you know *how* to deal with it? Will you know *why* it has been sent to you? We all have different individual problems, challenges, suffering, struggles, issues, and crises but the same need—for Jesus.

Suffering and in pain, we will respond in some way. "Hurt either makes us or breaks us. It moves us toward God or causes us to angrily run away from Him. It draws people to comfort and minister to us or causes us to chase them away and drown in our own bitterness. The latter response is a tragedy because if we ever need help, it is when we are hurting," wrote David Stevens, M.D., in the Fall 2007 issue of *Today's Christian Doctor: The Journal of the Christian Medical and Dental Association*. Experiencing pain can wake compassion. If not, the problem is likely a hard heart. It may take a lot of suffering for our hearts to soften enough to hear from the Lord.

Psalm 119:71 conveys a surprising message: "It is good for me that I was afflicted, that I may learn Thy statutes." We've never come across anyone who wants to endure pain, suffer hardship, be treated cruelly, know hatred and be ignored, or endure any challenge in life; but the lives of those who have seem all the richer. The very afflictions, hardships, and challenges that bring us to the point of breaking allow us to come to God, who will build character in us through our afflictions.

Experiencing pain can wake compassion.

When we learn the things He wants us to learn, we can, in turn, become more beautiful. We become compassionate, loving, caring, and considerate; acquiring a myriad of other wonderful character traits. When we cast our burdens on Him (Psalm 55:22), we learn to depend upon Him (II Corinthians 3:5) and gain our sufficiency from Him. Through our weakness we can be nourished by His strength. As we realize that He directs our steps, we can continually give Him our burdens.

In the meantime, He molds our character, teaching us how to love unconditionally, guiding us to pray more than we thought possible. He will put people in front of us, situations that will stretch us, issues that will bend us, crises that will crush us, all for us to realize how much we need Him. We'll continue to learn how little we know, how much we need Him, and how much he cares for us. It's all a part of His big picture for our lives. We are like immature pearls or diamonds in the rough. As the irritation of a grain of sand in an oyster produces a beautiful, shiny pearl or pressure and time turn coal into a sparkling diamond, our irritations and pressures over time will make us who we will eventually become and lead us—

From Trial to Triumph

We have choices.

Trials can make us bitter or better. Getting from one to the other may take a while, so the remainder of this book will deal with that process. What we make of these trials, using what we learned, choosing to be content and full of life that we might impart this life to others—that is how we triumph! When we let our mind dwell on what God wants instead of on want we think we want, we will have the opportunity to overcome what troubles us and in the process, others will see that attitude in us.

Trials have the power to make us sour, but we can triumph and become sweet. Psalm 34:8-9 says, "O taste and see that the Lord is good; how blessed is the man who takes refuge in Him! O, fear the Lord, you His saints; for those who fear Him, there is no want." Proverbs 17:22 says, "A joyful heart is good medicine, but a broken spirit dries up the bones." We can choose how we will act and how we will turn out!

Trials can cause anger, but we can triumph over it. Proverbs 16:32, says, "He who is slow to anger is better than the mighty, and he who rules his spirit, than he who captures a city." That is triumph.

On one hand if we don't properly use the trials we are given, we will likely become repetitive sinners, ungrateful, unhappy, nasty, manipulative, pushy, expectant, and contentious (you get the picture). Others don't want to be around this type of person. On the other hand we can triumph with the Lord's help and become sweet-spirited, kind, helpful, and caring (you get this picture, too). With whom would you prefer to spend time? When we choose to believe that God has a purpose for our pain instead of the lie that we were somehow the only one to be dealt "this" blow, we can go from sinners to winners from trial to triumph, but it's a choice.

What choices will you make? It all goes back to the source of our challenges. Is our thought life Christ-like? Do we model a proper attitude? Do we know what our values are and what our reality is? Do we know our options? Do we know Christ? Do we have a Christ-like perspective so that we can make proper choices, accept what He has for us, develop endurance, give encouragement, enjoy times of prayer, give thanks to God, and allow Him to build our character? Making the right choices will allow us to see that trials are temporary and triumphs are eternal. Pain and challenges always have a purpose. How that purpose plays out depends on us.

> *Making the right choices will allow us to see that trials are temporary and triumphs are eternal. Pain and challenges always have a purpose.*

Steve and Carol, whom we mentioned in the opening of this chapter, knew that Carol's mom would need a lot of help and attention, so they readjusted their thinking to meet her needs. They each had to give in order to move on together, but they accepted the challenge and altered their thinking and their lives to minister to her.

Brad and Shirley had been through difficult times before but not during a pregnancy. Firm about having the child, they never considered abortion, but realistically, they knew they would have to make a lot of adjustments in their thinking and in their lives. Together they determined the Lord could help them change their thinking and take hold of what they needed to move forward in a positive way.

None of the people we just described had a convenient, comfortable, fun-filled, or easy life, but each had the desire to please the Lord in caring for one who could not care for herself or himself as well as the determination to make it work. Because these people were dedicated to serving Christ, they knew He would get them through this challenge.

OTHERS' STORIES

- It's really hard to be around negative people (particularly when it seems that they are complaining about minor things in their life that don't look challenging at the moment; at least not to me). I have so many negative obstacles going on in my life that are also "ongoing" as I care for a special needs adult. It takes a lot of emotional energy to stay happy and be positive, so it is really a challenge for me to be around people who (without even knowing it) are so negative that they tend to bring me down. I need to be around people who are "life-giving" and positive and happy. Life is too short for others' emotions to rule ours.

- I know that I don't share my thoughts and feelings as I probably should. In the midst of a *life-threatening* hospital stay for my toddler, I responded to a call from someone who obviously needed me to help her check something off her "to do" list, but who showed no interest in my toddler. I caught myself sounding all "perky" saying, "I must run to the hospital to see how things are going." What I was thinking and maybe should have expressed was more like this, "This is not just a quick errand I'm running in my day. My husband has been there (not sleeping) all night, and now has to go to work. I'm going to the hospital for the next twelve to fifteen hours to sit there and watch my child in distress. I will emotionally have to keep it together for my little one, my husband, the rest of our family, and in front of all the doctors and nurses who will be talking to me and updating me on how things are going through this crisis. I am emotionally and physically spent, and I'm making it sound like it's no big thing, but it is, and you haven't even inquired about my child." I shouldn't judge whether someone doesn't seem to care, but when they don't ask, "How is your child doing?" when they know your child is in the ICU, I really don't see a point in sharing my pain. I'm not sure whether telling her how I felt or letting her check me off her list was better. I chose letting her check me off her list.

- I knew I had to learn all I could to deal with our situation. Prayer and knowing God were all highly important, but I still had to do the *work* of learning how to handle life, especially being patient. It is an ongoing, never-ending process.

- Joining a support group was helpful for me. It isn't an answer for everyone, but it helped me to accept the life of challenges before me. Some of these people have become life-long friends. Others I prefer not to see again, but that is part of making choices. With those who have remained in our life, we have positive, healthy relationships I cherish.

- Desiring to make life as *normal* as possible for my special needs son became my life's goal. It is a daily effort and struggle, but I try.

- We are thankful our grandson survived a premature birth and cerebral palsy. We also give thanks that his family is handling the dealings with many doctors, therapists, and surgeries. We appreciate that we are in a part of the country that provides great care. We are observing how God will carry out His purpose in this non-typical life!

- We could refuse to trust God, but that would leave us with fear and still nothing will change in our situation. Even though I sometimes feel deserted by God, I want to trust Him.

- Being given two special needs children has actually improved my life. They allow me to see in detail the clarity of the gospel, God's creation of these children for His purposes, and the way He will lead and guide us over their lifetime. I am more compassionate, and my pride is broken.

- Being more realistic from the start helped me enjoy the journey for what it was. My child will never function normally/typically, and I needed to accept the fact I wasn't going to change it, but I might be able to improve some things.

- The older my Down syndrome son gets, the more I realize that life is a challenge, and we have challenges with all our children and all of life. We must learn to look at each as a gift and a blessing.

- It hurts that one of my parents was ashamed of my sibling with special needs. It deeply hurt our relationship. It is a load one can't handle well without knowing God.

- There is no hope that my friend in a wheelchair will ever walk. To me that is difficult to deal with, but he is at peace with it.

- I've had several people tell me my one special needs child is like 10 typical kids. I'm glad they recognize that because it's true.

- I can hardly stand the thought of adding another condition on my child of "who she is." I sometimes have to take time and even leave the house for a bit to clear my head.

- I'm tired of medical mumbo jumbo and long for someone to tell me the truth, so I know what to do now and what to expect in the future.

- I realized I couldn't change the needs my parent have and how I'll need to care for those needs, but knew I had to change my attitude and develop some realistic expectations. If I think something should be a certain way, and it doesn't happen, then I'm frustrated. When my attitude changed, the way I looked at my circumstances changed, and then things improved.

- I got professional help for myself early because I needed help to have a right view of the future. I'm glad I did.

- As an Occupational Therapist, I have seen that the parents who accept their children for who they are and don't feel they have to "cure" or "change" them are the ones who handle things positively and stay together. Often they say finding out about the disability was the worst day of their lives, yet they have come to see it as the biggest blessing that holds them together.

- Natural humans see and believe. People of faith believe and see.

- Others need to know that our acceptance of our child's disability does not give them permission to make un-cool jokes or gestures. Kids who don't know better can get away with things that would be disrespectful from an adult. Having children with special needs has shown me how cruel the world can be.

- Watching my friends go through the journey of accepting their child has been exciting to watch. I know it was a long journey.

- Shifting from absolute belief that something is wrong with the person in my care to the belief that everything is just fine is such a struggle.

- We knew our special needs son would never walk. We took him to one healing service after another. Our intentions were only good, and we meant no harm. In response to Mr. Rogers' song about everyone being special, my son said, "Mommy, like me just like this?" I immediately stopped taking him to healing services because I loved him just the way he was. I stopped wasting emotions and energy on all the "what-ifs" and "could have beens" and started celebrating who he was. I wish the rest of the world would do that more.

  Having children with special needs has shown me how cruel the world can be.

- I've been guilty of calling people "psycho" and have never liked hearing people call others "retards," whether or not retardation is their disability. We have to teach others that those words are not acceptable and learn to accept the person and the special need.

- Accepting our adopted child's disability was what dedicated us to a higher cause—keeping him, loving him, and caring for him.

- I have had to stay focused on my two special needs children and not dwell on what our situation is or I can get very down. I know I need to accept each day and do my best.

- The toughest thing initially was hearing a geneticist tell me that my child had dysmorphic features (low set ears, droopy eyelids, widely spaced eyes, etc.). My child looked perfect to me!

- My seven-month-old son had a brain stem hemorrhage, was in a coma, and was to be taken off life support because the doctors said there wasn't enough brain activity to sustain life. He stopped breathing, turned blue, then grey, then pink and began breathing again. Obviously, God still has work for him to do—he is now a young adult needing full-time care.

- I wish others would accept that we all have different needs and abilities— and value. I also wish they would not judge us as parents.

- I used to say to my child, "Is there something wrong with you?" And of course, we came to find out, there is! I've stopped saying that about my child and others because we can't always see the disability the way you can see a person in a wheelchair.

- I needed to memorize scripture that comforted me in all the challenges. I realize that what caused my loved one to have a disability had been decided long before even I was born.

- Who are we to say what equals "quality of life"? The answer is in Matthew 25:35-40.

- I fear if our culture continues to shift toward evaluating people based on their perceived benefit to society, and as technology allows for "selective" births, special needs people and those who care for them may be seen as a strain on society. And we will miss out on so much that they have to offer us and to share, just like every other unique person God has created.

- Sarah Palin, 2008 Republican vice-presidential running mate to Senator John McCain, in an interview about her five-month-old son with special needs, said, "[I] prayed that my heart would be prepared for the changes to come."

YOUR STORY

What needs are you able to see in the lives of others who are being deeply challenged that might prompt you to offer to help (spiritual, emotional, physical, mental struggles)? Be creative in sharing what you think you could do to help: (Ex.: I see that _____ is sleep-deprived. I could _____. Or my friend is exhausted. I could keep watch while they sleep until they are refreshed.)

_____

_____

_____

_____

_____

Share specifically some of the struggles you face daily that you have either come to accept or are in the process of learning to accept?

_____

_____

_____

_____

Do you face any difficulties maintaining a good/positive attitude?

_____

_____

_____

How do you value this challenging situation? Do you value the life that is represented or are you questioning it? Do you see this as God's divine plan or some horrible mistake? Be honest.

_____

_____

_____

What stands in the way of your being able to accept this challenge? If you are helping others during their time of struggle, what do you see standing in their way that you might be able to help them through?

_____

_____

_____

How do you see this situation turning from a trial to a triumph? What changes must you (or others) make for this to happen? Where are you on the road to making this happen?

_____

_____

_____

What negative thoughts run through your mind? What positive thoughts run through your mind? Which tend to "stick"?

_____

_____

_____

Can we, like Abraham, submit to God so that any experience (loss, death, grief, or handicap) can be viewed as an opportunity instead of an obstacle?

_____

_____

We've seen how the Good Samaritan, Abraham with his son, and others responded to the challenge set before them. How have you responded to your challenge? Read Genesis 22:15-18 to see the Lord's response to Abraham's obedience.

_____

_____

_____

Are you able to experience peace in the midst of this challenge? If so, how? Explain.

_____

_____

_____

How has this situation affected your overall life and your faith in God? As a result, are you willing to trust God in all situations?

_____

_____

_____

What does "knowing" Christ mean to you? Do you know of Him, or do you have a relationship _with_ Him? Read Matthew 18:2-6 and explain what it means to you.

_____

_____

_____

Did you pray about your situation? If so, how? If not, are you willing to start? How do you think you might have prayed _for_ someone like Job or Joseph?

_____

_____

_____

Has your challenge helped you build endurance and character?

_____

_____

Read Psalm 107:23-31. What lesson can we learn about prayer?

_____

_____

_____

Settling In

"Settling In" may conjure up a thought of "getting comfortable." Maybe you thought—and hoped—that was where we would go with this section! However, when caring for your own special needs or the special needs of others, you may never find a place that is totally comfortable. Partial or total dependence on someone else, illnesses, constant changes in schedules, and needs to be met all add up to much less than comfort and fun! For us "settling in" meant accepting, moving on, enduring the difficulties, and making the best of life when life wasn't always the best. It has meant finding a **new normal**. Unfortunately, sometimes we have to find that new normal daily. Life and its limitations challenge us every single day, and we realize that this challenge always comes with a hidden cost. We may need to exchange sleep for fun, fun for sleep, hospital stays for time with friends, staying home for an impromptu dinner out. Different phases of life require different sacrifices. Life is not always convenient, comfortable, fun, and easy, but when we choose what we know to be right, we can live with ourselves and our consciences, knowing we will have no regrets down the road.

We also know that one size doesn't fit all. The physical demands of caring for another (or yourself if you are disabled), the emotional strain, the mental acrobatics, and spiritual implications will be as different for every person as a snowflake or fingerprint. Not every situation is the same, nor is every suggestion or learning experience expected to have the same outcome for each person. "Settling in" will be different for every one of us, but we can learn from one another no matter on which end of the spectrum we find ourselves.

As we share struggles we've encountered, victories we've seen or experienced, and what has worked for us, please keep an open mind. Be open to thinking creatively, asking yourself how something might work for you, knowing that it might need your own twist or turn in order to make it fit your particular situation precisely. Let's start by looking at where we are, realizing some have it more difficult and some have it less so. Either way, we are challenged and may have to look at new ways of doing things. We can likely do some of the same things others do but in a different way. Always remember, if we are following the ways of Christ, our whole life will change direction.

Birth or the addition of someone who needs care will bring changes to our family unit! When Joey was born, our world was turned upside down. Then we learned he was going to have difficulty in developing. Then we learned he was retarded. Then we started all the therapies and educational sessions to help him get a good start. We learned the critical importance of getting into an early intervention program to help him learn to do the things other children typically do on their own. Where we thought the bend in the road would make life easier, it got tougher. We had high hopes that he'd get better and life would proceed normally. Normally—a word we can hardly use anymore! You know the drill. What IS normal? What is typical? Different words, same root question. Life for us seemed complicated as we watched others who didn't have the struggles we dealt with. It was often frustrating watching other families do things with ease that were (and are) hard for us. It took a lot of adjustment in our thinking. It was harder at first, but it has become easier.

We purposed never to lose sight of the fact that others have their own and difficult struggles, and "comparing" our life to theirs is not only difficult but also dangerous. We held each other accountable when we started down that road, one that could lead to comparison and ultimately discouragement or even envy. We had to apply certain principles daily to our life like goal planning and finding our purpose.

As we applied those principles, we saw that although our life would be different from that of others, we still had a life. God had a specific purpose for which He would use us if we were willing. Over the years, He has helped us gain new perspectives and live life abundantly in the midst of constant challenge and change.

We relinquished our desires, wants, and needs to Him, gaining confidence through His reassurance. Every time we think we might know better, we rest assured that He knows what future plans are best for us and allow Him to take the reins of our life. James 4:13-15 says, "Come now, you who say, 'Today or tomorrow, we shall go to such and such a city, and spend a year there and engage in business and make a profit.' Yet you do no know what your life will be like tomorrow. You are just a vapor that appears for a little while and then vanishes away. Instead, you ought to say, 'If the Lord wills, we shall live and also do this or that.'" The last verse (17) says, "Therefore, to one who knows the right thing to do and does not to it, to him it is sin."

That's essentially "settling in"—doing the right thing because we know in our heart it is the right thing to do. We have learned that settling in has more to do with flexibility and willingness than anything else!

OTHERS' STORIES

- Life has been different and sometimes lonely caring for an elderly family member, but we eventually learned that life can still be fun; we just had to work at it differently. We get no time off for good behavior.

- Mild depression and physical exhaustion during certain times were difficult. I had to learn to set priorities differently and be flexible.

- It is a 24/7 responsibility caring for (anyone) who has a disability, who doesn't really have a place in society, just an existence. The caregiver gives this person joy in life, a place to rest, feel safe, and have fun.

- Not everything can be fixed, but we can learn to cope and adjust to life.

- Please stop feeling sorry for me and rejoice with me that we are finally adjusting.

- We're finally realizing everything takes longer when you are caregiving. Getting out the door on time every time is a future goal!

YOUR STORY

In an ideal and perfect world, what would you like "settling in" to mean?

_____

_____

_____

_____

_____

Do you often/ever see your situation as hopeless or senseless?

_____

_____

_____

Did you ever picture yourself where you are today?

_____

_____

_____

What do you think others think about your challenges?

_____

_____

_____

Seeing others in crisis mode or in a prolonged state of crisis can affect us. Have you ever been in a situation where you have been affected by someone's crisis, and how did you respond, help, or encourage?

_____

_____

_____

_____

CHAPTER FIVE

Yield Right of Way:
Life is VERY Different for Us

Chris and Carol were married only a short time before they saw Carol's mom's life falling apart. She heard voices and often accused others of things that were untrue. The accusations could be anything from "You didn't call me yesterday like you said you would" to something as complicated and dangerous as "I know my neighbor is trying to kill me." Life began a series of twists and turns that included calling the police, mental health services, someone to help with finances, and eventually a state institution. Life for them was very different from what they had planned or expected.

*Jonathan and Suzanne had a different set of circumstances. Their fourth child came into the world as effortlessly as their first three, but about eight months later, they realized little Gabriella was not developing as the others had. She liked to watch things spin. She liked music. She couldn't sit still. They realized their little girl had just become the one in 150 children diagnosed with autism (that the Center for Disease Control and Prevention indicated in their 2007 statistics). What they didn't realize then was that little Gabriella would never be able to be left alone—never. Their life was changing drastically. They had no idea **how** drastically.*

Carolyn, an only child and single mom, had two grown children, happily on their own, and doing well. She was one phone call away from the news that her widowed mom would be hospitalized with a massive stroke. Life would never be the same for either one of them.

OUR STORY

As we shared earlier, our early life and marriage had flowed rather nicely. But as it is for most of us, we don't *plan* on things entering our life that will change it profoundly from one moment to the next. Maybe you looked at your life as we did ours.

We knew what stages came when. For instance, when we were dating, we knew the next logical step was marriage, then children, building a career, guiding our children spiritually and educationally, participating in their school and activities, and eventually sending them off into adulthood to repeat the normal healthy process! Doing so was in a strange sort of way like putting money in a vending machine, expecting the piece of candy whose button we pushed. The problem? We got a different candy bar. Sure, we like this one OK, but it wasn't the same flavor, it wasn't the same size, and come to think of it, one of us liked the nuts, the other one didn't. We thought about kicking the machine to see if what we wanted would eventually come out, but then, what would we do with the one we had?

How Different Is It?

In 1987 Emily Perl Kingsley wrote *Welcome to Holland*, a sweet piece sharing how life changed when her family welcomed a child with a disability. Kingsley wrote, "I am often asked to describe the experience of raising a child with a disability, to try to help people who have not shared that unique experience to understand it, to imagine how it would feel. When you're going to have a baby, it's like this: it's like planning a fabulous vacation trip to Italy. You buy a bunch of guidebooks and make your wonderful plans. [She lists all the wonderful places she'll expect to visit, works of art, etc.] It's all very exciting.

"After months of eager anticipation, the day finally arrives. Several hours later, the plane lands. The stewardess comes in and says, 'Welcome to Holland.'

"'Holland?!?' you say, 'What do you mean Holland? I signed up for Italy! All my life I've dreamed of going to Italy.'

"But there's been a change in the flight plan. They've landed in Holland and there you must stay."

She acknowledges that although she isn't in some disgustingly horrible place, it's just different from what she had planned. Holland will require new guidebooks and travel will be at a slower pace and less flashy. She notices the famous artwork and scenery that Holland has to offer, but that they're very different from those in the intended destination of Italy. "But everyone you know is busy coming and going from Italy... and they're all bragging about what a wonderful time they had there. And for the rest of your life you will say, 'That's where I was supposed to go. That's what I had planned.'

"And the pain of that will never, ever, ever, ever go away... because the loss of that dream is a very significant loss. But if you spend your life mourning the fact that you didn't get to Italy, you may never be free to enjoy the very special, the very lovely things... about Holland."

Whether hoping for a particular candy bar or destination, when the deal doesn't deliver, we are disappointed. But when there is a change from what *life* might have been, we can be devastated. Disappointment can last a few moments with few and short-lived side effects! Devastation might happen in a moment but have lasting effects. How we adjust, deal with the devastation, and look at life will ultimately make a difference in how we make it *through* life.

Will we concentrate on what we don't have? Will we concentrate on what others have, what they get to do, places they get to go, dreams they get to fulfill that we don't, or will we choose to see the way our life has changed as God views it, seeing the big picture? Will we select just one instrument in the orchestra and listen to it alone, possibly able to hear a few mistakes, or open our minds to the beautiful sounds that all the instruments together will make under the direction of the conductor?

What Was/Is Different for Us

Becoming a Christian doesn't mean that life suddenly becomes perfect. Yes, we're forgiven of our past sin, and yes, we have the One who can help us avoid sin as well as help us gain new insights if we ask and rely on Him, but Christians and non-Christians alike will have trials and tribulations to work through. What makes it different then? The difference for us was going to be how we handled life with the Lord in control of it and how others might view it. The "happily ever after" life wasn't going to happen to us nor does it for many!

We decided we wanted to learn to handle this challenge in a way that would bring honor and glory to God, satisfaction to us, and help and encouragement to others. We realized that if we could handle our trials in this way, others might want

> *Becoming a Christian doesn't mean that life suddenly becomes perfect.*

to know who Christ is in our lives. Doing so wasn't and isn't easy, but we still try. We've made mistakes, all of which we openly share with those who care to listen or better said, all who care to ask. We have accepted that not everybody wants to hear about our challenges, so we've been careful in how much and what we share. But since you hold our book in your hands and are our captive audience—look out!

In the early days, the differences were there, but they were smaller. As our son grew up, the differences became more and more obvious as well as more and more challenging. We didn't always talk about them because not everyone could relate. (Who *really* wants to hear about someone potty training a child for five years or longer? Who could really understand how hard it was to nurse a newborn calmly while following behind a toddling Joey who did not know how to fall and catch himself?) Initially, we thought things were going to get better. We thought things would "level-off" at some point, and our life would be like everyone else's around us. It never happened. Every day was a new story, every day brought a struggle and a new way of looking at what *normal* was for our family.

We couldn't possibly tell you all the ways our life differs from yours any more than you could tell us all the ways your life differs from ours. To do so would be like showing someone the Grand Canyon from a vacation photo instead of seeing it in person. Explaining the grandeur of the Grand Canyon is impossible, and the same is true of our lives; we cannot explain or compare adequately. Lives are as different as snowflakes. Each has its own beauty, its own character- istics, and yet they are similar! That said we'd like to share some of the ways we have felt our differences. We'll share by category and story and include some of our frustrations in those areas. We share what is *real*—the feelings, thoughts, and ways we might have improved the situation to make the challenges and dif- ferences less stark, and what our frustrations were in the midst of it all.

Progress: Ours and His!

We all have hopes, dreams, and expectations for our children. It might be par- ticular sports, music, academics, or all of the above. For those whose children are missing milestones one after another, we realize that we have to continually reshape those hopes and dreams, and in some cases, eliminate them from any of our thinking altogether.

Because Joey's progress was so slow, we often had difficulty watching our friends' children passing him by almost daily. We tried to keep life moving as normally as we could for ourselves and our girls yet felt as if we were caught in a frozen frame in a film.

Sometimes we got tired of "rising above" the occasion. Sometimes we wanted to have a "terrible two temper tantrum" just to feel better. That's when we talked and cried and prayed to get through that tough time. Knowing our situation would never change, we had to learn to deal with each issue, each challenge as it came. We needed time. We're still learning.

We had to plan, talk, and make an effort to be sure that we would rejoice with others when their children did things Joey would never do, received honors that Joey wouldn't receive, rode their bikes when we knew Joey would never have the balance for that, got jobs and finished medical school, which Joey would never even dream of doing. We also were delighted as others rejoiced with us when Joey did things we never thought he'd do. Some people were very good at that, which in turn, was a great encouragement to us. We remember people sometimes taking notice and sharing things about Joey's improvement and development! Sometimes we were too close to the situation to notice some of the changes! Their noticing those changes made us feel as if they cared and loved Joey and us, too!

We knew we'd always be a part of his progress. We were involved in his IEPs (Individual Educational Plans) for the twenty years he was in school. From preschool until he was twenty-two years old, we met as often as needed with teachers, therapists, aides, and administrators to formulate his educational plans. They were a wonderful group of people we'll tell you about later. We needed their expertise to get us through not just this part of his life but also his whole life. They helped us prepare Joey for his adult years. Now we have a team that helps with his IP (Individual Plan) for his work. All of these people were the ones who helped us gain and keep the perspective we needed for the long haul. They were able to see the picture in the completed puzzle. They helped us move the pieces around until they fit in just the right places.

Lack of Progress

We also saw the lack of progress when we cared for our parents in their declining health. The unfortunate situation is that seldom does full recovery take place. In such cases we often see a major decline, then a slight improvement but not to the previous place, followed by another rapid and major decline, then only a slight improvement, and so goes the process until a nursing facility or part- or full-time home care remain the two options.

Marriage

When we were newly married, our time was our own. We had time to talk and dream and think! When children came along, that changed. Change is normal. We welcomed change because we were very excited to have a family. But when children have special needs, changes come quickly and radically and they don't stop. They never stop. When they're fifteen or thirty-five, they still need a babysitter. Some still need diaper changes. Many things had to change, and life continues to change from season to season.

We have had to protect our marriage through many seasons and for many reasons but can stand before you and say, "We have weathered the storms—so far!" Outside influences put strains on marriage, and if a husband and wife are strong, they can ignore or deal with them to keep their marriage strong. But when strain exists within the marriage or within the marriage family, a different kind of attention is required in order for the couple to stay together and keep the marriage strong. We strive for oneness in our marriage, which means meals together, conversations that are meaningful, not just business, and attending and speaking at marriage conferences. We continue learning and teaching what we know will help us stay strong, seeking counsel for ourselves and family issues when we just can't find an answer or resolution, always praying and reading God's word together when we are at church, teaching, or participating in small groups or together alone at home. We never neglect these things. But there are other things as well!

Married and Working Together as a TEAM

Yes, we work as a TEAM because Together Each Accomplishes More! This principle has been the glue that holds us together in marriage. It's like learning a dance together. One needs to lead and the other needs to follow. In a Christian marriage the husband is to lead. As he leads with the love of the Lord and with a servant's heart, the wife desires to follow (this is called biblical submission) because he has her best interest at heart. When a couple learns to dance, the man, who is to lead, can send his partner twirling, swinging, and moving with just the push and pull of his hand on hers. She doesn't fight it because she knows he has a plan to look good on the dance floor and to accomplish a routine! As they learn together, they discover what each push and pull means and can respond accordingly. When they work together, they both look good, blending in smooth and fluid movements.

If you're not a dancer and can't relate to that analogy, consider the tandem bike. The person riding the front position is the leader (captain) and needs the cooperation of the stoker in the second seat. The leader must provide ample warning when turning, when going uphill, and when passing others, so the stoker can help make the ride smooth. A good fire is built by stoking it—tending and supplying fuel (wood)—and the one riding as stoker does the same by pedaling harder to get momentum up a hill. They apply the brake to stop. Imagine the stoker who applies the brakes going uphill or pedals harder when coming to a four-way stop. The need is to work together for the sake of the whole and getting a better outcome as a result of that effort!

So husbands and wives, what does the TEAM approach look like for you? Do you recognize when your spouse is exhausted and offer to step in to give her or him a break? Do you wait for your spouse to come home and expect him or her to take over immediately upon walking in the door? The TEAM approach involves learning to read each other as well as communicate needs.

Cindi:

When the children were little, I had days when I wanted to throw up my hands and quit. Sometimes I'd expect Joe to walk in the door after a day packed with seeing patients at the office and take over what I'd been doing for twelve to fifteen hours already. Often he was very willing, but I learned that giving him some time to unwind after his long day was helpful to me in the long run. Unwinding for him involved washing up and changing clothes to get comfortable. On a particularly long day, especially if we'd had health problems and long nights with our son, Joe might take a power nap. This wasn't his usual pattern, but it was something he occasionally needed to get back into the game of being a dad for the rest of the evening. He often reciprocated not only by watching the children but also folding laundry or doing other household chores, giving me time to take a long, quiet bath. This was not our daily routine but certainly a good way to give each other what we both needed to provide better care for each other and our family.

Working together as a team is crucial to survival as a married couple in any situation, but marriage in the context of trying to raise a special needs child becomes more complex. Expressing unconditional love for each other in front of the children is comforting for them. It makes their world a nicer and safer place to be. It doesn't matter if a child is "normal" or has special needs: Children know when Mom and Dad are unconditionally in love with each other or not. Working together provides a stable and secure environment where the children can grow and flourish.

Married with Children

In our early years, we had loving parents, who were wonderful grandparents. They loved Joey and enjoyed taking care of him and his sisters. They were happy, we were happy, and the children were happy. We were one big happy family! We know not everyone has the luxury of parents who live five or fifteen minutes away and who are willing to watch the children, but we did, and we never took it for granted. Both sets of parents understood how to care for Joey during a grand mal seizure, knew his meds and food allergies, and other important health and behavior issues. They experienced firsthand what we dealt with and fully understood the amount of attention he required. God was so gracious in that way. We were able to get time away, allowing us a very active ministry, enjoying time with friends and occasional date nights to catch our breath and get refocused for the day-to-day challenges. But those times, which we cherished and appreciated, came to an end. As each parent became ill, it was our turn to help care for them and return the blessing and show our appreciation for all they had done for us those twenty years.

We considered it a great blessing not only to get away and have time alone as a couple, but we also appreciated the opportunities to invest in each of our daughters without always having Joey with us. When they grew a little older, the girls expressed that they didn't know when they were little if their grandparents loved them the same as Joey because sometimes they didn't go with him to their home. As they matured, they were able to see the beauty of uninterrupted time alone with us, and we were able to explain it to them, too! After both of Cindi's parents died, her sister cared for Joey for a week, so we could take a trip together with the girls and then sometime later, a special 25th anniversary trip that would have been impossible for him. Both trips were funny: We pictured the things we wouldn't have been able to do had Joey been with us—the escalator rides that didn't start and end with a fuss, cobblestone walkways that would not have accommodated a wheelchair or Joey's unbalanced steps, and dinners without worry about foods triggering his allergies. We experienced such freedom!

We always tried to avoid making our girls our permanent babysitters. We wanted them to do the things they could have done without a brother who was handicapped. We wanted them to learn to be compassionate, and so they were often included in helping, but we let it always be known by our actions that Joey was our responsibility, not theirs. As a result, we have found a sweet balance in our family of daughters who care deeply and help meet Joey's needs but also have very full and exciting lives of their own. We believe this delicate balance has allowed us to bond and work well together as a family.

Intimacy in Marriage

When couples care for others with special needs in their home, impromptu intimate moments don't or can't always happen! We realized early that planning for intimacy was essential. Planning may take some of the fun and thrill out of those special moments, but if it weren't for planning, they

We realized early that planning for intimacy was essential.

might never have happened! We had to work at making intimate moments together purposeful, relaxing, and fun. When both spouses are exhausted from caring for a special needs child or when a couple is at the end of their rope giving care to their parents or other loved one, sometimes it's difficult to prioritize sex. If you happen to be one of the caregivers we're talking about, and if you're honest about it, you know it's true. When all your energy, emotion, feelings, and thoughts are spent caring for another person all day long, it's easy to find yourself running on empty. For us, staying home while the kids were at the grandparents' house was more important than going out for a nice dinner or cup of coffee. It takes careful planning and good communication to make sure this part of life is not neglected.

Some may simply advise shutting and locking the bedroom door. That may be work for some, but remember, not everything works for everyone. Privacy is not always possible, especially if the people you are caring for are mobile, unable to reason, and make their way to your room. Their desire to reach you and your desire to be left alone might make this suggestion unworkable. In addition their safety is something that must be considered, and sometimes the safest time for the special needs person is when he or she is sound asleep.

The most important thing for couples is to work at open and honest communication. Is morning better than late evening? Might planning be better than impromptu? Each season of life will require different questions with different answers.

Privacy in Marriage

In addition to the exhaustion that all of us experience from time to time, the privacy issue also arises. At all ages and even now as an adult, we often hear Joey's pounding feet coming up the stairs (holding our breath, hoping he is holding onto the railing) and his knock at our door saying, "Thundering. Sleep with you?" The noises are as frightening and real to him as they are to any two- or three-year-old. Sometime we're so tired we don't want to get up and take him back in his room, so we simply roll over, and say, "Lie down with us," and he joins us! Picture three adults in a queen-sized bed! Funny, sweet, and uncomfortable all at the same time! When we have the energy to walk him back downstairs to his room, we lie down with him until he falls asleep, sometimes interrupting our sleep often more than once a night. One of the beautiful things about Joey and others like him is that they are children forever, and you can't make them grow up. Sleeping with parents to get through a time of fear is comforting to them. They are just big kids—sort of like Peter Pan!

Often we lock our bedroom door to keep out the early morning noise of the television or video game that Joey might start. That early morning noise might occur as early as 3 a.m.! The time of day doesn't even come close to fazing Joey! If he's up, he's up! We've been startled on more than one occasion at 3:15 a.m. to what we thought was the roaring of a lion and screaming. In a hazy fog, we ran to Joey's room, only to find him listening to *The Lion, the Witch, and the Wardrobe* with the volume turned to 35! (The volume registered at 9 in normally good!) Even a locked door can't keep that noise out!

Not long after that incident, Joey was up at 4:25 a.m. looking for an old remote control device that he once had as a toy. It hadn't been around for at least six years. What made him remember it was beyond our thinking! He would not let the idea go, so we pretended to help him look for it. When we could not find it (we knew we wouldn't but had to let him figure that out), he wanted to watch television. By the time we had him calmed down and back in bed, we had to get ready for the day ahead!

Privacy is something to aim for but not to be frustrated over all the time. We prefer to remember the days we *didn't* have an interruption instead of those when we did. We are less frustrated that way. We try to keep a sense of humor. We can find the humor in loud music but not in an ongoing illness that takes every bit of privacy away. So much of making this part of our life work comes from an examination of attitude!

Marriage for the Long Haul

The dreams we had for times alone, vacationing, retirement were dashed. We have other dreams, but they are very different from the ones we once had. We always thought it would be wonderful to travel to far off places together, holding hands, watching the sunset. We have a great marriage, are best friends, and have always enjoyed simple, quiet moments together. We are able to enjoy a walk together or sit on our deck and enjoy a cup of coffee and conversation. We love it. But *if* we have time alone, we don't usually spend it at dinner and a movie or on vacation. Those moments happen rarely and with much planning and preparation and only with certain caregivers when they have offered and are available. We had hoped to join our empty-nester friends for the last-minute "dinner and a movie," but to do so involves much planning. More later.

Social Life

Our earliest memory of our social life consisted of trips to Metro Hospital for early intervention for Joey. We met other parents with similar challenges, a variety of therapists and doctors, and plenty of staff people. Thinking we'd spend time in a gym for a mom-and-tot playgroup or at the playground playing catch with other dads, we found so much time in therapy rooms and hospitals somewhat disappointing. We were thankful for the people we met, and many have crossed our path over the years, and it's been quite fun and fulfilling. Because everyone we met was also dealing with special needs and doctors' appointments, we didn't establish long-term friendships. Everyone went in different directions with treatments all the time. We may have had plenty of people in our life but we lacked deepening friendships.

We have great friends and extended family that keep life fun! But in those early years, we got few invitations to join other families outside family occasions. We recall a few, and those times were challenging, so we weren't often asked to the homes of families with children. Joey could not tolerate noise and commotion. Very sensitive to sudden noises and movement, he would start screaming, hanging all over us, and generally making going out not worth our effort, much less worth someone else's effort to invite us! We didn't blame others, and no one ever said we were excluded; but for whatever reason, we often felt left out. Maybe we just felt that way because we *believed* others were out and about having fun and we weren't. We realize things aren't always what they seem for us or others. But honestly, we're not sure *we* would have invited us either! Joey's needs diminished our desire to go into those social settings, and when we did, we were often embarrassed about the way he acted, thinking others would consider us bad parents, unable to control our child. *He* couldn't help the behavior caused by brain malformation, but we had difficulty separating his behavior from how we felt about it.

Social life when our children were little meant having a lot of company in our home. We had to be selective. We couldn't invite ten small children at a time. We had to be sure the groups were small, and we tried very hard to be sure to make visitors comfortable in getting to know Joey. We also went to the playground often, allowing Joey to be out in public with others. Before having a child with special needs, we had been in situations where we felt uncomfortable with those who had special needs, not knowing what to say or how to respond. We know now that treating them as you would anyone else is the best place to start. Some with special needs may be nonverbal, but they may comprehend everything you say!

And then there is Joey's social life, which is actually more complicated. He can't pick up his cell and call a buddy to come over and hang out. Just kidding, he doesn't have a cell phone. Where we go, he goes. Where we decide he'll have a social encounter is where he'll have one. He doesn't ask to go out, and sometimes he doesn't want to. Depending how far from home we are going, we may allow him to stay home if he chooses. It's all been a growing process.

When Joey was small, we'd invite a classmate over occasionally for a dip in the kiddie pool or to play video games. If the parent were able to stay, we'd play board games or watch the kids play while we had coffee. These play dates could be very stressful for us because often both children were nonverbal to only slightly verbal. One time a little boy came over to swim without his mom. Without warning, he got out of the pool, came into the house, walked upstairs dripping wet, and lay down on one of our beds. Of course, I (Cindi) followed him (along with dripping Joey in my arms because I couldn't leave him in the pool in the backyard) to see where he was going and to be sure he was safe. When I asked him what he wanted to do, he said, "I sleepy." It was funny, but it was proof they couldn't be left alone to play on their own. Later the other mom and I shared a good laugh.

For the first twenty-five years of his life, we did not feel Joey could be left alone. It was too risky. Would he try to cook, go somewhere in the house and take a fall, get scissors to try to open something, go outside and lock the door behind him? (Actually, since he never closes the door when he comes in from work, he'd probably not lock himself out!) But as he grew and developed, and as we were able to see that he could do certain things, we felt more and more comfortable leaving for short periods of time to take a walk in the neighborhood or go for a quick bite to eat (alone or with friends) nearby.

People with special needs don't always get invited out, and sometimes they don't feel comfortable sitting for an evening when they can't participate. In addition, sometimes people don't know *how* to engage one with special needs in conversation even if the person with special needs is able to talk, has a strong mind, and thinks well. Sometimes people are frightened off if the individual is in a wheelchair. We remember how few visitors our elderly parents had in their time of illness and decline. Those who visited were precious and treasured.

While Joey could be very polite and sit and enjoy dinner with us and our friends, we are uneasy knowing that when he's finished eating, he'll want to do something else. Sure, our friends can ask him questions, but he is not conversational. And for us, honestly, when we go out for this kind of evening, we'd prefer to be alone and enjoy our friends without him. Put yourself here. Would you want your three- or six-year-old to join you for every event you attend? Would you want a little one with you to celebrate a special anniversary whether it's vacation or dinner in a romantic restaurant?

On the other side of this coin is the type of socializing appropriate for people with special needs. Thankfully, we know parents whose son has special needs; they set up routine outings at which the young people can socialize within their capabilities and with others like themselves. It's been fun to watch Joey's peers grow and mature with others like them.

Family Times

When the children were young, we were able to do some things together as a family. When Joey could sit up without assistance, we fastened him securely into a seat on the back of our bike. He soon grew too big, so we purchased a seat that pulled him along the back of our bike. It was actually a two-seat attachment so Kristina could ride, too! By the time Kathleen came into the family, Joey was already too heavy for the attachment, and our family bike riding days were over. Unfortunately, leaving one stage did not prepare us for a *next* fun family sporting event. There would be no skiing, sledding, jogging, or hiking as a family. Boat rides and train rides were good for us. We'd try to do new things on vacations, but those times usually turned into three people doing an activity and one waiting with Joey. We had a divide and conquer mentality.

Because Joey was accustomed to spending time with extended family, family social times usually went pretty well. He always loved being with family, but at times we, as young parents, planned activities that would allow us to "make memories" with our kids in our own little family. Not all memories fell into the "good" category, however! Try as we might, we often made memories we'd wish we could forget. I guess we can laugh at them now, but in the midst of some of these family times, we simply didn't think they were funny.

Joey was seven years old and Kristina was five; Kathleen was due in two months. We wanted to take the kids to the local fairgrounds for the Fourth of July fireworks and a movie. It was a hot July day. The movie was *Honey, I Shrunk the Kids*, and we all know now what we should have figured out then is that we were in for some trouble! You probably already see it coming. We did not. Our memory—and we're sticking to it—is that the kids were cranky because of the heat. The movie was on a big screen, so the bees and ants that were already bigger than life were *way* bigger than Joey could handle. One of us sat with Kristina, trying to act as if this was a fun experience, and the other stood in the back of the theater holding Joey. He couldn't talk, but he could scream! He was probably trying to communicate, "GET ME OUT OF HERE!" I'm sure the rest of the audience agreed! Removing Joey was a smart idea, so it was a while until we were reunited to then go off to the fireworks. It wasn't long before we figured out that fireworks are loud before they are pretty. More screaming added to our making of a memory. This outing, planned to "make a memory," ended with Cindi sobbing on the bed after getting the children to sleep.

Vacations for Family Times

After the memories we made that July Fourth, we decided to keep things simple while the kids were small. Vacations consisted of visiting Cindi's parents when they would be at their condo in Fort Myers, Florida, and day trips in Ohio that would be only a few hours away. One summer we took a "transportation vacation" around the Cleveland area, consisting of trolley, train, boat, and bus rides. It was perfect for our young family, but we also tried to branch out as the children grew older. For several years our plan was to visit each of the state parks in Ohio. We did the lodge, not the camping. We knew some of our limitations!

We've also had four trips to the happiest place on the planet. We will continue going until we get it right and find ourselves happy there! Joey and Kristina were four and two years old when we took our first trip to Disney World. Joey wasn't yet walking very well, so he could be in a stroller and we and Grandpa and Grandma Ferrini could take turns pushing both kids. Joey tolerated that for a time, but like most kids, he tired of it before we did. That trip wasn't bad, especially with all the assistance the grandparents provided in helping care for the two children; but we decided we just needed to do another one when they were old enough to remember! That was the trip that really challenged us. For whatever reason, Joey, then fourteen, had seizures on day two, which left him agitated and very exhausted. We rented a wheelchair because he was too exhausted to walk and too foggy to appreciate much. We were traveling with another family, and we didn't want to prevent them from seeing and doing the things they could do. They were so gracious and patient, helping to get Joey to want to do things we might not have been able to get him to do, but it still made for a very long day—make that week—with him!

We decided to try a third trip a few years later since Joe had a dental seminar in Orlando. We figured since all the kids were older and more mature, this might be a better time and experience. But Joey (almost twenty-one) was afraid of everything. The dark, the noise, the people, the music, you name it! We had decided to get a wheelchair once again because he could not keep up the pace of even slow walking. He was easily distracted by all the stimuli around him, often walking away from us totally unaware of the fact that he could get lost in the crowd. When we approached a ride, he would scream and hit us, and a few times tried hitting the workers! We would get on the ride totally exhausted, rubbing the new bruise he gave us, and about halfway through he'd say, "FUN!" We figured he would be excited to go to the next ride because the previous one had been such "fun," but he could not make the connection and would repeat his misbehavior at every ride. After a while, the routine became too much. Since Cindi can't ride some of the rides because of back problems, she was the one who stood in the hot sun and humid Florida summer weather, then pouring rain, while Joe took the girls from ride to ride. It seemed to be working out OK until dinner. As we all sat at dinner with shoes so wet that they were not going to be dry until we returned home, one of the girls said, "Joey, could you close your mouth while you eat?" Cindi lost it.

Cindi:

Yes, indeed, I lost it as politely as I could! I had pushed the wheelchair all day. I had seen every Disney store and trinket 6,000 times, and I'm NOT exaggerating. I had been running on empty since early in the day, "entertaining" Joey in the hot humid sun (where even a skinny lamppost was used for shade) and then later the pouring rain with lightning and thunder. Neither he nor I tolerated the steamy, bright yellow Disney parkas that we had to buy to stay dry. After some eight hours of this, I was tired of Joey's reaching out to touch things that could break, of my making funny voices to get him to laugh instead of hit me, and our standing in stores packed with people also dodging the raindrops. It was packed, hot, smelly, sticky, and miserable. I had a smile on my face all day, but I wasn't happy. I was even beginning to be annoyed that Joe and the girls came off all the rides laughing and having fun! Truth be told, I was tired of sacrificing so everyone else could have a nice time. So when someone at dinner wasn't happy to deal with a bit of noise from chewing, I lost it. I started crying, and I could tell it wasn't going to stop any time soon! Through my tears I quietly told Joe I'd be in the car with Joey. He said, "Don't you want to eat first?" (I know what the women reading this are thinking!) Although my meal had been ordered, I knew I wasn't going to feel like eating any time soon. Joey eats quickly, so as soon as he finished, I asked Joe to have my meal boxed for later, and Joey and I sat in the car while I sobbed until the rest of the family finished. I cried until I couldn't cry anymore. My eyes were burning as if I'd just finished a good swim in the ocean! I can't imagine their meal was all that delightful either. I was done with Disney.

We reluctantly took one more Disney trip, and had a full prayer team praying!

As we think about other vacations, we remember a trip to an Ohio park, where one simple fly had Joey flailing his arms in the air and yelling. No, not for one meal—the same fly joined us in the lodge for the several days we were there. And then there were the ministry trips for Campus Crusade for Christ—no air conditioning, small dorm rooms, dorm food, lots of people, and lots of kids running around. You get the picture. We would have had fun with ministry and networking if we hadn't had to plan for Joey to have at least one "meltdown" with all the windows wide open, swinging book bags at us while yelling usually at the worst possible time. We can hardly imagine what people walking by the windows or down the hall must have thought. We could only sit and watch and try to keep him safe from himself as any intervention would have escalated his bad behavior and made things worse.

And then there was the "make a memory" Olympics in 1996 in Atlanta. We enjoyed one event with just the girls, knowing that the crowds and noise might be too much for Joey. Wanting to be sure Grandma Ferrini and Joey had a chance to taste some Olympic flavor; we decided to take them the next day to the part of Olympic Village open to the public. Was it the heat? Was it the crowds? Was it just Joey's mood that day? What caused him to melt down and throw a tantrum in the middle of Olympic Village? We kept an eye on him, staying near him and watching him carefully, but knew if we tried to console him in any way, the behavior would likely have been worse. He wasn't hurting anyone, but he was definitely putting on a show that we wanted to pretend we weren't a part of!

And then there are the sporting events! The guys who might have had a little too much to drink aren't thinking they should be careful about what they are shouting. Joey doesn't have the ability to reason, "I should just be quiet and let those guys talk." Oh no, Joey says what he's thinking, and while it might be what we're thinking, too, it's not always best to have him voice that opinion or comment, all while pointing a finger and sticking his tongue out. Cute for a two year old, not a twenty something! Sometime we've had to find the right moment and leave. We think the noise and the emotion of it gets the best (or worst) of him. One might say, "Then why do you bother to go?" Well, the next game might prove to be wonderful and we think it will always be. Optimism.

We must always consider what *might* happen if we take Joey and decide what we are willing to "deal" with. It might mean a totally ruined vacation or a perfectly lovely one. We've realized that the best vacations were ones with little to do and few pressures to be anywhere or do anything on a time schedule. Grandpa and Grandma's Florida condo was that special place where we could simply go with the flow. Anywhere else always involved a guess, speculation, risk, chance. With those odds, maybe we should consider Vegas next time!

When Cindi's dad's dementia struck, her parents could take few vacations because of the very same kinds of pressure. When dealing with issues of the brain, we cannot plan for a person's behavior to be consistent.

The List Goes On

Safety

A gate across Joey's door kept him in his room when he was little. Most kids wouldn't have needed this safety precaution, but he was too big for a crib, yet unable to stay in bed without rolling out. We had him in a bed with the mattress on the floor next to the wall, and the box spring next to the mattress, so he was somewhat enclosed. He could crawl out at the end of the bed with only a 5" drop. He couldn't do the stairs alone and did not understand the danger of stairs, so we were fearful that he would get out of bed and dash down the hall, plunging down the stairway. We hated using that gate, yet doing so allowed us peace of mind. (We should all keep these things in mind the next time we want to judge someone we hear about on the news who may simply be keeping their child from their own self-destruction.)

We had a deck built off our kitchen that was designed so no children could put their head through the slats. We installed a small latched, gated doorway so they couldn't get off the deck without help, and then fenced in the yard just in case that happened! Living on a corner lot on a relatively busy street, we felt the need to have a fence built in order to make sure that Joey would not drift out of the yard and onto the street. In order to have that fence built, we had to go before our city council to get approval to build the fence. We knew that one of the council members had a minor form of cerebral palsy but clearly was not mentally impaired. As I (Joe) stood before the council to present our case, one of the Board members said, "I am not in favor of building this fence because it won't stop your son from climbing over the fence and out into the street." I was stunned. "Climb the fence? Are you kidding me? Right now my son can't walk down or up the stairs without help." I repeated my position that we believed a fence was necessary to build so that Joey would not drift off and wander onto the street (looking into the future with hopes he would walk someday), which was less than fifteen yards from our back door. The council member with the mild cerebral palsy just shook his head and said, "Mr. Ferrini, you can build your fence, and no one on this board is going to stop you. It is clear that some board members don't understand the situation. Please build your fence." As I listened to the interaction of the Board members that was taking place, some tears welled up in my eyes either because I wanted to strangle the insensitive council member or because I appreciated the councilperson with mild CP sticking up for me or because I could not make this person better understand our situation. I was slowly learning that she, like others, could make decisions only through the mindset that she developed through her life experiences. As I thought about the latter option, I was able to keep my composure under control and leave the council chamber, appreciating the final decision to allow us to build our privacy fence so that we could protect our son. People can make laws to build ramps and have door openers and parking spaces for the handicapped, but unless people's hearts are changed, little is accomplished for the overall good.

> *People can make laws to build ramps and have door openers and parking spaces for the handicapped, but unless people's hearts are changed, little is accomplished for the overall good.*

We know when we are out in public we need to have Joey hold our hand or shoulder so he can negotiate curbs, steps, and uneven walkways. He needed that help when he was young and he continues to as an adult. He doesn't think ahead to obstacles that might present themselves quickly to him. Escalators are another story! We hear in his loudest voice, "No, no way! Not there!" all the way to the escalator. Once Cindi gets him on the first step and steadies him he says, "That was easy!" We say, "*For whom!?*"

Forms of dementia and other memory loss issues create safety concerns as well. As this type of disease progresses, the small increments of decreasing abilities can leave caregivers wondering how to keep the person safe. Sometimes a wheelchair is a blessing more than a curse because the person is confined and can't wander off—as with both Cindi's dad and eventually Joe's Mom. Confusion, trouble with organizing and expressing thoughts, losing items, changes in personality and behavior, and inability to swallow must eventually be considered for the individual's overall safety.

Joey's severe allergy to peanuts has caused teachers to make sure lunchroom seating was safe. We've had to watch where Joey was seated on airplanes and be sure the trays were clean. Inhaling the aroma of baking peanut butter cookie or touching or ingesting it can be fatal. Fortunately, Joey has learned that he is not to eat anything unless someone checks the ingredients. Previous emergency room visits obviously made a lasting impression on all of us.

Because Joey would go with anyone, we had to be sure teachers and aides had names of approved drivers for Joey. That didn't end in elementary school. A list of approved drivers is still observed at his workplace under the watchful eye of an onsite supervisor. Joey must have supervision at all times.

No matter how carefully parents or caretakers keep watch over a child or adult, in only a moment he or she can dash out of sight. MedicAlert (www.medicalert.org or 1-800-ID-ALERT/1-800-432-5378) offers an enrollment program with personalized identification products (necklaces and bracelets) that carry information with the number of a toll-free emergency response system (twenty-four-hour service). If your loved one has Alzheimer's disease or dementia, you can secure your peace of mind by enrolling him or her in the MedicAlert® + Alzheimer's Association Safe Return® program which provides family notification services so that you can be easily reunited with loved ones who wander or get lost.

People with special needs can wear a necklace or bracelet to identify their medical conditions. For example, Joey's necklace states, "Asthma, epilepsy, mentally retarded, cerebral palsy, severe peanut allergy, routine medicines needed." It does not provide the full scope of his issues; however, MedicAlert can coordinate efforts to take care of him or anyone wearing MedicAlert jewelry/tag in an emergency. For those with other medical conditions, MedicAlert features twenty-four-hour emergency response service:

Instant Identification:
Your Membership number shown on your emblem enables you to be identified by emergency responders by a simple phone call to our 24-Hour Emergency Response Center.

24-Hour Emergency Response:
MedicAlert relays your key medical facts to emergency responders, so you receive faster, safer treatment for your medical conditions, and avoid harmful or fatal reactions.

Family Notification:
MedicAlert calls your family contacts and notifies them of your situation, so you won't be alone in an emergency.

Records

We keep Joey's medical records in a book now six inches thick. We thin it out occasionally, keeping only what we feel is absolutely necessary should we need to educate someone about him or should we need to refer to things that have happened along the way in his health care and education. It has also been a great tool to take to meetings so the people around the table know we keep good records, of which that particular meeting will be included. Those we've worked with know we keep good records, and we want the best for our son. If we are to deal with the challenges of his care, we don't want to deal with people who for whatever reason don't want to be helpful. Everything takes so much time, so this book lets them know, we simply mean business. We have had wonderful experiences with all those in Joey's life. We think this is part of the reason. We've planned and prepared well and expected the best for our son. We've represented him well, and his teachers and doctors have, too. Documentation helps everyone to stay on the same page.

Journaling

We have kept journals for the children from before they were born to help us see how they have grown and to document their lives. They enjoy looking back at them, and even Joey enjoys our reading from his. Journaling is another way of seeing positive growth when we couldn't see it up close. We have recorded people's words of encouragement when they've noticed good things going on. Journaling not only gives us something to hold onto when nothing worthwhile seems to be happening in our lives or the lives of those we are caring for, but it also serves as a way to look back at God's faithfulness in each of our children's lives.

Charting

When our parents needed full-time care, we made schedules for family members (and a few willing friends) to fill in their names when they would be able to take a turn caregiving. We seldom had blanks. Some stepped in to change diapers. Some stepped in to help bathe. Those who came to read, or visited and tried to make conversation with our loved one even when there was little response, are treasures in our hearts.

We have watched as young parents learn the ins and outs of caring for their child and make the necessary adjustments to allow others (many whom they can't possibly know well) care for their child in order to get out for a walk, a date, or errands. Charting the nursing staff or helpers can be time-consuming and irritating, especially if they don't show up as scheduled. One unexpected change changes everything. Some will need to make these kinds of adjustments and plans every day in order to have time even to make phone calls.

Dressing, Showering, and Personal Care

Someone we knew for a very long time expressed her surprise that we continue helping Joey with showering. What surprised us was that this daily regimen of care surprised her! We came to realize that we didn't share some of our "care" issues with others because we just didn't think they'd be all that interested, and we didn't want to be a broken record, sharing every detail of our day. We proceeded to share with this person that showering Joey is only one thing he still needs help doing and likely always will.

Joey has progressed a long way and can help get himself dressed and undressed, usually at appropriate times. But there are those times that we wonder what he is thinking. Whether we hand him a shirt or pair of pants, there is only a slim chance that it will be put on correctly. It doesn't bother him if it's upside-down, backwards or inside out. If it's on, it works. That's fine as long as we're not going somewhere. Once on, it's staying on. We want him to be as independent as possible, but we also realize that he is limited in his understanding and needs help to do things thoroughly. For instance, he is able to turn the shower on by himself (we have a regulated one that keeps the temperature the same), but if we were to leave him there to shower himself, we'd likely find him with an empty bottle of shampoo and the water still running. We daily hand him his shaver, and maintain hope that he'll someday do it thoroughly; but without some guidance he'd shave one patch and think he was done, the shaver still running! If we didn't remind him to use the bathroom—and we've tried this—he will go all day without toileting himself.

Although developing a routine can be the highest priority for showering, we also found creative thinking on our part could *get* him there! He doesn't particularly like to shower and fights us on it every day. (By the way, so did Mom Ferrini when she needed assistance showering; this worked well for her.) Saying, "It's time for your shower," would initiate every possible answer known to man. "I just showered." "I don't *need* to shower." "I don't *want* to shower." So we now begin our routine like this: "Joey, let's go into the bathroom and change your clothes." Once there, we would put the shower on, take his hand and gently guide him from the toilet to the shower. We did the same with mom. It worked most every time. They didn't see it coming! Instead of all the verbal combat, we just prompted them from one location to another, guiding them with hands instead of words. We did it carefully and thoughtfully with a sense of routine.

Something else that made this battle easier was putting a terrycloth robe on them right after we turned the water off and before they even got out of the shower. It warmed them, dried them, and made them feel secure. For those who may have an understanding of being showered by someone they don't know too well, being covered up helps those uncomfortable feelings of being unclothed in front of others. Having a shower seat outside of the shower, allowed them to sit down in their robe (so they did not struggle with balance issues while drying off), and only their legs and feet needed drying. It was a great routine for us, and really helped when we had two to shower!

Whatever we do for ourselves, we must do for Joey. It isn't that he can't do some things; it's just that they aren't done thoroughly, and it doesn't bother him or occur to him that it's not thorough. We have developed routines in caring for

Joey that help him to know what to do next, how to arrange clothes so they get put on correctly (i.e., the position of the tag inside clothing needs to be a certain way for him to know how it goes on), and what to anticipate so he doesn't get frustrated. Showering and shaving are two care tasks, but we also need to help him finish brushing his teeth, toileting, keeping his nose clean, and other interesting things!

We've seen some homes being built or adapted for the care of someone with special needs. Building up a bathtub to a higher level to accommodate a parent's bad back (and inability to bend and lift a heavy child) and installing ceiling tracking with hammock-like seating to move a disabled person from room to room and to lift them from a sink level to a tub is part of what some people have to plan in their homes. We might be talking about a new home or new addition, but we are not necessarily talking Better Homes and Gardens décor.

And what makes it continuously different for those of us in this situation is that we will always have to consider who will help our loved one bathe or shower. Leaving for a long weekend requires more than simple "adult-babysitting" services.

Humor

Proverbs 17:22 says, "A joyful heart is good medicine, but a broken spirit dries up the bones." We couldn't do without it! But let us say that we have the freedom to joke about some aspects of our life that those outside our family do not. Because we know the pressure, we can say and do some things that are funny to us that we would find hurtful and insulting if others did or said them. For instance, in a private moment away from Joey, one of us might say something just like Joey that would be cute, humorous, funny, and even tender. But it would not be funny to us for someone else to "enter" our private family moments with the same humor.

Humor keeps us going, and we are thankful that Joey seems to understand some aspects of humor as well. We make sure we laugh with him, and we encourage joking, light-hearted teasing, and having fun. We are thankful that although he has some behavior issues, he has a good sense of humor and laughs when appropriate.

He reads at a fourth-grade level with lower comprehension and often reads road signs and billboards. While riding in the car on the way home from work one day, he saw a billboard advertising Fish Furniture, an area furniture company. He read the billboard out loud, "FISH FURNITURE." Then he looked at me, "FISH? FURNITURE?" He and I (Cindi) burst out laughing. My mind never went in the direction his did, but he clearly attributed the ad to selling furniture for fish! It was hilarious! I love that he has a sense of humor.

Cindi:

I had taken Joey to his annual neurological examination. He generally fusses, knowing he'll have to get a blood test after the doctor visit, but he's a good patient and went through the exam well and even did well with the blood draw! We were all sharing "high-fives" as the cotton ball and Band-Aid went on the tiny dot of blood. Forty-five minutes later I pulled up to our mailbox and asked Joey to hop out and grab the mail, our daily routine. He looked at me and said, "With my ARM!?" I burst out laughing and followed up with, "Your arm isn't broken. Get the mail!"

> *Sometimes we have to look for humor even when it's most difficult to find.*

The journal we keep for each child is full of funny things each of them has said and done, but we also realize that at times we have to have good humor in the midst of very stressful situations. That's harder but still very important. Proverbs 14:13, "Even in laughter the heart may be in pain, and the end of joy may be grief." Humor and laughter can help release stress even during challenging times. Sometimes we have to look for humor even when it's most difficult to find. At those times we feel we can't do it any more, we have those people in our life who we know will add that element of joy and laughter appropriately and get us back on track.

When Joey was little, I had called my prayer partner to share my frustration about his misbehavior. I said, "I just want to throw him out the window." She got me to laugh when she responded, "Is that from the first floor or second?" She knew the importance of hearing me out but broke a tense moment by understanding my frustration while keeping the reality of the moment in perspective!

Travel

Cindi:

Joey and I were recently traveling together without Dad. We've mastered escalator's, moving walk-ways, and bumpy airplane rides as we travel from point A to B, but there are still some things that remain harder to deal with. I needed to use the bathroom in an airport, and no family bathrooms were to be found. In a family bathroom, I can have Joey stand in the corner and hide his face so he doesn't watch me. But this time, I had Joey stand outside the women's bathroom, clutching my carry-on, hoping he would not talk to anyone. I was thankful he didn't need to use the bathroom because (I have had to do this) most women don't look too kindly upon an adult male in the women's bathroom. I've had a few nasty looks, but I dismiss them, knowing he needs assistance. I won't risk his being alone in a public men's bathroom. It's great when my husband or son-in-law (or someone we know well) is there to help him, but on my own, I can't risk his wandering out with his zipper down, making a mess trying to wipe himself after a bowel movement, or having a problem while alone in the bathroom or anything else you can picture or imagine.

Any time we travel, we need to play out each possible scenario and decide how he might act, and at best it's a guess. Our response is to plan what is most necessary. All in all, it's best for us to travel alone, so we don't inconvenience others with our need to time all activities carefully. Also, less is better. If we plan too much in too short a time span, we usually pay dearly.

Planning

Everything is planning—and planning is everything. Just as planning for a special Christmas takes time, so does planning anything with people who can't care for themselves. We always need to stay a step ahead of the game, whether it was planning a simple outing to the park when the kids were little or considering housing needs for Joey as an adult or taking our elderly parents out for a meal. The list seems to be never-ending, and the phrase "pick up and go" has no meaning for us.

If we take Joey in a wheelchair to make it faster and easier for us to get from place to place, we must consider the availability of ramps and elevators to get us where we need to go.

For most families when the children grow up, they are done with bottles and strollers. But when caring for someone with special needs (whether young or old), bringing special food, special medicines, special clothing (or diapers), special medical supplies, wheelchairs, feeding supplies, suctioning tubes and apparatus is always an issue. Sometimes the planning and preparation isn't worth the effort. And with all the planning, everything still moves at one speed. A mentally or physically disabled person cannot be rushed.

Frustrations

We are frustrated by people who fail to get what we're going through and don't even try. When they respond to us by comparing apples to oranges, we are reminded of the importance of thinking before responding. For example, sharing with someone about Joey's sleepless night, we were told, *"Well, my kids are popping up and down all night just like yours!"* So what is our frustration with that comment? Are they almost thirty? Have they been doing it for three or thirty years? Are your kids really *just* like mine? We're not saying their situation isn't frustrating and tiring, but we are saying it's different from ours.

Perhaps a different response might have been one that showed caring instead of comparing: "How do you get the proper rest you need when you're up a lot at night every night?" "It must be hard to be rested when you're up so much in the night time."

Here's another example of a person's response to how long potty training took. *"Yes, I understand completely! It took me two weeks to potty train my little Johnny!"* When it has taken someone five years to potty train their child, or perhaps it's never happened, and they're still changing a "poopy" diaper on a seventeen- year-old, people can't possibly and completely understand unless they've been through the same situation day after day after day. Never engaged in that thought process? Then please think it through.

Here are some examples of caring responses: "That must be hard to still be potty training all this time." "I never thought about how hard it would be to potty train for five years. I'll bet you're thrilled that you finally helped your child accomplish that task!" Then let the caregiver talk. If at all possible, try not to give advice. After five years, she or he has probably heard and tried everything and is already frustrated that it hasn't happened yet; we were.

Want to comfort a person who will likely do the same thing for the rest of someone's life? Then say something like this: "I can't imagine what it would be like to change diapers on your seventeen-year-old." The caregiver will appreciate that so much more than advice.

At times people say they understand a medical issue. *"Yes, I understand how difficult seizures are. My little Sally has really bad bouts with the flu and some bad allergies, too."* Usually the flu is something people get over. Yes, the flu can have lasting effects but generally does not. Most people don't "get over" seizures or Alzheimer's or muscular dystrophy. When people have made comments like this, we tend to think, "Oh, does she fall on the floor convulsing? Is she unresponsive during her bouts with the flu? Does she nearly crack her head open from the fall? Does she turn blue and choke on her vomit? Does she stop breathing?" Of course, we would never say these things because it would diminish Sally's flu, which is a very real issue as well; but the situations are very different. We would hope to respond like this: "I hope Sally feels better after this bout with the flu." "I imagine that really set Sally back a few days. How is she now?" We hope we would *not* blurt out something that would be hurtful even though it might go through our minds! All of us need to think ahead to a response that would be caring and kind.

Caring responses by Sally's parent might be, "What is it like when your child has a seizure?" "It must be hard to watch your child have a seizure and not be able to do anything to make it better or stop it." "When did your child first experience seizures?"

Take a moment to picture exactly what the caregiver and person with special needs is really dealing with, and then think about a caring response the next time. We can all learn to respond in a more caring manner with a comment that relates with the issue instead of making unsuitable comparisons.

The key to good responses can be found in scripture. Philippians 2:4 says, "Do not merely look out for your own personal interests, but also for the interests of others." And when someone says something that they don't even realize has hurt or shocked us— like "I feel like such a retard"—let's remember Proverbs 19:11: "A man's discretion makes him slow to anger, and it is his glory to overlook a transgression." Let us be gracious to others so they will be the same for us when we unknowingly say something thoughtless. And then we must let it go according to I Peter 4:8, "Above all, keep fervent in your love for one another because love covers a multitude of sins." Not every comment is intended to hurt. We all have those times when we say something we wish we could grab and put back in our mouths! We include ourselves in the learning process. And that learning process is life-long.

Decision Making, Daily Coping Skills

Environment

Caregivers must make many decisions on behalf of others, and many factors, including special challenges and frustrations, influence those decisions. We must think about the environment—sounds, smells, and anything that will affect the sense of touch. We have to maintain an environment where our son feels safe. If you have a loved one whose illness or disease causes her or him extreme sensitivity, considering the effect of new situations and places is important.

When Cindi's dad was in a nursing home for rehabilitation following a mild stroke and also suffering from dementia, he was very sensitive to sounds. An attached alarm would sound if he moved certain ways to alert the nurses to make sure he was safe, not trying to get out of his wheelchair or bed. By the time they would get to him that sound would have him an emotional wreck; and one time we found him on the floor in a pool of urine. How long was he like that in our absence of two hours? Joe's mom was in a nursing home also with dementia and had the same type of monitor. She didn't like the sound, but it didn't affect her in the same way. She was annoyed but not emotionally distraught.

To this day, Joey watches the fast movements of a small dog, a tiny insect, or the activity of small children and can become very upset. His emotions and moods change like the Cleveland weather, and like forecasters we have a hard time predicting what will trigger a change for better or worse. We can experience the full range within moments! (For those who don't know Cleveland weather, one afternoon in late October we enjoyed watching sunshine followed by rain, snow, and hail, in a twenty-minute time period and a thirty-degree temperature change.)

Life becomes very different for those dealing with issues that cause such daily disruptions. Although some therapies can help reduce these annoyances and frustrations, they don't usually disappear completely.

The Individual's Personality

A person's afflictions as well as personality will affect the way she or he acts or reacts in various situations. People in pain, no matter how nice their usual personality, will likely be challenged in different situations. In public, our son has an overall pleasant personality. Many people, especially at church, see him as quiet and docile. He is not. If he becomes irritated—and one can never be sure when that will happen—he can become very nasty. He is 6'3" tall, and when that testosterone starts flowing, he is very strong. He has swung and missed and swung and hit. It can be very frightening. It can be borderline abusive to us, the caregivers. Because we can't always know or anticipate how he'll react or respond in different situations, we sometime feel we can't take the chance and need to opt out of plans. What is particularly difficult for us is that not everyone has seen the rage or even the simple misbehavior, and that makes us *feel* as if people might not believe us. Kicking a hole in a door because he didn't want to get in the car and go for a ride one Sunday is not typical of his daily or even normal behavior, but it happens; and we can't always say when or why. Sometimes he needs to be restrained. Although Cindi is much smaller than Joey, she is able to get him off balance enough to settle him down on the floor. This technique has only been used a handful of times when damage to property, people, or himself is looming. We wonder what *that* would look like to someone observing for the first time.

Both parents who had dementia/Alzheimer's and Joe's dad with brain cancer dealt with personality and behavioral issues. Some people become very agitated; others become sweet and docile, sometime the exact opposite of their life-long personality. Some of the change may derive from the frustration of being misunderstood. Cindi's dad was upset when he was no longer "allowed" to carry a wallet. In reality, his sweat pants provided no place for him to carry a wallet. It was just easier to fit these pants over his diaper; they could more easily be lifted up and down and just happened not to have pockets. Zippers, buttons, and now wallets had been taken from him, and he didn't like it. We didn't either, but simplicity trumped his old comfortable khakis. We eventually found some nice pants that had an elastic waist with pockets, but by then, he didn't remember he ever had a wallet. Mom Ferrini, complaining about her ailments, may have been more frustrated about her state of life in general than about any one ailment. Joey is always with someone but maybe he wants some "alone" time. It's a tough place to be. If he somehow understands that he doesn't have the freedom or privileges that others his age have, perhaps that is when frustration, miscommunication, personality changes, and poor behaviors result.

Damage, immaturity, a disorder, or changes in the brain can alter the personality of the individual we care for in a flash, making reading about care for the particular special needs person essential because many illnesses and diseases initially or ultimately affect the brain. A book that helped us in the care of Joey as well as three of our four parents is *The 36-Hour Day* by Nancy L. Mace and Peter V. Rabins, M.D. It contains over 400 pages of helpful advice for every person involved in patient care. We have read it at least four times and find it a valuable resource that we recommend often. Read it by section or chapters that pertain to where you are and what you need. You don't have to read it from cover to cover, but all the information is very valuable. Even though Joey does not have dementia, Alzheimer's, or other related dementia illnesses like memory loss in later life, many symptoms manifest themselves similarly in intellectual ability, daily functioning, vocabulary and speech, mental processes, lack of judgment, physical abilities, and even personality changes (if you know the multi-personalities of Smegel from *Lord of the Rings*, you'll have an idea). We recommend it as required reading for anyone caring for someone whose brain has been compromised in any way. We also encourage extended family to read it so everyone is on the same page. As you determine your level of commitment to the one you are caring for, the more you understand, the better you will be able to walk in her or his shoes, and the better caregiver you will be.

Become an Expert on the One You Care for

Proverbs 31:8-9, "Open your mouth for the dumb, for the rights of the unfortunate. Open your mouth, judge righteously, and defend the rights of the afflicted and needy." If we don't do it, who will? They can't take care of themselves. Looking up a phone number to make a call is way beyond Joey's ability. To formulate his needs into words is not possible. To report to someone that he is being mistreated isn't even on his radar screen. To ask someone how to get something he needs—please! He needs us to care for his needs, to open our mouths, and get him what he needs. It's not a life of wants, only needs.

As parents, we feel as if we know our son better than any doctor, therapist, or teacher; but we've always listened to and appreciated the help and support they've given. At times, however, you know what you know, and you must be firm in demanding what you need or want for your loved one. Knowing what our roles and responsibilities are is also helpful. Keeping a notebook, writing notes to teachers or medical personnel in it, letting others add to it, and reading and reviewing what has been written makes for better communication, providing everyone uses it!

Having helped in the care of our parents, we found that becoming experts on their care was different. We hadn't "grown into" their issues as we had with Joey from birth, so we had to rely on the help and advice of others to help us make decisions in the best interest of each parent. In addition, if another person was in charge of that parent's care, we voiced opinions but supported the final decision of the primary caregiver, whose responsibility was to listen to advice and concerns but do what was best even if others were critical of the decision. We trusted that the caregiver was truly interested in the person's care, not money, material goods, or some other interest that would interfere with giving and getting the best possible care.

Read all you can to become educated on health, mental, physical, spiritual, and emotional issues. Depending on the loved one's ability to think normally, she or he will appreciate your efforts to learn about specific needs. For those lacking in the ability to think normally, you are still ahead of them as you learn to deal with them in many ways.

Take Care of Yourself

This can be a tough one. Caregivers can go on and on, day after day, month after month, doing what they do, and not stop to realize their own health is becoming a problem. We will discuss this in more detail in Chapter 11. If you feel this is an urgent issue, turn there now, and return here later.

Interruptions in Life

A report from the Alzheimer's Association indicates almost ten million Americans caring for someone with Alzheimer's. With the possibility of four to six years of survival after diagnosis (or as long as twenty years), 8.5 billion hours of care will be provided by caregivers and valued at almost 83 billion dollars. That adds up to some big changes and interruptions in the lives of caregivers. We can choose to see these challenges as interruptions in life or as opportunities to show who God is in our life and lead others to Him.

Often people have said to us, "How do you do it?" For us, it is clearly and sincerely with the help of the Lord. People ask how we can be happy all of the time (not all the time— really! Our close family and friends know the real us!). We simply point them to the Lord. We explain that He gives us what we need when we need it, and because of that we have joy. We know joy and happiness aren't the same. Sometimes we aren't happy, but we can experience joy in doing what we know to be right. People are amazed to see someone handling a difficult situation with joy. People have said things like, "I've prayed that something like this won't happen to me because I could never handle it the way you do." We say, "Look out!" No one is exempt!

On a day-to-day basis seeing the blessings might be difficult, and it was for us in the early years. When we look back and see how the Lord has led, guided, and helped, the blessings become more evident and obvious, and it becomes natural to point others to Jesus. We couldn't do it ourselves, and we know Who helped! Matthew 6:25-34 teaches us that when we seek Him first, He will provide us with everything we need just when we need it. When we see His provision, we realize that we have experienced the *full* blessing!

Interruptions will be easier to handle if you can answer the following questions for yourself:

✓ What is my purpose in life?

✓ What are my desires in life?

✓ What are my values in life?

✓ How has God gifted me? Am I using this gift?

✓ What are some goals I'd like to accomplish in life?

✓ How will I respond when these purposes, desires, and values, are challenged in some way?

✓ Who is *really* in control?

If we can learn to work out these answers day to day by prioritizing what is most important, we will be able to view interruptions as opportunities and some day look back without regret. In Luke 10:41-42 Martha wanted to spend her time preparing for guests. Mary knew that sitting with Jesus was most important at that moment. They both prioritized when something unexpected occurred in their lives. Would we know which role to choose? Do we choose properly?

Yes, our lives are different—different from what we expected or what we may have planned, different from the beginning to the end and everywhere in between, and even different from the lives of many others. But we recognize that all people have struggles. Theirs may be temporary where ours are permanent, but their struggles are no less valid. They have frustrations and so do we. They are just different ones.

Enjoy the Journey

We have many ups and downs in life, and the addition of caregiving responsibilities doubles them! We will never probably "get over" our challenge, but we will "get through" it. Certainly not everyday will be enjoyable. Certainly we won't choose to repeat certain days, but can we determine to enjoy the journey?

Romans 8:18-30 offers encouragement to all of us. Verse 18 says, "For I consider that the sufferings of this present time are not worthy to be compared with the glory that is to be revealed to us." Verse 28 says, "And we know that God causes all things to work together for good to those who love God, to those who are called according to His purpose. For whom He foreknew, He also predestined to become conformed to the image of His Son." He reveals the journey to us day by day. He has done so for us, molding us into the people He wants us to become in the process.

What we do for others in our families (teaching, training, nurturing, loving, protecting, and leading) is what we do for the one with special needs. The difference is extra work, time, effort, patience, and endurance. Having raised two daughters without special needs, we know the difference! We must adjust our thinking and our attitudes in terms of what God has planned for us. We haven't changed our call in life or our mission or gifting. All of these are a part of the journey.

When we mentor young couples with children with special needs, we explain that we often felt like "jumping ship" because the world out there has so much to offer. When we feel trapped by the roadblocks of life, it's easy to feel like quitting. But when we feel as if we need to "get a life," we quickly remember that Joey is our life. Our daughters are our life. The sooner we surrender to what God has for us, the sooner He can work in and through us!

As Plan A turns into Plan B, then C, then D, we adjust our thinking and our lives to surrender to Him. We learn to take on different roles and responsibilities. We learn to be creative to get things done in a timely fashion. We learn to discern. Like Emily Perl Kingsley, we might not be in Italy, where we wanted to be, but Holland has much to offer. Let's not miss it! Let's learn to enjoy the journey!

Yes, our lives are different from what we had expected and likely different from yours whether or not you are caring for someone with special needs. If we all keep an open mind about what others might be going through, we'll probably be able to show compassion and kindness to one another through our struggles.

OTHERS' STORIES

- It is very frustrating to live among other families with children who are having fun and doing normal things while we are in therapy for our child. Trying to live in both worlds can be stressful and often frustrating. Sometimes it's easier to retreat into the world of doctors and therapists because others don't seem to understand the constant emotional drain and our lack of energy. If that isn't sad enough, it seems they don't really care enough to understand.

- I love it when others caring for people with special needs share how they really feel in the midst of the challenges. I don't feel so alone then.

- I have tried to embrace the talents and giftedness in others' children even though mine will never be able to do the same things. Watching my son on stage at a special needs camp and seeing helpers carry him in a sports relay helped me to know that my son and I can enjoy the same things as others—only differently.

- Because of having several ongoing issues with our special needs child, it is very difficult for us to be active in our church. The leadership has criticized our lack of involvement. Some of the things they want us to do occur at the same time our child needs to get to sleep. In addition, if we *could* participate in the things they are requesting, who would interact with our child who is wheelchair bound and unable to play with the other children? Who would meet the special needs if there were a problem? Would they want to listen to the noises my child makes if we go past the scheduled bedtime—which is very likely?

- I notice that my church family is happy to listen to the "facts" of our special needs situation (i.e., pray for Susie, who is in the hospital for therapy four days a week), but they don't want anything to do with the "feelings" part (i.e., "I am so tired, I really could use a break." "I wish I could get over the feelings I have of frustration every morning when I wake up.") I sense that others prefer I stuff the feelings.

- Our child's behavioral issues are very challenging. When he gets upset, it's hard to calm him down. If we respond the wrong way, we find that his behavior spirals downward quickly. It's very hard to deal with his behaviors because no two situations are ever the same. I've sought help, but it's very difficult to find resolve. I wonder if getting older will escalate the behaviors or tame them.

- My neighbors petitioned to keep me from constructing a fence in my yard. It was the only thing we could protect our autistic son yet give him and us some freedom. They held us hostage in our own home because they were insistent on keeping the neighborhood *looking* a certain way.

- I can't accomplish things in big time slots like I used to. I am learning to be one who works in "spurts," being consistent and persistent in baby steps. Trying to make things happen for everyone every day puts my list on hold.

- Our special needs family member is very disciplined, organized (once trained and practiced). These attributes are wonderful but have taken years to instill. The highly scheduled regimen is often hard to follow but necessary.

- The "acute" times of our son's illness were all-consuming, physically, emotionally, and time-wise. They involved more than just remembering his medication! During these intense times, we wished people would've understood when we asked for no visitors. We were exhausted and needed to give what was left of our energy to each other. At times people made comments that were impractical. I know they were made with good intentions, but sometimes they hurt.

- I wish that others didn't assume that I have everything under control and understood how demanding and time-consuming this caregiving is. It takes a toll on my body, time, energy, friendships and finances.

- Something my friend has made me aware of is the *daily-ness* of caring over and over—and not seeing progress of the person to the next stage of "growing up." Also I've seen what a *lifetime* commitment it is—never getting to that "empty nest" stage.

- Finding good doctors and specialists does not mean always finding them locally.

- As a teacher, I say, "Get rid of the nonessentials on those IEPs (Individualized Education Plan). Who cares if they can tie their shoes if they are able to get them on and off?" Try Velcro. Be creative. Don't let every detail wear you out.

- The logistics of getting my adult friend in and out of a car, transporting the wheelchair, etc., makes me realize what he and his family must deal with daily.

- Our child has a mental illness. I am careful to tell only certain people who need to know because it is stressful enough without everyone having comments and remedies. I've learned no family is perfect.

- Because caring for my brother with special needs took so much time and effort, my parents made decisions that affected our family finances greatly. Although our family income dropped dramatically, no one could tell. Both parents managed to provide us with everything we needed.

- Being on call 24/7 is tough, yet it's become normal to us.

- I have taken care of my handicapped elderly mother for twelve years. I really don't like to be told how to take care of her by people who have never taken care of someone besides their own children who are now grown and gone.

- Don't give me solutions that work for your typically developing child for my special needs daughter. The dynamics are not even close. It's not the same.

- If you have a third cousin with the same condition my person with special needs has, please don't act like you know how hard it is unless you've been a caregiver.

- Finding time to do my son's therapies is hard, and because he can't do anything on his own, he is completely dependent on me for every single thing.

- Putting my child on certain medications to help in one area has caused regression in others.

- Taking my child to the county board of mental retardation and having him declared incompetent was a hard pill to swallow.

- I had hoped to continue teaching but chose to stay home to care for my child with special needs. There were no day care facilities able to care for his needs and I ultimately wanted to be the one to provide him with what he needed.

- As a husband, I choose to put my wife, daughter, and son with special needs first by serving them, but I battle against selfishness.

- I had no idea how different life would be for us. Others simply don't have a clue and seldom ask to understand our life. I wished I'd known how hard it was for others in my life. Now that I'm caring for someone with special needs, I wish I had been more compassionate, caring, and helpful. I hope to help and mentor others as they go through difficult times when I am a bit further down the road in my journey.

- I subscribed to LifeAlert for Dad. The machine arrived one day, I set it up the next day, and the following day Dad fell in the bathroom with the door SHUT. (I am serious about the timeline!) His voice had grown so tiny by that time that I was amazed that he could be heard by the device downstairs and through the bathroom door. I got the call and was there within five minutes. Had we not had the device he would have lain there bleeding and shivering for several hours until I arrived to get him to an appointment. The sad thing is that when we left for the hospital that morning it was the last time he was ever in his home. I sent the machine back right after that. We only had it three days, but it was definitely worth it.

YOUR STORY

What are some challenges you have experienced in your marriage as a result of caring for someone with special needs?

_____

_____

_____

_____

What are some blessings you have experienced in your marriage as a result of caring for someone with special needs?

_____

_____

_____

Describe some things that you've had to adjust to in the area of privacy or intimacy in marriage. (Give only examples that both you and your spouse are comfortable sharing.)

_____

_____

_____

_____

What dreams have been dashed in your life?

_____

_____

_____

Do you have any vacation/travel stories you'd like to share with your group?

_____

_____

_____

How have you been able to maintain a safe environment? What things have worked? What have not?

_____

_____

_____

Can you share a humorous story that has helped you keep a good perspective as you enjoy the journey?

_____

_____

_____

How have you handled the challenging comments people have made?

_____

_____

_____

What are you learning? What wisdom/advice can you give and share?

_____

_____

_____

_____

CHAPTER SIX

Road Blocks and Delays: The Long Haul

Immediately after Bill became a quadriplegic following a motorcycle accident, he said he'd rather be dead than stuck in the wheelchair. Trapped inside a body that no longer worked, he regretted not having worn a helmet. He regretted his foolish riding. He regretted having to sit in a computerized wheelchair, but as time passed, he adjusted to using just one finger to move his wheelchair wherever he wanted to go. He eventually understood the value of life and appreciated those who fed, dressed, and cleaned him.

....

Luane has changed her daughter's diapers for seventeen years, much longer than she ever expected. She has learned to appreciate serving this way, making a difference in the life of her daughter and in the lives of those watching. She still longs for "breaks" that don't come often enough but enjoys them when they do! She is grateful for ten minutes of free time and makes sure she always thanks those who have helped her.

....

For two years Edward has tended his wife with Lou Gehrig's (ALS) disease. No longer verbal, she is restricted to her wheelchair or bed. He is still able to lift her but realizes he will soon need a mechanical device to transition her from one location to another. He makes sure she is turned and repositioned throughout the day to avoid the painful bedsores she has developed on occasion. He knows this job will not last forever, yet he's tired and looks forward to the one day a week that his only child comes to give him a break.

....

OUR STORY

A few years ago we took our girls to Hawaii. We were thankful that Aunt Susie had offered to watch Joey because on this trip we wanted to do what we could not have done had he been with us, for example, taking the road to Hana. We soon learned why we were told to hire a driver who "knew the road." Sure, we *could* have driven it, but we wouldn't have known the courtesy expected by other drivers who also knew the road. The long and winding roads, the cliffs, the waterfalls, the narrow passageways, the bumpy areas, and the constant unexpected curves made us glad to have someone else in control!

Having Joey in our lives is like the road to Hana—bumpy, narrow, curving yet with some beautiful views. To enjoy the ride, we are glad someone else (God) is in control! When life sets us upon a road that is longer than we expected, when we stand at the edge of an emotional cliff after days, weeks, or months of caring for him through an illness, when the narrow passageways of decisions need to be navigated quickly, when the bumps are too jostling to keep holding on, when the waterfalls are shedding more water than we can tread, and when the curves of life are coming at us way too quickly, we know we have to rely upon the One who has sent us on this journey!

Looking back, we see life as a journey, an adventure, and we realize we have actually lived to tell about it! Yes, sometimes we are "sick of it in the thick of it," but we always have someone in control of what's going on in our life! After recognizing and accepting that life was to be different from what we had expected, we could prepare for the long haul. The preparation came by way of a significant attitude adjustment like the ones experienced by the three people whose stories we shared above. We've had to adjust to new life goals, the changes, the frustrations, and all the work. We've had to admit that we can't impose a time frame on our situation, which may last longer than we think we can handle. We've acknowledged that we are in for the long haul, so we'd like to share with you *some* of the things that have affected us for these many years. Perhaps you or someone you know will relate. If we share something that seems to fit your situation in even the slightest way, consider how you can "fine tune" it to help you.

Prayer

Individuals may have thought they were doing fine in their relationship with Christ prior to the challenges they're given, but day-to-day frustrations take a toll on those whose faith is minimal, who pray only "as needed," and who are happy with a religious experience instead of a personal relationship with Jesus Christ. In Chapter 3 we talked about how a group of people weathered a storm (Psalm 107:23-31). All of us experience sickness, grief, death, accidents, problems and these can cause us to fall to our knees and pray. We have the opportunity and privilege to go to God in prayer. When the wind is taken out of our sails, when life is so demanding that we can't function anymore, He is there to guide us. He simply wants us to ask for help. And when we ask and take time to listen, He always has an answer and a way to help us get through each situation. We must make prayer a first priority instead of a last resort.

Please read all of Psalm 116 and record below how these verses speak to your heart:

_____

_____

_____

_____

A Lifetime of Service

Some Christians pay lip service to acting as servants of Christ by saying they will surrender to God, and do whatever He calls them to do – even if that means suffering; but when asked to serve those who are helpless, the words *servant, surrender, called,* and *suffering* are redefined. All these words add up to sacrifice. We sacrifice time, energy, our own dreams, our child's dream, our spouses' hopes, our present, our future, our family's desires, or a combination of all these! One of Webster's definitions of the verb *sacrifice* is "to accept loss or destruction for an end, cause, or ideal." Making a sacrifice in baseball provides a perfect analogy. One player on base must be called "out" in order for the overall goal to be achieved, in this case a better opportunity to score. For us, sacrifice creates an opportunity to allow other events to take place in our lives that will yield a perfect ending!

What is the "end, cause, or ideal" for which we are willing to sacrifice? According to Psalm 138:8, "The Lord will accomplish what concerns me; Thy lovingkindness, O Lord, is everlasting. Do not forsake the works of Thy hands." That ideal might entail developing a greater compassion for others. The end might be that we finally give ourselves to the Lord. The cause might be that we give up selfishness and trust God to help us serve when we would not have chosen to do so—not something that comes easily to us and possibly something we don't really want to do. After all, do you know anyone who has asked for a challenge or difficulty in life?

We can't hold onto bitterness in our heart and expect to show grace. We can't express our disappointment and anger in sinful ways and expect to be an example to others. Once we realize that we're on the road to our own learning experience, we must first yield to His will for our lives and become more like Jesus Christ. Others are watching. What are we teaching them by our example?

We hope that others see how God has kept us going, kept us on the straight and narrow path! Colossians 3:17 says, "And whatever you do in word or deed, do all in the name of the Lord Jesus, giving thanks through Him to God the Father." He's supplied us with endurance, willingness, and power, and we recognize that we derive our adequacy from Him! (II Corinthians 3:5, "Not that we are adequate in ourselves to consider anything as coming from ourselves, but our adequacy is from God.")

Constant Changes

Whether we care for a child with a disability, an older child who has had a tragic accident or injury, or an aging parent with an illness, we learn that everything our loved one experiences will affect us. Change for him or her is change for us. We may see constant changes in health issues, caregivers, teachers, aides, bus drivers, Social Security, government assistance, therapists, medications, hospital visits. The list is endless. We must understand that this life is a testing place, not a resting place!

Ongoing changes have occurred in Joey's life as he's grown and developed, and many of them have surprised us. The changes in the care of our parents affected us as well. Although we did not assume full-time care of all of our parents, we were very intimately involved in their care during their declining years. The first change we personally experienced was they could no longer help us with our son and daughters. We were suddenly without babysitters and knew we needed to rise to the occasion and help those who had previously sacrificed to help us.

Cindi:

At one point Joe's dad was in a nursing home for rehabilitation following chemotherapy and radiation. His roommate was my dad, who was recovering from yet another stroke. Visiting both at the same time was convenient but also very draining. My dad's early stages of dementia were such that leaving him alone caused him a great deal of stress, so my mom, two sisters, and I made a schedule; and someone stayed with him at all times. He couldn't eat by himself, and help wasn't always readily available from aides. He needed help toileting and could not request it on his own. So we were there to help where and when we could. This went on for weeks. Over the course of his care, the last three and a half years being the most intense, he was in a hospital or nursing home probably ten or more times. Each time required us to change our "plans." Everyone sacrificed to help. I had to continue caring for my own family, yet this other dimension of life was equally exhausting, time-consuming, and top priority. These difficult tasks and situations became our lifestyle and a labor of love.

Later on down the road, we cared for Joe's dad at his home, giving Mom Ferrini some time to run errands and catch her breath as the primary caregiver. We had the luxury of a large family who all took turns. His "long haul" lasted a mere seven months before cancer took his life, but in the midst of the caring, seven months seems like a very long time. We were very thankful to have several nurses in the family, who helped immensely.

My dad's total one-on-one care was required for almost seven years. As a family, we determined to keep him at home. Mom, the primary caregiver, had an addition built onto the house to accommodate a wheelchair and a handicapped-accessible bathroom. (Anyone who's ever "built" a home or added onto one while living still in it knows the changes, aggravations, pressures, and frustrations that are added to life!) They were able to hire someone to tend to Dad through the night, so Mom could actually sleep; and my sisters and I continued to care for Dad during the day for a very long time. Mary Jo helped on Tuesdays; I spent the day on Thursdays; and Sue, who lived with Mom and Dad, was there in the evenings and on weekends. During the times Dad was in and out of hospitals and nursing homes, we saw a bit of an improvement after various rehabilitations (physical, occupational, and speech therapy), but he never returned to his previous level of capability. We needed a van with a lift when he could no longer transfer from the wheelchair to the van. Thus, there were always changes in the care he needed. We were continuously readjusting. Life was always changing.

Joe:

After Mom Ferrini was diagnosed with advanced vascular dementia, we knew that she would need additional interventions in her life from others. Because my father had given me power of attorney for my mother should her health ever fail, I was the one to tell her she could no longer drive her car. This was a particularly difficult thing to do because she was very independent and loved outings with her church and senior citizen friends. We loved to see Mom do these things on her own, but we knew she could no longer drive when one day she knocked down her mailbox pulling out of the driveway. Granted, we all have had our little accidents, but in this case, despite admitting that she hit the mailbox on the day it happened, the next day Mom could not understand how her mailbox got on the ground. I told her, "This time you just hit a mailbox. What if next time you hit one of the neighborhood children?" This was just one of several things that led us to decide for her that she had to stop driving.

Gradually, as a family we realized that we needed to make provisions for Mom so that she would be able to transition to a simpler lifestyle. We tried to do this as sensitively and diplomatically as possible. The next big issue was to sell the house, which was in need of some major repairs. Thankfully, my brother-in-law George, a skilled plumber, and Ed, one of our life-long friends, were able to get Mom's house ready for sale. Prior to putting it on the market, we knew we would have to convince her to move in with us. With the passage of time, a lot of patience with Mom, and eventually her own awareness, she knew she could no longer live alone. We did our best to help her feel comfortable in the mother-in-law suite, making it her own. Once she agreed to live with us, she gave us the blessing to sell her house, which sold quickly. Clearly our life was going to change— again—and in fact it was changing every single day. Unfortunately for Mom Ferrini, her health continued to falter after moving in with us. The timing of the sale of her home was perfect to provide funds to cover her medical expenses and an eventual room in a nearby nursing facility.

Daily changes for us occurred from the spring of 1995 until the spring of 2006, caring for Joey and one parent after another. Doing so was a privilege but also wearisome.

A Matter of Perspective

When our kids were small, Mom Ferrini used to say, "These are the best days of your life!" Those words resonated as many times as she sweetly repeated them and certainly every time we were up all night with one child or another, every time we had an extended stay with Joey in the hospital during his seizure activity, when all the kids were acting up at once or throwing up one after the other. We remember saying, "If these are the best days of our life, does that mean it's only downhill from here? Stop the world—I want to get off! Can I get a pink slip or am I still employed?"

Cindi:

I sometimes questioned Mom's wisdom in those early days, and on a few occasions asked her whether she remembered things the way they really were! She helped me to realize that appreciating life is a matter of perspective and we can't always see it clearly when we're in the midst of it!

I've had to learn to assume a proper perspective on each and every situation and to bend like a willow, not to be like the old oak tree, strong but rigid! I'm not there yet, and I'm still practicing to "get it right," but I'd like to share with you what has helped me immensely. No matter what we go through, I do my best to keep things in perspective, realizing many have it much worse than I do and some have it easier. I try to remember that these days will soon slip through my fingers, never to be held again, except in a faint memory. In some ways I make a game of it! Let me show you how it works!

When Joey had seizures for hours on end (sometimes twenty- to sixty-minute seizures every hour in a twenty-four hour period), keeping us up all hours of the night, then being out of commission for the next few days until his strength returned, I needed to train my mind not only to say but truly believe the following:

✓ I was privileged to be a "stay-at-home mom," who didn't have to call off from work—again. Thank you, Lord.

✓ In a few days life would get back to "our" normal. Over the years I'd met some families with special needs children, literally unable to leave their homes without a lot more effort, help, and planning than we needed. Thank you, Lord, that once Joey's better, I can get out and run errands again.

✓ Everything that happens has a good side and bad side. What is the GOOD side here? How can I concentrate on that? Help me, Lord, to see it.

✓ I'd run through questions that would help me see what God saw. What has God been teaching me through this? Am I relying upon Him as He has invited me? (This required having a broad vision of who He is, which is more easily found when reading His word faithfully and daily!)

Here's one more scenario. When we were young and the little boys of our friends or family members played sports that Joey could not or now when our empty-nester friends call to ask us to an impromptu dinner or when others tell us about the next trip they have planned, I have to run through a similar drill in my mind. I have to remember to "take every thought captive to the obedience of Christ" according to II Corinthians 10:5. Here's how it works.

When I sense a "twinge" of envy coming into my thought life directly from the adversary, it sounds something like this: "Oh, if you had a normal son, Joe could have played catch with him. Instead, you're stuck watching everyone else's children play sports. You have to listen to their dreams and watch them being fulfilled." Instead of staying in that mental "groove," I pray (and sometimes I've had to do so out loud), "Lord, you have given me so many blessings on a daily basis. Please help me to understand that this one thing is only a little thing in Your overall plan. Help me to rejoice in the joy that other parents have for the success of their children." When we have to decline a dinner invitation because we don't have a sitter for Joey, my mind could easily run into the ditch that says, "Oh, you poor thing. You have to sit home again. You are so deprived. Everyone else can pick up and go out, and you are stuck at home." Again, I need to recall God's faithfulness, and the *many* times I've had opportunity to do other things, just not *this* one thing. When friends tell me about a trip they are planning, I need to replay in my mind, the times I've had wonderful trips, the dear family and friends who have helped us so that we could travel. I just need to realize it's not the same for us as for someone else. Besides, they have their own set of troubles and challenges; they are just different from ours.

> *"Lord, you have given me so many blessings on a daily basis. Please help me to understand that this one thing is only a little thing in Your overall plan. Help me to rejoice in the joy that other parents have for the success of their children."*

When things go our way, we naturally feel good and have right reactions and responses. But when things aren't going our way, we need the supernatural help of the Lord to put things into the right perspective so we can respond and react properly.

To sum up, Colossians 2:6-8 says, "As you therefore have received Christ Jesus the Lord, so walk in Him, having been firmly rooted and now being built up in Him and established in your faith, just as you were instructed, and overflowing with gratitude. See to it that no one takes you captive through philosophy and empty deception, according to the tradition of men, according to the elementary principles of the world, rather than according to Christ." This principle is short, sweet, and simple, and if we are to become an example to others we must practice it every moment of our lives. Easy? No. Possible? Absolutely!

Behaviors

As noted previously sometimes a person's illness, disease, disability, or disorder causes her or him to have personality or behavioral challenges that sometimes embarrass us or our families. Behavior challenges might manifest themselves in acting out or acting inappropriately or poor table manners or personal hygiene resulting from their physical or mental limitations. A behavior caused by an illness may last only as long as that illness, but when long-term behaviors result from mental retardation, mental illness, or other "ongoing" situations, the long haul can be exhausting.

Consider the Alzheimer's patient who experiences "sun-downing," a term used to describe the time of day as well as the turn of events in that person's day. She or he becomes more confused and agitated in the late afternoon and early evening perhaps because of greater fatigue and a reduced ability to tolerate stressful situations along with the shadows and darkness of night. Making late afternoons and evenings as simple and relaxing as possible can reduce distractions. Keeping lights on until bedtime can also help.

Looking into Joey's journal made us realize some of Joey's behaviors have not changed and likely won't. Talk about the long haul! We know we've seen maturing along the way, but let us share something that happened just after his eighth birthday.

August, 1989:

"You have been quite 'contrary' lately! One day Kristina showed us an outfit that she was going to wear that said size '6'. You said, 'NO, 7!' I showed you the tag and asked you what number that was. You said, '7!' So I agreed with you and then you said, 'NO, 6!' You can be a corker!"

156

Fast forward to exactly the same situation, only the subject might be the Indians' score, a Browns player, or a trip destination! Sometimes we have to ignore Joey, lest we be swept into what we call "Joey's world" and have conversations as silly as the one we just shared!

Cindi:

When Joey was eight, he went through a very trying time. His behavior was very erratic and challenging. He bit, spat, hit, yelled, kicked, screamed, no matter whether we were at home or in public. Embarrassed and exhausted, I just didn't know how long I could put up with it. For me, the primary day-time caregiver, days were very long. You can imagine how I would want to "dump" the kids on Joe the minute he walked in the door after his long day at work. I thought, "Your day couldn't have been this bad." I knew he would have challenges in the dental office daily, but when he came home, I wanted to be as done with my daily job as he was done with his. He was great with the kids when he came home, and always helped out. He could tell Joey's behavior was taking a toll on me, but sometimes all his help and encouragement weren't enough for me. He could tell I was at the end of my rope, and honestly, I wasn't sure if I *liked* Joey let alone *loved* him. That may sound awful to someone who's never been in the place I was, but every ounce of my being, my day, my emotions, my stamina, my thought life—you name it—were being tested moment by moment.

Today, when we listen to the news and hear about a parent who has beaten a child, I am curious to know more about the situation. Was the parent mentally ill, depressed, distressed, or stressed? I am much less judgmental when I hear those reports. Although I've never beaten our children, I can tell you I was close at times, not because of their bad behavior or trying to "get to me" but because I was not getting the necessary respite. When a parent listens to a crying, sick, cranky child or when an adult cares for another adult day in and day out, hearing the same repetitious and monotone speech, uncontrolled sounds, and crying or dealing with the same behavior without much-needed breaks, the caregiver grows weary. And then consider the caregiver who does this not just day after day but year after year after year. No matter how much love and patience caregivers have, they reach the breaking point. The key is to know when you need to ask for the help of others so you don't cross that line. If you are a family member or friend observing someone caring for one with special needs, your careful observation and then willingness to intercede is very important. We will discuss this further in Chapter 11.

On one of his days off, Joe invited me to take the whole day and go out to do whatever I wanted! He even offered suggestions like a spa day, shopping at the mall, or lunch with a friend. I was so exhausted that I honestly wasn't even excited about going out. I'm not sure *what* I would have preferred to do, but my "day away" was neither satisfying nor refreshing. When I walked back in the door, I realized I was right back where I started. The hitting, yelling, biting, spitting and otherwise poor behavior Joey was unchanged. (If this is where you are right now, please consider reading Chapter 11 now and come back here later!) Joe looked at me and sensed my frustration. He apologized, and said, "I know you didn't expect this, but I have an emergency at the office, and the patient is meeting me there in 30 minutes." Joey wasn't in bed yet, and I wasn't ready to tackle that struggle. Jolted back to reality, I asked Joe to bring his *Physicians Desk Reference* with him when he returned home. I didn't really even realize the words had slipped out of my mouth, but in retrospect I am glad they did. Later when Joe returned home, we looked up the medication Joey was taking for his seizures and learned that he exhibited every possible side effect listed. The next day as early as possible I called his neurologist and said, "We have to find a different medicine for Joey. If we don't, we'll have to find one for me!" Immediately we changed his meds, and although we still had some issues to overcome, the majority of behaviors subsided considerably!

On other occasions, Joey's behaviors have been embarrassing and exhausting. Remember the family visit to the Olympic Village in Atlanta in 1996 that we shared with you previously, and other vacation snapshots we shared? Remember the sporting events we told you about? Don't think we didn't consider walking the other way. Somehow, though, the Lord has always given us the patience and endurance needed at the very moment we're ready to quit!

Our hope is that others can "see" that Joey is different and that they will not carry things further in a bad way but instead extend grace to us, the ones who deal with this daily!

Behavior Boundaries

We've been straightforward to show that sometimes life doesn't go as hoped or planned. Over time we have learned that we can help Joey through his poor behavior but not when he's in the midst of it, when too much emotion and investment in those emotions are in play. Here are a few measures that have occasionally helped.

✓ Set boundaries. If the person understands boundaries, you can both choose which battles to deal with and which to ignore.

✓ Maintain your composure. Don't become angry. Don't yell. Don't hit even when they strike first. (We've failed at this one a few times. It's so easy to yell because you feel as if you've had your say, but unfortunately, that usually gets the other person going downhill faster and doesn't work.)

✓ Figure out what the issue is, and if possible, try to resolve it. What does your loved one want? What doesn't she or he want? Does something hurt? Is the individual angry with you, your spouse, a television program, or something they've made up?

✓ Watch what the individual communicates verbally and nonverbally to see if you can determine the cause of the anger or acting out. If the person doesn't talk, figuring out what's wrong is difficult; but even if she or he talks, sometimes the anger gets in the way of communication.

✓ When the behavioral issue has passed and life is calm, review what happened, and maintain open, nonjudgmental communication to resolve this and future issues.

✓ Realize those who have brain-related issues are not always able to reach the same conclusions you can, not today and perhaps never. At those times, discuss with your spouse and/or other family members whether or not the person is able to remain in the home. Safety is a very important factor. Waiting until an accident or tragedy happens is too late.

✓ Don't model words or actions that you don't want your special needs person to imitate. For whatever reason, those seem to etch firmly in their minds and become habits without our even having to try!

The Behavior of Others

When we have hosted other special needs people in our home, we were the ones to tolerate and understand the behavior of someone else. Always trying to reach out to people in our community, we agreed to have a mother and daughter visit Joey, the girls, and me (Cindi) one summer day. This little girl was likely to be in Joey's classroom during the next school year. We were told that she was very aggressive and that the parents and teachers were assessing whether she would be able to integrate into this classroom with other multi-handicapped children. We had some games ready, so we'd get to know each other as we played. Kathleen, about three years old, was learning how to behave graciously when playing with others. To my surprise she sweetly permitted this little girl to choose her favorite yellow game piece. All three kids and all three adults were playing nicely when in a fury this little girl leaped across the game board, attacked Kathleen, pulling out a huge clump of her thick black hair. Thankfully, I sat right next to my daughter and cushioned the blow, which could have landed

> *Think twice and respond either by offering help (if appropriate) or a smile of reassurance that says, "I get it and you have my admiration and prayers. Hang in there."*

her onto the brick fireplace. Kathleen did not cry or fuss but was visibly shaken. I held her tightly as this little girl continued to lash out furiously. The mom was embarrassed, and I hurt for her, knowing that she deals with this behavior day after day. But it was clear the party was over, and I later learned that this little girl would not be in Joey's class after all. I felt bad and relieved at the same time. I know the girl's parents had their hands full.

The next time you're caught in the middle of someone else's trying and embarrassing moments, we hope you'll think twice and respond either by offering help (if appropriate) or a smile of reassurance that says, "I get it and you have my admiration and prayers. Hang in there." Remember, incidents like these can happen to children, adults with a special need, and elderly with declining health needs. During those challenging moments caregivers deeply appreciate and welcome the grace extended by others.

Medications, Hospitals, Nursing Homes

Having a loved one in a nursing home does not eliminate the caregiver's responsibilities. If you remain attentive and attuned to their care, whether you have their power of attorney or are a caring individual, family member, or friend, you have much to do that keeps you busy, keeps you connected to the individual, and may leave you exhausted. We had three parents in nursing homes or in need of around-the-clock care for varying problems, some at the same time. All told, I'd say we had some four years "invested" in visiting hospitals and nursing homes. Joe's mom, who lived with us under our care for several months, eventually took up residence in a nursing home within walking distance of our home. We were delighted to have her close! We could visit daily and even more than once a day if we needed or wanted to. The employees knew us and knew we came often, so they took care to be sure she was always dressed nicely and cared for well. (All the residents were, but when family members visit frequently, nursing home personnel will likely be especially attentive to your loved one.) Being nearby allowed us the opportunity to keep Mom's room neat, make sure her clothes were always clean and cared for, and most importantly, assure that she received the best care possible. The nurses and aides knew us, and we knew them. They loved Mom and treated her wonderfully. When she was no longer able to use the telephone, they allowed her to use the one at their desk, and they'd even dial for her! Sometimes Mom called just to say she missed us, loved us, or needed another visit—even when we'd been there twice that day already!

Even when the loved one lives elsewhere, emotional attachment and drain continue; but the burden of physical care, sleepless nights, and medications, is lifted in a trade off of sorts. When we love someone, her or his care is still on our mind, even if the individual is no longer in our home. We still receive phone calls at various times that alter our day.

Whether caring for an extended family member or our Joey, we struggled trying to balance the rest of life when the urgent need for care required monitoring medicines, a hospital stay, or nursing home care. For several months, we cared for both Mom Ferrini and Joey at home, and doing so took its toll.

Safety Concerns

We were most concerned with safety issues when Joey was little. Because he could not perform physically like others his age and did not comprehend danger until much later, keeping him safe and away from what could injure him was an urgent matter. Learning to read and experience taught him to recognize danger signs himself. He can read the word *danger* and knows what it means. Because he needs constant supervision, someone is always with him and can see the sign, too, just in case he was distracted!

When he was young, we gated everything; the deck in the back yard, the back yard, his bedroom, and all stairways. As an adult, standing at six feet three inches, we are concerned primarily for Joey's safety (and ours) when he is angry. We have a walkway overlooking our family living area. Because Joey is so tall, the railing touches him quite a bit lower than his waist. When his bedroom was on the second floor, his bursts of anger would make us nervous as we sat below in the family room and watched him extend his arm and point his finger from upstairs. Realizing it would just take one simple move for him to tumble over that railing, we soon moved him to the in-law suite on the main floor. We did not want to find ourselves in the headlines: "Christian Parents Fail to Supervise Adult Handicapped Son – Falls to Critical Injury from Second Floor Balcony!" Those who understand the dangers of keeping any child safe know something of these challenges, but it's different with a full-sized adult with the mind of a child. Guaranteeing safety is tough enough when children are small, but with age come hormones, making them unstoppable.

Additional safety concerns stem from Joey's severe allergy to peanuts, peanut oil, and the like. His diet has always been a concern. Almost always, before he eats anything, especially if we are out, he will look at us as if to say, "Can I go ahead and eat this, or might it have peanuts?" We have come to learn the hard way that even being in a room with peanut butter is a concern. We can't bake peanut butter cookies because it triggers a throat reaction even though he has not ingested it. He can't be in a room with people making peanut butter craft bird feeders. We've visited the ER on several occasions following these classroom learning experiences. Even the packaged items, like PLAIN M&Ms, include the disclaimer that they might contain peanuts. Joey always carries an "EpiPen," an auto-injector that delivers a 0.3 mg intramuscular dose of epinephrine. Injections into the thigh help counter any life-threatening allergic reaction. An EpiPen is a vital medication (by prescription) to have on hand if someone you know and love has severe allergies that could be fatal.

While Joey has learned some lessons and keeps safe most of the time, we realize we will always be responsible for his ultimate safety. He doesn't have the alertness and quick processing necessary to know when, where, and how to cross a street. He is easily distracted, so even when shopping, he is looking all over the place! He loves everyone, so if a stranger came up to him and said, "Your dad and mom said I could bring you home," he'd likely trust that person and go with them. When people question why we drive Joey to and from work everyday (a 2-hour daily commitment) instead of allowing him to take public transportation or hire a taxi service, this is why. With low verbal skills he could not express concerns or tell us if additional stops were made, or if he arrived at his destination on time.

Whenever we think of the steps and actions necessary to keep a baby or toddler safe, we must remember that a person with special needs requires the same attention. Considering wheelchairs, medical equipment, and supplies, is necessary. Someone with special needs is totally dependent on a caregiver.

Here are a few tips:

- ✓ Post emergency telephone numbers where caregivers and others can easily locate them.
- ✓ Have good lighting on stairways, in bathrooms, and kitchens at night. Nightlights can illuminate hallways and small areas.
- ✓ Don't use throw rugs. Special needs people often walk with a shuffle and can trip on rug corners.
- ✓ Use devices if needed to monitor the one you're caring for.
- ✓ Keep a telephone near the person with special needs if she or he is able to use it properly.
- ✓ Keep all electrical cords out of the path of traffic.

Spirit of Adventure!

Cindi:

Sometimes when I'm driving, my family sees more than they had bargained for. Asked if I'm lost, I'll say, "No, I'm not lost. I'm on an adventure!" I point to the great view of the parking lot where I just turned around or the scenic view from the next in a series of gas stations where we've stopped to ask directions. Sometimes I'm frustrated, but if I'm not too off course or too late, I consider it an adventure!

That same spirit of adventure helped while caring for Joey and our folks, and it will sustain us in the future for whatever or whoever might come our way. Because the day-to-day duties can be very challenging, we can easily become frustrated when things don't go the way we had planned or had hoped—and that's every day! To make the best of what is happening, I try (*try* being the operative word!) to keep a good attitude and spirit of adventure. Because life isn't perfect, I openly share my frustrations, disappointments, and tearful times with family and close friends. Having a good attitude all the time is challenging when nothing ever goes as planned, but God has given me a lot of practice, so I'm learning the lesson!

Making the "day to day" into an adventure takes some creativity. My goal is to find ways to laugh! We never want to make fun of a person or situation, but we definitely need to take time to laugh when we can. For instance, every day Joe and I have the privilege of

> *Because life isn't perfect, I openly share my frustrations, disappointments, and tearful times with family and close friends.*

getting Joey up for work and preparing his breakfast. We have our routine jobs and responsibilities and Joey maintains his routine is to stay in bed! So nearly every day, OK, *every day*, I try to find a way to make it *fun* for Joey to get up. Joe gets the breakfast going so I can work my "magic"! I might hide one of his Disney characters somewhere so he'll want to get up and find it. I might make it a game to see who can get to the bathroom first, him or me. I might be the voice of his Raggedy Ann doll talking to him to coax him out of bed. I've had to think creatively so I don't become frustrated! Do I *like* hiding Belle and the Beast? Do I *like* making a funny voice for Ann? Well, not usually, but it beats the alternative which is Joey's not so subtle obstinate behavior or anger.

When caring for adult parents or other adults whose mental age is more in line with their chronological age, this kind of humor would be inappropriate; but because Joey is very young mentally, we can do this and he responds to it. But let me give you an example of something I did for my father when he was home under the care of my mom and his three daughters.

One Thursday when I arrived at 9:00 in the morning to care for Dad so Mom could get out for the day, he was facing the window looking out at the pond. When I said, "Good morning, Dad, how are you today?" he said, "Oh, Cindi, I had such a nice day. I took the boat out on the pond today, played a round of golf, and went skeet shooting. It was such a nice day." I looked at Mom for some clue as to a conversation they might have just had and wondered if any of the scenarios could possibly be true! Mom shrugged her shoulders as if to say, "He hasn't left this room or his wheelchair." As I went to give Dad a kiss, I said, "I am so glad you had such a nice day. I'm here now, so I'm glad you had fun before I came, because I'm not sure the haircut I'm going to give you will be that much fun!" I didn't say what my first thoughts were, "Oh, Dad, come on! It's 9:00 in the morning! How could you have done all that, and for heaven's sake, you can't get out of your wheelchair to do that stuff!" Instead, I enjoyed the spirit of adventure with him, happy he had a nice morning in his mind.

I tried very hard to make the most of those pleasant thoughts because at times his mind played disagreeable tricks on him. When "people" in the other room planned to harm him, I'd go there, talk to the invisible people, and come back with a reassuring word that they were leaving. When Dad saw worms on the floor (clearly the swirling design of the carpet), and also saw them going up the wall, I got a cloth and pretended to clean them up. Somehow, as silly as I felt, it calmed my dad, and I didn't have to engage in the battle of who was seeing things in the right way. Of course, I was waiting for my dad to laugh and say, "Gotcha! And you thought I was losing *my* mind!" He never did.

Sometimes the spirit of adventure takes the form of humility and the willingness to give people with special needs their dignity. Sometimes it's difficult to make an adventure of or find humor in putting clothes on inside out and backwards, putting shoes on the wrong feet, repeating the same thing for the fiftieth time that day (not an exaggeration), performing the same medical procedure, cleaning soiled clothes, etc. No matter their age or condition, as we work toward giving them dignity, we must be willing to humble ourselves to do what is needed to make people with special needs feel valued. It's not easy, but it's worth it!

Some of those challenging and funny times can be endearing when we look back at them. Just as we kept a journal for each of our children, we kept a log of humorous moments we experienced with our parents. We knew that if we didn't write them down, we'd forget them. Thus, we were able to share with family and friends some of the sweet remembrances. We'll never forget the really hard times, but we were able to soften the harsh memories of the gradual loss of a loved one and dealing with tough challenges day after day by recording fun, pleasant, and funny things to hold on to in our memories.

Scripture always provides answers and reasons that we should act certain ways and do certain things. When we purpose to have a joyful heart, it will show on our face and we will have a good disposition. What's more, people will want to be around us and spend time with us. Proverbs 15:13, "A joyful heart makes a cheerful face, but when the heart is sad, the spirit is broken." Who wants to spend time with a sour, dried up, crabapple?

Trust God to show you a creative way. Ask Him to show you what not to miss in your usual day. Embrace special moments. Trust Him to make each day count! We've heard it said, "He who laughs, lasts."

Helping Others "Figure It Out"

Because we are "in it" all the time, we become immune to our own life! Others may be startled to see what has become normal to us. We have become so accustomed to life as it is that we are startled that others seem startled! How funny!

One time our whole family was riding an elevator when a boy entered. He was obviously mentally retarded, probably with some degree of cerebral palsy and very low verbal skills, acting just like our Joey but perhaps five years older. We said hello to him, and after he left the elevator, we all just looked at each other as if to say, "Oh my! Is *that* what others see in our family? How we have come to see it as absolutely normal!"

Figuring out what's "wrong"

Because we're in this for the long haul, we want to help others, especially little children, understand so they don't have to go away wondering. They tend to stare and ask questions in a most sincere and precious way! Adults, on the other hand, tend to stare with facial expressions that show attitudes that sometimes hurt our feelings. Thankfully, Joey doesn't comprehend such responses, but others who are handicapped physically but fine mentally may feel hurt. The bottom line is that both children and adults want the answer to the same question: "What's wrong with that person?" Some adults wish their children wouldn't be so inquisitive, but we're glad they are. They ask because they are inquisitive. The comfort level kids feel with computers and other technical devices that frighten us is the same comfort level they feel with those who have special needs. They are not at all intimidated!

So when someone (young or old) questions or is sincerely curious, we love the chance to introduce Joey to him or her and explain a little bit about Joey. We usually then ask them if they like sports. If they do, we tell them how much Joey loves sports, and if they ask the right question, they'll push the "I won't stop talking" button on Joey! It's then fun to watch them proceed slowly. Joey's enthusiasm about his sports teams is contagious and soon, they are engaged in conversation.

During Kristina's fifth-grade year she read *Welcome Home, Jelly Bean* by Marlene Fanta Shyer, the story of a little girl with mental retardation. She was sent to a training school before eventually coming home. From the younger brother's perspective, the author shares the family struggles, lack of sleep resulting from the little girl's banging her head on the wall during the night, sitting on top of the piano, and other very typical annoyances faced by a family caring for a child with special needs. Eventually the father leaves because the situation becomes too much for him. The reading culminated in Kristina's inviting Joey to visit the classroom and writing her own story that found its way to the pages of *Exceptional Parent* magazine.

Kristina's classmates, teacher, and principal welcomed Joey; and his visit opened the door to questions about him (answered by Cindi in a visit that preceded Joey's). The students were pleased to show Joey things they could do, and he in turn showed them what he could do. The visit provided a rewarding learning experience for all.

Figuring out how to have conversation

At a graduation party, Joey was standing by himself, and a dear man approached him and pursued conversation. He pushed all the right buttons for conversation, and Joey became a talking machine. Because his verbal skills are limited and he is not always easily understood, this man could not figure out everything Joey was saying. We were both engaged in another conversation and didn't want to be rude and walk away to help Joey. By the time our conversation had ended, the man had completed his time with Joey and was talking to someone else. We had fun watching that little episode! We later had the chance to thank him and let him know how very special that scenario was to watch! He was most gracious toward Joey, but we really appreciated that he asked us questions about Joey and seemed sincerely interested in learning about him. Situations like this make us wonder whether he had perhaps had a special person in his life at one time or presently, whether he had compassion toward individuals with special needs, or whether he simply pursued information with a genuine and sincere heart without reservation. Sometimes we ask, other times we don't, but no matter the reason, we were blessed! Talking to this man gave us the opportunity to make him feel more comfortable about people like Joey, and come to think of it, he made us feel pretty comfortable, too!

Figuring out the ten-second rule

Having difficulties in speech, hearing, or comprehending information conveyed verbally, a special needs person might have a delay in response. For some the delay can be uncomfortably silent. We sometimes advise people asking Joey a question to wait ten seconds before repeating or rephrasing the question or comment. We watch for the same delay when his Cleveland Browns' make a great tackle, score a touchdown or kick a field goal. One, two, three . . . ten. "WOW! Yipppeeee! Look, they did it! Ahhhhhhhh! Ohhh!!" The silent processing can take longer than the final reaction.

Figuring out typical responses

When someone asks how Joey generally acts or responds, we just giggle. We aren't making fun of the questions; we just haven't quite figured out the answers yet ourselves! When we think Joey will behave in a particular way, almost without fail, he will make us liars every time! How does Joey respond when a dog comes into the room? We'd predict he'd be frightened and come near to us. Of course, that's the time he says, "Oh, little doggie" and waves at it or surprises the whole family and pets it! How will Joey respond to riding an escalator? Some days he holds our shoulder, steps on the escalator and says, "That was easy! No problem!" Other times, he's swinging at us, telling us there is no way he's getting on! We'll grab his hand, put it on our shoulder, make him keep moving onto the escalator, and ten seconds later he'll proudly say, "I did it!"

Figuring out how to deal with repetitive words and phrases

We have grown accustomed to a routine of Joey's that can irritate others: Every morning, he states the day, what the next day will be, and then the next until he goes through the week. It doesn't stop there. One day I counted that he did that over 50 times—during two car rides. Other times he'll repeat his displeasure over a situation or thought. Example: If Dad didn't win at some video game they play or isn't going to be home to play, Joey may express his disappointment via anger. It sounds something like this, "Dad is not playing games. Dad will go to jail. Dad will not have it. I will win. I will play." OK, that can actually be funny the first time, but when the conversation groove doesn't change for the 30-minute drive home from work, it isn't funny anymore. Yes, it's worse than someone telling the same jokes and stories—all the time. The only way we have dealt with this one is to ignore him when he gets stuck in this groove. We initially address it, and then have to pretend that we aren't hearing the repeated comments. It's tough if we're actually trying to hear something on TV or the radio, and without fail the repetition comes with increased volume at the point we really needed to hear what was being said. It's not so different from caring for people with Alzheimer's because they don't realize they are repeating themselves. It can wear on caregivers, and they must be willing to relinquish their perceived rights to quiet them or to yell at them unless they want to enter into another issue—a battle!

Figuring out what makes people with special needs tick and what ticks them off

On more that one occasion, people who know Joey loves sports have said things about his particular team losing. Those are fightin' words! In Joey's case, it's best to lead the conversation to concentrating on the next game rather than focusing on the loss. When we're with others with special needs, we follow the leader (their parent or caregiver) to see how they handle different situations. If the caregiver seems to be steering the conversation in a different direction, we go with it. Example: If you tell Joey, "Man, what about those OSU Buckeyes! I can't believe they lost!" We can be sure (we can never be sure—whom are we kidding?) he'll say, "They won. Not lost!" We'll probably steer the conversation to discuss the next game or how the Browns are doing or some other topic. If you decide you want to pursue the conversation you just started, you're on your own. Good luck!

Figuring out the track the person with special needs is on

Sometimes we have no idea what causes Joey to start conversing about a subject that seems totally unrelated to the one under discussion, but we're getting better at it. We call this phenomenon "Joey's rabbit trails." One thing for sure, the listener must get on the right track—the Joey track. Here's an example: We can be talking about the Prince of Wales in the news. Joey will gasp with excitement and say, "The Prince!" That leaves it wide open for us to guess what he's thinking. Although we sometimes dismiss his comment, we don't want to treat him rudely; but we know from past experience we can be stuck here for quite a while. So we start guessing—Prince Caspian? Jesus, Prince of Peace? The Princess and the Pea? It can be exhausting. Occasionally, we will know of something he just read, looked at, or saw in a movie, and can only hope we guess correctly on the first or second try. This "track" or trail that Joey is on is important for others to grasp, lest they be stuck on the Prince of Wales for a long time in a conversation that does not end happily ever after!

For those involved with people who have problems in thought processing, stuttering, or ability to express their thoughts, here's a list of some things that might help (and have with Joey):

✓ Ask them if they want help in what they are trying to communicate.

✓ Speak slowly and clearly to them so they can process what you have said.

✓ Use simple words and sentences.

✓ Ask them if they can spell a word you have trouble understanding.

✓ Ask them to speak slowly and let them know you didn't understand. (Generally they will repeat things patiently, more times than you'd imagine in order to get their one point or word across to you! Our usual with Joey is about ten times.)

✓ Ask them if you can ask their parent, caregiver, or someone else to help.

✓ Always be kind and courteous, so that you don't embarrass them. If you don't know or can't figure something it out, say so, politely. Don't talk down to them.

✓ Maintain good eye contact, even if they struggle to have it with you.

- ✓ Pointing, smiling, hugging, and other nonverbal communication is good if they are willing to accept it.
- ✓ If they become argumentative, don't enter into a verbal war of words. You will seldom, if ever, win.
- ✓ Ask questions with clear choices, not open-ended questions. Example: "Do you want to watch TV or listen to music?" not "What do you want to do?" The latter is often too hard to process.
- ✓ When all else fails, avoid conflict and redirect them to something else, saying you'll talk about this another time. Excuse yourself politely. Perhaps in time you'll be able to put the pieces of your conversation together, and complete it on another occasion.

Yes, dealing with a person with special needs can be like putting a puzzle together with ten missing pieces! But when and if you "get it," you have such a great feeling of accomplishment!

And if you figure out some things we've yet to learn, do let us know! We are teachable, trainable, and appreciative! We know we're in it for the long haul, and we welcome anything that helps us to get along better in this life!

Figuring out what is allowed and what isn't

Those outside the family of a person with special needs must be sensitive to what family members can do that outsiders cannot. Some words, some actions are appropriate for family only. Let what appears to be a joke among family members be just that. It's unwise to engage in jokes even if the family does. If we do or say things to copy Joey, we know the difference between making fun and having fun. What might be funny to us within our family circle just might be completely inappropriate for someone else to do the same thing. If an outsider is unsure, she or he should avoid humor at the expense of hurting someone's feelings.

Learn to Say No

Although we tend to say yes as often as possible, we've had to learn to say no sometimes. It's not that we want to, but we have to. Some things are impossible for us to do with Joey. We can't do some things as a couple unless we have someone to care for him. Sometimes we'd like to participate as a couple and really don't want Joey with us. A date plus Joey isn't a date. One of us always has to cover for the other. If we have the opportunity to attend an event, we often have to choose who will go and who will stay home. Thankfully, we work well as a couple and are able to do and accomplish many different things but not always together.

The Practical Side of Life—There Is So Much More

We have so much more to say about the long haul. Because we'll cover additional situations in other chapters, we'll briefly list other issues that take place daily to carry you over. Just remember that the long haul differs for each person and is unique to each person and situation. Your list might be much longer than what we have listed here.

♦ **Life:** The initial change is a shock, and then the reality sets in that life has changed forever. The shock may linger in troubling and challenging places for varied lengths of time before a new normal settles. We ebb and flow in the sea of the daily grind. We learn the dance, but new steps are required from time to time!

♦ **Grief:** Because we handle things differently, we have grieved losses in different ways. Thankfully, when one has been weak, the other has been strong. We've learned to be sensitive to each other, to talk through the grief together, to talk about decisions and challenges until we reach a common goal. The most difficult part of this occurs when we're at different stages of grieving and we see things differently. Listening carefully and thoroughly to each other is very important.

♦ **Marriage:** The union can be severely challenged. Time is often taken from each other and given to the person needing care. With high divorce rates among caregivers, the need to keep the marriage strong and healthy is of utmost importance. As a couple spends time in God's word, growing individually as Christians, the more likely they are to grow together as a couple and the marriage will more likely be strong.

♦ **Family:** We call it family dynamics. The number of people in the family, their ages, and their personalities will determine the complexion of that family unit. We have noticed that when one person is missing, all the dynamics change.

♦ **School and Work:** Whatever happens at home affects school and work. And often, what happens outside the home is brought home! It's difficult to separate the two, especially in times when the loved one who needs care is in a critical state. We feel it's important to be open with educators and employers but to be careful not to overwhelm others with details if they cannot comprehend or empathize.

♦ **Relationships:** Friends and family, other caregivers, doctors, nurses, aides, therapists—many in our circle have become our friends. Those who go through this long haul together really understand the struggles and victories and often develop strong bonds that can last a lifetime.

♦ **Free Time:** Sometimes we have none. Depending on the role a person has in caring for a special needs person as well as the severity of the disability, free time can range from "some to none." We'll cover this in Chapter 11, but we've learned the hard way the importance of time for ourselves. Free time ranges from something as simple as time to read a chapter in a book to getting away for a week to recharge! Another issue with free time involves creativity in finding it!

♦ **Vacations:** Vacations are not always vacations when we take someone who needs help with everything. But then again, we might not get a vacation unless the steps are taken and plans made to include that person, the supplies, the helpers, and whatever else is needed to be able to see a new place.

♦ **Sleep or Lack Thereof:** This goes hand in hand with free time. Sometimes we shave time from one end of the day or the other to find that we are neglecting our own sleep. We have learned that sleep as well as rest and relaxation are critical for the caregiver. We can't think clearly, might not respond properly, and can't stay healthy ourselves if we don't get proper rest. In addition, if our health is compromised, the only way to heal fully is to get needed rest.

♦ **Daily Coping Skills:** Sometimes we have them, and sometimes we don't. For us, we know that sleep, Bible reading, and knowing when to ask for help are all *parts* of what is needed to be able to cope well in a stressful situation. Learning good coping skills will prevent burnout. The hard part is doing what we know will help—humbling ourselves to ask others when we know we are losing it and giving up our pride in thinking we can do it all alone!

♦ **Emotions:** We could be "all over the board" on this one! What emotions don't we experience when life throws us a curve ball and we realize our life will never be the same? We must strive eventually to get to the point where we are able to express ourselves well. Tears, anger, grief, loss of control of whatever emotion we're feeling at any given moment—these accompany the reality as it settles in, and it almost always does at some point. We also have to "get a grip." We've talked about the need to rely upon God and His word, and we'll talk about the importance of solid, healthy human relationships shortly. We need God and we need each other.

♦ **Social Life and Loneliness:** We've had to make many adjustments in this area. So often we wish we could just pick up and go for a ride in the car, a walk in the park, or on a vacation—alone. Arranging for activities like these takes so much effort that sometimes we forfeit the social aspects of life and stay home. We have often had to be the ones to invite people to our home in order to enjoy the fellowship of others. Sometimes we long to be asked out where we don't have to do all the work and planning. Again, we are still learning the steps to this dance!

♦ **Finances:** Some disabilities, illnesses, and diseases can be very costly. Joey's early years were financially burdensome to our family. This burden can spill over and affect emotions, causing members of the household to work a second job or affect social and other areas of life. We'll discuss some options and solutions in Chapter 8.

♦ **Safety:** We need to live as if we have a toddler. Sharp objects are put away where only we know where to find them. We post notes on our front door alerting guests whether or not we can have callers. Objects left on the floor might cause a problem if we need to move quickly out the door or if emergency personnel need to get in, so keeping order is always a necessity. Peanut butter is located where only those of us who can eat it know where it is and can enjoy it when Joey is in bed! Each caretaker will have different safety issues to accomplish.

♦ Add your own issues to the "long haul" list.

_____

_____

_____

_____

_____

It's a Commitment

The long haul is a commitment to the responsibility of caring for another for whatever reason and duration. Even if the long haul lasts five months, it's a long haul for that time period. When the road takes many twists and turns with no end in sight, unconditional love and commitment will take the caregiver from one point to the next. The journey, not the destination, is paramount. Most of us will not wake up tomorrow to a miracle that has changed life back to what it was. Even the person who has extended family to help on occasion or government assistance for respite care realizes that when these helpers go home, the challenges remain unchanged. Helpers have their own challenges in life, but probably not this one. We must deal with happiness, contentment, sadness, and challenges on a daily basis one step at a time: Each emotion is but one leg of the

> *The long haul is a commitment to the responsibility of caring for another for whatever reason and duration.*

whole journey. We can be thankful for those who help, but we always have the responsibility on our mind and in our heart.

We have also had to face facts: This *is* our life. The sooner we surrender to what God has in store for us, the sooner He can work in and through us; and the sooner we can help others when they struggle. If we are open, we can grow in the process.

It's OK to Be Human

Sometimes we have difficulty admitting how tough life can be at any given time. If we can set our pride aside and let others know when we are overwhelmed, exhausted, frustrated, frightened, or off the charts with excitement, we believe we will have a greater impact on our family and friends. We learn quickly who wants to hear about our frailties, frustrations, fears, and joys and who doesn't. The circle of helpful and committed family and friends might become very small, but when we find that circle, we'll find the greatest blessings!

In addition, because we are human, sometimes we need more help than our family or close friends can offer. Seeking professional help might be a necessary option. When we face complex issues, we might need an outsider's perspective, permission, or authority to act when we are at the end of our rope. We might need a change in medication for the person with special needs or an opinion or a way to turn in a different direction that a professional will help us clarify. Deep disappointment for some may lead to depression. As a result, we might feel as if we lack the faith to follow this path to the end, or we might even question or be angry with God. When we are in the midst of challenge every day with little respite, those doubts and fears will surface. We're not doing a job we were trained to do, and for many of us, it wasn't a job we wanted in the first place! We are doing a job that requires much responsibility for which no foreseeable break may come. What differs for us as Christians is that we have a choice. We have God, who hears us in prayer and will help us through. We may choose to go with our feelings or with what God wills for our life. It's a choice we make over and over in our Christian walk. Daily we yield and surrender to His will, and we need to take care of ourselves so we can help care for others.

The Future

How can any of us know what the future holds? How long will the illness, disability, or disease last? How long will the person for whom we are caring live? Is there a life expectancy for them, or are we in it for the long haul—however long that may be? How can we deal with the long haul for the next 20 to 50 years when we're at the starting point of the journey?

Can we plan for our future and theirs? Do we have to take guardianship or assume power of attorney to care for their affairs? What happens if our own health is compromised at some point? In the face of many other questions, the bottom line is always "What will happen when I/we die?"

The future is never definite, but we can make plans and seek help to feel as secure as possible in the situation in which we find ourselves. Every day needs to be taken one step at a time. Finding a mentor/helper earlier in a life-changing crisis can be of great value. Although we missed out on having someone in our life that could get us from one steppingstone to another, we always found the answers to our questions. Today, we cherish mentoring younger couples in our area who have questions and concerns about their challenges. As we meet, we want to impart what we've learned along the way that might help them in their unexpected journey.

The Long Haul Summarized

Clearly, we all have our own story. For each of us, a day is made up of 24 hours, but for the caregiver the list of daily challenges is never-ending: frustrations, medications, housing issues, family issues. We individually aim for the various goals we had for the day, and yet we all likely want the same final result. May our end result always be "And whatever you do in word or deed, do all in the name of the Lord Jesus, giving thanks through Him to God the Father" (Colossians 3:17). May we wake to a new day filled with hope to make it through with thanksgiving!

As His children we have the privilege to claim His promises from His Word (the Bible). Read and study it to make it through the struggles, gaining endurance and making it for the long haul.

OTHERS' STORIES

- As I struggle with my dad in a nursing home (Alzheimer's), I'm reminded often *my* plans have to change. I finally had a chance to go to a very nice hotel overnight with my husband. We hadn't been away together for a very long time. At some wee hour of the morning, we got a call that my dad was rushed from the nursing home to the hospital after a fall. He wasn't conscious, so we all agreed to meet at the hospital immediately. I had to pick up the kids from the person watching them and spend hours at the hospital, only to find out that he wasn't dying but had some kind of infection that hit him hard. We got to go back to the hotel, but the mood was definitely changed. It would even be okay if this was the first time, but it happens more often than others would want to hear about.

- Our special needs child gives us most of our "illustrations" in life!

- Because some issues aren't physical handicaps (ADD, ADHD specifically), we have some unique challenges. These "invisible issues" challenge relationships and communication.

- It's tough to think my child will never drive, go to college, or marry, but she talks about those things all the time. We just take the "we'll see" approach.

- When dealing with medical treatment and behavior issues, I want to tell my daughter that everything will turn out all right with her child with special needs. The reality is not giving the pat answer that flippantly says "all will be fine" but instructing her that what God has it all under control and *that* is all right.

- The sheer administrative work I must do (doctors' appointments, therapists, providers, insurance, state programs) is overwhelming.

- Doing this alone as a single mom is very difficult. I know it's hard to be patient when I feel such pressure, but I have to shoulder it alone.

- As an observer, I wonder what I can do for people with special needs—to lighten their load on this long journey. (Keep reading!)

- As an occupational therapist I think parents of children with special needs should present "just right" challenges (that we can help establish) to go to the next level or step towards independence. The long haul can be made a bit easier by presenting the right challenges that allow children to succeed. (The same goes for adults who find they require OT.) Don't enable dependence by unpacking the book bag, opening the car door, putting on their coat, picking out clothes when or if they are capable of doing those things.

- I never thought about asking others if I could help, but I interact easily with those who have special needs.

- I cannot always do what others do, for example, going to weddings and funerals or the beach or to church on Wednesdays after four therapies, and wish people would not be offended when I have to say no. I need to do what is best for my child and our family.

- A therapist we go to once said that she thinks people don't want to get too close to kids with special needs because they think the disability will somehow rub off on them or that being your friend will be too emotionally draining.

- My child's loud noises, constant crying, and outbursts make me want to put my hand over his mouth to quiet him. Sometimes I've done it out of anger and too roughly, but because I know the Lord, I ask Him for the strength I need to be gentle. I have hope. And that hope is in Him. People who feel they might take their anger too far should find someone to express their emotions to and people who can give them time off from the constant pressures.

- I know what it takes for our friends to take care of their son, and I appreciate that they continue to make sure he is clean, shaven, has up-to-date clothes to wear, and nice teeth. I believe it makes it more pleasant for others to approach him.

- I literally have not been able to finish a TV program without some type of interruption from my loved one with special needs over the last thirty years.

- I need to tube feed our child, so I continue to wake up at least twice a night to feed him and more if he has seizures or other health-related problems.

- I have learned how to fight for my child, and I will not stop fighting until all options have been exhausted.

YOUR STORY

What bumps in the road (past or present) have you or someone close to you experienced in caring for someone who can't care for himself or herself?

_____

_____

_____

What bumps do you anticipate in the future if you're riding the smooth road right now?

_____

_____

_____

How would you picture your life changing if you had to care for someone 24/7? If you are caring for someone, what is most challenging to you?

_____

_____

As you care for another, do you feel as if your day or life is constantly changing? If it's presently stabilized, explain how that came about.

As a matter of perspective, can you find others who are more or less deeply challenged than you are? Share an example:

What behaviors in those with special needs make you uncomfortable? Can you think of a way to overcome it? If you care for some one with behavioral issues, how can you help others become comfortable with that person?

What might you help others "figure out" about the person you care for?

How can you look at one of your challenges with a spirit of adventure?

The long haul—how are you doing in the midst of it (emotionally, coping, relationships)?

Have you ever sought professional help for yourself or the one you care for? Would you be willing, if needed?

_____

_____

Formulate a thought and then write a statement that will help you determine what you need to do today to "end well" down the road:

_____

_____

_____

_____

Write a mission statement if that will help you keep on track for the long haul:

_____

_____

_____

_____

CHAPTER SEVEN

Road Work Ahead:
We Are Family

Darlene's brother Pete, who has Down syndrome, could be a real challenge. When they were kids, he treated her badly, both verbally and physically. She loved to see her parents at all her high school track meets, but she was embarrassed that they had to bring "him"! Now that they are adults and she has children of her own, she has come to realize that his special needs are what have made him dear to her heart.

....

Melanie cared for both of her parents in their declining years. Because they didn't want to leave their home, she did her best for several years to manage the house, their health care, and her sanity. She did very well but was always exhausted. Although she had siblings, the most helpful one lived out of town; another was in town but made it clear that caregiving was "not her thing," and the other was nasty and criticized her decisions. Melanie's ability to accomplish all she did with limited help was amazing.

....

Peggy had numerous health issues, her mental stability the most difficult to manage. She was thankful for family support, but when she chose not to take her medications, her personality was very abrasive. She pushed nearly everyone, including her husband, away from her and wondered why others didn't want to spend time with her. Their divorce was soon added to her list of challenges.

....

OUR STORY

Many of us have awakened surprised to find that we are no longer sleeping next to the person we married! Somehow over the years, we've both changed to the point that we're unrecognizable to each other, no longer the way we were so many years ago! Our journey has taken us to places where we have become new and different from the people we were in those early days. In some ways we've become softer; in others we've had to get tougher. On one hand our family has benefited from the detours on our journey; on the other hand, we feel we've missed out on some "attractions" along the way. God knows the plans He has for us, and that's why we're who and where we are, two people learning to trust Him with every detail of our lives and helping our children to do the same!

A Strong Marriage

The challenges of everyday living, not to mention the daily, never-ending, and all-consuming responsibility of attending to another person's needs, might have led us to throw up our hands and shout, "I want out. Let's divorce"; but we vowed never to speak those words in our family. Imagining the difficulty of being the one left alone with such a serious responsibility may have kept our marriage from becoming a statistic! Don't think of us as completely noble here: We were probably selfish in thinking, "I don't want to be the one stuck with all the work while my spouse moves on in life!"

We knew the hard work, the long nights, and full days, so we simply made a vow to do everything together, no matter how difficult life might get!

> *We knew the hard work, the long nights, and full days, so we simply made a vow to do everything together, no matter how difficult life might get!*

With such a high divorce rate among couples caring for someone with a disability, we are thankful that we have weathered the storms of life together and have been there to support and encourage each other. Life in our house may look different from yours, but we've had to make it "work" for us. What has helped immensely is the three-cord strand mentioned in Ecclesiastes 4:9-12: "Two are better than one because they have a good return for their labor. For if either of them falls, the one will lift up his companion. But woe to the one who falls when there is not another to lift him up. Furthermore, if two lie down together they keep warm, but how can one be warm alone? And if one can overpower him who is alone, two can resist him. A cord of three strands is not quickly torn apart." For us, that three-cord strand is the Lord and the two of us.

If any one area particularly needs tuning up, special care, and pampering, it's marriage. A marriage conference like FamilyLife Weekend to Remember (see www.FamilyLife.com) teaches couples what tears a marriage apart and how to build theirs up. Couples concentrate on making marriage work through the tough times that all experience. Without a strong marriage, caring for someone with special needs is much more difficult and challenging.

We have known many couples to divorce because the frustrations are so high in a marriage when another person's special needs require so much day-to-day, moment-to-moment attention. Some can't handle the guilt (perceived or real); some can't handle the strain, and because of it they simply quit. We're not here to judge those who quit because we can assure you we've had thoughts of it, too. Some have told us that we "make it look easy." Trust us, it isn't! We've simply kept renewing our decision to "go the distance." The pressure that this kind of lifestyle puts on the marriage is intense! Often this pressure causes the spouses to withdraw instead of unite, and the walls of isolation rise to the point that divorce seems the only option. What some people don't think about long enough is that right around the corner from divorce are financial hardships, making other matters harder to deal with as well. We'll address single parenting shortly.

One prenuptial agreement we recommend is this: "We will never discuss divorcing, no matter how tough life becomes." We think this is covered in the "for better or worse" clause of most ceremonies, but many couples think only the richer, the better, and the health will happen in their marriage. We've had the privilege of taking part in and witnessing couples renewing vows after fifteen, thirty, or fifty years of marriage. When these vows are exchanged before a congregation in a church ceremony, you won't find a dry eye in the sanctuary. Why? Because the couple has experienced the poorer, the worse, and the sickness, knows the real pain of life, and has a realistic perspective after going through life's rough spots. They shed tears of the sadness for the sorrow they have shared and tears of happiness for having persevered and remained together!

To keep a marriage working well, we advise that decisions not be made until both husband and wife agree. Should a decision need to be made quickly, when time is too short for lengthy discussion, and when one spouse is unwilling to compromise in the interest of time, then the husband should decide and the wife should support his decision. We seldom disagree on major issues, but often need to discuss the little ones. We have come to know each other's strengths and weaknesses and rely on those to help us make choices.

Making Marriage Work: Divide and Conquer!

Making our marriage work has taken time, sacrifice, and creativity. Both of us must work together to find a ways to do things we have on our individual agendas and schedules. Having Joe attend a meeting while Cindi stays home or Cindi taking a class while Joe stays home has worked for us. You get the picture. "Divide and conquer" is our motto! We'd "divide and conquer" for meetings, classes, activities with other kids, church, chaperoning school events, and driving places if Joey couldn't come with us.

Cindi:

For *years* we had to attend Sunday services separately because the nursery was too noisy for Joey's ability to adjust to the overwhelming stimulus, and he was too noisy for the sanctuary. So we worked out a routine: Joe drove to church in his car and participated in the early service while I stayed home with Joey. I'd pack Joey up and drive to the front of the church just before the late service was to begin. Joe would exit the church, get in the driver's seat, and go home with Joey. I would then attend the service and drive home in Joe's car. That worked for a good many years, until Joe's dad volunteered to stay at home with Joey occasionally so we could attend together. That worked well, until Joey was mature enough to sit still during a church service, somewhere in his teen years.

Marriage—Pamper It!

Everyone has different options and choices. We were blessed in the early years with time away to be alone. The grandparents were willing and able to care for Joey, so we tried to use that time for "us." Not all couples will have this particular option, so before you close the book and say, "This doesn't work for us," realize that some of us might need to be more creative than others in getting what we need. If we don't try to figure out ways to make things work for us, it is doubtful that some stranger will approach us and say, "Perhaps I can help." Creativity and flexibility must stay high on our list as we work through taking care of our marriage, and all of life.

We might want a week away but need to settle for three hours. We might want a trip to Europe but need to be content with an overnight stay in an adjacent city. We need to find ways that will work practically and financially.

For us, pampering our marriage ranged from staying home and going to bed together early when the grandparents took the children overnight, to a weekend away forty-five minutes from home, to a nice twelve-day vacation out of the country. We liked the out-of-the-country pampering the best because short of an emergency, no one would call us. Selfish? Perhaps for some, but for others it's self-preservation. When a caregiver is on call 24/7 every day, getting away without interruption seldom occurs, so when an opportunity arises, take it! *Every* married couple needs time alone, time to focus on each other, time to rejuvenate. When a person with special needs is involved, that opportunity is harder to find. You can't just pick up and take off—ever, without involving and including others to help make it happen.

When we had just the two children, we had a chance to take a cruise, not even a business or ministry related trip, just pure fun! If memory serves us correctly, it was the first or maybe second trip we'd taken alone since having children. Someone had said to us, "*That* must be nice. I wish we could do that." Perhaps our response should have been "Oh, thank you so much for sharing in our joy" and might have been, had the comment not been made in a condescending tone that we heard as "It must be nice to leave your kids and go off on a trip alone.

I'm envious." Our response instead, was "Well, we are very much looking forward to it. Since we have parents who have offered to watch the kids while we're away, we need to take the opportunity. Someday when all of our kids are grown and gone and we're retired, you'll be able to travel; but we'll still need a babysitter for Joey and won't have grandparents to help as they do now. We need to seize the moments now."

If enjoyment comes from playing golf, diligently search for someone who can handle the responsibilities of special needs long enough to get to the golf course to play nine holes! (Be happy with nine even though eighteen sounds better!) Of course, some of us then need to learn how to relax once we're on the course! If not golf, then perhaps running, swimming, or taking a dance or foreign language class will give a couple the sense of enjoyment and rejuvenation that will allow the pair to go back home to life as usual. We can't do life as usual for very long without some kind of relief from the pressures of caring for another's full-time needs.

> *We can't do life as usual for very long without some kind of relief from the pressures of caring for another's full-time needs.*

Marriage: Good Physical, Emotional, and Spiritual Health

Because good health is most important to each spouse as well as to the couple, stress reduction, proper diet, exercise, enough sleep, time away, intimacy, laughter—all these promote good physical and emotional health. But we also need to continue engaging in activities that will establish good spiritual health like prayer, reading God's word, and fellowshipping with other believers. Church is one of the best places for these along with Bible studies and small groups where people share life with one another. The healthier we are, the better we can care for others and the better attitude and outlook we will maintain.

Make no mistake: The care of folks with special needs requires teamwork through much pressure and challenge, yet due to the tragic divorce rate, the results are often many single parents. Over the years, we have seen firsthand the divorce or separation of the parents of several of Joey's former classmates. Taking care of the marital relationship is essential in preparing the couple to go the distance together. Going it alone is an added pressure physically, emotionally and spiritually.

Marriage: Talk It Out

Sometimes the grief and frustration of the challenges make us reluctant to talk—to anyone—but getting the feelings, frustrations, grief, victories, and joyful moments out on the table for discussion is very important. If you wait to talk only when a crisis erupts, you will experience the highs and low but nothing in between. We need all the "in between" normal conversation to maintain a healthy marriage! We need conversation about work, other children, ministry, friends—everyday topics.

Sometimes we sit outside on our deck or on the couch with a cup of coffee and catch up on our day. Joey is in the next room playing a game or watching television. He can see us, but we are alone. We can talk, laugh and discuss issues that need resolution and catch up on conversations we've neglected. Making the time to talk is not always easy and takes planning, but it's worthwhile for our relationship!

Marriage: Help Each Other

This is not the same as "divide and conquer." Helping each other involves the willingness to sacrifice time each day to assist with routine responsibilities so neither partner burns out. Part of our learning to divide and conquer came from hearts willing to assist and serve each other even at times when we felt as if we had been doing that more than we wished we'd have to!

Each of us has certain chores and jobs that are mostly ours, but neither of us is "above" doing the other's chore. Sometimes we are pleasantly surprised when we realize we don't have to do one of our regular chores. For instance, right now, Joe is emptying the dishwasher at 10:45 at night so Cindi can write. Cindi is thrilled she won't wake up to a full dishwasher in addition to getting Joey ready for work, making breakfast, and packing a lunch. Cindi took out the garbage tonight, so Joe wouldn't have to do it when he came home after a twelve-hour workday! We helped each other, and we both appreciated it! We still did chores, but not the ones we typically do; so we felt we had a break from our own chores, and we knew we were helping each other! Think: Be considerate.

When spouses withhold from each other, thinking or saying, for example, "You never help me with the dishes, so why should I help you with the garbage?" they fall into a trap that moves them farther from the person who should be a helper and an asset. Why would we do something that would make things worse for us? Pride and anger are two starters, and they both constitute sin. Ask for forgiveness, turn away from that sin, and move on together. Work as a TEAM (Together Each Accomplishes More)! Philippians 2:3,4 says, "Do nothing from selfishness or empty conceit, but with humility of mind let each of you regard one another as more important than himself; do not merely look out for your own personal interests, but also for the interests of others." When we work like that, we can't go wrong!

Marriage: Make It Your Ministry

When we speak about marriage through the ministry of FamilyLife or in other venues, we offer hours and hours of excellent information that can help married couples "make it," but the bottom line is this: If you make marriage your ministry, the chances that you will make it for the long haul are very good. When we make marriage our ministry, we desire to serve our spouse as Jesus served others. No matter what we say or do during our day, if we (both the husband and the wife) make every effort to be like Jesus, we will continue to fall in love with each other every day, serve each other, communicate in healthy ways, and grow together. If just one person is making the effort, the marriage may be pleasant and even decent, but it won't be vibrant and thriving. We each must choose to make the effort.

Extended Family

We have been so wonderfully blessed to have a supportive extended family. When the children were little, the grandparents loved spending time with them, giving us needed breaks. With all four grandparents now deceased, we see that the Lord has continued to provide help: Cindi's two sisters help out on occasion with Joey. Even our two daughters help in ways we would never have imagined.

We realize that not all extended family members will share the same interest in helping, and we have never wanted to "dump" any of our kids on anyone; however, when others offered or we had a need, we appreciated their willingness to help. Our motto has been "Accept help, but don't take advantage of it."

If extended family members are willing to help, and you know the person with special needs will be safe, and their health and well being not compromised in any way, we urge you to accept help! Those offering to help will gain a new appreciation for what you go through every day.

Extended Family: Grandparents

All the grandparents were great with the kids. We attribute Joey's fourth-grade reading ability to the tender loving care and hours of reading they all did with him as well as the girls. We'd start dozing two pages into a simple reader, but they could read for hours! And the kids would sit! They invested their time and energy in our children, and we benefited knowing they were making precious memories with them and giving us time to nourish our relationship or catch up on things around the house.

We remember times when Dad and Mom Ferrini would call on a Friday morning and ask whether they could take Joey for the weekend. When Joey's bus was due at the end of our driveway, Grandpa and Grandma Ferrini would be waiting there to help Joey off the bus. They loved to see his excited face and tell the bus driver what they had planned. We treasured watching the whole scene take place! Joey would barely give us a kiss goodbye as he got into their car! He was so excited to go to their house (right in our development), eat dinner on the TV tray and then snuggle with Grandpa on the couch watching a game. It was priceless. They blessed us by doing this often.

We took vacations at different times with both sets of grandparents and spent casual time with them over dinners in our homes. They were fun to be with, and they were helpful with the children during those times. We invested in one another, and we were all rewarded. For several years after Grandpa Ferrini's death, we took Grandma Ferrini on vacations with us. Those times happened because we all worked to make them happen. We got along because we purposed to do so. None of us is perfect, so let's not pretend we didn't have differences of opinions and situations that needed to be discussed; but we worked at these precious relationships, and doing so benefited all of us.

Whether or not they have an issue with caring for a family member with special needs, many families have problems with members of their extended family. They wish they had them in their lives, but for whatever reasons, they don't communicate well or perhaps don't communicate at all. We know that some issues are tough to handle, for example, in-laws who are controlling, manipulative, or perhaps even abusive in some way. In those situations, it's never wise to leave any child with such people, let alone a person with special needs who can't express what is going on. But sometimes, family differences are a matter of not seeing "eye to eye" or simple communication problems. In those situations, we recommend considering counseling. Why sacrifice the loving relationship and help that extended family can be for the sake of having to have things always go our way or theirs. Sometimes just a bit of "tweaking" in the relationship is all that is necessary to improve it.

Because we learned how to handle one another's personalities (both strengths and weaknesses), we benefited by having our parents involved in very loving and wonderful ways with all of our children. We could write pages about the wonderful influence the grandparents were, so the grief we experienced losing all four of them within ten short years is understandable. Caring for them was a long and difficult commitment, but because of the influence they had on us and our children, investing our time and energy in them during their challenging years was our privilege. We spent countless hours visiting hospitals and nursing homes, waiting for doctors, participating in therapy sessions, keeping them overnight at our house, changing their diapers, holding their hands—and were thankful for every moment of their declining years. We doubt that the number of hours we spent in caring for them were even close to those they spent with our children, but we did all we could for each of them during the challenges of their declining years just as they helped us during some of our most insurmountable challenges.

Our Own Siblings

Cindi's two sisters have always helped out with the kids. Mary Jo has four of her own children, and sometimes we've had opportunity to help her out as well. Sue is single and has always welcomed each of the ten nieces and nephews into her home and life. She takes them to dinner, movies, and sporting events, hosts sleepovers, and will even stay at our home if we are out of town, keeping the kids' schedule as routine as possible. Everyone wants to adopt our "Aunt Susie"!

Aunt Susie has said it well, "Joey gives you such a 'look at life'—if you're not trying to do other things!" She knows: If Joey is in his sweet and simple mode, life is good. If he is acting out, life comes to a screeching halt. She also knows how much we appreciate her giving us a break. While Cindi was writing this very section, in fact, she called to ask if Joey would like to join her at a nearby retreat center for a concert and overnight stay with some friends that we also know well. Joey was excited about going, and we had the opportunity to enjoy an impromptu dinner with friends, a sunset at the lake, conversation on a boat, and ice cream afterwards. What a thrill! We felt as if we were in our dating years again. Sue dropped Joey off twenty-four hours later, and we felt refreshed and renewed. She went home to get some rest! She gets the picture. She's been involved in Joey's life, so she knows she can't plan a lot when he's part of the picture. Sue also knows that Joey has a way of teaching us things we all need to learn without saying a word.

Sue recently took him to her house overnight and was caught in the middle of some nasty "Joey behavior." At midnight she called and asked if she might bring him home. Whatever the problem was, she could not quiet him as she usually can. He wanted to come home, and Sue knew the train was on the wrong track; and trying to get it back on the right track might be more than she could handle. She brought Joey home, we put him to bed, and he was fine. We can't always get into his thought process, but we can learn how to try to resolve some issues. This was a good move, and she recognized what she had to do because she has involved Joey in her life and understands him. Uninvolved people do not understand most of what we deal with, so coping with others' comments is difficult at times. Someone who is not in the midst of helping may think he or she has all the answers, but that's for the next chapter!

Cindi:

My sister Mary Jo also offers to help out. One Friday I received a call from her. She was on the road near Joey's workplace, located a good thirty-minute drive from our house. She said, "I am at a place in my day that I could stop and pick him up and bring him home to you if you haven't left to get him yet." I was so excited because that total of sixty minutes of drive-time was now mine to spend as I wished. I was beside myself with joy! Moments later Sue called and said, "I just had some plans change, and I wonder if I could take Joey after school (she teaches) to come and stay overnight and maybe for the weekend, depending on what happens with the rest of my plans." I was dancing the jig packing Joey's bags! I didn't just have sixty minutes; I had the potential of a whole weekend!

Can you believe the goodness of my two sisters? Because we have involved ourselves in one another's lives, we look out for one another, helping where we can, yet remaining realistic about our own and one another's situations, families, and personal limitations. This type of family relationship will weather the storms better than those who compete or simply don't want to "get involved." This type of relationship requires giving and taking. Most people are smart enough to realize at least at some point that if they keep taking, they must at some time give in return. Some simply don't want to make that effort. They don't know what they are missing in learning to love our loved one. We are thankful for family members who have reached out to our family, and we do the same for them in ways that we are able.

Our Children

When Joey was little, a friend told us that Kristina and Kathleen would someday be excellent helpers. In the midst of diapers and daily duties, we could not see that far ahead. We thought we'd always be in the diaper phase of life, and no one would be there to help tie Joey's shoes or dress him. But sure enough, as the girls grew and matured in all ways, they became sweet little helpers to him. God allowed us to have two very special and helpful daughters who have blessed us in every way!

At three, we remember waking Kristina in the middle of the night, asking her to grab a coloring book and coat. She met us without question at the garage door as requested to make an emergency run to the hospital with Joey. We also remember the first time Kristina tied Joey's shoes. She was probably four years old and did so without being asked and sought no attention for it. Hers was a loving action, and it touched our hearts. We also remember finding her helping Joey in the bathroom; she had toilet paper everywhere as she attempted to wipe him. These are just a few examples, but they were the first of many. We always encouraged them, and they understood early in life, the joy they would experience continuing this type of kindness to others beyond our four walls.

While the girls were growing up, their teachers often noted how caring, kind and helpful they were. Often, the teacher would not know about Joey, and when they would eventually meet him, their reactions were usually the same: "Oh, now I see why they are as helpful and caring as they are." The beauty of this at-home training is that it's later seen outside our box, and now that everyone is grown up, we see that this life training has given them a heart for helping in their own homes, in ministry, and in their community.

When we traveled for FamilyLife and other ministry organizations, Kristina and Kathleen offered to help care for Joey when we were gone. Even with an adult caregiver at the house to oversee our children when they were under eighteen, the girls helped keep the ship on course! We have always told our girls that the day that anything comes between us as a family or in our relationship with the Lord, we would drop whatever it is we're doing outside the home. We routinely asked the girls whether they felt we were giving them enough attention and spending enough time with them. They have always said we spend enough time with them, and on one occasion, Kathleen in her mid-teens said, "Too much time!" with a laugh. But it was great to have them come alongside us and help care for Joey. In the earlier days, Kristina was the one who helped Joey the most. But when she married and moved out of state, Kathleen stepped to the plate and helped beautifully. With both girls on their own, now, we see family dynamics constantly changing, and others have stepped up to help in ways that we never expected.

Having grown up with Joey, both girls are very sensitive to those with special needs. We never worried whether they would stick up for Joey if someone picked on him because we watched them tell others to be kind to other kids. One time while in high school, Kristina heard a big football player teasing and trying to get one of the boys with special needs to do something inappropriate. Our little five-foot three-inch gal marched right up to him and in front of the whole table of guys said to the football player, "You should be ashamed of yourself. You are not treating him nicely, and you should be a good example to him and others because people look up to you." The football player changed his tune.

You might be wondering whether the girls always looked after Joey's best interest. Well, um, no! They have their limits, too! We won't mention names, but we've watched our share of hitting and pushing during those early years, times when the girls had "had it" with Joey and weren't going to let him get away with something. We remember a "push" that resulted in Joey almost losing a tooth. To this day we are amazed that the tooth has not needed a root canal! We remember a few yelling matches and a few good slaps. They were things we neither modeled nor encouraged, but they happened in the everyday frustrations of life. We used those situations as teachable moments for the girls, teaching patience, discipline, forgiveness, unconditional love, and yes, protecting and standing up for themselves.

We made sure that we thanked and praised our daughters for helping, protecting, and caring for their big brother. Probably one of the greatest blessings for us as parents has been observing growth in our daughters as they have matured through the ups and downs of having a brother with special needs. We'll let them share their stories:

Kristina:

We made sure that we thanked and praised our daughters for helping, protecting, and caring for their big brother.

I was aware of Joey's disabilities at a young age because I helped a lot. I was like a second mother to him, helping tie his shoes and getting him ready. Communication with him was not always easy because he can't express his thoughts. He can make most needs known, but sometimes he's just hard to understand! I'd love to have had a traditional big brother who protected me and took care of me, but that wasn't in God's plan; and I never knew any different.

Growing up, I felt my parents were overprotective of me. I didn't understand it so much then because I felt sheltered and as if they were keeping me from different aspects of life. Now as an adult I realize that they had better plans for me than I could've hoped. They kept me safe from the "world" around me, and now I feel that I have more to learn from them because one day I hope to be a parent.

As I was growing up, I decided that if I ever got married, I would want a man who would love my brother because I was willing to have Joey live with me some day. When I was fifteen and dating the man who is now my husband, I felt I needed to ask the big question: "If we were to get married and something happens to my parents, I'd like to have Joey live with me. What do you think?" Whoa! I don't think he was expecting that, but I'm glad I asked because I wanted to see his heart sooner rather than later. Thankfully, he has always loved Joey, appreciates his specialness, and is willing to have him with us someday.

I am so grateful and wouldn't ask for any other brother. I am still protective of him and care for him when I return home. I wouldn't change anything in our life, but sometimes I wish people would see the reality and difficulties of the day in and day out struggles and routines. He's helped to make me the person I am today and us the family we are today. Joey's helped us to learn to be patient, to serve, to protect, to care, and to show unconditional love. Joey is God's special creation, and God knew what He was doing when He made Joey especially for our family. Joey is so special, and he has blessed many others. He loves God in a way I may never understand.

One thing I know—we should never blame God for sending us someone special because I know that Joey is a major blessing in disguise! My husband Cos said it accurately: "I think Joey's the one who has it more right than the rest of us."

Kathleen:

Because I've always known Joey, I really never knew he had special needs. Perhaps the one thing I remember is that he was always given more attention. But as I've grown up, I understand better why he needed so much help and attention.

I feel he's taught me lessons I would not have learned had he been normal. Talking to him normally would be nice, but we really can't. He answers and makes his needs known, but he can't really carry on a conversation with us. For instance, when driving him places, I'd love to be able to talk about a sports game or how his day was without constantly saying, "Say that again" and having to listen so carefully to his every word to figure out what he's trying to say.

Having Joey in my life has helped me to stay in control. I think he's helped all of us keep things in focus because we all know how important we are in his life, and we wouldn't want to do anything to jeopardize that. When you have someone to care for, you don't have the opportunity to do some things that might take you off course; and that can be a good thing.

I want others to know that taking care of Joey is not always as easy as it looks, and that it's hard for all of us. When you initially meet Joey, he tends to be very happy and you become Joey's number one "buddy"; but Joey is not always like that. He's not always friendly, nice, happy and cooperative. We get frustrated sitting and listening to him yell and fight when we have no idea what has set him off and no way to reason with him to try to understand why he is angry. It's hard to sit and listen to him yelling and hitting the floor. It's frustrating trying to watch a movie or a sporting event as a family because he might get angry about something, stand up and yell, point at the screen, block our view of the TV, and get angrier if we say anything. It's frustrating trying to understand his needs unless he makes it very clear, which he is not always able to do. Joey is a wonderful brother, but we live in a world totally different from the one an outsider sees.

I have gotten better at handling Joey. I have learned to be more patient with him. When he is upset, I have learned to walk away and ignore his outbursts. My first instinct has always been to go to him and ask what's wrong, but that seldom works. I still struggle to be patient when getting him ready for bed or even just getting him to come to the kitchen table. When we are trying to do anything with Joey, it's on Joey's time. If we want to have dinner right now, that could mean ten minutes from now. Joey has to make sure his game is paused and in the right place; he has to remind us what the score is, and then he tells us not to touch it. He has to make sure he brings his favorite toy to the table and that all his other toys are strategically placed so he knows right where he can find them when he is done with dinner. A simple thing like getting him to the table takes a lot of patience.

One thing I fear about the future is taking care of him when Dad and Mom die. I fear he will hurt one of us when he gets mad and yells and starts throwing punches or running away from us. Joey is a strong man, and I fear that one day his anger will really get the better of him and someone will get hurt. I am also afraid that he won't be taken care of as well when our parents are gone. I would want Joey to either live with my sister and her husband or myself to know that he is in good hands.

Family Dynamics

Each person in a family affects the others. When one of us is out of the family picture for whatever reason, life plays out differently. Some dynamics are better than others! Each of us in our family has a relationship with God and relationships with one another. A family of six, for example, will find ample opportunities for various relationship dynamics. Throw in a person with special needs whose personality, behavior, and requirements vary from moment to moment, and the number of relational dynamics increases dramatically! Then, add extended family, friends, doctors—interesting!

When the children were young, dynamics were difficult because toddlers are unpredictable. Well, teens weren't always predictable either, but that's another book! Anyway, without going into the psychology of personalities, let's keep it simple by saying that we all have our own distinct personalities; and as we grow to know people, we learn about how they think, react, and respond and how life affects them. As an example, we'll discuss a scenario from our family.

Joey tends to single out one person when he acts up. Thankfully, he usually targets one person at a time. This has been his usual pattern in our family, at school, or at the ballpark. He may seem like a very docile, agreeable, loving person—and for the most part, he is—but when something (and we seldom know what that "something" is) upsets him, things can change dramatically from one moment to the next in public or private, when he's rested or tired, happy or sad, on Monday or Friday. (Remember Smegel? Get the picture?) Because every situation is a guessing game, we don't always know what triggers an outburst or for that matter what will stop it. We can be sitting at the kitchen table, talking about "the ride to work." Joey might be thinking something totally different, but it doesn't matter because he's on the "Joey track." If we don't understand where he's headed on that track, it can look something like this:

Cindi: (Talking to Joe - Dad) So, it was a nice ride to work?

Joey: NO RIDE TO WORK!

Cindi: (Said nicely) I'm referring to Daddy's ride to work.

Joey: NO, MY RIDE TO WORK!

Joe: (Said nicely) Yes, my ride to work was nice.

Joey: NO! NO RIDE TO WORK!

Kristina: (Said nicely) Joey, it's OK. It wasn't your ride to work. It was Dad's.

Joey: NOOOOOOOOO! YOUUUUUU! YOUR RIDE TO WORK!

Kathleen has remained silent and not even in the conversation but suddenly becomes the person on whom Joey focuses.

Joey: (to Kathleen) OUT! GET OUT! GO TO YOUR ROOM!

Now with both girls grown, gone, and out of this family picture, that same scenario might end like this:

Joey: DAD, YOU! OUT! YOU GO TO JAIL! GET! GO AWAY!

Same general ending, but pointed in the direction of someone else! It all matters who's in the picture at the time. So who can figure out what track Joey was on? Good luck!

Because Cindi is the one who generally helps Joey shower, she has had to learn to be creative to get him there! Here is a scenario with an ending more favorable than the last one:

Cindi: Joey, you'll get a shower when we get home.

Joey: NO SHOWER!

Cindi: Oh! No shower right now, but how about a haircut today and then a shower? (Cindi had no intention of giving him a haircut that day.)

Joey: NO HAIRCUT!

Cindi: OK, no haircut, but how about just the shower?

Joey: Yeah!

We have learned that if we feel we must *win*, we have already lost! We have to be creative, realizing that sometimes what we try will work and sometimes it won't. We know in our situation we can't wage a war of words and get anywhere. We have to reword, restructure time, and do whatever it takes to get done what we need to get done. Joey got a shower. Mission accomplished.

Family Dynamics: The Pecking Order

Be on the look out for interactions with the person with special needs when he or she singles out one family member. In our case, we personally think Joey picks on one person over another because he has a sense of the family pecking order (Webster's definition of *pecking order*: "basic pattern of social organization within a flock of poultry in which each bird pecks another lower in the scale without being pecked in return and submits to pecking by one of higher rank"). In the first scenario above in which the girls were present, Joey would not target Kristina even though she spoke up because she helped care for him to a greater degree than Kathleen. However, in the second scenario, without either sister to target, Joey targeted Dad. What we have learned, and trust us, it doesn't work all the time, but we have simply had to ignore him. We all walk away and ignore him. At some point, he gets the message and apologizes to the person he yelled at. Sometimes it has taken days, but we have found it works better than trying to address an issue we can't figure out. And when it's over and done, we still don't know what his issue was with "the nice ride to work." And once that is resolved, we can expect the next conversation about "an ice cream cone" to be the issue.

Cindi:

Very recently, I took a trip with Kathleen and one of her friends, leaving Joe with Joey. I hoped they would both be alive when I got home. I wondered how the "pecking order" would play out with the boys being alone! And as we had guessed, Joey was perfect. He wasn't about to bite the hand that feeds him! He must have sensed who was in charge and how much he could get away with. He may be a whole lot smarter than we give him credit for sometimes! And some would say that sounds just like their teenage son! I guess we need to keep a sense of humor about some of these things!

The hard part for us is that Joey does not speak and think rationally all the time. Transfer that to other special needs situations like mental illness or Alzheimer's. Although they are different diagnoses, they present similar challenges. You can't argue with someone who is irrational. Through this challenge, we have tried to teach our daughters how to respond and when to walk away instead of react. Reacting tends to inflate the issue. Reacting in the previous scenario would have involved one of us raising our voice and say, "JOEY! Come on. Get with it. It's not your work. It's not your drive. Let us talk!" We seldom get him to understand it, so talking louder or more does no good. He's already down the "Joey" track on a runaway train! The more we say, the worse it gets.

Family Dynamics: Communication and Discipline

What has been helpful for our family is for the girls to observe us interacting when we are having communication problems and how we correct them. (Check resources on our website for books that can help in this area.) Joey cannot be included in most of these because he simply doesn't have the ability to understand the process. We want our daughters to understand how to communicate well and work through problems, and we have seen them do so wonderfully in friendships and Kristina in her own marriage. Because we don't always do everything right and have at times lost it with Joey and shouted at him, we also have had plenty of opportunities to ask for forgiveness and talk about how we handled things badly. Even Joey has learned that when he gets off the track, he has to get back on and ask for forgiveness. When he is calm, he knows how to ask forgiveness in a very simple way. But sometimes it takes a while and sometimes only after a long, hard battle. Let us share two scenarios with you.

We recall the day we decided to go for a Sunday drive. Nice weather and nice day to spend some family time together. The girls were getting into the car when Joey (about thirteen years old) out of the clear blue sky, started hitting both of us before making our way outside. He was getting strong and it hurt! Because the anger seemed to be toward Joe, Joe left the room, and Cindi stayed with Joey. After kicking a hole in the door to the garage, Cindi wrestled Joey to the floor to protect him from damaging anything else or hurting himself. He has poor balance, so that is not hard to do. As an adult, his poor balance still allows us to get him to the floor, even though he is over six feet three inches tall, much stronger, and not easy to keep down! But at times we must do that. It's not a pretty picture, but on occasion these unprovoked behavioral issues have to be dealt with aggressively. On that Sunday we had little time for communication, and corrective discipline that leads to training wasn't even on the radar screen. We were in survival mode at that moment. Eventually Joey calmed down, but the Sunday drive never happened.

Cindi:

On another occasion Kristina's college orientation (just a few miles from our home) was to take place on a gorgeous summer day. Joe and girls were up and ready to go, and I was on "Joey duty" because he was ornery and turning to nasty. I am usually the one who can calm him and talk him into joining us or changing direction, but this morning the "magic" wasn't working!

We determined it was best that the three of them should go ahead, and I'd catch up with them later. I probably tried too hard and should have stayed home with Joey, but I kept trying to get him to come because I didn't want to miss this "special" occasion. He began spitting and yelling, "I hate you, Mom. I am NOT going." A scripture verse came to my mind Psalm 66:18, "If I guard iniquity in my heart, the Lord will not hear." As I watched Joey misbehave, I realized this is probably what I look like to the Lord when I am behaving badly, and He is not listening to me. Oh, He *hears* me, but He is not responding. I decided to do the same to Joey. I eventually got him to come with me, but I told him I would not be talking to him until he said he was sorry and could talk nicely. I communicated my intentions and followed through with the discipline: I didn't talk to him.

Somehow we finally got in the car. I continued to ignore him while he kept yelling. We got to the college, and he followed me around the campus pointing a finger yelling at me the whole time. I pretended he wasn't with me. We went from one building to the next, realizing not everyone on campus was informed about what things were taking place where. At one location, Joey fell and skinned his knee. He kept pointing to the blood on his knee, but I ignored him. I kept on walking. I didn't look around at others who were undoubtedly watching, and I don't even want to think about what others thought of me. I just kept walking to get to my destination.

Missing several meetings because of the mix-ups, I finally got to the part of the day reserved for a picnic. I said to the rest of the family, "We are *not* talking to Joey today. He must first apologize and talk nicely." My family knew I was about ready to cry and because of how late I was, they knew I had dealt with a lot that morning, so like a lifeguard jumping off his post to make a rescue my family was instantly on the same page as I was. No one talked to Joey. Tears were just about ready to stream down my face, but I remained composed, thankful for a supportive family and determined to enjoy what was left of orientation for Kristina.

Some of you might be saying, "Why didn't you leave him home? Why didn't you call a sitter? Why didn't you—fill in the blank?" Well, making such arrangements involves much more than simply picking up a phone. In retrospect keeping Joey at home would have been the best thing, but other people have their own plans, and last minute doesn't always work for them. In addition, leaving an angry twenty-one-year-old with someone else isn't very considerate. Dynamics are not always easy. It would have been best to stay home, but even in that, sometimes we tire of being left out to stay home.

We did what we felt we had to do, and although it was a long and awful day, at the end of it and with great remorse, Joey came to all of us and said, "I am sorry." We were grateful for the apology, wishing that and the good behavior had come sooner. We all learned some valuable things that day. The girls learned that we valued them as a priority, no matter the challenge we faced. They knew we would still try to include Joey because he is a part of our family. We learned we individually needed to shift our thinking and plans for the sake of the whole. We also learned that we may have chosen better options if we had more time available to develop them and that we can't give in to Joey's behavior. We have to communicate the best we can and discipline creatively. Doing so is always a challenge, but we learn from it every time.

In a follow-up to this scenario, a year or two later, I was waiting for Kristina at one of the campus restaurants, when the waitress said to me, "Oh, I remember you from orientation day." My thought was, "I'll bet you do!" She went on to say, "I remember thinking you did such a great job with your son. You looked like you were ready to cry, but you were firm with him and you kept moving on. I could see you were having a bad day, and yet you were trying to make the best of it. I think of that situation quite often, and it has encouraged me when I have a bad day." I was able to share with her the scripture verse that sparked my thinking, and how later Joey apologized. I don't know what she thought of all that, but what she shared with me was an encouragement.

We can often second-guess ourselves, and we will never say we do everything right; but I was happy that something positive came from that very trying day. We don't always find out how others are affected—for good or bad—but I was happy to close the loop on that day with something positive and encouraging.

Have we always handled every situation with grace and ease? No. Have we always talked in quiet, sweet tones? Well, no! We're human, and we have sometimes had to apologize to our kids! But you cannot deal with a person with mental retardation or other brain-related issues, expecting the same results in the same time frame as we do with other members of our family who have no such issues. Not all disciplinary measures will yield the same results. Because of his limitations in communication, we often wonder if his out-of-control yelling, name-calling, spitting, and hitting (which we have never modeled) are his last resorts to try to get "some" point across, and/or a malfunctioning brain that he can't control.

Over the years we have tried different things to get him to communicate when he is frustrated so that we can eliminate these behaviors. Our goal with our children has been to use discipline not as punishment but as training. Some things work, others don't; but we must always keep trying.

Family Dynamics: Never the Same Answer

We share these things because we've had to learn to recognize potential conflict and tread carefully. We've had to deal with the power struggles and learn what affects Joey's behavior and what he responds to. If it were always the same, we'd write a book that would solve our problems and probably a lot of yours, but the formula is **seldom** the same. The best we can do is the best we can do. You might need to come to that conclusion as well. When others criticize, we must move on. They don't get it, and further discussion probably won't help

197

them to understand any better the challenges and frustrations we face. Our solution, when we talk privately is this: "I wonder if they'd like to take Joey for a week and see how they'd solve it?" Are you laughing? Is that something you've said or thought?

For those who wonder if we've ever just thrown up our hands and said, "Well, Joey can't learn, so oh, well! Act out, hit us, kick the doors, and walls, and we'll all be fine later." No, we don't do that. Joey knows that his behavior has consequences. We have had to learn to be creative and cautious in every situation.

Here is an example of something that happened within the first year of Joey's supervised employment. He works at a manufacturing company doing light assembly. The job is perfect for him, and his supervisor is, too! She is a believer, understands how to deal with Joey, treats him well and cares about him. For someone like Joey, this is truly a dream job! Yet like the rest of us, on some days he just doesn't want to go to work. Of course, the supervisor invariably calls after we have dropped him off and returned home, a trip requiring an hour in total. We then take another hour, drive back, and bring him home. One morning, however, we could not motivate Joey to get out of bed and ready for work.

Cindi:

I had tried for some forty-five minutes to get Joey out of bed and in a good mood for work. He kept putting his blankets back over himself, fussing, saying, "Not going to work! Not see my friends!" When I finally got him to think about changing, he'd put his socks on and then take them off again; the same with the shirt and pants. He grew belligerent saying, "YOU CAN'T MAKE ME! I STAY HOME! DADDY TO JAIL! KATHLEEN NOT GO TO SCHOOL!" You can see that Daddy, who has never been to jail, is always being sent there when Joey is angry! At some point, I knew I was not going to get him to work. I prayed as I often do when these things happen, and the Lord reminded me of a verse. I went to my Bible, looked it up, and returned to Joey's room. He was in his pajamas, in bed, yelling at me. I have to admit, I almost laughed. He was throwing the biggest two-year-old tantrum I'd seen from him in a while. He's a grown man, needing a shave and lying in bed fussing like a toddler.

I opened the Bible, and he quieted for a moment. I said, "Joey, you know we live by this Bible, God's word. And I know that you love Jesus and want to do what His word says, so I'm going to show you a verse, and I'd like you to read it for me." He sat up, reading the words from II Thessalonians 3:10b, "If anyone will not work, neither let him eat." It didn't even take the usual ten-second delay for him to understand. He looked at me with shock in his eyes, as if to say, "Oh, no, you wouldn't do that!" I calmly closed the Bible, looked at him and said, "You are a grown man, and you can make this decision on your own. If you choose to stay home, you can stay in bed. You may not play your music, watch TV, or play computer games. You can have your medicine and some orange juice, but you will not have anything to eat until you choose go to work. Do you understand?" He nodded his head showing he understood, and the whole day, he either sat on his bed or lay in it, but he did not leave the room. At bedtime he got his evening medications and went to sleep. The next day, he got up, got dressed and said, "I will eat today!" He also apologized for the way he acted.

Although most things don't happen twice the same way, we did have a repeat performance about a year later. I opened the Bible and let him read the verse, and he started getting dressed. Off to work we went!

Can I figure out what triggered it? No. Can I expect it to work that well every time? No. But he seemed to understand something! Not every situation runs so smoothly, but that was a good one. He missed a day of work, and as a result my plans changed; but he learned a lesson. It will happen again, and we have no way of knowing which choice he'll make or the choices I'll have to make.

Just so you understand us clearly, we'd never starve our child! Missing two or three meals wasn't a problem. He is a big guy and was not at risk with any health issues that would hurt him by missing a few meals. We would never do anything to injure our children, but when they are hungry enough, decision-making suddenly gets easy for them! We know not every mentally challenged person will be able to come to the conclusion Joey did, so we are not saying everyone should try this. It worked for Joey because he had the basic understanding of what we said, and at that moment he wasn't traveling at 200 mph down his track; so he was able to listen and understand! Had he continued yelling, ranting, and raving, I might not have been able to talk to him the way I did. Each situation requires creativity, caution, and always seeking His wisdom. Matthew 6:33, "But seek first His kingdom and His righteousness; and all these things shall be added to you."

Each family member affects the others. Although the dynamics may change from situation to situation, each of us follow certain rules to make the best of whatever the dynamic! We always agree that we are a TEAM, and we want to work together as one. Earlier we shared the acrostic to the word TEAM—Together Each Accomplishes More—and we have seen that to be true and helpful. Here are the rules we have established as a TEAM, based upon the Golden Rule in Matthew 7:12, "Therefore, whatever you want others to do for you, do so for them" and Mark 12:31, "You shall love your neighbor as yourself. There is no other commandment greater than these."

✓ Treat each other kindly. We all have value (I Corinthians 10:24, Romans 15:2, Philippians 2:3, 4).

✓ Talk nicely to each other. Yelling, calling names, and belittling do not constitute kindness.

✓ Don't start trouble. You'll find what you're looking for.

✓ Be fair. Don't play favorites.

✓ Keep your word. Let your "yes be yes" and your "no be no." Work together, helping each other whenever possible.

✓ Never exclude others.

✓ Even when you are tired of listening to your loved one repeat herself or himself for the hundredth (or more) time or she or he has misbehaved or embarrassed you once again, be patient and love the individual through the challenges.

Family Meetings

We felt our family needed "check ups" from time to time. Living in a home where one person requires so much more time and attention than the others, it's easy to neglect by default the very relationships you want to nourish! So we check up on those relationships and make sure they are thriving. Our family meetings included reviewing our calendars, communicating about things happening at school and work, and then taking time to share frustrations or concerns. Having this open communication allows for discussion and attentive availability and fosters openness outside family meetings as well, but we always know we'll have this focused time to get problems out in the open. We talk about issues of importance, which for us include our walk with the Lord, our family relationships, our friends, our work, and ministry. During these meetings we make sure that we know which direction we're headed and where we can help one another. Working together, we can accomplish more. The goal is to be sure each person is heard and understood in an effort to move forward together in relationships and life.

> *The goal is to be sure each person is heard and understood in an effort to move forward together in relationships and life.*

For families with a parent or sibling with special health needs, meetings held from time to time with extended family members can be very helpful in deciding treatments, reviewing medications, discussing difficulties and how to resolve them, and keeping everyone informed and on the same page. We have seen both sides of this coin. Some families work well together, and all members seek the best for the person needing care as well as how they can best use their gifts and talents to help. In some situations, however, one family member will not be happy with anything anyone suggests or does.

Handling caregiving is easy when one family member says, "I just don't want to deal with this" and jumps ship; however, when one member says, "I'm not going to do anything you ask of me, but I'm going to be in on every discussion and decision," difficulties arise. So what's a person to do? In our situation, we decided that no one could spend time alone with the family member who made the latter statement. That immediately eliminated the "she said, he said, you said, I said" silliness. We took notes, documenting each meeting. (Joe has always done this in his dental practice, and we know that what isn't documented can't be properly discussed or disputed whether in simple conversation or, if needed, in court.) Documenting only facts and the details of what happened; we told those involved that these documents were available for anyone to review. If the reader of the document came to a particular conclusion, that was fine; but we just stuck with the facts. Yes, some people like to throw "court-related" words around, even family; so we recommend taking meticulous notes in front of them (family, case workers, anyone involved), dating and recording them (we used the computer for all notes), and always having the notes available to refer to if needed. Documentation will provide you with an accurate accounting and verify who said what if referring to conversations becomes necessary down the road. Because phones calls always ended with insults, threats, and accusations in our particular situation, we asked that only emails be used for communication so that all details could be documented and verified.

When keeping documentation, "stick with the facts." In other words, we didn't say things like, "I feel that _____ was being unrealistic." What you *think* an individual was trying to do or say doesn't matter, only what was actually said or done. Sadly, some people just don't want to work together with the group, so for them additional efforts that will "cover *you*" are necessary. Ironically, when we take notes and document everything, we seldom need them!

Family Time: One on One

We tried to have time with our daughters, one on one as often as possible. In order to do so, we had to implement the divide and conquer mentality if we wanted to have solid relationships with them. Good conversation isn't always possible when Joey is around. He speaks out whenever he thinks of something. Because we've given him a lot of practice, occasionally he can wait patiently for everyone's attention; but sometime he can't let go of an idea or phrase, and so we knew we needed to give our girls time to be heard. We each took them on dates, which included shopping, the zoo, walks, an occasional trip, and breakfast or lunches out. We were intentional about making sure they did not feel left out. No doubt we failed at times, but they knew our heart and intentions, and we felt that was helpful. Now grown, they better appreciate the efforts we made in this regard.

Family Dynamics: Roles and Responsibilities

No matter what the size, complexion, personalities, or dynamics of a family, certain people will take on certain roles and responsibilities. Not all firstborn children will take charge, but that often happens. The roles and responsibilities are likely to change from person to person and time to time, depending who's home and in charge, who can and who is willing to do what.

In our family, Joey is the oldest, but because of his disabilities, Kristina always seemed older. And because Kathleen was born nearly six years after Kristina, we realize she has many firstborn qualities as well. Add that to Joe is a third born after a ten-year gap, and Cindi a firstborn. We have a lot of natural leaders! This situation serves us well most of the time: We are all ready and willing to help out. When a crisis occurs, we all get in gear to do whatever is needed; yet some of us are more willing than others, and some personalities adjust better to change than others. Some of us work better with Joey when he is in a tizzy, and the ones who don't, know they are better off remaining quiet and even leaving the room. We've learned the dance, not in a way that skirts the issues but in a way that acknowledges we each have our ways of dealing with stress, handling a crisis, and doing what we need to in order to see the best outcome. Coming to this point didn't happen overnight, and we've not arrived yet. We still make mistakes and continue to talk about ways we might handle things better another time.

In families that care for others on a full-time basis, many dynamics are in play. The family is just one of those dynamics, but we have worked very hard over these years for each of us to understand our own strengths and limitations so we can work best together as a TEAM. We all know what medications Joey takes and when they are given, his routine of showering, toileting, eating, and bedtime, how to distract him and how to keep him on task, when to push issues and when to leave him alone. So if Dad and Mom go out for the evening, and one of the girls is caring for Joey, she knows what to do.

Cindi:

During times when I have struggled with severe back pain, I have watched my family lovingly pick up where I had to leave off. Each member knows how to do laundry, even though that is my usual job. We all can cook—some better than others—but the results are edible. Because we want to work as a team, we do so, helping one another, knowing someone else will need our help down the road. The same thing can work in extended family situations when all parties are willing, able, and helpful.

We have always appreciated the support of our daughters in Joey's care, but we have respected their social lives and have not expected that every time we need a caregiver, they are available. We want to honor them and show them how much we appreciate them. (Philippians 2:3-4, "Do nothing from selfishness or empty conceit, but with humility of mind let each of you regard one another as more important than himself; do not merely look out for your own personal interests, but also for the interests of others.") Because we have tried to work well together, we generally asked ahead of time if either daughter could commit to a certain date for us. When they were of "babysitting" age, we paid them as we would if we'd hired any other paid babysitter. We wanted to make the job worth their while and also allowed them to have a girlfriend over. This would make it worthwhile for them and us. We enjoyed time away, they had time with a friend, and they made some spending money!

While we each know Joey's routines for waking, toileting, eating, medicines, and, work; some of us have the main responsibilities, and no one does those tasks unless a transfer of title has occurred! That way, we have a better flow to our day. Cindi gets Joey up and dressed for work while Joe makes his breakfast. Cindi takes care of Joey's medicines, and Joe plays computer games with him. Cindi showers Joey because he is less confrontational with her than with Dad. Kristina or Cos can get Joey out of one of his stubborn moments more effectively than Kathleen, who as the youngest has had to make many adjustments in learning how to deal with Joey but has weathered the storms quite well.

In case you wonder how we got to this point, let us show you the flip side. When Kristina was in elementary school, she helped us get things cleaned up around the house, doing things as we "directed" her. Her ears heard it differently. In a funny and very sweet way she said, "I feel like Cinderella doing all these chores." She wasn't alone in doing everything, but her concise description of the situation made us stop and redirect our efforts that day and every day since. She was capable, able, and even willing to help; but that didn't mean we were handling things properly. That day we made some changes. We gave her a choice of which chores she'd like to do with a time frame instead of "doing it now." There are teachable moments for all of us, and this time it was our turn to learn.

Different ages, different needs require different dynamics in our roles and responsibilities. We need to be flexible to achieve the best outcome. Trial and error is the name of the game!

Routines and Priorities: Goal Planning

If you are a caregiver, you know the importance of routines and priorities. You know that if *anything* is to be accomplished, planning is essential. You also know the difficulties of relating those routines and priorities to others who aren't in the loop on a daily basis! Sometimes you wonder whether you want to bother "getting out" and having to go through the whole list of what to do and what not to do just to get out the door. Staying home almost seems easier! However, when we have established those routines and priorities and others are willing to help within the framework that has been created, all benefit!

In our own family we have learned that Joey simply cannot be rushed. No matter what routine and priority we might have in place, we may need to redefine it or simply wait and be patient for things to work out. We are careful not to include in our plans people who don't understand that "this is the way it is." If others must maintain a certain pace, having things go their way all the time, and don't have patience, we might not be able to keep up with them, and it's better to say so up front.

Joey and many like him function better with routines that remain the same every day. Subtle changes can catch them off guard, flustering them. Fast changes can put them into a tailspin on the way to a nosedive! Caregivers must recognize the signs that throw them off. The frustrating part for many of us is that we do not always know *what* will set them off. Being attentive is important. When we miss the sign(s), we then need to be creative in figuring out an alternative plan, realizing what works this time may not next time! Our patience, love, and understanding will go a long way in helping people with special needs deal with change.

Our family is busy and active, so we have found that conducting the family meetings mentioned previously has been very important in keeping us all on the same page. Planning goals for ourselves individually, as a couple, and for the family was both helpful and necessary. Usually at the end of January, we write on a sheet of notebook paper ways we want to grow spiritually (as individuals and for each family member), what we want to accomplish in business and ministry, and what we desire to do as a family. We looked at this paper throughout the year and make necessary adjustments to see all goals through to completion. Sometimes we don't hit the goal, but most times we do. We figured, if we didn't write them down and try, we'd have nothing to aim for and thus miss the target every time. During times when we felt as if we were standing still in a tough place in life, these lists show us that we indeed have some movement in a positive direction!

Sometimes a goal planner who sets things up a certain way can be very successful but not necessarily when working with one who has special needs. We could write a separate book about all the times we planned activities and had to cancel because of illness or behavior or had to arrive late or rearrange our day or week (this is a big one!), or simply sit in a hospital room for days on end, none of which had been "scheduled." Others may not believe, agree, or understand what we deal with (or have dealt with), but we have learned to remain focused on what we must do. It all boils down to surrendering our day to God's plans, our thoughts to His mindset, our desires to His desires, and ultimately our life for what He wants to accomplish through us.

Have More Children?

Surprisingly, many if not most of the children in Joey's classes over the years were first children instead of the last in a family. We often hear that children with special needs are born of mothers conceiving in their later years. For most of us in the circle we knew, we were young parents having our first children.

If the person for whom you care is your child, you have certainly asked the question we remember saying out loud: "God wouldn't do this to us twice, would He?" Yet time and time again families with more than one child with special needs have crossed our paths. Joey had a set of identical developmentally disabled twins in his class one year. Someone we knew had three adult children, all with varying degrees of the same special needs. We have had the privilege of mentoring a lovely young couple with two children with special needs. Each child has different needs, but those needs add up quickly because the parents must manage all medical issues, each therapy, and ongoing home care needs as a family. We don't share these situations to add fear but to be realistic. We are always amazed that people challenged with more than one child with special needs get through it as we all do—one day, one crisis, one loving touch, and one frustration at a time.

Sometimes becoming pregnant without planning is best! We know several families who found out they were pregnant in the midst of the medical challenges of caregiving their children or parents who were requiring much assistance. We know one family who was discussing whether or not to have another child, a sibling to their child with special needs. This tired mom was taken by surprise when she found out through a routine blood test that her decision had already been made for her and her husband! In all of these cases as it was in ours, we had to rely upon the Lord for strength to get through another pregnancy with a good attitude, without fear, and with assurance that He would guide us through this child's care just as He did with the first, no matter what the needs.

We were certain we wanted another child or two and equally certain that we would not choose to have another special needs situation. We know how that sounds, but it is the truth. Our hands were so full with medical issues, doctors, meetings, and lack of sleep that we wondered whether we would want to start all over on that same road. The truthful answer was "no"! We wanted to experience a "normal" birth, "normal" infant and toddler activities, and "normal" life! Of course, we knew our life would never be "normal" because our Joey would always have special needs, but we really wanted to have more children. We had to ask ourselves whether we were ready to have another child, no matter what the outcome. That challenge was more a matter of the heart than anything else.

To have a second and third child was the best decision we could ever have made.

Our life would have been full with whatever number of children the Lord had given us, but we are thankful for the rich way the Lord blessed us with Kristina and Kathleen. Kristina came into this world on time with a breeze of a C-section (compared to the first one), ate well, slept well, cried well and a lot, but we could handle that little issue. And she went through life like that, too. She was a wonderful kid, superior student, had very few issues to deal with, had nice friends, and met a wonderful man she dated for six years, graduated from college, and less than a week later, married her sweetheart, sharing their first kiss on the altar. Yes, they had never even kissed during those six years of dating.

Kathleen was a different story. She was ready to enter this world earlier than the planned C-section date by almost a month! Soon after her birth and a quick glimpse of her, she was whisked away and transported by helicopter to a city hospital to spend the next two weeks in the NICU (Neonatal Intensive Care Unit) because of breathing difficulties (Hyaline Membrane Disease.)

Many things ran through our mind. Joey's birth, although difficult, did not send to him the NICU. We could only imagine what might go wrong this time. We were told the oxygen Kathleen was given could challenge her eyesight and even cause blindness although the risk was minimal. She had needles and tubes everywhere—the one in her head was a particular concern—yet she developed fine, doing everything right on schedule, was also a superior student, loves life, laughs often, and lives well. Even though her lungs were a problem at birth, today Kathleen is a soprano vocalist able to hold those high notes for a very long time!

Our children are proof that God has a plan we may not be able to foresee, grasp or figure out! We'll all have concerns, but the bottom line is doing what we believe is right for us. If we believe the Lord has spoken to our hearts, how will we respond to Him? The Bible says, "Behold, children are a gift from the Lord; the fruit of the womb is a reward. Like arrows in the hand of a warrior, so are the children of one's youth. How blessed is the man whose quiver is full of them" (Psalm 127:3-5).

Cindi's brother enjoyed archery. We asked him, "How many arrows does it take to fill a quiver?" To our surprise, the answer went something like this: "Each quiver holds different numbers of arrows, depending on what the hunter is hunting. Some hunters need more arrows if they have different-sized targets. Hitting a large animal might be easier than hitting a small one, but you'll need more arrows to kill it unless you hit it just right. Arrows come in different sizes, too, for different animals you hunt."

The moral of this story is that we shouldn't think we should all have the same size family. We will all differ. We need to go before the Lord and ask Him how many arrows will fit in our quiver. What will He have us accomplish with the children we have? Where will we "send them out" for His glory? Are one, three, or ten needed to accomplish what He wants us to do? We need to be very careful not to judge others because they have too many or too few compared to us. We knew our quiver was full after the third child. We don't know whether we can even explain how we knew, but we prayed together about it; we prayed individually about it, and we asked the Lord to make His will clear to both our hearts. We would never suggest making any decision without spending time together in prayer and both in total agreement.

Counseling

At times issues within a family simply can't be resolved without some outside help. Don't wait to get help. Don't be embarrassed to ask for help. Find a counselor who is a good listener, who will keep your conversation private, and who will help direct you. We recommend a Christian counselor so that Christian principles (how to deal with people, how to pray, how to respond) are followed. A counselor is often able to see what we cannot see clearly and trained to get to the core of some issues that may take us years to figure out on our own. Sometimes individual counseling is needed before group counseling can be beneficial.

When Joey was about ten years old, we felt we needed some help. His behavior was sometimes explosive, and we did not know whether our discipline methods were good for him or not. We did not want to continue in the same way and cause future damage to him or to our family and its dynamics! We sought the help of both a Christian counselor and a school psychologist. The school system provided whatever was needed for us, and we were most grateful; but their way of thinking was not always consistent with what we read in the Bible, so we listened and learned from both sources, sifting through what we felt was most beneficial for our situation. We believe we received great counsel all the way around, and it helped us to know what direction to take.

The Christian counselor met with us only three times. He suggested some reading material that we discussed regarding discipline methods, teaching us how to remain consistent in teaching Joey with his multiple handicapping issues and also to understand what we could realistically expect from him. He encouraged us by sharing the ways he felt we had a healthy handle on things yet was able to point out some things to help us for the long haul. In some ways that was such a boost to us! When you're in the midst of the battle every day, it can seem as if you do *nothing* right. Had we needed more than three sessions, we would have made additional appointments; but the counselor felt we were heading in the right direction with Joey as well as the girls. If we feel we need counseling in the future, we'd go again.

We suggest that spouses agree prior to seeking counseling whether or not they'll share with others their counseling experiences and outcomes. Some families want to know more about the situation than those in counseling really need to share. Some friends might have opinions that will muddle the thinking of the counseled. Consider this ahead of time and save some aggravation. When agreeing to share with others, be sure to agree on what is permissible to share and with whom. Our website has information on how to find a counselor in your area.

The Future

What will happen to my loved one if we/I die first? This is a hard question to answer. Yes, many options are available, but not every option is right for the person you care for. We have had many meetings over the years, talking with private, county, and other governmental agencies, private housing options and learning what is available or provided for our son. In addition to meetings, medical appointments and psychiatric evaluations are necessary to verify needs; these are accompanied by endless forms to fill out and sign. What is most necessary, however, is the faith to believe God will take care of our loved one when we can't.

One of Joey's coworkers, a young man with special needs, had dinner with us; and upon returning him home, he asked us to come to his apartment (government assisted) to look at a few things needing to be fixed. He shared with us how his mom prepared him to live on his own. His humble little apartment was the topic of our family conversation on the way home; we remarked about how uniquely God provided for all his needs. He doesn't know exactly how everything gets paid, but he is taken care of and able enough to care for his own basic needs. We know much assistance is available for those in need. Having the right advocate (parent, guardian, or trusted friend) is very important in providing for the future. Such individuals can help make the provisions so that you know the person will be well cared for.

The process starts by making one phone call to an agency that you work with or learn about, or talking to someone who is a step ahead of where you are. Hundreds of follow-up phone calls may be necessary, but those who are persistent can find answers for each question. The process takes time, and only the strong survive the pursuit of all that is available!

Family Support and Beyond

We have been blessed to watch our two daughters grow into young ladies, caring and kind women at home and in the community. While finishing college, Kristina enjoyed a summer of helping care for a young boy who was blind and mentally challenged. His twin had neither of those disabilities, but they both loved Kristina and enjoyed having her come to spend time with them. Because their mom did not have family support during the daytime hours, she was wise to hire Kristina, a hard worker with experience caring for someone with special needs. We all have to be creative to get the support and help we need.

When our children were young, we occasionally hired a young gal from church to come over while we were home to watch the children. While she did so, we were able to finish tasks like ironing, Bible studies, and writing. The caregiver provided us uninterrupted time, and yet we were available if a need or emergency arose. This was also a great way to peek in on how the babysitter was doing, to get to the point where we felt we could leave a particular caregiver with the children.

Family support was the best because they knew the routines and personality complications, but family wasn't always available; and sometimes the change was nice for the children. We had to achieve a certain comfort level before we left our children with others. That same principle flows over into those who'll care for an adult. We have to consider some things that differ from the usual babysitting criteria.

✓ Can this substitute caregiver change a diaper on an adult if needed?

✓ Can this substitute caregiver lovingly help dress and bathe the person for whom they are caring?

✓ Is the age/gender an appropriate match? (Example: Joey is an adult. We would not be comfortable having a fourteen-year-old watch Joey. We were also careful about having our girls caring for some of Joey's needs until they were older. (Example: We weren't comfortable with having them help toilet or shower him. Helping a three-year-old is different from helping a grown man.)

✓ Do you feel your special needs person is perfectly safe? If not, don't put them in a situation that is uncomfortable or unsafe in any way. You may be their only advocate to watch out for them.

In our own family, we have had to make choices. God has provided people in each generation who have lovingly supported us and loved Joey and the girls enough to invest in them. He didn't motivate *every* relative, but our needs have always been met; and we are grateful and appreciative to Him and those He has provided for us. He didn't inspire *every* friend, but we have a lovely group of devoted friends who have helped with driving (when we speak out of town) or staying overnight (in a pinch usually!) or meeting some need we hadn't thought of but God asked them to do for us. It's wonderful to watch the hand of God at work and we deeply appreciate each of these individuals.

The Single Parent

Many single parents head households that include someone with special needs. In addition to taking care of one who can't care for himself or herself, some were abandoned by a spouse because the job was too much for the other person. We'd like to meet personally with some of those people. No, maybe not. Sometimes we actually have to stay in marriages for the "worse" part of it. Marriage isn't always easy. That said—and we could say more—we want those of you who are performing this duty alone to know that we admire your perseverance, endurance, and unconditional love. This life might not hold the rewards we hope for or want, but somewhere in the midst of what we know to be right, we are rewarded by our faithfulness to the call. It can't be explained, but it can be understood in our hearts.

Those who have been abandoned carry a heavy burden. If those who observe the life of anyone caring for someone with special needs would take time to read this book, particularly Chapters 8 to 11, we believe many eyes would be opened not only to what we go through but especially those who are doing it alone. Those chapters are important for the single parent as well because they will need to gain the support of others who are willing to help.

We know some couples who are on the brink, ready to jump ship. STOP! Abandoning ship carries a cost, too. They will feel regret. Life isn't always easier when you walk away. You will have to carry with you the guilt of leaving your spouse and family. We know life *seems* as if it would be easier and more fun with less responsibility; but quitting is the coward's way out. You will leave behind the hero, the person who approaches this obstacle with the willingness to do what *needs* to be done, who is faithful and asks the long list of questions, knowing the list of answers doesn't always include what she or he wanted to hear. The hero is the one who remains available to the person who has needs and who gives up her or his own time, talents, and treasures to do what is right. The hero is the one who will humbly do his or her duty, even alone.

Not every situation is the same, and in some cases, a single parent caregiving option is the only option, like in the death of a spouse. We know of some single parent options that have resulted in having to find housing (government facility or group home) for their child because they could not do it on their own. None of us should make judgments. We want to encourage you. Make the best of it in all ways possible. For those who are married, don't quit now if you can see any way to go the distance together. You'll find rewards along the way, maybe in a smile or an obstacle overcome. The rewards might not be big, but they line the road all along the way.

Parent, Spouse, or Caregiving Advocate

Whether you are a caregiver to a child, spouse, or parent, you must be an advocate. When the person you are caring for can't think, speak, or act independently, he or she would be at the mercy of others without your help. Meticulously recording all information from the county, the state, the doctors, and lawyers is crucial to the individual's getting the attention and care needed to live the best life possible. We can't be embarrassed or lazy when it comes to asking for help and guidance. We have scattered various ideas throughout your reading for you to consider and choose from.

Family Humor—A Necessity

- When Joey was little, he liked to be chased up the stairs to bed. We would pat him on his behind to hurry him up, laughing and saying, "Get going! Get going!" One day we wondered what this might have sounded like if neighbors heard what was going on. Although he meant, "Don't get upstairs ahead of me," he could be heard yelling, "Don't beat me! Don't beat me!" We are thankful social services never wound up on our doorstep!

- Somewhere in his early twenties Joey went shopping with me (Cindi). I was picking up plastic dishes for picnicking. He had made it clear that he did not want to come with me and kept fussing about being there. I put eight dishes and eight cups in my cart, contemplating buying a few more before they were gone because the supply was limited. As I stood looking at something else, Joey had taken the eight dishes and eight cups and put them back on the shelf just behind me. When I looked at the cart and realized what he had done, I quickly went to reach for what he put back when I noticed a woman filling her cart with the very ones Joey had put back on the shelf. I was disappointed, but as I thought about it, I realized he had gone through quite a thought process to do what he had done. I didn't want to laugh and encourage it, but it was funny! The laugh was worth far more than the dishes!

- Joey enjoys looking at sports magazines. In one of them he saw a picture of athletes with missing limbs. When asked what he thought about this picture, he said, "Missing a leg. She is missing an arm. He is missing two legs," and so on. We asked Joey if he had anything missing in his life, and he boldly said, "No!" It's good that he doesn't have a clue that his mental abilities and intellect are lacking! We are so thankful for that!

- Sometimes the things Joey repeats over and over can get really tiresome, but we never tire of hearing him say, "I love you." He follows that up with, "Do you love me? We are family. I stuck with you. You stuck with me. We are family." It usually ends in a family group hug and kiss that he initiates. The girls didn't like that at some stages, but it is a tender moment to us now!

- And one more thing—Walt Disney World Trip Number Four went fairly well. We're not sure whether that was because Joey had grown up and was further along in the maturation process or we'd finally adjusted as a family or the prayer team praying made the difference, we don't know. We are just thankful we finally had a pleasant trip!

- One time at dinner Joey told Kristina, "YOU CANNOT TELL ME WHAT TO DO!" We were all shocked that he said it and that it came out so clearly. Trying not to laugh was just as funny!

OTHERS' STORIES

- A FamilyLife conferee, who was engaged to be married, wrote, "I have a special needs brother. Cindi, what you shared during the Mom talk gave me a view of my mom's perspective, and for that I am so grateful. I will think of her differently even though I have always thought highly of her."

- Our family has enjoyed the family retreats that Joni Eareckson Tada's ministry (Joni and Friends) sponsors. They know how we feel, how frustrated we can be, and how hard life is day to day, and they make every effort to pamper us, encourage us, and listen to us.

- I was planning to meet my husband at an extended family function with my son (age two), daughter (six months) and special needs son (age eight). I made four trips into the house, watching everyone watching me. I had diaper bags, feeding paraphernalia for my son's feeding tube, a special seat for him to sit in, and a baby seat with the baby in it, and a two-year-old accompanying me back and forth because I didn't want to let him loose. Not one person offered to help. Later someone apologized for not helping. That was nice, but honestly, my disappointment in my family made it almost not worth the effort going.

- My special needs brother gets treated specially by some people, but others call him names. My parents give me more allowance, which I like. My brother does not lie. Sometimes others try to use him or make fun of him. He doesn't know what they are doing. He is good company and easy to love because he loves you right back. He doesn't ask for much. He can't be rushed. He can't do most "boy-type" things.

- I appreciated my husband taking over when I was overwhelmed, caring for my parents, one with cancer, one with Alzheimer's.

- "Our family has grown closer because of our challenged family member." This comment was repeated over and over in the surveys. Different challenges and scenarios, same result. Some expressed the blessing of kids coming home from college to help with grandparents; others found their special needs person to be the "glue" of the family. Many shared that their quality of life was improved caring for another because they were more compassionate and caring. Some said their loved one with special needs brings much joy and is sensitive to difficulties and reminds them to love each other. A number said that siblings are willing to care for their special needs person when the parents no longer can.

- The person I help care for has been made a recluse by his mom. The past has been a problem for both of them—abuse issues—but being overprotective doesn't help.

- Family loved our daughter and was supportive, but they did not feel comfortable babysitting her to give us a break.

- Intimacy in our marriage was lacking because of fatigue and stress.

- Many family things we couldn't do together (not even bike rides).

- Having been raised with a special needs sibling, I wondered if I would have any special needs children.

- I have been a caregiver in several homes on a daily basis, doing everything including bathing, meds, dressing, and brushing teeth. I know the caregiver that lives with that person does so much more. I could leave and be free of the stress.

- I've asked family and friends whether they knew of anyone who could help me out (the nice way of asking them). No one had any leads. Going for coffee with my husband or running a few errands alone would be such a welcome treat.

- One set of parents is extremely helpful, which helps make our challenges more manageable; but the other set play no part in our life, which adds more conflict and misunderstanding. They live locally and could be of great help to us.

- We learned that spanking does not work with all special needs children as it does with typically developing children with the ability to think and process their actions.

- I wish the grandparents would do what we ask them. It's so important to what we are trying to accomplish. Denying the problem and then not helping as we ask is counterproductive.

- Our life is good and we are grateful we can help our children and grandchild have a better life with our physical, emotional, spiritual, and financial support.

- Events must be well planned to incorporate his needs, stamina (physically and emotionally). Overstimulation is a problem.

- I explained to our other children that our son would have a harder time learning things. We celebrated each time he learned something new. All of us rejoiced.

- When my brother was adopted, he was malnourished and had a flat head because of lying in a bed all day. I really didn't think anything was wrong with him. I have so many fond memories of my childhood. Because he couldn't walk, I would drag him into one of our rooms to play. He had a lot of rug burns growing up until I figured I could put him on a blanket and drag him on that. Today he still needs help in his assisted living with doing laundry and grocery shopping.

- These challenges have brought a deeper, more sacrificing type of love into our marriage. We have had to be creative in expressing love to each other. We have gone for weeks not seeing each other outside of the hospital. We rarely go on dates because it is extremely hard to find someone able to watch our child. Our extended family had been great, but we don't live nearby.

- I feel as if I enjoy life more than some others because I know what really matters in life, appreciate the little victories, and I enjoy it to the max!

- My father lacked compassion for my brother, who has special needs.

- We are parents to an adopted son with special needs and felt our life as a couple was always on hold. Extended family could have been more involved, but weren't. We've enjoyed watching his sister and her friends include him. He is now in a group home, and we are adjusting to being a couple. After almost 30 years, I'm beginning to find myself as an individual.

- When our son was diagnosed, the neurologist asked if he recognized us. I stated, "Not only does he recognize us, he recites the alphabet!"

- My husband sometimes says I'm too protective, and I tell him that is why the Lord gave us a child like we have—because I'll protect.

Your Story

What special need(s) are you dealing with in your marriage and how has it impacted/affected you and your spouse?

_____

_____

_____

_____

If you are no longer married, what was the course of events that led to the ending the marriage? Who is the primary caregiver of your loved one with special needs?

_____

_____

_____

If you are still married, what things do you do to strengthen your marriage? What do you wish could be different?

_____

_____

_____

Do you make your marriage your ministry? If so, how; if not, how could you make your marriage your ministry?

_____

_____

_____

_____

What part does extended family play in helping with your special needs situation?

_____

_____

_____

_____

How are you dealing with unhelpful/helpful family members? The family member who denies that something is wrong with the person who needs your full-time care?

_____

_____

_____

_____

How do you facilitate and encourage healthy communication within your immediate family and extended family?

_____

_____

_____

What recurring family dynamics might always continue?

_____

_____

_____

What are the roles and responsibilities in your family structure? Are they working?

_____

_____

_____

What goals and planning strategies help life run as smoothly as possible?

_____

_____

_____

Are you now or were you ever considering whether to have more children because of the impact a person with special needs was already having on your life? What does/did your decision-making process look like?

_____

_____

_____

_____

What future plans have you put in place for your special needs person and yourself?

_____

_____

_____

_____

CHAPTER EIGHT

Slow Down Ahead: Everyday Issues

David and Esther have three children with various special needs. All the children are of elementary school age, and they find themselves putting out one fire or another when it comes to school issues. They have three Individualized Educational Plans (IEPs) and are grateful to have a say in what their three children will learn from year to year, but their biggest problem and greatest issues involve communicating with the therapists and teachers. David and Esther want more services, yet the school personnel feel they are doing all they can for the children. The parents wonder whether they are expecting too much or not enough of their children and those teaching them.

Joan has been caring for her husband Martin for several years. His diabetes has consumed his life. He goes from hospital stay to hospital stay, trying to tackle another of his health problems with each visit. He refuses to eat the way he should, and his body is starting to fail. Insulin is being used but it's very hard to keep his numbers consistent. She's tired of hospitals, medicines, therapies, dealing with Medicare, all the phone calls and paper work in dealing with these issues, including her husband's mismanagement of his own health.

Carolyn has been in a wheelchair since her sporting accident four years earlier. At age twenty, she has trouble making friends and getting places and sadly feels left out. Her parents can do only so much to facilitate a social life for her. She is mentally and verbally doing well, but physically she needs someone to help her with everything. Her overriding issue is wondering what will happen when the day comes that no one is willing to help her.

OUR STORY AND THE STORIES OF OTHERS

We all have issues. Like fabric our challenges are rolled up in layers of issues.

And sometimes when we're in the thick of it, we get sick of it! We'll share with you some of the issues that we have faced in the past as well as some we'll continue to face. We'll share our own joys, frustrations, thoughts, and stories from others at the end of each section. We trust what is shared by others will open your eyes to needs out there. We all have issues, but some of these may have you thinking, praying, and considering how to serve differently than ever before.

Activities

We are disappointed that we can do only a handful of activities as a family. In the infant stages of Joey's life, we could take him anywhere, but it wasn't always easy. His nervous reaction to noises and then the crying that followed often placed us in uncomfortable situations. How long do you let a child cry before you put others out of their misery and leave so they aren't disturbed? The difference in children with special needs is that they cannot be calmed unless the stimulus is removed. If too much noise was the stimulus, we'd have to leave.

In summers when the children were growing up, we'd keep an ongoing list on the refrigerator with activities we could do together. This was much more advantageous than suggesting something, then and saying "we can't do that." It kept things more positive. Another list was helpful for "Dates with Dad" or "Moments with Mom," which included activities we couldn't accomplish as a family. These outings allowed our girls to see that we made efforts to be a family but also made time for just the two of them in activities they liked and could do but Joey could not.

Consequently, we've learned to divide and conquer in the area of activities, and whoever *could* do something did. A family trip to Niagara Falls was to include a helicopter ride. We all wanted to do it in "theory," but as we approached the helicopter, Joey just lost it. Even though decisions leave one person disappointed, we know that forcing the issue is not the way to go, especially when fear is involved. One of us usually decides to stay behind. Sometimes, if the activity is something we all really want to do, we'll take turns. It isn't a "family" thing anymore, but it has to do. It also takes more time to divide and conquer, and that needs to be factored into the decision.

Fortunately Joey can travel, but other issues prevail. Can he eat the food? Can he handle the tours? Can he handle the pace, the noise, the commotion, the heat, the cold, etc.? Is medical assistance available should he have a seizure or severe allergic reaction? We must consider more than just packing a suitcase. We have learned to appreciate the places we can go—some people can't even leave their home.

Adoption

We know couples who have adopted children with special needs—a few knew in advance and others did not. We have been blessed to see these families welcome the children as their own and for the long haul. In increasing numbers children with special needs are ready for adoption in other countries as well as our own. These children are blessed to have the advantage of joining families with the capacity to love and the ability to provide financially for things like surgeries and care that they likely won't receive otherwise.

Before adoption is considered, a couple should talk to other families who have taken this road and become as well informed as possible about all the issues they will face. Disabilities may range from missing or extra fingers to mild or severe cleft palates to severe mental, physical, and intellectual handicaps, and everything in between. Initial medical observations don't always map out what the future holds, so the more information that can be gleaned, the better one can plan for the child's future!

- When we adopted our daughter we had no idea of her special needs. I love her and would never leave her, but it has been more than I ever bargained for.

- We have adopted three special needs youngsters, and although it's not easy, we find it so very rewarding. Their needs vary on the autism spectrum.

Advice

We always appreciated advice, took what might work and left the rest at the roadside. People who give advice don't always need to know if you try it or not. Our two favorite responses were "thank you" for advice we might try, and "that's interesting" for advice we needed to really think about! Both responses are polite and appreciative, but we knew some things weren't for us.

- Don't suggest miracle cures. We've heard most everything.

- Please don't tell me how I should feel or what I should do unless you've helped me a few days and actually know what you are talking about.

- Please don't act as if you know how I feel or give advice if you have not cared for someone 24/7. Ask questions, offer help, show concern before offering advice.

Advocate

If you are the caregiver, you may be the only advocate your loved one with special needs has. If you aren't overseeing the individual's affairs and standing up for her or him, who will? Our bottom line for our son was always, "What will be in his best interest while also looking out of the interests of others?" We can't always expect the person we are caring for to get her or his way (or our way) every time, but we can expect that the individual will be treated with dignity and fairness in each situation. That is actually the law.

Thankfully, our country has laws that protect those who can't care for themselves, but having someone who will advocate for you is of great advantage. Joey would have never made it without us. No, we're not bragging at all. We wished we didn't have to spend thousands of hours with phone calls, doctors' appointments, testing schedules, meetings, writing letters, talking to lawyers and judges, filling out IEPs, and signing legal documents. We would have had much more fun hanging out at the soccer or football field with other families or going to music events; instead, we are the ones who took him to therapies, who made sure we knew the laws so he was not on his bus rides longer than the state law allows, who have set up appointments for work assessments and county programs, taken him to and from work daily (13,000 miles a year!), and made sure every personal and daily need is taken care of for him. Lest you think that was a list of complaints, let us assure you that we are thankful to be the ones who care for Joey. Doing so requires a lot of time, planning, and effort to carry out all that must be accomplished for him.

As advocates, we must learn to be diplomatic, not demanding or unreasonable. No one wants to talk to uninformed monsters demanding their own way. When we behave rationally and sensibly, we develop trust with whom we work. They come to realize that we are not there to do battle but to help our loved one. And others are there for the same reasons but not with the same personal attachment we bring! Our need to communicate well is important if we want to establish great relationships with those who work with us.

What are you willing to do or give up in your own life in order to make "it" happen for the person you are caring for? You will give up a lot, and you won't be living a life that is comfortable, easy, and fun. You won't have any regrets either because you have chosen to do what is right.

- I count it a privilege to advocate for my child, but the amount of time needed for meetings, phones calls, filling out and filing papers is overwhelming.

- Becoming the POA (Power of Attorney) for my parents put me in a situation that kept me very busy. I had to make all the decisions and field all the phone calls (whether crisis or everyday). At times the responsibility was so much, and I would have loved for one of my siblings to pick up the slack somewhere else—like visitation—but they never did.

- I am a person with special needs, but can't always get the things I need. Having a friend who advocates for me has been a great blessing. I know this friend takes a lot of time to help me, but if I were to do it myself it would takes ten times longer. I am very appreciative.

- Having someone mentor us in the area of setting up our will and a trust for our loved one's care was very helpful. It saved us a lot of time when talking to a lawyer to set it up.

- It's important that two people understand the paper work, governmental and health agencies and issues, etc. For someone to pick up where I left off in handling the many papers and issues would be nearly impossible to figure out unless they were "in" on the process all along.

- My mother and I had to have many conversations with a social worker in the nursing home to be sure that my one brother, who wanted information he was not to be given, was handled properly. She couldn't do it alone and wanted me (as POA) there to help her voice her own concerns.

Allergies

Some people might not consider having allergies a "special need," but when you must read every label before you put something in your mouth or the mouth of the person you are caring for, it becomes a special need. Allergies can go from just making a person uncomfortable to killing them. We have some friends who have such restricted diets that we truly wonder how they can stay alive. Yes, their food is healthful, but they have little choice and variety.

Joey is allergic to one degree or another to about 80% of what he was tested for. The worst allergies are to outdoor allergens, cats and dogs, but he is severely allergic to potatoes and peanuts. His peanut allergy was detected when he was less than three years of age when he had his first bite of a cookie. He was finally on table food at this point and had previously had one lick of peanut butter that made his voice sound scratchy. This little nibble of his first cookie immediately gave him severe reactions, including body hives, a swollen tongue, watering and swollen eyes, vomiting, severe wheezing. We have been told that all future encounters with peanuts, like the one he had, would cause Joey to go into an anaphylactic shock. Since that time, he carries the EpiPen on him for his safety.

His allergy to peanuts is so severe that walking into a Sunday school room at age five when children were making bird feeders out of peanut butter, one of Joey's eyes swelled to the size of a golf ball. Thinking "the smell probably won't bother him," we attempted baking peanut butter cookies at home. We had to remove Joey to the outdoors! Others don't often realize that if people with peanut butter on their fingers touch a doorknob and someone who has a severe allergy touches that doorknob and in turn touches her or his eye or mouth, it can be deadly for the allergic person. Joey's allergy is not just to peanuts but all kinds of nuts as well as their oils, which are used in many processed foods and snacks.

As Joey matured and learned that not everything goes into his mouth, he also learned from these near death experiences that he doesn't eat anything without permission. The next time you hear someone snicker at this idea being absurd, have them read the ingredients in plain M&Ms. Or better yet, have them take charge of the trip to the hospital and watch the reaction.

In addition, Joey's allergies often produce a domino effect, triggering his bronchial asthma, then flu and cold systems, difficult and labored breathing and two to three weeks of recuperation at home. Another mom once said that Joey needed to "get with other kids" to become immune to all the "bugs" going around. Later, when her youngest had the same allergy-related health problems, we listened to how hard it was to be out of the loop of life when she had to be home caring for such a sick kid. Our first thought was to say, "Maybe she just needs to be with other kids to become immune to the bugs going around." Instead, we asked the Lord to give us listening ears and a sympathetic heart to the difficulty we **knew** she was now enduring.

- Most wouldn't think that allergies would cause people to have special needs, but their diets must be regulated, what they smell, touch and eat cause major issues; and if they are unable to understand or comprehend their severe allergies, that is another difficulty.

- For years my daughter could hardly eat anything because of severe allergies. She couldn't go on school trips unless her food was prepared in advance. Around puberty things began to change, and today she eats anything she wants.

- My father never had allergy problems to foods, etc. but when he was tested for different things at the hospital, certain dyes and then follow up medicines were causing serious allergic reactions to him.

Appearances

We understand completely that "man looks at the outward appearance, but the Lord looks at the heart" according to 1 Samuel 16:7 and that the issues of the heart are more important. We also realize that people with obvious outward special needs are already noticeable, and thus we wanted to draw less attention to the already obvious by dressing and grooming Joey (and Joe's mom and Cindi's dad) the very best we could. People with special needs are not always kept neat and clean. Caring for their needs is difficult because many don't like being showered or bathed, and clothing has to be kept loose instead of fitted so they can be easily toileted and changed with quick and easy access. The declining health of three of our four parents at various times made changing them difficult. We shopped for comfy sweat suits in nice colors, but let's face it, styles are limited. Function must override style, but we still wanted them to look nice.

Looking back at pictures of Joey, we tried to keep him as up-to-date as possible in clothing; simple, clean, stylish but not trendy, casual but not shabby. We would ask our girls if his appearance passed the test. They were always ready to tell us the truth on this one because they didn't (and don't) want to be embarrassed by how he is dressed.

Because of a fall he had, one front tooth was badly misaligned, causing the rest of his teeth to get into positions that would later possibly cause some speech problems. We didn't expect it, but he did surprisingly well with the whole procedure of getting braces, including impressions. When he was done with the braces, the difference in his appearance was remarkable! Making sure he has a nice short haircut, is cleanly shaven, has clean ears, nails, nose, clothes, and that his safety glasses for work are clean are parts of the whole package. We are glad he doesn't want to be in dirty clothes, but he can drive us to distraction if one little thing isn't quite right (like toothpaste on his shirt). Only one item might need to be changed, but he will insist on changing the whole outfit, right down to the briefs. It takes some good psychology to get him to change his mind and only the clothing needed. He needs assistance getting things on properly. He undresses with no problem, but left to his own, putting things on usually winds up inside out, backwards or on the wrong foot. Putting "L" and "R" inside his shoes helped him know what to do!

Those kinds of special touches make those who can't care for themselves more acceptable to others who might already feel uncomfortable or uneasy about approaching them.

Clothing and cleanliness are very important, but those with body or facial deformities have other issues to deal with as shown in the following:

- My first child was born with a facial deformity. People did not know what to say when they looked at him. No one could say the usual things, "Oh, what a beautiful baby! He looks like his dad!" Oddly, it wasn't just family. It was the doctors and nurses, too. I would have liked someone to say something positive! They might have noticed that he has beautiful brown eyes with long eyelashes or that his dark hair was so beautifully wavy! I suppose the shock of the deformity was such that no one could think fast enough. But what about the medical people who see malformations every day? I would have liked for one of them to encourage me with something in a positive way.

- Our daughter is seventeen, and in many ways appears to be a typical teen, but her inability to communicate well and sometimes acting like a three-year-old sets her apart immediately. It's hard because she looks normal but is extremely socially undeveloped.

- Kids make fun of my child's _____, and it hurts me terribly.

224

Babysitters and Caregivers

Most people considered to have special needs can rarely be left alone. We've never had a time where we've had freedom to get up and go without much preparation. When the children were small, it was fun to have the grandparents watch them. The girls grew to the age when they did not need babysitters and babysat others, but we still needed and continue to need someone to watch Joey. The girls were great about watching him and helping him with some daily tasks. As the grandparents died and the girls grew, our source of help diminished. We never expected anyone to be there all the time because we wanted family and friends to be just that, not our source of child or adult care. If we experienced a need, we asked; but we didn't want others to feel the pressure of expectation to help.

We find ourselves in a new place with both girls out and on their own. Joe is in semiretirement with some free time but nowhere to spend it alone together without a lot of effort and help. We're at a different place in life than we dreamed of early in our marriage. Joey is pleasant company most of the time, but for those times we want to have a dinner out alone or with friends or take a trip, we must factor in what to do with Joey. We will never have the empty nest so many of our friends enjoy. We are adjusting, but we are also in the process of finding out how we can get caregivers who will give us a break when we need one.

We will talk about this more in the chapter on relationships, but one situation that has worked out nicely is a couple we have known for many years who are empty nesters have come to our rescue a few times! In an emergency another couple stayed with our children for a few nights when we had to be away and had no one to help at the last minute. The girls were older and capable enough to "run the ship" but not at a place where we felt they were able to stay overnight alone without an adult. We have neighbors who have said they are available to help if an urgent need arises and others along the way who have offered to help in various ways. We have their names on a list and have occasionally made calls to see whether someone could get Joey from his bus in earlier days or from work now, or other smaller things. Asking others to care for Joey for days at a time is another issue, but we are most grateful for whatever bits of time we have to do small and special things.

- We cannot get away—ever—without first contacting a respite care facility. We've used several. One was good; the others were not. We felt our adult child was overmedicated at one facility, and we never went back there. Those things are hard to prove when you are not present to watch them and see how the child reacts and responds while in residence. In our years of marriage, we have been away twice. It's very discouraging.

- Because my son is a fully developed young man and still in diapers, it is very hard to find someone to care for him. Changing a baby's diaper is far different from an adult's. We have had family members care for him but because they don't do it very often, helping totally stresses them out. I wonder whether they ever try to imagine how we feel having the job 24/7.

- We have an adult son with special needs; who needs care if we go out. Adult caregivers are hard to find, and the thought of a high school boy or girl watching him just doesn't seem the right thing to do.

- We can't have just anyone watch our toddler. His care requires minimal skilled nursing care for feeding tubes and medications. That means we seldom go out.

Boredom

Yes, boredom is a complaint difficult for us to hear. We can't relate in the slightest and wonder what we'd do with ourselves if we were ever bored. Anyone who is bored, please give us a call after you read Chapter 9. We have nothing to write about this issue, and not one person mentioned it in their surveys.

Children

We talked about the issue of whether or not to have more children in the last chapter, so this section will not address that issue. We want to consider issues regarding all the children in our families and things they encounter. Our goal was to try to do all we could with each of our children individually and as a family to promote family. It was difficult, given their ages, abilities and interests to find things to do together. Because Kathleen was nearly six years younger than Kristina, they took a while to become interested in some of the same things.

We always encouraged the children to help, spend time with, and be nice to one another. Each child and situation had her or his own challenges and limitations, but as we look back, our goal was a good one. We remember trying to teach Joey how to read before he could talk. We would put words like *table*, *chair*, and *door* around the room and play games with all the kids. Later they would be given the word and have to place it on the proper item. It was fun to put the girls in charge as teachers and us as students with Joey. That made it more fun for them. The basic idea was always to include everyone.

We found we needed to spend time with the girls individually. By doing so, we could invest in their lives, talk to them about things that would not have been possible to discuss around Joey, and do things in which we could not include Joey. As they grew, they began to see how valuable this time alone was. They could talk openly, and we were able to listen without the interruption of noises or Joey's needs.

- When the children were small, it was hard to have one-on-one time with each of them. All our time seemed focused on the child with special needs. Now that they are older, we have developed a routine that works for us and allows us time with the children away from the child who takes so much time and effort. We have enjoyed having this special time with them, listening to their hearts, being a part of their plans, and understanding their frustrations.

- We would like a larger family (our first child has special needs), and we think all our children will be so blessed to know and love their sibling, who is wonderful!

Clothing

For us the key to clothing was "easy." Joey continues to wear pants with elastic waistbands although he has a few nice pair of pants for dressy occasions that have a regular waistband and zipper. What difference does this make? The difference is how much help he'll need when toileting. He can pull down and pick up elastic waist pants but has great difficulty manipulating a zipper and even more difficulty getting a button into a buttonhole.

For Cindi's dad and Joe's mom loose-fitting clothing was a must as their health and abilities declined. We purchased Mom Ferrini all new clothes when she went to the nursing home. They were all colorful and easy to put on and take off. She had lost so much weight that it was good to update her look with the right size and pretty colors. We wanted her to look nice for visitors even though I don't think she knew or cared how she looked or what she was wearing. We also stopped getting her hair colored and permanents because it was too hard for her to sit that long. She had a beautiful new hairstyle that was very attractive for her. Cindi's dad did not like his new clothing because it didn't have the right kind of pocket to hold his wallet. He liked having money in his pocket. Joe's mom always wanted to be sure her purse was near her because she did not like being without it. Because of their inability to remember things, we had to watch when they had their wallets and where they put them. Not all clothing is accommodating.

- My daughter is in a wheelchair and her clothing needs to be "least restrictive." Elastic pants, blousy tops, and no ties or buttons—that's the name of the game for us!

- Dad just needed a bib-type apron because he was messy when he ate. We couldn't move him forward to tie the ties behind his back, and the aprons with ties would catch on the wheels, so they were not needed. I made aprons for my father without ties (or would cut ties off of other aprons).

- We labeled mom's clothing with her name so she knew it was hers and the outside of each drawer in the dresser at the nursing home so she could coordinate what to wear and to remember where the items of clothing were. It helped for a while until reading even became difficult.

Communication (or Lack of)

We knew Joey's verbal skills would be limited. Even in the early years most of our communications with him were half verbal and half charades. We learned along with him when he learned sign language in his special preschool—much better than the charades we had been playing! We had decided that we would learn what sign language we could, and if Joey were able to speak, we would use words when he was able to use them and sign when needed. Because he didn't say much that was intelligible until he was almost twelve, we had to come to grips with what his pediatric neurologist asked us: "Do you realize this may be as good as it gets?" We knew he was right, but we also knew that much of what children learn and retain is a matter of how much time we spend with them helping them to learn. Cindi went to many of Joey's school speech sessions, so we could work with him at home. Sometimes after dinner we all did mouth exercises, which ended in many a laughing spell! These exercises were good for speech but also helped Joey learn how to lick his lips when he had food on them. They were good for us because they helped us appreciate the difficulty Joey had grasping how to do what came so easily to us. We learned never to take for granted how God blessed us to be able to do such things easily.

When Cindi's dad had speech therapy after his ministrokes and for a time throughout his Alzheimer's, we were able to use what we learned with Joey to help Dad. When Dad's speech was nearly inaudible and so garbled that most could not understand him, our family (and those who had invested in Joey's life) could understand Dad pretty well. We often felt like his interpreters as we were for Joey. What a blessing to help him be understood!

The first words Joey said and actually knew what he was saying were *mom* and *dad*, but we are often reluctant to share the first two words Joey put *together*. For a bit of comic relief, they were "*Shut up*"! Interestingly, we do not use this expression at home, but we applauded him because we were proud of him for putting two words together! Many months later another pair of words came out at school. He must have learned them at school because we were told they came from a show we never watched. The words were "*butt head*." We had to suppress our laughter when disciplining him, but we found humor in that one, too!

Since that time, Joey has learned many words and has a fairly good vocabulary; but most of his talking is done in phrases. The most words he's used at one time in a phrase or sentence was thirteen! His comprehension of verbal cues is fairly good, but his verbal expression is low and mostly incomprehensible to those who don't know him. Of course, we can generally understand most of what he is trying to say. If we don't understand, sometimes we'll ask him if he can spell it. If he can tell us the first letter, sometimes that's enough to help us figure it out. For occasions when his sports teams aren't doing so well, Dad, his sports buddy, taught him a few tough words like *pathetic*! That is quite a big word for someone who's challenged in speech!

In addition to speech, we were pleased that Joey learned to read nicely. Sitting across from him as he reads a book, you would say, "I think he's making things up." But if you sat next to him and read along, you would understand him and realize he can read a simple reader pretty well. Joey can read at the fourth-grade level and understands most signs, which is great for his safety; and he listens to children's music and storybooks and reads along. He can enjoy a simple book, looking at pictures and reading most of the story. He may not be able to tell you all about the story because his expressive abilities are minimal, but he is able to answer questions that require one- or two-word answers. We also love to watch Joey read many words on the screen during worship time. Because singing words is usually slower than speaking them, he can generally sing along. He and mom make a joyful noise at best!

Just after Joey turned twenty-seven, he used a word we'd not heard him say before. He said, "Today is not a good day *because*...." We couldn't believe it! He had never been able to answer the question why? "Why are you tired?" "Why did the teacher correct you?" After those questions, he'd give us a blank stare. We could see the thoughts processing, but nothing came out. So we'd guess, "Are you tired because you stayed up too late?" "Are you tired because you woke up early?" Lucky for us if we guessed right. Very *unlucky* if we didn't. The more we'd guess, the more frustrated Joey became. But on this particular day, he tried to connect the dots; and yet he could not get the rest of that thought out in words. He's also never asked us the question "why". Maybe someday.

Both Joey and two of our parents had difficulty coming up with names as well as answering simple questions. Joey often says, "Help me with the name." We then ask him to give us hints. He'll say things that remind him of that person. "Your friend, Dad. The funny guy. OSU fan." The more clues he gives the easier for us to give him a name. Having a full conversation is difficult when most of it is a guessing game. When asking Joey (and our parents with Alzheimer's/dementia) questions, we learned to say the full question and then simplify it. This way they'd hear it twice and be able to answer more easily. For example, "Joey, do you want to go to bed or play computer games with Dad? Bed or games?" Sometimes it needs to be repeated more than once or twice, but repetition and simplification are helpful. Too many ideas and questions in one sentence cause confusion.

We purchased a communication device for Joey to use at work. Because he has had a few verbal "altercations" at work, we have him record into this device expressions like "Leave me alone, please" with his own voice. When he is frustrated with someone, he can push this button; and the device plays the words he can't get out fast enough. It has helped remedy a few problems!

- As a friend of someone who has a son with special needs, I appreciate when the parents help me understand what their son is saying. Knowing what he likes to talk about gives me ways to converse with him.

- Anyone who tries to make conversation with my mom, who is unable to speak, thrills me. I know she still understands things, so the person who takes time to talk to her is a dear.

- A young man at our church is unable to communicate at all, but we know he understands. I try to touch his shoulder and say hello to him until his eyes meet mine. Then I say a few things and wish him a good day.

- Offer to help or simply touch him (the person I care for) and talk to him.

- Give special needs people *time* to respond to a question and to show an emotion. It all takes time to process.

- My son verbalizes what we all wish we could, but we'd never get away with it!

Concepts

Something we saw as difficult for us with Joey as well as Joe's mom and Cindi's dad with Alzheimer's is that concepts are hard to understand and formulate. For instance, Joey can understand that 1 is less than 35. He can read numbers, but he can't calculate them. Why can't they do simple math but they can identify 345? We've read enough to know a brain issue is involved, one that can't be fixed. Many other concepts are hard to grasp as well. Joey understands a lot of how the game of football is played, but he can't understand why his team doesn't always win; and he gets upset when they don't. He'll say, "The Brown's are winning by 7," when the score is 7–3. He's fine while they're winning.

Cindi's dad knew he wasn't well, yet he insisted that if he could just get out of his wheelchair, he'd be fine. He could not grasp the reality that his feet no longer worked because his brain told him something different. Even after six years of illness, nearly four in a wheelchair, he would say that *when* he got better, he'd go golfing.

Brain dysfunction is difficult to understand for those of us whose brains seem to be working as they were intended, but imagine the difficulty those with brain-related injury, trauma, or stroke have when they are trying to communicate something and their brain won't let them.

- Sometimes following the speech of people with special needs is hard when they can't express themselves because they aren't capable of grasping reality. Even when people try to help, sometimes they just can't figure out what the individual is trying to communicate.

- It's been educational for me to watch teachers help our child learn from one concept and transfer it to another, for example: his IEP in the early years was to learn to roll Play Dough; in high school he rolled out dough and cut out biscuits. He learned to sort blocks by shape and color and later learned to sort silverware in the drawer and clothing for laundry. He learned to put small objects into a small opening on a bottle and later learned to put coins in a vending machine.

Conversations

We find that people who don't know us seem uneasy around us if we have Joey with us. We generally introduce Joey, but sometime people don't know what to say or how to say it. Here are a few suggestions that have helped us.

✓ Introduce the person with special needs. Allow her or him to shake hands if able to do so or let the other person know what is acceptable. "Sally can't shake your hand, but she'd love a pat on the back."

✓ Don't shout. Deaf people still won't hear us if we shout, and a person who is mentally slow won't understand us any better. Find out whether the person with special needs can hear you and speak normally to her or him, looking to the caregiver for clues about how to respond. In addition, if the person with special needs has any kind of auditory stimulus issues (too much noise sets them off and causes them frustration), talking loudly or abruptly could make for a very difficult conversation. Lowering the volume, speed, and tone can help.

✓ Loud noises can distract a person from concentrating. Wait until he or she is calm before continuing the conversation.

✓ Ask about the disability if appropriate. Give the person with the disability the freedom to talk about it if desired, and the freedom not to.

✓ Using a word like *see* with a blind person or *hear* with a deaf person or *walk* or *run* with someone in a wheelchair is usually nothing to worry about if you are using it in general conversation and not a hurtful way! Example: If we say to someone who is blind, "I see" for "I understand," that is normal conversation. If we say in frustration, "Don't you SEE?" it lacks sensitivity and could be hurtful. If we can think ahead fast enough to avoid these words, we are better off. The bottom line is sensitivity.

✓ It's OK to ask people with special needs to repeat themselves. If we have to ask too many times, though, seeking the caregiver's assistance can ease an awkward situation. The worst tactic is dropping the subject, especially if the person is really trying to make something clear. At times, however, the severity of lack of verbal skills may necessitate our gently moving the subject into another direction without disregarding the individual's ideas.

✓ Keeping conversation short and simple is a good idea if it becomes difficult. Always end the conversation politely.

✓ Ask one question at a time and wait patiently for the individual to answer. Don't worry if waiting a few seconds is a little uncomfortable.

✓ When speaking to a deaf person who has an interpreter, make eye contact with the deaf person.

✓ When conversing with a blind person, do not "make friends" with her or his Seeing Eye dog. Do not pet, offer a treat, or otherwise distract the dog from the job for which it has been trained.

✓ If a person is in a wheelchair, stoop down to talk to them face to face. Remember that being in a wheelchair doesn't mean she or he can't talk or understand.

✓ Stay positive and pleasant.

✓ Don't correct the person unless you are sure they understand what you are trying to say and what your motivation is for the correction.

When Joey listens to others, he has a hard time making eye contact. Sometimes we will gently touch our hand to his chin and guide his face to the person he is talking to. It usually helps, but sometimes he doesn't like that. We try to be sensitive to this.

• Be careful not to use words in conversation like, "I feel like such a retard," or "Oh, I'm brain dead." Someone, sooner or later will be offended or hurt.

• I love it when people initiate conversation with me (I'm in a wheelchair) because I know they are making an effort that shows they care.

Crisis

We are thankful that we are still functioning in spite of weathering our share of crises resulting from illness, seizures, allergies, ER visits, and behavioral issues! We didn't say we're functioning normally, but we've come to realize that "normal" is a matter of perspective. When we're in the midst of crisis, we often feel at the end of our patience, endurance, and joy. One particular time of crisis occurred when Joey was having seizures. I (Cindi) was already tired from the daily care of small children, and Joey wasn't feeling well. During the course of the night, the seizures happened. When we heard him, Joe ran to Joey's room, found him blue, and began administering CPR. As I called the emergency squad, cleaned up the vomit, and began changing the bed sheets, I remember saying, "I just don't know if I can do this anymore." Joe said, "Let's just give it until the morning." The medical people came and went, the room got back to normal— Joey was still in the process of getting back to his normal—but the next day things indeed looked different, and I was ready to go another round. We need to gain a perspective during and after a crisis.

Crisis, we have learned, looks different to each person. We have learned to be careful when people tell us about their present crisis, not to respond facially or in words that say, "You are kidding, right?" Whatever any of us are going through at the time that presents itself as a crisis, no matter how big or small, it is a crisis. We are served well if we listen carefully to one another and not judge whose crisis is bigger or worse or worthy of discussion. Here are some things we try to do when we know others are in crisis:

✓ Listen attentively and carefully (attentive = paying attention to their crisis, carefully = hearing all the details, not just waiting to share your own crisis.) Not sharing an answer unless asked because we simply don't have all the answers.

✓ Make a meal and deliver it. Send it in a foil container so it can be frozen if they happen to have too much food already. Add paper plates, plastic cups and utensils, and table napkins so they have everything in one place and don't have to return anything.

✓ Pay a visit but keep it short unless you can do something to help them. They won't know how to ask you to leave politely, so keep it short and simple. If they want or need you to stay, we hope they will say so.

✓ Pray *with* them not just *for* them. Don't miss this golden opportunity to minister to their pain. Keep it short because their minds are on other things. Keep it sincere because they need to hear your love. Keep it true to the reality of the crisis so they know you understand (or are trying to understand) what they are going through.

✓ Offer advice if those in crisis ask for it or seem receptive. Advice from people who have not endured the same crisis is often of little benefit. Just listen at that point. But if you've been through similar events, test the waters and say a little something about what you've been through. If they don't pursue it, drop your experience and advice and wait for another more appropriate time. When things are initially "sinking in" during a crisis, people have difficulty hearing what has worked or how others' situations turned out well. (If you've never been through it, don't be a know-it-all. When you're the one going through the crisis and the other hasn't, being polite is difficult.)

✓ Be sensitive to the fact that people in crisis may have no idea what is really happening. If you ask questions (which can be very thoughtful), be sure not to get too personal. If they want to open up, they will.

✓ Send a note, postcard, short letter, or card. Personally written sentiments are always appreciated. If you want to offer help of any kind, write a time and date that you will call them to talk about how you can help. That gives someone in crisis the option to take your call or let the answering machine get it. It also shows you are willing to help! In addition, if your words are encouraging, they can read and reread or replay them over and over again when they need them!

✓ If appropriate, include the person in doing something fun, an activity to lighten their load a bit. They are likely in a place where they can't think about what might refresh them.

✓ Do something. Doing nothing may result from your feeling that you don't know what to do or you aren't creative enough to *think* of something on your own; but don't let this stop you! We've given some suggestions, and this is just to get you started. Be as simple or elaborate as your time, treasures, and talents allow. If you can't spend the time but can afford to purchase something for someone in crisis, what about a gift card for a massage or pedicure or money for a round of golf or to buy dinner? What about picking up the children to do something or running errands for the family?

✓ If you don't know what to do or say, say something like, "I am sorry for _____. If I can help in any way, I'd love to. I'll call you _____, and if you think of something, I will be happy to do what you need."

When we were in the midst of a personal crisis, we could hardly think about what we needed. We were only able to live "in the moment" and not always well. Those who creatively and lovingly helped or listened became our heroes. They met a need we couldn't meet on our own even if it was something we normally did daily. Crisis affects people differently. Some may be angered, sad, frustrated, numb, or confused; so meeting a need that will be appreciated and accepted is not always easy. Tread lightly, and your sincerity will be recognized and appreciated.

- A dear friend of mine was dying of cancer. The family didn't always receive guests because my friend's care was becoming more intense; however, she was willing to have guests one particular day. A visitor spent almost four hours with my dying friend, going on and on about her personal family trials past and present. As my friend lay dying, she didn't need to hear about problems that were only temporary. This individual was the last visitor the family allowed except for family and a small circle of caring and helpful friends.

- I just wish someone would have sat and cried with me.

- Spending two nights in the ICU with my dying mother could have been easier to handle with a friend at my side. Siblings, who were also taking turns, needed to tend to their families, and my spouse was with our children—one with special needs.

- An annoyance is something that can be fixed over time. A real problem (crisis) is something that won't be changing any time soon, if ever. We need to learn to discern the difference so when we listen and when we speak, we know the direction our conversation should go, being sensitive and caring.

Daily Coping Skills

We learn daily coping skills as we practice doing what we **need** to do, day after day without grumbling, complaining, whining, and crying. Expressing frustrations to our spouse or a trusted friend may be acceptable, but if doing so becomes our way of life, we become bitter and ugly people. Those who care for the needs of others clearly give up a great deal. They sacrifice their own time, treasures, and talents to be able to do what they feel God has called them to do. Each of us will make different choices to get through each day and cope. Unfortunately, some people may choose vices like drinking, drugs, alcohol, or other unhealthy choices. To enjoy a better life in the midst of crisis and challenge, we must be proactive in looking to do what is healthy and positive, not destructive.

We will touch on this in more depth in Chapter 11, but think about enjoyable activities that help you feel as if you've accomplished something, been energized by, or have a great sense of satisfaction having completed or participated in! Caregivers need to be refreshed and rejuvenated now and then in order to be able to give back.

As a young couple we enjoyed a season when the grandparents watched the children and we took golf lessons. We weren't any good and weren't trying to get into a league or be competitive, but we spent pleasant time together without crying kids or responsibilities for a few hours. We have always enjoyed ministry together and travel when possible. Individually, Joe has taken time to meet with other men to learn from them and to teach them through discipleship and Bible studies, and Cindi has done the same but also enjoyed sewing projects and more recently learning watercolor painting. Choosing the right "vice" (healthy and positive) to help us get through the tough times is very important.

In addition, we must learn to cope daily because at times we can't "get out." Sometimes we need to go to another room and look through a magazine or read a book. We might need to call a friend or balance our checkbook. Whatever it takes to get away and get refreshed to be able to cope in a healthy way is important.

When it comes to the daily coping skills of our loved ones with special needs, we need to show them first our example and then a way for them to cope. We've had to provide a variety of means for Joey to cope. Sometimes we remove him from the excessive stimulus that causes him to lose control of his emotions. Music can inspire emotion from any of us, but it can move Joey to tears. We are pleased he shows an emotional side, but doing so can also upset him and cause him to become confrontational. We don't know if he's embarrassed or simply doesn't know how to handle his emotions (like a two-year-old). We have tried various techniques—distracting his attention, whispering to him, making light of it, hugging him—but we never know which of these will work. So as the airline attendant instructs, "Put the oxygen mask on yourself before assisting children and others needing assistance," we try to cope first and then assess what Joey needs. We sometimes watch others try to help, looking at one another as if to say, "Good luck!"

- It is really hard to listen to others tell me how to cope, when they have no idea what I deal with.

- Our daughter with special needs loves music, movies, and all kinds of media, so allowing her these interests in the privacy of her bedroom is one way she learns to leave a stressful situation (lots of noise, too much company, etc.) in our own home.

Death

Dealing with death is difficult no matter when it occurs. Sudden death brings shock and grief; a lingering illness preceding death brings grief and then sometimes shock or relief. The loss of a person with special needs is compounded by the loss of the caregiver's identity. Doing everything for another person closely identifies the caregiver with the one needing care. Upon death everything changes drastically and dramatically. We've talked to others who didn't know how to act once they were no longer "Kathie's mom" or "Richard's daughter" after caring for loved ones through long illnesses or disabilities.

Those failing in health may have living wills and particular directives regarding their care and treatment during the course of their illness until death, but for those who have not made those arrangements, the decision of what life-saving measures are to be taken can be very difficult to discuss. When does the DNR (do not resuscitate) order take effect? Will you choose a feeding tube? The more that can be discussed and documented for caregivers and medical personnel, the better. Thorough information on these issues appears in an article by Carrie Gordon Earll entitled "Be a Voice for Life: The 2008 Sanctity of Human Life Handbook" in the January 2008 issue of *Citizen* Magazine by Focus on the Family.

Drawing to a close all unfinished relationship issues helps as well. As we cared for our parents in their declining health, we had the privilege of knowing that our last words to them were "I love you." We know that is rare, and we don't take it for granted. For those whose relationships are as frayed as the edge of burlap fabric, take note: If there is clear mental ability and time, don't waste the opportunity to get that estranged relationship back on track.

As difficult as this is for us to say, the truth is that we desire for Joey to die before we do. We do not wish his life to be over, but we desire to care for him as long as we can without having to put him in the care of someone else. Although Cos and Kristina have offered to take Joey someday, our desire is for them to meet the needs of their own family. We'll see how the Lord will answer this prayer.

We have been amazed by how well Joey has handled the deaths of our five family members. He never cried. He never became angry. He never asked questions. He does say from time to time that he misses his loved ones, and he's excited to see them again in heaven someday. We have a lot to learn from him in this regard. Perhaps this is how God would have us grieve for our loved ones—with the anticipation that we'll see them again instead of questioning why they are gone.

- I pray our special needs adult daughter dies before we do. I don't want her death to come soon, but I want to know she doesn't have to go to someone else. (Many made similar comments.)

- After my special needs child died, I felt I had to reinvent myself. I didn't know how to act without the routine that kept me busy 24/7.

Decision-Making

Depending on the person's disability, decision-making can be difficult. The article in the Focus on the Family publication previously mentioned was extremely informative with regard to legal terminology and caregiver decision-making. Although it's good to let people make as many decisions as possible on their own, the time will come when they are simply unable to make good and right choices. Having everything written out ahead of time for people whose health is failing is imperative. For young children, the decision to award guardianship over their affairs at age eighteen is just as important.

- It was important to know that my parents made certain choices of who would take care of them because one sibling was not very cooperative and would probably have not handled the money properly. They looked ahead and made wise choices.

- My husband and I have learned to "meet in the middle" on most issues, and this has strengthened our marriage.

Development

Children develop differently from one another. Recognizing the markers of development is important, but we must not expect every child will hit those markers on schedule. We hear of the child who walks at eight months, so when ours is thirteen months old and not walking, we think something is wrong. This may be so but not always. We are all on our own timetable, but we also need to be diligent in looking for details that would point us to a problem. Regular visits to the doctor and reading material to educate and inform are great ways to keep updated on what a child should be doing. The Internet is great; however, we can read information that doesn't really apply to our situation, and that can be dangerous.

We never thought Joey would understand things like Christmas and birthdays. We could see he was developing slowly and learning some things we'd never thought he'd learn, but events that occurred once a year seemed hard for him to comprehend. After many reoccurrences of days, dates, and holidays, he learned the concept. Crawling, walking, potty training, and learning colors presented the same problem. What took other children once or twice to grasp took months or years for Joey. Someone we knew who had a grown son like Joey told us that her son needed to have reminder markers year after year to learn these things; the more he heard it and experienced it, the better he would remember it. And it was true. The first time Joey said that Thanksgiving comes before Christmas, we were surprised. He was probably twenty, but he got it! He needed a marker, a frame of reference from which to remember and learn.

- It's very hard to deal with the initial news that your child will not develop normally/typically like other children.

- I appreciate when others notice that my child is finally doing something that took a long time to learn.

Denial

Although denial is a real issue that plagues most of us, we can spot it more easily in others than in ourselves. We all want our children to be healthy and develop normally according to the charts; however, because we are so close to our children, we might not see the obvious as others do. We often wonder how many people heard us echo the doctor's words, "He just needs a little therapy, and he'll catch up to everyone else." When we see small children whose parents say those words, we cringe, remembering how we were; and we wonder how to respond to them. Maybe it will be true for them, but for us it wasn't. Often we listen and later pray for them when we are on our own because we may not know where they are on the continuum of acceptance.

For those who see a developmental delay in their child and have accepted it or are in the process, we also make ourselves available should they want to talk, run ideas past us, pray, and even cry with us. As we found to be true, many of them discover that most people either just "don't get it" or choose not to (because that would mean they would have to respond in some way) and need someone who will help them be accountable for the way they handle things and move forward in the life-long journey of caring for their loved one.

Denial is often the first response when hearing any diagnosis and trying to deal with the shock of it. When Joe's dad was diagnosed with lung cancer that metastasized to his brain, brain surgery would never heal him. When Joe's mom and Cindi's dad were diagnosed with dementia, we thought this might be one of the first times the doctors misdiagnosed that awful disease. As we see declines in health and abilities, we grow more realistic in our thinking and approaches to dealing with the issue.

We planted a clematis vine at the base of our mailbox intending that it would grow up and around the mailbox. Joe's dad, whom we hired in his retirement to do our yard work, continued to cut down that vine, thinking it was a weed. We told him a time or two that it was a flowering vine, but he continued to hack it off. His work was meticulous, so much so that we chose to forget about our hope of purple flowers ever growing on the clematis vine! Each time he cut that plant down he denied the plant the opportunity to grow, thinking it was one thing when it was another! When Dad was no longer able to do yard work, the clematis suddenly began to grow! It bloomed as never before because it was finally permitted to grow naturally. When we don't see our loved ones with special needs "as they are," we hinder them from growing to be all they were intended to be; and we, too, miss out on becoming all we are intended to be.

Although we can hardly deny severe autism, retardation, muscular dystrophy, Alzheimer's and other situations, those early stages during which we "wonder" can be most difficult. We sometimes need others who will lovingly help us see what we deny! Mart DeHann of RBC Ministries said in his December 2006 pamphlet entitled *Mental Health*, "If troubled people need our help, we don't do them a favor by ignoring or indulging unhealthy thinking when there is reason to believe they could be making better choices. Love needs to be strong, and sometimes even tough, in dealing with those who are profoundly impaired. But this is where we need to use wisdom and patience rather than the presumption of ignorance."

Paul tells us in I Thessalonians 5:14, "And we urge you, brethren, admonish the unruly, encourage the fainthearted, help the weak, be patient with all men." We have an obligation to take action and not remain in a state of denial.

> *Some family members say things like, "Honey, why don't you pick up your head? Why don't you roll over yet?" I want to tell them, "Because he has brain damage."*

- A family in my life has a daughter who is very slow. What little I know about disabilities, I think she may be a higher functioning autistic child. She doesn't communicate very well and makes very little eye contact. Because I volunteer in the schools, I see the parents coming in for meetings and have had opportunity to talk with the mother. The mom can't see that her daughter has any problems. She's asking for things to be done for her daughter (general education classes) that are unreasonable because she thinks her daughter is fine. I wish she would observe in her daughter's classroom and see how socially behind and odd her behavior is and how others (including children in the class) need to help her to get along in the regular classroom. This mother's denial is hindering her daughter's growth, I believe.

- Some family members say things like, "Honey, why don't you pick up your head? Why don't you roll over yet?" I want to tell them, "Because he has brain damage."

Diet and Exercise

For most typically developing and healthy people, exercise is important. For a person with special needs, exercise is critically important but often takes the form of therapy. The time-consuming, slow stretching movements keep the person flexible and movable for as long as possible; and they help young children to get moving by making repetitive movements until they can do them on their own.

If we as caregivers are in the midst of scheduling many therapies, the last thing we want to think about is exercising our loved ones or ourselves. We are not exercise experts, nor do we have dietary expertise except to say that both are important in keeping a person as fit as she or he can possibly be even in the midst of illness, disease, and handicapping conditions. We must talk to the doctor to know the acceptable weight a person should be as well as the kind and amount of exercise they should receive. As caregivers we also need to be concerned for ourselves in this area. We are less likely to be able to care for others if our health is not good.

- No doubt about it, having a good diet and exercising regularly is necessary for a persons' well being whether he or she is the special needs person or the caregiver.

- Taking care of a very heavy person is extremely difficult. We had to put our dad on a diet that got him into a good range of weight. When people are dead weight because they can't help lift themselves or move, the caregiver has a tough time.

- We are soon to put our child on a special diet that will hopefully control the 110+ seizures he has per day. It will be under a doctor's strict supervision and guidance as we feed him through his feeding tube.

Driving

As we mentioned earlier in the book, Joe's mom was driving much longer than she should have. We knew she had become lost (before we knew she had dementia) after taking us to the airport. The twenty-minute drive home took her two hours. Beyond that, her driving became unsafe because of her lack of ability to respond. We expressed our concern to her and she said, "Well, if I die, then I won't have to worry about it." We said, "But if you live and kill three other people, how would you feel? And what if one of those people was one of your grandchildren?" She said, "I didn't think about that." We let her know that was what worried us.

After one of her cardiac rehabilitations, she was given a driving assessment through a county organization and stopped at our house with the instructor to say hello. She drove off, wiping out one of our sprinkler heads and crushing a few plants. She later was given clearance to drive by that instructor. We share this because we knew she shouldn't be driving, but she wasn't ready to give it up. At one point, we simply had to take her keys away and lovingly tell her it was unsafe for her to drive. Doing so made things harder on the family because she then needed transportation to all her appointments and social functions.

The Bureau of Motor Vehicles (BMV) and USDOT will help you locate driving assessment programs, programs for special needs/adaptive needs, and adult classes. Asking yourself (if you are the one who wants to start driving again) or asking the person who has some special needs the following questions will be helpful to determine whether they can drive safely or not.

✓ **Vision**: Do you have problems reading highway or street signs? Do you have trouble seeing lane lines and other pavement markings, curbs, medians, other vehicles and pedestrians, especially at dawn, at dusk, and at night? Do you experience more discomfort at night from the glare of oncoming headlights?

✓ **Strength**: Do you have trouble moving your foot from the gas to the brake pedal or turning the steering wheel? Can you raise your arms above your shoulders?

✓ **Flexibility**: Do you have trouble looking over your shoulder to change lanes or looking left and right to check traffic at intersections? Do you feel pain in you knees, legs, or ankles when going up or down a flight of ten stairs?

✓ **Health**: Do you have heart disease? Do you have Alzheimer's or another disease that causes memory loss and confusion? Do you have any illness that affects your eyesight or causes problems with concentration? Do you have Parkinson's disease? Are you on kidney dialysis?

If there are any "yes" answers to the above, choosing another mode of transportation is highly recommended. Those options include senior or special needs transit programs, taxis and community ride services, ridesharing, or carpooling.

- When Dad had been on kidney dialysis for about a month, he totaled his car at age 89. He had fallen asleep at the wheel. I had heard the same thing happened to the much younger husband of a friend, but I didn't realize dialysis patients were often very tired and shouldn't drive. Dad was so banged up. I felt really bad because he was on his way to a florist to get flowers for my birthday. For the next year until he went into a nursing home, I drove him everywhere. I couldn't justify the expenditure for private transportation when I am retired and available!

Eating/Feeding

Our issues feeding Joey were minimal because he nursed well and was eventually able to feed himself. We spent a lot of time teaching him how to hold utensils and get the food to his mouth without being too messy in those early years, but he learned to do a fairly nice job. Keeping his mouth closed while eating and keeping his tongue in his mouth while drinking still elude him, but don't think we haven't tried. At some point you settle for the best you can get.

We have several friends with small children being fed with a feeding tube via their abdomen. Without this medical intervention, these children might be labeled "failure to thrive" in part because of traumatic deliveries or other serious health and delayed developmental issues. The parents' job is not an easy one,

242

yet they know it is sustaining life; and they do what is needed. Special needs individuals on feeding tubes are often unable to use their mouth to chew or their throats to swallow. Stroke patients may have the same issues. At some point, especially in the case of Alzheimer's, the person actually forgets how to eat. If no one intervenes, other health issues can result, such as loss of weight, susceptibility to illness and disease, and of course eventual death by starvation.

Many caregivers need to work one on one with the person they care for to help them eat. The time commitment involved in feeding via feeding tube as well as trying to feed by mouth to maintain the sense of taste and the desire to eat is tremendous. Techniques can be taught to caregivers to encourage their special needs person to eat by mouth. The caretakers learn to manipulate and stimulate the person's lips manually, to massage the inside of the mouth and tongue in preparation for individual to accept willingly and chew food as well as reduce the gag reflex when food enters the mouth. Speech and occupational therapists teach how to do these manipulations with small utensils or the caregiver's fingers. Giving the special needs person the right amounts of food and the right consistency of that food is important if the desire to eat via the mouth is eventually to be accomplished. This takes much time and patience for both the caregiver and person with special needs to learn.

Dealing with drooling, messiness, and choking as our parents declined was challenging, especially when food just didn't taste good to them anymore. When a person doesn't *want* to eat, forcing them to do so is impossible.

- I really appreciate seeing a person with special needs using nice table manners. I can see someone must have taken a long time to teach those skills.

- Our baby has so many needs that I could not continue nursing because she was not gaining weight. We did not want to put her on a feeding tube, but because her mouth muscles were so weak, she could not nurse properly and even through a bottle was not getting enough nutrition. Even though I wanted to continue nursing, everyone told me to do what I felt was best, and I knew the feeding tube was the best for her.

- Our daughter makes loud gurgling noises when we give her medicines and liquids. It sounds awful—like she is drowning. We know she is fine, but others often panic when they hear her.

Emotional Issues

Do we want to discuss here the emotional issues of the caregiver, the patient, or both!? Much is wrapped in this package, and certainly more than we have time for or expertise from which to draw! But let's talk about both briefly because of the many issues facing both parties. What do you do when nothing seems to be going your way, and when nothing can be done to alter the situation that has changed your life forever?

From the perspective of the individuals being cared for, great frustration can result from their realization that they are not healthy or whole and are not going to improve. Some recover from the shock, get a healthy perspective, and move on; but some never do. Some will never accept a diagnosis or devastating accident; however, some will not only accept it but also do all they can to maximize their opportunities. Personalities, drive, motivation, and other factors play into how a person responds. From the standpoint of one whose health and being are diminishing, she or he must deal with many personal adjustments. How long will I be able to drive? How long will I be able to walk? Will I be able to travel? Will friends still come and see me? Will I have to go to a nursing home? How long can I expect to live with this before I die? All of these questions and more point only to grim realities.

For those in this situation, we suggest a good Christian counselor, who can help them and their family deal with the issues they face. A third party may be able to clear some of the fog to give direction and guidance before someone goes off the deep end to depression. Issues like isolation, anger, and depression can be discussed and dealt with before they occur and will hopefully be avoided. Ideas and suggestions are available to maximize the loved one's situation while remaining realistic.

Cindi's mom was the primary caregiver for her husband. Even though she could count on time for herself every Tuesday and Thursday when Mary Jo and Cindi came to help and for companionship and help in the evenings and weekends when Sue was home from school, the majority of the weight of the clock rested on her. Visits from family and friends gradually dwindled. Dad could be nasty at times, and that was hard to deal with. Exhaustion at the end of the day could be very emotional. We have learned from our own situation that help and visits are wonderful, but sometimes nothing is enough when you are emotionally spent. The emotional devastation can be debilitating. Personally, we feel that Mom's massive heart attack and death at age 69 was probably the result in some degree of the exhaustion of six years of caring for Dad at home.

As Joey's caregivers we've learned that we need to cope daily and work toward doing things we enjoy for our own emotional well-being. Add to the ongoing care he has needed all his life, the dump truck of life showed up with an additional load of issues that lasted just over a decade. Within ten years we endured the loss of Cindi's brother, Joe's dad, and Cindi's parents within five days of each other as well as another severe back injury for Cindi, the beginning of caring for Joe's mom in our home along with continuing to meet Joey needs, helping a daughter plan a wedding, getting our youngest through high school, and eventually making the decision to establish Joe's mom in a nursing home. Responding with little compassion to several people brought us to the realization that we were emotionally spent. Truthfully, our level of compassion had diminished during ten years of caring for loved ones with health issues, hospital and nursing home stays, and deaths, none of which constitute a reason to treat others without compassion; but we weren't just running on "low"—we were on "empty." At a time when we needed to be ministered to, shown compassion, and given encouragement, two church leaders who had met with us, perfunctorily prayed a cliché prayer and left the room, leaving Cindi in tears and Joe stunned. This whole scenario—from our lack of compassion to the lack of compassion shown us—taught us that we should make no excuse for our actions but instead look to respond properly at all times even when under emotional duress. It's not easy but it is possible with the Lord's help.

- I have a special needs child and so value my parents' help. My mom has been depressed for a while, I think, in part because of our child. She loves her dearly, but I think it's too much for her to handle.

- Don't be too quick to judge a kid having a tantrum. You *never know* what the circumstances are.

- My son with special needs has the same emotional needs as everyone.

- The challenge of fatigue, our loved one's getting up three or more times a night, and frequent hospitalization mean little or no sleep for the caregivers. We're drained.

"The" Diagnosis

On one hand sometimes doctors can't diagnose an illness or condition immediately, and sometimes when they can, they don't want to label someone too soon, especially a child. Such a decision may be wise to a degree, but when it hinders securing immediate help for a child, we have to hear the tough words that a diagnosis brings. On the other hand we wonder about some diagnoses made these days. Without specifics, we wonder whether some doctors too quickly slap a label on a child, prescribe some medicine, and hope the child improves. Parents may feel an initial sense of freedom when a child's behavior changes immediately, but if the change is a result of medication to sedate the child instead of deal with the root problem, other perhaps bigger problems may occur down the road! Any time a doctor wants to start medication right away, parents should first research the medications and learn about the side effects as well as how long the medication can be taken and whether or not blood tests must be done routinely to be sure other body parts are functioning properly while on this medication. Talk to others who have gone this route.

Anyone suspecting a loved one is not functioning normally, whether an infant or an aged adult, securing medical help is important as is sharing the results of medical consultation with family members; so everyone understands what is happening as well as what can be expected in the future. Some will deny the information, some will think you're making things up, and some will support you. No matter what others do, you have to get the help you need as soon as possible.

- Our family battled trying to agree on the way to take care of our dad. The medications "whacked" him out worse than his illness.

- We have been so grateful to finally have our son's seizures controlled after many years of being unable to find the right medication. Finally! One that works well!

Embarrassment

Yes, embarrassment is an issue. As much as we love our loved one, sometimes their behavior, table manners, and social skills can cause embarrassment. We remember being in a conversation with a group of people when one of us said out loud but in a quiet manner so others could hear, "I think Joey needs to use the bathroom." Clearly, everyone noticed the aroma—and Joey just stood there waiting. It wasn't an accident, but he probably didn't know how to interrupt us in our conversation or couldn't get the words out fast enough or didn't understand that he had to use the bathroom at that moment. Who knows what things do or don't go through his thought process? No one made a big deal of it, but it was uncomfortable and embarrassing.

Some with special needs (youngsters going through puberty as well as adults with Alzheimer's and other issues) may do sexual things in public. They may not have the awareness that touching themselves or others in "private" places is inappropriate and socially unacceptable. Depending on mental ability and retention of what they've been taught, they may not be able to remember from one correction to another what is acceptable and what isn't.

Talking to others in our sphere of influence to help us figure out how to handle some of these situations is a good idea. Family and friends can help provide consistent reminders to the loved one about what they should do and how they should act if they are reasonably able to comprehend and comply. Counselors may offer some solutions. Those unable to understand may need to be removed from situations if they are behaving unacceptably. Some issues are tough calls. In those situations, prayer for wisdom is always a great place to start followed by consulting with doctors and counselors.

- My daughter has a special needs classmate who is continually fondling himself, and we have a very difficult time knowing how to respond or react when he does so. I've volunteered in the classroom, and the teacher will gently take his hand and put it on his knee. Sometimes that works; sometimes several reminders are necessary.

- When our son gets nervous, he tends to reach for his private parts. We move his hand, and that is usually the only reminder he needs. He doesn't seem to be doing it to stimulate himself, but it's a mannerism that's become an embarrassing habit.

- Our mom is in a wheelchair and failing. We still try to take her to enjoy lunch or dinner out occasionally. She is beginning to make noises instead of conversation even though she still understands that we are in a restaurant. I know others look at us and it's a bit embarrassing, but I still want her to be able to enjoy these outings until she is no longer able.

Faith

The body may be ravaged by disability, yet the individual may have complete understanding of spiritual things. Because God is spirit and truth, we believe it's probably easier for those with special needs to know and understand God because they are mentally simple, and that's how God wants us to come to Him— simply like a child. We complicate things with big questions, trying to figure out what only God knows. When we observe special needs people at church, we clearly see that they are connected to God. They worship without the worry of who is watching and analyzing them! They know the words to the songs and don't stutter or stammer when they sing them. The words flow. Although we don't know for sure, they seem to be able to concentrate because they don't share our worries and distractions, which keep us from focusing. Joey isn't worried about whether he has enough gas in the car to get him to work on Monday morning or whether he has enough money for the groceries this week. There is a beauty to that. He lives his life in faith moment to moment.

If we as caregivers could remember that principle, we'd be better off! We worry about so many things that don't have answers anyway, and sometimes we merely need time and patience to see certain situations through. In Luke 12:6-7 we read that God values us and even knows the number of hairs on our head. If He cares about how much hair we have, He must be involved in ways in our life that we will never comprehend, and thus we should put our faith in Him.

When Joey brings us his Bible and says, "Read to me," we oblige him immediately. He enjoys reading nightly from his children's Bible and probably understands things that we never will. On some occasions, we have watched him look past us almost as though he is observing other things going on in the room that we can't see. We'll never know but often feel he is connected to the Lord in a way we will never experience. Undoubtedly, we are the ones handicapped in this area.

- The favorite day of the week for our son is Sunday. He loves the worship music at church.

- Seeing those we consider "handicapped" serving at mass and being a part of that celebration is absolutely beautiful.

Finances

Many great resources are available to help us learn to handle our finances and stay within a budget, and some can be found on our website. Those who are buried under the weight of financial obligations resulting from health care expenses can turn to some great resources, agencies, and private programs and agencies as well as county, state, and community funding and organizations when the financial weight of responsibility becomes overwhelming. First, we'd recommend talking to doctors and social workers concerning your options for financial help, including the institutions from which you might receive help. Many local agencies have been established for both research and care of patients with particular illnesses and diseases. Then call organizations according to the particular illness, disease, or disability for help. People in those organizations can help direct you to other people and organizations. Continue with the Yellow Pages, the Internet, and people in the same place as you (or perhaps a step ahead) who can guide you, or others who are simply willing to do some legwork for you!

Since Joey has multiple handicaps, we were referred to a number of different agencies. Over the years, we've received referral assistance from United Cerebral Palsy, our County Board of Mental Retardation and Developmental Disabilities (CBMRDD), Social Security, Family Services, and numerous others as they helped us find out where to seek help. This process, however, is not for the faint of heart! Every aspect requires a tremendous time commitment and large amounts paper work! You'll have a paper trail to verify needs, complete follow-up procedures, and enlist assistance. Most people we know who have a special needs person in their family live on one income. Many caring for an adult with the onset of an illness or disease, thus putting them into the special needs category, go from a two- to one-income family. In most cases both spouses cannot work. Meetings, dealing with finances, and getting to therapies require a person to commit to these as a full-time job.

We won't go into the monthly financial burden of different categories, but suffice it to say that nursing homes can drain savings accounts quickly because of the costs to the individual families. Depending on the care needed, we can be talking $5,000-$10,000 monthly to care for those with severe special needs.

Some people make their homes the place to care for their loved ones. We have personally not had those kinds of monthly totals in caring for Joey, but even the cost of sending our son to a private preschool for children with special needs was as much as paying to attend a local community college in those early years. Most young couples are not prepared financially for that kind of commitment, yet without that kind of start, young children with special needs fall even more behind; and making up for lost time is extremely difficult.

Consider the financial needs of a family who must diaper their child for the child's entire life. Add doctors' visits (specialists cost more!), hospital stays, medications, on-going treatments, caregivers, and supplies. The cost of all these adds up very quickly.

- When our child finally turned 18, we were so relieved. We immediately signed up for Social Security Income (SSI), and at different ages, medical help and other things were added to help us with the huge financial burden. Medicines we paid almost $100.00 for were now in the $5.00 range.

- Our daughter had many medical bills and medication costs. We struggled financially for many years, but our needs, not necessarily our wants, were always met.

- My husband is in sales and our financial situation changes monthly. Planning for all the needs of our children is difficult, but we see that somehow God always allows us to have what we need.

- We have great insurance yet still pay thousands a year out of pocket.

- At one time we had twenty-seven different medical bills. We were thankful to people who donated money and gave financial gifts at just the right time!

- We have some dear family members who had a fundraiser and raised over $10,000 to help with our medical bills and other health-related debts. We deeply appreciate their efforts because SSI and Medicare turned us down a few times. (Note: Many restrictions including age, ability, family size, and income are used to determine whether a person will get the help the family is seeking.)

Free Time

During some seasons of our life, we've had no free time whatsoever; and other times, some. We've never known the luxury of free time, including vacation time spent traveling or staying home for some time off. We've been able to "sleep in" only a few times in our marriage. Every moment of every day we have to think about Joey and ourselves (and for a while our parents, too). We keep in mind that *everything* we do for ourselves needs to be done for Joey. We have to think in the moment about what is happening and think ahead about what might happen and what we must do to make life work. When Joey was growing up, we trained him to do as much as possible for himself. He can play his video games well, but we would not trust him to open a new game wrapped in cellophane with a pair of scissors on his own. We have to think about the things he can "get into" if we aren't looking, and be sure he stays safe. That will never change. Joey may look like an adult, but we have a child forever in our home. He will always need to be watched, guided, and cared for.

Although we have little free time, Joey actually has plenty of it! His mind is free from responsibility and care. He works daily at a supervised job, but he doesn't need to worry how he gets to and from his place of work or whether or not tomorrow is a day off. He doesn't fret over whether he's assembled the right number of pieces at work or what he'll make for dinner. His mind is free from all that clutter because his mind doesn't hold it. We're pretty sure he doesn't even comprehend that all these things are being done for him at the sacrifice of someone else's time or effort. When he comes home from work, he knows he can listen to his music or watch television or his movies because his time is his own. He can and does help with some chores around the house, but thinking anything needs to be done is not even on his radar screen.

> *I do not know "free time." If I get time away, it is for errands and catching up.*

As our parents went through their health issues, their ability to *think* and *reason* was very limited and thus all of their time was planned for them. The same is true for Joey as he proceeds through his life. Depending on the stage of dependency, nothing happens unless someone plans and makes it happen.

- I struggle with envy listening to what others get to choose to do.

- I do not know "free time." If I get time away, it is for errands and catching up.

- Free time? What's that?

- Loneliness. Even if I had the free time, I can't plan outings. My husband and I take turns going to church and running errands. I'd love to have time with my other child but simply can't unless I have someone to give me that free time which then becomes planned time once again.

Future

The future may be the most difficult topic for caregivers and their families to discuss. We've covered many subjects throughout this book (e.g., future housing, deaths of parents whose children have special needs). We've omitted a few, including but not limited to the following: birth control, sterilization, hormonal treatments to keep children from growing, and stem-cell research and implementation. Doing research on those topics leads us to say that none of us can judge what another should do. We've come away asking more questions (to help us understand) instead of having any answers.

How a family deals with things like puberty, pregnancy, carrying and lifting a grown man or woman has allowed us to think differently and withhold judgment. Preparing for someone else's future is a great deal more complex than preparing for our own.

- Our daughter with special needs wanted to marry. She had enough skills to care for herself, but she would be unable to care for a newborn and raise it. We had many conversations with counselors, doctors, and her to come to the conclusion that she should undergo a tubal ligation to prevent pregnancy. It's not a decision we told others because we did not want to hear their opinions. We had heard them all as we went through the difficult and heart-wrenching decision-making process.

- I read about a little girl whose parents wanted to use hormones to halt her growth (permanent growth attenuation) so they would not have to be concerned about carrying her when she was a full grown adult and also so she would never have her period. As I discussed this with others, I found people on both sides of the fence on what these parents should do. I came away knowing that it must be hard to make a decision like that unless you are the one having to make it.

Grief

This is not going to be a happy section. Sorry! We believe that we may be able to *get through* whatever situation we're enduring, but we might never *get over it*. We can cry at the drop of a hat, thinking about what we've missed in Joey's growing up. We can cry over the things we've missed as a family, and the things we wished we could have done.

We know that it's OK to grieve for a time, but we have always known we can't dwell there. Grief can result in isolation. One who desires to be productive and purposeful in life cannot continue to wallow in grief every day. Yes, many find themselves in far tougher situations than ours and may feel the need to grieve forever, but in doing so they miss golden opportunities to serve and show others how God works in a life that is constantly tested.

We have read about and met many whose lives have taken a detour because of an accident or illness, confining them to a wheelchair, bed, or home. In such situations we must remember that we have the most impact when we move through the process of grief and find a reason to go on. We have to get our bearings on this road and eventually accept the particular condition, step up to the challenge, share struggles with others to help them cope, and in turn glorify God just as He intends. (Reread Section One "Starting Out," Chapters 1 through 4 if you feel as if you have not yet overcome your grief.)

Of course, grief follows not only the death of a vision but also physical death, which can in turn bring relief. When one has been in the caregiving mode for a long time, a sense of relief often accompanies the passing of a loved one. For us, after Joe's mom died (the last of the parents) we felt relief for two reasons: First, we knew she was in heaven; and second, our work and care for our parents was complete. We still miss all of them, but we welcomed the sense of relief.

We need to be patient with others and ourselves moving through the stages of grief. No time frame for working through grief will work for everyone. We need to accept our feelings, ask for help, and take steps to get back into life as we are able. Helping others is often a good way to start making our way back into life.

- For many years I cared for my husband, who died after a long and debilitating disease. I grieved his death the whole time he was dying, so after his death, I was very ready to move forward in my life, even feeling ready to date. I know others did not understand that, but I had had years of caring, crying, and grieving. I had already experienced what usually takes place after a more sudden death.

- Since the diagnosis of our child's special need, we are having a hard time getting through what we know of the grieving process. Everyone says each person takes a different amount of time to move through it. I wish we could move a little faster.

Guilt

Guilt—yes, the gift that keeps on giving! Those of us parenting a child with special needs must face this issue somewhere along the journey. Are we guilty of causing the condition? Are we guilty of neglecting her or him in any way? Are we guilty of feeling bad because we are losing it? Are we guilty of suppressing our frustrations and true feelings and emotions? Are we guilty of doing too much for the child? You'll notice that these self-questioning thoughts seldom sound like this: Am I guilty of having too much time to myself? Am I guilty of spending too much money on me? Am I guilty of being selfish and doing all the things I want to do? Our thoughts about guilt seldom run down these paths because most of us never have this kind of time to spend on ourselves!

Guilt magnifies our weaknesses. Think about a time when you've felt guilty. Was it at a time you were most vulnerable? Was it a time when you melted in a puddle of tears on the floor? Was it when you couldn't take any more? And what happened before these situations? You were probably vulnerable, having had no sleep, little food, no time to get refreshed, and _____. You fill in the blank.

- It's easy to stay in the place of guilt; however, blaming ourselves will neither help our loved one get better nor get us moving in better ways to help them.

Handicapped Parking Places

Oh, yeah! Now we've pushed a button! If you don't need a handicapped parking decal or hanger, don't ask for one. If you don't have one, don't park where you shouldn't. And if you do have one, but the handicapped person is not with you, don't use it for yourself and your convenience.

We have a handicapped sticker to use when we drop Joey off at work so we are out of the way of others coming and going, and we have used it when we know the walk will be too long or strenuous for him or if he is extremely fatigued or ill.

Pulling up to a handicapped spot only to find a car parked without a decal or hanger displayed is extremely frustrating. Those who park illegally can't possibly know how difficult they are making it for one who really needs that spot, and if they know the problems involved in transporting a handicapped person and they still use the spot for their convenience, they are rude.

- When we have seen cars parked in handicapped spaces without the proper tag, we have occasionally reported the car and license number to police. People who park in these spaces without the proper authorization are not only committing a parking violation but they are also inconsiderate and rude in keeping someone (us, in this case) from using the space when we need it. Those showing their lack of consideration today may experience the same frustration themselves someday.

- Sometimes I see people getting out of a car and walking fine. That bothers me, but then I realize I don't know what their situation is; and I just hope they aren't abusing the use of that tag.

Health

Health is a topic for a book of its own! We have dealt with of a range of health issues in our immediate and close extended family: bronchial asthma, asthma, severe life-threatening allergies, congenital heart conditions, cancer, Alzheimer's, dementia, hyaline membrane disease (lungs), pleurisy, pneumonia (many times and many people!), epilepsy, mental retardation, bipolar, brain aneurysm, chronic back problems, rheumatoid arthritis, and osteoarthritis.

We've been through the revolving doors of hospitals, mental institutions (those doors lock, they don't revolve), nursing homes, and rehabilitation facilities a lot! When you care for those in your family, you will find yourselves in these places, too! We know that many of you could add to this list and have already said, "Wow, that's nothing. We have been through so much more and for longer periods of time." Our hearts go out to you. We know the exhaustion, confusion, and frustration ongoing medical issues can cause. Going through this is difficult, and having others around us to care and pray is most helpful.

For those just learning your newborn will always be on a feeding tube or your husband has just been diagnosed with a debilitating disease, we know that your health issues are only beginning; and you may have years ahead of you with little to no hope in them. You will need to learn to live one day at a time, not trying to solve tomorrow's health issues because all we have is today. If your loved one improves, rejoice. If your loved one declines, weep. Find friends who will join you. Today, pray for how you would like God to answer your heart's desire, and be open to His teaching as you gradually see things differently. Then welcome the adventure tomorrow will bring.

Health issues make for challenging and difficult times, and they often lead us to sincere prayer and utter dependence upon Him because we simply lack the power to improve the situation on our own. You might want to reread Chapters 5, 6 and 7 for a new perspective on how life will be different. During this time, God might reveal to you to eat better, to take better care of yourself or your loved one; and He might lead you to some unique answers. Listen carefully to what He might be teaching you about why He has you in this place.

- There's nothing like poor health to make us turn to the Lord and prayer.

- My poor health and special needs have made me realize how much I need others and God.

- "When you have your health, you have everything." People who say that know what they're talking about!

Heart for God

A heart of God is what we need to develop and allow those who can't care for themselves to develop, too. We should not hinder their searching or inquiring. If we know the Lord, we should certainly consider our responsibility in leading them to Christ and teaching them what they are capable of learning. Even those near death are often able to hear prayers whispered.

Cindi:

Whenever I visited my mother-in-law in the nursing home, I also planned a visit to see Mary, a woman in her late eighties with the sweetest disposition. She knew the Lord and was grateful for each day. In constant pain, she reflected a disposition that revealed she had a heart for God. Her last days, just before her ninetieth birthday, reflected to others that her heart was for God. While she may have appeared to be in and out of reality, those of us who knew her heart for God could see she was in and out of heaven! She talked about seeing flowers that were more colorful than what she knew here. She would reach out with her thin, tired arms saying, "Jesus is on His way for me." The day before she died she whispered to her son, "I don't have any shoes. No one has any shoes." He was concerned for her and asked if she wanted to have some socks and shoes on to keep her warm. She faintly answered, "Oh, no, honey, no one wears shoes here; it's lovely." We all wondered why Mary took weeks to die when all her vital signs and health issues pointed to her leaving us sooner than later. Those of us who know the Lord could see that her heart for God caused many around her to see the reality of heaven, the need for Jesus, and the sweetness of a home-going for one who had a heart for Him. In her last moments, she asked her son to lay his head on her heart. With that request, she breathed her last. Workers cried. Workers shared what they learned from her. Some even came to know the Lord—all because of Mary's heart for God!

- Some of the most patient, sweet, and caring people are the ones afflicted. Like the chicken and the egg, I'm not sure which came first—their sweet disposition and their heart for God or their illness or disability.

- I have never had more purpose in my life than I do now. I feel the Lord has given us this amazing opportunity to care for this little one who has special needs.

- I find great satisfaction in caring for patients in a nursing home, and being able to share my heart for God with them. Most are very open to hearing.

Helps

Many items are on the market to help us care for our loved ones. Posing our many questions to therapists, doctors, and medical supply representatives has been one way to help us get Joey and our parents what they needed to keep them as "independent" as possible. These include gadgets to lock doors as well as to open them more easily, gadgets to raise toilet seats, make showers safer and kitchens more user friendly, walkers to help with balance, etc. If we didn't ask, we didn't learn, and we had much to learn! Don't stop asking until you've traveled every possible avenue. Then you can rest assured that you did all you can do.

If you are reading this book because someone you know is caring for a person with special needs, take a moment and do a search on the Internet to find a wide variety of helpful products. Start with products for children, and then look into products for adults. Make a mental inventory on the costs of these items, and add up the out of pocket expenses (many not covered by insurance, government assistance, or other agencies). Factor in the replacement costs, realizing that many of the products available for helping children will need to be replaced periodically as they grow. As you familiarize yourself with what others deal on a daily basis, put yourself in their shoes as you take a mental journey through their day, remembering they do it day in and day out.

Beyond discussing products that are helpful, helping others in practical ways is most always appreciated as well! When you don't know *how* to help, consider what you would need or like if you were in that person's shoes.

✓ If you notice someone needs help, verbally offer them help before just doing something for them.

✓ Opening doors is nice for anyone, whether they're walking in normally or using a wheelchair, walker, or cane.

✓ Invite friends with disabilities to accompany you when running errands or traveling, but remember that your pace will be different from what you are accustomed to. Know ahead of time what type of help they might need and appreciate from you.

• As a teacher, I welcome parents coming to help in the classroom. I wish more did.

• As a disabled person, I appreciate having the door opened for me. Then I can make eye contact and converse with someone showing me kindness.

• As a full-time working woman I have needed help in caring for my ill mother. Managing life and my mom is difficult. I've had to consider whether I need to take time off without pay, quit working, be satisfied with lower productivity at my place of employment, or job share with someone if our employer would agree. I feel I am giving help but often need it myself!

Hidden Disabilities

So many disabilities, illnesses, and diseases are not "visible." Children with mild disabilities may be regarded as troublemakers because of their odd or poor behavior, but because they look normal in size and appearance, their needs may be tragically overlooked. Consider how life is different for such children and those caring for them. When Joey was very little, he did not look too different from other children. As he grew older the differences in his abilities, his gait, looks, mannerisms, sounds, and verbalization became more and more obvious, making it easier for others to realize that his misbehavior or lack of ability to communicate had something to do with a disability. People whose disabilities are masked have a much more difficult time persuading others (sometime including their families) that life is difficult because of their daily struggles.

We've known quite a few parents whose children look normal, speak normally, and even learn certain subjects quite well yet can't perform daily living tasks because of their disabilities. These children may never be able to learn how to work a microwave, ride public transportation, or balance a checkbook. We know one such adult with whom we can talk about a topic from history or about geography, his forté, and everything seems rather typical, but he is unable to be on his own because lacks the abilities.

Even after two of our parents had been diagnosed with dementia/Alzheimer's, some people still said, "They seemed just fine to me. I didn't notice anything was wrong." The problem? Spending ten minutes or even half of a relatively trouble-free day won't always reveal struggles in their health, communication, care, or behavior; but spend a day or two, and pretty soon you'll begin to see that something is different. Both Joe's mom and Cindi's dad had conversations with others about things that never happened. Those people thought everything was fine and some even insinuated that nothing was wrong with them and that we didn't know what we were talking about. A few even whispered how terrible it was that Mom Ferrini was in a nursing home. A ten-minute visit does not reveal someone's long-term toileting, showering, and emotional needs. Unless you have become the expert on someone's care, you can't possibly know all the hidden disabilities that might be present.

Although hidden disabilities don't make you a bad parent or caregiver, you may have difficulty convincing others (if you choose to do so) that something very real is hindering the health, development, or well-being of the person you're caring for. Such challenges as bipolar disorder, autism, ADHD, even depression, do not always "show" themselves in a way that is obvious to others. Some people with special needs have one or more of these hidden disabilities; thus, we must all learn to be patient with others and tolerant of things that seem out of place without an understanding of how to "fix" it as well as maintain a good listening ear so we can engage in the learning process.

- Our teenaged daughter has the mentality of a three-year-old. She looks very normal, but once you try to have conversation with her, you see that something is wrong.

- Many childhood diagnoses are such that the child looks normal but is unable to behave like others their age. This is very difficult particularly because onlookers who don't know the situation tend to be judgmental.

Home Alone

For the most part, we can't leave Joey home alone. Someone needs to be with him to be sure he is safe. Although he can operate a microwave with assistance, he would not consistently be attentive to whether he put 1:00 or 10:00 minutes on the timer. This could make a big difference in allowing him to prepare his own dinner.

When Joey was in his late twenties, we realized he had never really been home by himself. Discussing how we would feel if *we* were never left alone to our own thoughts, space, and quiet, we decided to experiment with leaving him home while we took a ten- minute walk. We assured that all his needs had been met and situated him with TV or a movie and then took a short walk in the neighborhood.

On occasion, we have gone to a meeting early on a Saturday morning, leaving Kathleen to sleep in, and Joey to get up on his own. We can leave a simple note for Joey outside his bedroom door that lists what he should do. He will usually follow it. It will have boxes for check marks, so he can check it off. It looks something like this:

❑ Go to the bathroom

❑ Wash your hands

❑ Put TV on (We have it ready for cartoons that are acceptable)

❑ Sit at the table

❑ Eat (We put a spoon in the bowl with cereal and bananas, orange juice in a glass, and then milk in a measuring cup so he can easily pour it on his cereal.)

❑ Put dishes in sink

❑ We will be home soon. Kathleen is in bed if you need her.

He will get a pencil and check off each task as he does it. We spent many years—almost thirty to be exact—training him finally to be able to this. It started off with pictures, and as he was able to read, we began writing lists. He might not do everything on the list, but he'll definitely eat!

In time, and as we were sure he could handle times alone, we then taught him how to use the redial feature on our phone to call us. Before we leave, we dial in one of our cell phone numbers on our home phone, a private line. He knows he needs to press "start" to answer the phone if we call him. Only a few people have our private number, so if the phone rings and it's not us, he knows the callers; and they know Joey well enough that they can talk with him and tell him who they are. In several instances, we have been pleasantly surprised that he remembers to tell us who called. Because he follows the one routine, even when answering a call, he *pushes the "redial" button!*

So whether he is calling out or taking a call, the caller must first listen to the beeping of our cell phone number automatically dialing. In ending a call, we all know to tell him to hang up the phone and we wait to hear it click before we hang up, so he doesn't leave the phone open and unable to receive other calls. Otherwise, he would set the phone down and eventually be listening to a recording telling him to hang up and dial again!

Joey's acquired ability to handle the telephone allows us to take a forty-five-minute walk, go out to dinner locally for ninety minutes or so, and be comfortable knowing we can call him, and he can call us. We stay local so we can stop home and check on him if we have any concerns. We make sure he is well fed, toileted, and has a snack in the kitchen if he feels like one to remove all possible scenarios of danger. We call him every half hour and have several questions we ask him. ("Are you OK? Is anyone there with you? What are you doing? Do you want us to come home now?") Most times he hasn't moved from playing a video game or watching a movie. Occasionally he has climbed into bed, the phone at his side, and the bedroom lights on. Two out of three is pretty good!

When Mom Ferrini lived with us, leaving her at home alone was dangerous. She would hold the remote control for the TV or ceiling fan and ask us why the phone wasn't working. She had tried to heat food in the microwave, but fortunately, she could not comprehend the series of buttons she had to push to get it going, so she quit trying, keeping her from danger. She was unable to ignite the gas stove top, which requires a momentary delay before the flame ignites, thus the kitchen became an unsafe place for her. Often, we would find Joey showing her how to work some of the simple mechanisms he knew how to operate—like the TV remote. Watching Joey be the teacher was quite humorous!

Cindi's dad was confined to a wheelchair (the very chair whose wheels and foot plates he designed) when he was in decline. This was both a blessing and a curse. We never had to worry that he'd wander off or push buttons on stoves or microwaves that might put him in danger, but we had to watch him carefully because sometimes he'd think he could get up and walk and wind up falling from the wheelchair. He was not a tiny man, so two people were required to get him back into the chair—and only if he cooperated.

- We could never leave our special needs adult home alone but know many who are able to. Perhaps someday.

- Leaving at home someone with challenges like dementia or Alzheimer's is never a good idea. One never knows what she or he will do when no one is around that could be harmful. That has changed our life drastically as well.

Hospital Stays

When any of our parents or children required a hospital stay, someone stayed with him or her. Joey was never left unattended. We alternated nights and slept on a cot with one eye open on nurses who would check on Joey through the night, and the other eye trying to get some sleep. The same held true for our parents, particularly when their minds were failing. All the hospital noises, people coming and going, the poking and prodding, and the unfamiliarity can cause confusion and frustration to the patient. Staying with them gave them a sense of stability and comfort, which far outweighed our getting a good night's sleep. Returning in the morning to a loved one who has been uncomfortable all night adds frustration to others as well as the patient.

- My special needs daughter has been hospitalized numerous times for surgery and each time has been life threatening. Either my husband or I spend the night, but he has a hard time when he has to work the next day. If someone close to us, whom we could trust, offered to stay a night here or there, we would be grateful. After a week or two of us dividing our time like that, we wear down and often get sick.

Housing

Joey has always been with us, and we plan for him to be with us for a long time. Because we don't know what the future holds, we have him on a county list for group home placement should a drastic and sudden need require his placement somewhere. That would happen if we both died suddenly. Although our will stated a caregiver for the children when they were underage, things changed when they turned eighteen. We have tried to keep a step ahead of where we are to be prepared in case of an emergency.

Cindi's dad worked hard in his own business and had the means to provide care for himself every night and occasionally during the day. Dad could not be left alone, and because he did not want to go to a nursing home, our family worked very hard together to provide him the best care possible in his own home for over six years. Mom had an addition built that was handicapped accessible in every way. That was helpful, yet his care took a toll on all of us. It was exhausting. Mom and Sue took the biggest hit in the time they invested, yet both Cindi and her sister Mary Jo gave up time from their own families' needs to help with Dad once or twice a week for over three years. Everyone helped; everyone at one time or another was weary, but none of us have any regrets!

When Mom Ferrini's care was more than could be handled by us at home or by Joe's sister, the decision, after much prayer and consideration, was made for her to be placed in a nursing home facility. Many of her caregivers were Christians and loved Mom dearly. Our almost daily visits kept us aware of the quality of her care, and the aides and staff always knew they could expect us. She received excellent care that we could not have provided, particularly because our hands were already filled caring for Joey.

> *Nursing home, group home, assisted living, community housing, and institutional care are just a few of the housing options for those with special needs.*

Nursing home, group home, assisted living, community housing, and institutional care are just a few of the housing options for those with special needs. The decision can be very difficult. Some make the decision after many years of hardship caring for their loved one at home. Sometimes we become so exhausted that we can't care for the individual in a healthy way, and it's best that she or he take up residence in a facility that will provide the needed care. A social worker can help make the necessary assessments to determine the best time to make the move as well as what would fit the person's needs best. The best interest of the patient regarding health and safety must be the primary concern. When family members differ in their opinions on this issue, a social worker can provide objectivity.

- We wondered whether our daughter's special needs would have a negative impact on our son's future wife. We knew that the Lord chose the right woman to be our daughter's sister-in-law and son's wife. We trust that if something happened to us, they would be sure our daughter was well taken care of in the group home where she lives.

- Our adult son with Down syndrome had lived in a group home for quite some time when he was diagnosed with a life-threatening disease. We chose to bring him home where he died peacefully with us at his side. We were blessed to care for him as an infant and in his death. We try to tell others of his death before they ask because people always asked about him. He was a great joy to us.

- Keep an open mind about things like special needs boarding schools and nursing homes when safety becomes an issue for the patient or the caregiver.

- I worked in a nursing care facility and loved my job. I'm thankful for such residences so that these people have safe places to live. I think our society is coming to a place where those with special needs will be eliminated. That troubles me. I loved them as if they belonged to me. Not everyone treats them nicely, and some of the patients do realize it.

- I had to keep my options open for housing for my son who had several severe special needs. As he got bigger, he was just too hard to handle; and I had to find a special facility for him. I didn't want to do that, but I had no choice. I could no longer care for him the way I had been able to in earlier years.

- We had someone say to us, "How dare you put your daughter away." We were shocked. This person never helped or offered once, and had no idea how our forty years of caring for her had affected us. In our aging years, we had to figure out a plan that worked for us. We wanted to say, "How dare you judge what we have been faithful to do for over forty years." We had been preparing for this difficult move for many years, but no one knew, because no one ever asked.

Hygiene

The hygiene of those we've cared for has posed quite a challenge. Joey never liked baths or showers (but loved the swimming pool), and getting a disoriented, frail, or ill person in and out of a tub or shower is very difficult, especially when they oppose you. The battle becomes physical and emotional!

When Joey was too big for the tub and unable to shower alone, Joe would get in with his bathing suit on and assist Joey in the shower. On some occasions Cindi had to do the same thing. Joey is now able to turn the water on, get in, and get wet. We still assist in cleaning him because he is not thorough. Joey can wash and dry himself but misses a lot of places. He needs a bit of help and generally asks for it. He often asks for help dressing because he'll warm up faster. If he's cooperative, we're happy to help him. If he's not, we let him do it alone! For each, we developed a routine based upon what did and did not work. We used trial and error, but once your loved ones have a routine they like, the job can get easier. The hard part is settling on the routine.

The caregiver for Cindi's dad made sure Dad was sponge bathed when he could no longer be taken to the shower. The caregiver said to all those who helped when she wasn't there, "Always wash him good on the neck and behind the ears, so when people give him a kiss or hug, he always smells good."

- Even though showering routines can be difficult, they become more and more important particularly if the special needs person is in diapers or soiling himself or herself occasionally or often. Until an adult needs to be in diapers, it might prove helpful to put plastic covers on furniture since the smell of urine and feces is very difficult to remove. With none of those familiar "nursing home smells," family and friends will be more inclined to visit.

- Building a home with handicapped accessible bathrooms has been the biggest help in caring for our special needs child, who is approaching adolescence.

- Having a daughter with special needs further complicated teaching her how to care for herself when she had her period. Much of that care was put on us as parents. We learned to do what we didn't think we could.

Illnesses

Sometimes illnesses create other problems. For instance, Cindi's dad had been on a downward spiral with ministrokes coupled at times with various infections. The combination left him very confused and extremely agitated. Add the Alzheimer's diagnosis and our suspicion of Parkinson's, and we had our hands full. He not only needed help transferring from bed to chair, but he began to weaken to the point that everyday functions as well as surprise illnesses became a daily problem. When he was no longer mobile, normal bowel movements were difficult for him; and even though he took stool softeners, he was often constipated. At times his bowels were impacted, and it resulted in his being seriously confused. Each situation complicated another! We often think if one thing is wrong, that should be it; but one thing can trigger another. We remember saying, "It's either one thing; or one thing after another, after another!" Whenever these things happened, we made sure to tell the doctor all of the symptoms even though they might not seem related.

Jobs

We are most grateful that Joey has been able to hold a job. It has not been without incident, however. His anger and inability to get words out clearly and quickly can get the best of him. He has benefited immensely from having a daily routine that includes work. The company he works for is a plumbing manufacturing company, extremely clean, and very family-oriented. They have wonderful business ethics, are rated among the top ten in the city of great companies to work for, and the people are very friendly and attentive to the special needs population.

The job is good for Joey's sense of self-worth and personal satisfaction. His day is like that of a half-day kindergartner. We provide transportation to and from the job each day, totaling ten hours a week and about 13,000 miles a year. Having Joey work is worthwhile for his sake and ours because it allows us a few hours in the day to run errands, attend meetings, and go to work while he is busy and productive. Then he can enjoy his weekend at home like the rest of us watching TV, listening to music, playing computer games, helping with a few chores around the house, and going to church on Sunday. We get a break from each other during the week and enjoy time together on the weekend!

- Our mentally retarded son got a simple job wiping off tables in a fast food restaurant. He has such a sense of purpose and worth having this job!

- Our daughter got a job bagging groceries. You'd think she was the CEO!

Jokes

Jokes are no laughing matter! But seriously, joking can be a release from the pressure of the day-to-day grind of care, frustration, and life for caregivers; however, joking can be awkward for outsiders, who may wonder whether we are insensitive or uncaring or both. Caution on both sides is important and considerate!

A friend once told us how rude we were to let Joey say, "Ha, ha," because he was making fun of others, implying he made fun of her. Apparently he said, "Ha, ha" when he reached an area of seating before she did. What she didn't understand is that our family (in the spirit of fun and competition in getting Joey to the car, up the stairs, into bed, or out the door when he was less than motivated to comply) would tease each other and say "Ha, ha" when we would be the winners getting wherever we wanted him to go. We found it sad that she would even consider our using Joey to make fun of her or anyone else. If anyone has taught their children not to make fun of others, we did. Why would we want to make fun of others and teach our children to do that? This little family silliness was our way of getting Joey moving in a playful way. She was out of line in her thinking and took our joking way too personally. No amount of explanation seemed to satisfy her. In those situations we simply move on and let other people deal with their issues. We have enough issues of our own to deal with.

> *Joking can be a release from the pressure of the day-to-day grind of care, frustration, and life for caregivers...*

Here are several unspoken rules that will help in knowing how to deal with family jokes and joking.

✓ If you *are not* an immediate family member, you don't automatically have the "right" to partake in family jokes. No one will tell you that—it's just true. You might think something is funny and even cute, but the family wants their jokes to remain their own. In fact, they might even feel that you've rudely pushed your way into their private world of caring for the special needs person. An exception: *If* you have invested time and effort to care for that person with a level of understanding that the family has, it might be OK. Watch their expressions. If you sense at all that they don't like you participating in their private joking, either ask them if you've overstepped your bounds or silence yourself. We hope they would be honest with you if you were honest and caring enough to ask.

✓ If you *are* a family member, be careful how you joke around others who might not get the humor. Joking can make others uneasy and unsure how to respond appropriately. If you sense you've pushed them away with your joking, take the time to explain yourself, and then be careful not to exclude them.

✓ Never *make fun* of someone; but always *have fun* with others!

....

- As a caregiver, what bothers me most is seeing people laughing, mimicking, or snickering at the person I care for. They wouldn't appreciate it if they were the one being targeted.

- It's not funny to call people *retards* or other derogatory names.

Lawsuits

We've never been a part of a lawsuit, but some cases belong in court. We've known of several cases where malpractice was certainly the cause of a special needs situation, and we feel that those cases need to be handled in the legal arena. NO amount of money will ever make things "right" or restore a normal life, but some things will be "better" as a result like providing for medical bills, therapies, ongoing mechanical devices, prostheses, chairs, wheelchairs, and other provisions.

One of the difficult things about going through litigation is that you don't stop having to care for the person with the special needs in order to turn your attention to the necessary paper work and phone calls. Volunteering to file papers, answer questions on forms, make phone calls, or help care for the special needs person so that the caregiver can complete the legal work would be very helpful and much appreciated.

The article entitled "Be a Voice for Life: The 2008 Sanctity of Human Life Handbook" by Carrie Gordon Earll mentioned under the **Death** section contains the most complete information on what the Bible says about life, fetal development, alternatives to abortion, end of life, living wills, power of attorney for health care, discussing medical wishes, and making medical decisions for loved ones. It is a complete resource that we keep on hand and refer to often. We suggest contacting Focus on the Family for a copy of it.

Mannerisms

Twitches, jerking, flailing arms, noises, monotone voices, stuttering, unusual sounds and words of people with special needs can make others uncomfortable. Educating others who are willing to learn and understand what makes people with special needs act the way they do helps to eliminate awkward feelings.

Sometimes we don't know why they say, act, and do certain things, and even sharing that with outsiders can be helpful. We don't have all the answers, and that's OK for others to know that!

Some of their mannerisms may show up in behavioral patterns. Joey likes to have his "props" with him when he plays. Every movie, every song has something to go with it. If he watches the *Wizard of Oz*, every character he has must come out to be a part of the show, and sometimes there are pieces of clothing he must put on to be in costume. If a character is missing or costume not available, look out! He will require help finding it before he moves on!

- Our child makes the same noises all day long and it will always be this way. Sometimes listening to the same volume and one sound all day drives me crazy. One day I was so frustrated I wanted to stuff my child's mouth with a sock. I didn't, of course; I knew it would be wrong, but sometimes the frustration level is so high I can't help but think those kinds of things.

Medication and Medical Treatments

This is often an area of hard decisions for people. Knowing that side effects can be worse than the ailment, the choice of medicines and treatment must be carefully considered. Talking to doctors and others who have dealt with what you are dealing with, going to prayer, and using common sense are factors to consider before making a decision. (Emergency situations, of course, must be handled differently and quickly.) If siblings are part of the decision-making team, everyone must know the facts and draw the same conclusion; all must be on the same page, not arguing about the best care for the family member. One person needs to be in charge, so if a "stalemate" occurs, she or he can make the call and stick with it. Others then need to be supportive.

When the doctor, pharmacist, and family all work well together, it is a beautiful thing. Knowing how the patient can take the meds (swallow, chew, orally, IV, or through feeding tube) is important as is being able to read and understand the label. Some questions to ask are:

✓ What is the name of the medicine?

✓ What should I expect it to do? Not do?

✓ Should the meds be taken alone? With water? With food?

✓ What side effects might occur? If they occur, what course of action should I follow? What should I be looking for?

✓ Should the medication be stored in the refrigerator or my medicine cabinet?

✓ What should be done if a dose is missed or forgotten?

✓ What foods/beverages should be avoided with this medicine?

Joey's initial medications for epilepsy did not work well. One medication actually increased the number and length of seizures. Clearly, not every medication works the same on all patients. A new medication was recommended, but because of one of the side effects, we tried other things. Because of the severity of his seizures, we simply had to try the medicine. It was the right medicine, and the dosage worked for him. He hasn't had a seizure in years, but he must have blood tests annually to be sure the side effects haven't damaged his organs. We must be thorough in his dental hygiene since swollen gums can be a side affect of his medication.

All side effects must be considered as well as whether the medicines are doing what they should be doing.

- As a doctor I'd like to tell caregivers not to toy with medications and doses that they give the person they care for. Some medications require weaning; others can be stopped cold turkey. Let the professionals make those determinations for you. You can do more damage than good not knowing how medicines are absorbed and used in the body. Also getting proper med levels can be tough, so give each option a fair chance.

- Don't dismiss or ignore when doctors (or other parents) suggest a medicine that might work.

Others' Opinions

We have something to say right up front: "If others have not walked in our shoes, if others have not been a caretaker for months and years on end, if others have not had their lives disrupted by a life-changing issue (not just a minor surgery or two or an occasional illness), they simply will not understand what we do." OK, we said it. If you are reading this and are the parents or friends of someone who is a caregiver, we hope you will read this section with a very open mind as well as the section entitled **Words: What Others Say**.

Not everyone will be happy with the way we choose to do things, but everyone will have an opinion on it! We have learned, when someone shares an opinion with us about how we are handling things, we listen and pray about it and consider whether a change is needed or dismiss the advice or opinion. When Joey was an infant and even through his growing up, several people close to us flatly denied that anything was wrong. It was very hard for us to deal with that attitude because we were spending many hours at various therapies to try to get Joey to where he needed to be. Any book on child development that we'd read showed

Joey was far behind others his age. Our positive attitude and excitement in seeing him learn, however slowly, was often suppressed by well-meaning others trying to convince us that he was fine. We wanted to shout, "You've got to be kidding! He's over two years old, and we still have to walk behind him because he doesn't know how to fall," or "What are we missing? He's seven years old and is still only saying 'dada,' 'mama,' and 'ahhhh'! Everything is not fine!"

With every ounce of strength we had, we pressed forward, seeking the help Joey needed, enrolling him in a costly private preschool, arranging therapies, CT scans, EEGs, and any other kind of test that could tell us what caused his problem and what, if anything, could "fix" it. These efforts didn't take just a week out of our life—they took years. Finally, when Joey was in his preteen years, the neurologist labeled his condition. The medical term is pachygyria; it is a brain malformation and not heredity. Joey's brain simply had not developed beyond a certain point, and no cure, solution, pill, or remedy could take it away. The doctor wanted to run additional tests, but we simply responded, "If there is no way to fix what is wrong, there will be no further testing." And that was that. Our days on that path were over. We had done all we could, and now we were finished. We continued therapies to improve his abilities and skills, but Joey would have no further tests.

Some people felt we should continue testing; some said we did what was right, and still others thought we had wasted our time and money because nothing was wrong. We wanted all those around us to accept things as they were and emotionally support us from there. We all need to remember that most caregivers are truly concerned about their child/spouse/patient and will do all they can, considering every avenue, remedy, pill, therapy, doctor, aide, test, idea, or nutritional supplement that they feel might help. Coming alongside them to support them is the best response.

While we were speaking at a conference, one couple took a special interest in Joey and his condition, telling us that they would be willing to test him and tell us what vitamin supplements he needed so he wouldn't be "developmentally delayed" anymore. We had been through some different nutritional regimens but figured, "Why not?" and arranged for time with them. The tests they conducted on Joey seemed silly to us, but we watched and waited for their diagnosis. We sat patiently through their testing to hear their final conclusion: "The fillings in his teeth have to come out. That is what has caused his condition. After those come out, we'll get him on a series of supplements that will build him up; and he'll be fine." We almost burst out laughing. None of our children have ever had a filling in their mouths. At that point the testing and meeting were politely concluded because we knew these people were misguided. We sensed it from the beginning but thought we'd try this one more thing. Most of us are always up for "one more thing" if it has any chance at all to work!

We will share more in the section entitled **Words**, but in summary people's opinions should be taken seriously on some occasions and lightly on others. We've had to be careful not to become angry at suggestions or opinions we consider silly. And you'll find plenty of them out there. We try to make sure the looks on our faces do not say, "Your comment is absolutely ridiculous." We've tried not to laugh or respond meanly, but sometimes we have a hard time. We truly desire to keep an open mind, knowing that one silly thing might actually work. And then, what would we have to lose?

- I have two special needs children very close in age. I was trying to figure out how I might be able to get to a church-related class and have my children's needs met when someone said to me, "Just put the kids in the nursery." I graciously smiled and said thank you for the idea, but this person had no clue how much help and attention my two children would need. For someone to meet their needs along with those of a whole group of others their age would be a physical impossibility. I wished this person had first inquired about my children's needs before telling me what to do with them. The individual meant no harm, but I was still frustrated.

- What troubles me most are people who offer unsolicited solutions but aren't willing to be a part of what they think the solution is. The other challenge is for me to be polite.

Outings

Outings, vacations, even just trips to the grocery store can be very challenging. Anyone who has little children knows the effort needed to get them ready to go anywhere! Play out that scene with an adult in a wheelchair or a young adult who doesn't understand why we're getting her or him dressed and undressed, moving and changing them and then doing it all again to come home.

Joe always said he wanted his own business, so he wouldn't have to go to work on Monday mornings. During the early days of our marriage, his day at his dental office was scheduled from 2:00 to 8:00 p.m. When we had children, Joe stayed home with them while I (Cindi) ran errands without children. On occasion I took them with me, but doing grocery shopping and other errands quickly, particularly when Joey was little and could not sit up on his own in the seat of a grocery cart, was truly a luxury.

As Joey grew up, some outings became more difficult instead of easier. He still needed to sit in a stroller for longer walks and when we had to move quickly in crowds. People looked at him as if to say, "What is that big kid doing in a baby stroller or wagon (with a belt to hold him securely in place)?" At some point he graduated to a wheelchair if one could be rented. Wheeling him is easier than having him hanging on our shoulder trying to keep up and then possibly becoming distracted and wandering off. We cannot hurry Joey, so if there is a mission to be accomplished, he must be contained so we can keep moving!

We have always tried to give Joey and our girls a broad range of experiences, and for the most part the experiences have been positive. We've had to keep in mind their abilities and attention spans for the type of experience we wanted to provide for them. We all love music, so we often had outings to the Cleveland Orchestra, the ballet, or plays. Usually Joey can sit politely and has learned the polite "theater" clap. He loves music, but he can become emotionally overwhelmed and excited at musical crescendos and loud unexpected percussion to the point of crying. Practicing at home is helpful, but sometimes Joey's emotion cannot be contained.

We spent the duration of one orchestra concert in the foyer with Joey having one seizure after another. He howled through an OSU football game, and not everyone around us was as polite as the young special education teacher behind us who found Joey's level of understanding of the game quite fascinating. We chose to leave an Indians' game early because some beer partakers a few rows behind us were verbally making their opinions known. Joey didn't agree. He stood up, pointed to them, and said what we were all thinking, "You! Outta—here! You! Get out! Get out!" We can only hope they could see that Joey was special. The incident was simultaneously embarrassing and funny.

Taking either of our parents on outings at different stages of their Alzheimer's was too much. Much like Joey, they needed to be held onto or prodded to keep moving, were easily distracted and more easily annoyed, and often needed to make more trips to the bathroom than one could provide if sitting in a theater or sports facility. We lost count how many times Mom asked to use the bathroom at any given event.

We have come to realize if you don't laugh, you'll cry, and why spend all your time crying!?

- We took my dad to a sporting event in his wheelchair. It's hard to stop and start a wheelchair with a heavy adult in it. People totally ignored us, and I felt many times that I was going to bump into someone because of the momentum of the wheelchair. Sometimes I wanted to! I wanted to say, "Hey, this thing is not easy to push, and I can't just stop on a dime! Help me out here if even just to move out of the way."

- I was in the grocery store with my son, who is autistic. He shouted, cried, and screamed possibly because he was overloaded with too much stimulus for his system and acted out. So many people watched and looked at me as if I were a horrible mother. This is my life and it can't be changed, but I wish it could. I would have liked someone to come up and say, "I can see this is a challenging day. Is there something I could do to help you?" Or if I knew I could grocery shop alone and have someone watch him at home, what a treat that would be!

- Advance plans needs to be made to be sure of wheelchair access wherever I take my son.

- My relative is handicapped, and I am often invited to her "get-togethers." Talk about feeling awkward. Being the one person *not* handicapped gave me a bit of a perspective on what it might feel like to be the only handicapped person in a room.

Paperwork

If you've never been able to visualize eternity, we have two examples we think might help: laundry in most of our households and paperwork for those overseeing the care of someone with special needs.

Keep hard copies of all your records—everything from meetings, doctors appointments, family discussions, therapies, social security, paid bills, insurance, whatever doesn't go as it should to how you are feeling and coping and what people have specifically said during appointments. We have a binder for Joey that begins with his birth records. As soon as we knew he was going to need special assistance, we kept records. As a result, we have information and answers to any questions anyone may have when we attend assessments and meetings.

Every so often we purge the binder of information, retaining only what is pertinent and necessary from the past, keeping future needs in mind should we require a particular item later. The binder is presently about six inches thick. It can look intimidating, especially when we think about how much we've purged over the years. This book travels with us to all meetings and will go with Joey wherever he goes—someday. It truly contains a wealth of information!

- Unless you've cared for someone with special needs—you have NO IDEA the paper work that is involved!

Puberty

Going through puberty with our typically developing teens is problematic, so you can imagine the challenges when those with developmental disabilities can't understand what is happening with their bodies. Both children and young adults, special needs or not, have to deal with the emergence of hormones in their system. One questions we might ask when we get to heaven is, "Okay, God, I'm starting to get a handle on the special needs stuff, but why the hormones?"

- This time of life for my special needs daughter was good in that her allergies subsided, but we traded those for a lifetime of helping her every month caring for her during her period. That is extremely humbling for her and us.

- Our son seemed to get through puberty fairly well, not fondly himself or doing other things that could be difficult to get him to stop; but he experiences "wet dreams." We taught him to change himself when he awakens, and while it only happens once or twice a month, we are thankful he can manage that himself.

- Our daughter is able to understand what menstrual periods are but is unable to care for herself, so we (my husband and I) must take complete care of her. Because she could not transfer herself from her wheelchair to the toilet, we need to help her do that and manage all the necessary "equipment" (pads, wipes). It is not something my husband ever wanted to do, but I am not always available at the moment she has a need. We have developed a good routine, making sure she is clean (having to educate my husband regarding the necessity of cleansing her from front to back so that she doesn't get bladder infections from being wiped improperly. If that happens, then we deal with the pain and frequency of urinating with that type of infection.) My husband, who never understood the difference between a light or heavy day of bleeding, understands very well now and knows what type of pad to use for her. When we have caregivers in our home helping with this issue, they wear plastic gloves, and we always carry them with us when we're traveling even for us to wear when we take care of her. My husband also had to learn things we woman take for granted; for example, you can lift her skirt up to change her. It doesn't have to come off. He was accustomed to caring for her as a little girl with elastic-waist pants that easily pulled down, but it's not the same with a dress or skirt. Once my husband had to take our daughter into a men's room, asking the men to leave for a few minutes because no family rest room was available. Our daughter is embarrassed at times, but she is gracious and thankful for the care she receives. We have put her on the pill, which has reduced her flow, making it lighter and easier for us to deal with.

- When our son was young, he would play with his private parts and excite himself. He would often lean up against people or objects to further stimulate himself. It was horribly embarrassing for us and not a habit we wanted him to continue, but he did not know any different except that it felt good. We talked to a behavior counselor, who helped us to manage his behavior in this area. She gave us ideas how to divert his attention and get him busy doing other things with his hands (read a book, play a game). Training him took time, and we and the teachers had to be very consistent; but now as a young man he controls himself and refrains from doing anything in public.

- Our daughter started her period very early. She does not understand what it's all about, so we have chosen to put her on a pill keeping her from having her period at all. It took some time to "kick in," but that has been very helpful.

- Keeping our daughter well cleansed during her period is important. She knows that keeping clean will help her from having offending odors or possible infections.

- Our daughter is not aware of having a period, but does have the premenstrual discomfort and attitudes! We have found it easiest to keep her in an adult disposable diaper (no overflow accidents with those) instead of sanitary pads. Tampons would be totally out of the question.

- We have had discussions with our doctors about the possibility of a hysterectomy. Much controversy surrounds this option, but I prefer discussing it with someone who has had to care for a young woman with a heavy period seven days a month, not someone who has a daughter who takes care of all her needs herself.

- We carry Wet-Ones for thorough clean up everywhere we go.

Respite Care

Our church has a program that offers parents a night out as other members watch their special needs child. What a blessing! But what about those times where a couple might like to get away for a weekend or a short vacation? That poses other issues that take a lot more time and effort.

- We have some area homes that will take people for respite care. Our situation was disappointing. We felt our child was overmedicated because of the level of activity of her personality. We continue to look for the right options.

- We have told younger families seeking the "perfect" respite care options that no one will do things as well as you, and you need to let the care available be good enough. (We are not talking about abuse or neglect.)

Routine

Routine is such an important factor. A predictable daily schedule is a must for most people with disabilities. Anything out of the ordinary often brings disruption, frustration, and then behavioral issues. Although we cannot always make each day flow with the ease we'd like, trying to keep the "surprises" to a minimum when possible is definitely beneficial.

In television interviews (2008) the mother of Olympic gold medalist Michael Phelps explained the importance of keeping her son (diagnosed as a child with attention deficit hyperactivity disorder or ADHD) on task, on schedule, and in a routine. He tried various sports, but she explained that the fixed lane markers defining his task helped Michael focus more easily than when he was out on a baseball field or doing other sports without well-defined boundaries. She said she kept him on his medication to help him focus during school days but not on weekends and not in the summer. During those times off from medicines, she worked diligently to keep him focused, taught him to stay on task, and made sure he understood his boundaries. Eight gold medals later, we can be impressed with all her efforts!

Safety and Protection

Stairs to fall down, carpets to trip on, fireplace corners to fall into—all these pose safety threats for those who have difficulty walking, picking up their feet, seeing, or maneuvering around a room. Gates, pillows, and moving rugs and carpets are a part of everyday life.

We are the first to admit that we have been overly cautious for a very long time, and still are! Our girls wore helmets for bike riding and weren't allowed to ride horses or go white-water rafting for a long time. Too long! In our defense we didn't consider that the girls were capable of doing things simply because Joey wasn't! The girls were probably shocked that we allowed them to drive and get their licenses on time! They were glad we didn't make them wear helmets while practicing driving!

When dealing with a first child who can't sit up for their first year of life, stuffing pillows in every direction surrounding them so they don't get hurt, the children who follow are sure to suffer the ramifications of that necessary protectiveness. Because Joey's progress was so slow, we never considered that the girls might be passing him up and able to do things that required balance and that were fun! Of course, our goal was to keep all of them safe, but we overdid it. We needed to loosen up a bit and did so over time.

Joey had to be watched carefully on the stairs. His lack of balance and his age hindered his ability. His ability to walk at age ten didn't mean he had the mental ability to think about getting down the stairs. He even had to be helped walking down three steps from one room to another. As a grown man, he can go up and down most stairs fine, but will he remember to turn on a light so he can see? Will he keep one hand free to make it down the stairs while holding the railing? The answer to both is "no" for the most part. And that's part of the issue. He sometimes "thinks" and sometimes the thinking process is not even on his radar screen! Our watchful eye is ever present.

When Joey was in his teens, he was angry about something and decided to run away. Wanting to protect him, we tried to talk him out of it. Then we thought, "What would he actually do if he walked out the door?" From past experiences we knew he would go with anyone who might approach him, so we wanted to be sure we let him think he was running away, but it was under our supervision! So with his coat and a bag with his pajamas out the door he went, satisfied to run away from us. The girls and we were laughing in the house, watching from the front windows, wondering what he would do. He got to the end of the driveway and just stood there. He didn't know what to do. We don't know what he was thinking, but we hoped it was, "Where will I go? How will I care for myself? How will I cook? How will I do my laundry? Will my family come after me? Will they ever visit me? Where am I going?" Ironically, at that very moment of his indecision, a high school friend of ours (a police captain) pulled up to drop off some reunion information. Joey didn't know why our friend was there, and we think he thought he was "busted"! He walked to the door with our friend and sat on the bench inside the house, hanging his head low. Our friend played along with the "runaway" story. Joey was very contrite. Perhaps he thought about all those questions after all, and he's not run away since!

The basic idea is to always protect loved ones with special needs. We are their advocates, and if we don't take care of them, who will? Even though we built our deck right off of our kitchen, enclosed with a gate and latch, surrounded by an eight-foot fence around our whole yard (also with a latch), there were still times he'd take a tumble somewhere else! We can only do the best we can. We want to keep our loved ones out of harm's way but must take whatever opportunities we have to teach them how to keep themselves safe.

- My son is autistic. Because our neighbors would not approve our putting up a fence in our yard, we mostly kept our son in the house to play. The neighbors did not understand that without the fence, our son needed supervision outside every minute. A fence would give me freedom to work in the kitchen while keeping my watchful eye on him. Eventually, the fence was approved, but I was very disappointed that my neighbors were more concerned about how the fence was going to look and whether it was going to devalue their property than what it meant for my son and our family to have freedom in our own yard.

- My husband was in a wheelchair for several years because of dementia. We were not comfortable letting him use things like the microwave and stove even though he had been able to use them before. His inability to remember the sequence of using these appliances made it dangerous for him to be left home alone.

Support Groups

Getting into a support group can be wonderfully helpful, a way of learning more about the challenge you are enduring and finding treatments and a good medical counsel and advice through the years. Finding a support group that meets your needs while you are meeting the needs of others is ideal. It's a great place to meet friends who will go the distance with you and people who truly understand your situation.

It's a great place to meet friends who will go the distance with you and people who truly understand your situation.

We found our family to be our greatest support. An early support group proved to be less than helpful because each person seemed to want to volunteer a worse scenario than the one previously shared. We decided it was too much verbal competition for who needed the most help and who had it "worse." We were better off to be involved with our families. Each person gets a different perspective on support groups, so if one doesn't work out and that is where you think you'll get the most help, then continue to pursue and participate until you find the perfect fit for your situation!

Staring and/or Making Fun

We all try to figure out why someone talks or walks differently. We all do it. It will never change. We all try to guess why someone is in the wheelchair but talks perfectly well, or we wonder why a child is acting oddly when she or he looks perfectly normal. When someone stares at our loved one with a handicap (visible or invisible), we sometimes take it personally.

Our girls really dislike it when people stare at Joey. We've caught them staring back, and if we're truthful, we've wanted to do it, too! When they were little, they stared back to show their protection of him. As adults, I think we want to stare back to show our annoyance. That may be what we want to do, but we mustn't. Scripture teaches us the following: Proverbs 12:16 (NIV), "A fool shows his annoyance at once, but a prudent man overlooks an insult"; and Proverbs 12:16 (God's Word Bible), "When a fool is irritated, he shows it immediately, but a sensitive person hides the insult."

We must never make fun or give someone who is different a hard time for whatever reason. Leviticus 19:14, "You shall not curse a deaf man, nor place a stumbling block before the blind, but you shall revere your God." Deuteronomy 27:18a tells us, "Cursed is he who misleads a blind person on the road."

Sometimes others may be simply trying to figure out the situation. They need to look longer to do that, thus the stare. Joey had to be taken into a public women's restroom (because there was not a family restroom) on one occasion by Aunt Susie, and Kathleen overheard a woman say, "What is that guy doing in a woman's bathroom? Oh, he's retarded." Kathleen was taken by surprise, and cried, feeling bad for Joey.

Another situation occurred when Joey was little. Joe sat with him at the airport looking out the window at airplanes landing. A woman with a little boy about the same age as our son, but who was walking and talking and toddling around, said hello to Joey. Without waiting for Joe to respond for Joey, who could barely walk and did not talk at all yet, she moved her son along saying, "We don't need to be with unfriendly people."

Unfriendly hurtful comments take us by surprise and fortunately tie our tongues! But we can be gracious and smile back if we see others staring. We can ask, "Is there something you'd like to ask that I can help to answer. I know sometimes we have questions we wish we could ask." We've never had the chance to do that because most people quickly look away once our eyes meet. We hope to say this someday. A right heart is needed.

If Joey begins talking to a stranger and we see that he is not being understood, we will "interpret" for him. If the stranger is willing to continue engaging him and us in conversation, we take it from there. If they want to understand more, we'll share; if not, we are polite and let the individual know how much we appreciated their talking with Joey and how much Joey enjoyed that. We want to be the bridge from Joey to the world and hope that others will learn how meaningful it is for them to take an interest—beyond rude and questioning stares to meaningful conversation and caring!

If you are one who wonders what to do when in the presence of someone with a disability or suspected disability, here are a few helpful hints:

✓ Offer your hand to them. If they shake it, great; if they don't (or can't), ask, "How are you?" Because people who can't care for themselves almost always have someone with them, engage the caregiver in conversation first. Ask what you can do to engage the special needs person in conversation. The caregiver will be happy (usually) to teach you and include you! (We realize that it may be very uncomfortable to offer your hand to the special needs person who is drooling or perhaps not very clean because of their inability to swallow properly or their poor eating habits. In that case, gently touch their arm as you say, "Hello." Touch is very important to most and will be appreciated, but realize some may be overly sensitive to any stimulus, so listen with your heart as you try to enter their world.)

✓ If the person is in a wheelchair, stoop down to the level that your eyes will meet theirs. Even if their eyes are looking all over the place, they may be able to see you, hear you, and understand fully what you are saying. As you inquire of the caregiver, they'll invite you to understand more!

✓ Don't yell. If they can hear, you will be rudely loud. If they can't hear, you will still be rudely loud.

✓ Speak at a normal rate until you observe the caregiver. If the individual speaks more slowly, give the person more time to respond than you might think necessary. Take that cue and do the same.

✓ If you're unsure about something (to say or do), ask the caregiver, who will likely be pleasantly surprised at your willingness to learn and welcome your question!

✓ The more you learn—pass it on. Then instead of staring we will start caring!

✓ Don't ask a list of questions and then criticize or make fun.

Teachers, Aides, and School

Whether you have a special needs child or not, teachers and helpers can always be an issue. Thankfully for Joey and us, we had the most wonderful public school experience! For the sake of representing everyone, we'll explore both sides of this coin!

Inclusion and Mainstreaming: To do or not to do!

Let's start by pressing the big red button right away! Every parent of a child with special needs has an opinion of where their child should be, some wanting their child in the regular classroom at all times, others wanting special education only. Is there a happy medium or some middle of the road!? What about the group of teachers who don't want the special needs population in their regular classroom? See how red that button is!?

In our years of volunteering in the schools and having the opportunity to observe many classrooms, teachers, aides, general population, and special education students, we've seen and heard plenty of conversation on both sides of the fence with this issue. In our situation we definitely took the middle of the road! Our son would never have thrived, let alone survived, in a regular classroom all day long. And we would not have expected the teachers to survive the day either! As we worked with the teachers in developing his yearly Individualized Educational Plan (IEP), we made suggestions and shared our thoughts about where we wanted him. Often, we sensed their relief when we neither expected nor wanted Joey in a regular classroom all day. We felt, and they agreed but could not demand it, that Joey would wind up being babysat instead of in a situation where he could learn life and communication skills. The question that we asked and that the teachers were happy to answer was "Where will Joey learn the best, be most productive, and not hinder others in his classroom?" We did not want Joey in a classroom where everyone had to help him in order to fit in. Yes, it's important to have regular education kids helping special needs kids, and we were all for that. But if Joey couldn't do third grade math, why would we want him in that classroom sitting in on the math lesson on multiplication? If he needed to learn simple addition through a special math program, could he learn it with the other kids while they were learning multiplication and division or would his educational needs take away their opportunity to learn? When it was a tough call to make, we would yield to the professionals at those turns in the road! But often, the calls were easy.

Early educational decisions can be easier to make than those in the secondary school years. As the years progress, the chasm between the differences in a child special with needs and the children in regular education widens. Although Joey could do some of what a five-year-old did in kindergarten, he could do very little of what a high school student could do. We knew parents who insisted their child be in a regular high school math program when their child couldn't grasp easy addition. Both parents and teachers would express frustration. Teachers want to teach, not babysit. Parents want their kids to learn but sometimes don't get the picture of what their child is really able or unable to comprehend. We wanted Joey in the special education classroom for things like simple math and simple cooking and life skills. We loved having Joey in an adaptive art, physical education, or music class (elementary) where regular education kids would come in to help. Everyone benefited. It was great. Joey had the opportunity to play simple percussion in the middle school band (he has a sense of rhythm!) alongside kids who really knew what they were doing and make great art projects for his level of interest and ability. He was able to mingle with other kids through these opportunities, broadening his horizons and theirs! But by high school, he could not have been on an even playing field with a regular education student!

We can't tell by looking at a special needs person as to whether or not they can learn normally, and some excel at subjects like history or science and enrollment in regular education should be considered. Some may have great intellectual ability but lack social skills or have behavior issues that keep them from placement in the regular classroom. The bottom line for everyone involved is looking to the best interest of the child in the context of all of the children in the classroom as well as looking to the ability to learn, comprehend, and use the information. Special education teachers have the expertise to help make that decision. Let them guide you. They can be your best allies. Don't deny your child the help she or he needs nor hinder the child from situations that could expand his or her abilities. Be there to help, but be there to help the teachers, too. (See also the section on **Denial** and **Advocate**).

What about the teachers who don't really want special education children in their classroom? Personally, when we knew that to be the case, we'd prefer Joey not be there. If the teacher's heart isn't in it, why push it? We didn't want Joey where he wasn't wanted. But we also knew of teachers who "gave it a try" and wound up really enjoying having this population in their classroom.

When it came to the bus drivers in our district, many wanted the special needs kids in spite of all the in-service meetings they had to attend to learn how to take care of special needs emergencies. They loved spending time with the kids!

Here are a few helpful hints to get you started:

> *When you don't know what to do, ask for help.*

- ✓ Don't deny that your child has special needs.
- ✓ Make your child your priority. Advocate for him or her.
- ✓ Your school system should give you the information on laws every time you have an IEP conference for your child. Be sure to read and understand this information before confronting people about things you want for your child.
- ✓ When expressing what you want, be firm, helpful, kind, and polite.
- ✓ Be realistic about the needs and abilities of your child.
- ✓ Don't always expect to get your own way. Be flexible.
- ✓ When a problem arises, talk to the teacher first. If you get no results, consult the head of the building or district special education department or principal; and if you still get no results, speak to the superintendent. Don't start at the top. You'll burn bridges that way, and they won't like seeing you coming.
- ✓ Don't demand. Ask how you can help and be part of the process and solution. Demanding verses helping are two different approaches. One works.
- ✓ Offer to help in classrooms. (We volunteered to help in art and basic computer skills class, sat in on speech therapies, and so forth. It was a great learning tool for us as well as seeing what our child was learning and who was in his life!)
- ✓ When you don't know what to do, ask for help. Talk to counselors, other teachers and parents who can help you to sort things out and set you in the right direction.
- ✓ Get involved in your child's IEP, special education meetings, committees, and seminars. Far too many parents don't do a thing—unbelievably!

✓ Encourage, thank, and appreciate all the people who work with your child. Send notes to express those feelings. An occasional small, inexpensive gift (e.g., stickers to use in class) that conveys your feelings is a great way to establish yourself as one who is caring and kind. When you need to meet and discuss something that is "difficult," they know you are approachable, logical, and will listen to all the facts.

✓ Remember to also show appreciation to the aides, bus drivers, therapists, and administrators who educate and care for your child. Be the same person to them that you want them to be for your child. They are all important in the care and educational concerns of your child.

- I have a friend who teaches special needs children. When I hear her say how exhausting her day is I understand but am a bit frustrated. She tells me how rough her six-hour school day is, but I'd like her to remember that the parents have the child the other eighteen hours.

- As a teacher, I appreciate parents who are willing to listen to our suggestions and who work with us rather than against us.

- We had a notebook that was sent between home and school to keep up good communication from teacher to parent and vice versa. It reduced phone calls and unnecessary meetings.

Teachable Moments

We shared in the section **Behaviors** (Chapter 6) the time when Kathleen had a clump of hair pulled from her head by an angry little girl with special needs. That was a teachable moment! We could never have given a lecture on how to prepare for such a situation nor how to respond to it nearly as well as when it became a teachable moment and we taught a lesson in the midst of it.

We have also allowed our times with Joey to become teachable moments for our own family and for those in our sphere of influence. If we ignore them, pretend they didn't happen, or act as if they didn't happen the way they really did, we are not learning anything except how to deny reality. We need to know how to treat different situations, and dealing with them as they come our way is the best means to learn. In times of crisis, a teachable moment may occur; however, waiting until life is back to a "normal" state may be necessary.

- I try to use the times people "feel sorry" for me to let them know what a privilege it is to care for my loved one.

- Helping able-bodied people to appreciate their health is something I try to do when they inquire of the special needs person I am caring for.

- One time at a playground, a little girl made some nasty comments about how my son looked. I wanted to smack her. It gave me a glimpse of what others see (my teachable moment) and how I will need to teach my child to deal with it in the future (my child's teachable moment). I know my child will need to be well prepared.

Time Commitments

In general, the subject of time commitment is one with which we take issue! Too many people don't show up when they say they will, don't show good manners with the consideration of a call to indicate a change in plans, or make and break plans because bigger and better things come up. Everyone's time is important, so we want to honor the time we put aside for others by keeping our commitment to them. In our family, we have an added factor in our commitments, and that is making sure Joey is taken care of. We can't pack our day with everything we want to do without checking to be sure someone is on "Joey duty."

We have always been involved with our family, the children's activities, school, ministry, work, speaking, enjoying time with our friends and extended family, keeping up a home and dental practice, and meeting with people in and through all these avenues of life. We have explained that we were able to balance various commitments because we had our parents who helped and now we "divide and conquer" the activities to which we are committed. If one of us has a commitment, the other may need to pick Joey up from work, shower him when he gets home, and then remain at home until the other returns. We have learned as a TEAM to check in with each other to see if we are needed at home or to decide whether we can add something to the day that wasn't planned. It's like being a two-car family with four or five drivers. You can't always have the car!

It's important for us to keep several biblical principles in the forefront of our minds as we commit our time.

Psalm 15:4b, "He swears to his own hurt and does not change." When we say we will commit our time to something or someone, we do not change our mind when something more interesting, more fun, or better comes along. If we must consider a change for any reason, we contact that person and explain the conflict, stating that because we scheduled with them first, they continue to be our first priority. If they see the importance of our changing, it's only with their consent that we would change plans and reschedule with them.

Matthew 5:37a, "But let our statement be, 'Yes, yes' or 'No, no.'" When we say we will do something, short of an emergency, you can count on us. If we say we will call, we will. If we say we will get back with you in a week, we will. When we say we can't do something, the reason is that we want to honor those things to which we are already committed. Sure, on rare occasions we forget to call or write something incorrectly on the calendar and aren't where we said we'd be, but they are rare and people know it because of our track record.

The bottom line is this: Everyone has the same twenty-four hours. Everyone's time is valuable. Everyone is important. Honor it all. Recognize that if I arrange and schedule time with you, doing so affects at least two other people in my family directly. And you can expect that I will do the same for you. At the dental office Joe does not schedule three patients at one time. If your appointment is at 2:00, he will see you at 2:00 unless there is an emergency, and you are informed. Time is important to everyone.

Those caring for individuals who can't care for themselves cut their own personal time in half. We do the same for Joey as we do for ourselves, so we don't have endless hours of free time. We get free time when one of us takes the responsibility of Joey so the other can do what she or he has committed to. Meeting with and engaging in Bible study with others is a top priority and we do so at the expense of exchanging personal time for ourselves for time with others. That is why we and others in our situation are extremely frustrated when people call and make last-minute excuses like, "I can't come for the Bible study because the hamster is out of the cage, and my spouse can't take care of it." It's kind of like "The dog ate my homework" that the teacher hears. It becomes a time commitment as well as a manners issue. Our time is just as valuable as everyone else's!

- I try very hard to commit to only that which I know I can do. Others might not like my infrequent involvement, but I can only do so much while caring for someone full time.

- It's tough to commit to things because my spouse demands so much of my time and attention. I know this season is going to be short, and I will soon be alone, so I try to remember the importance of committing my time to my spouse knowing someday down the road, I'll have more time to do the things that sound good to me right now.

Time Management

Cindi:

Although I'd like to delve into this subject with you, I've already written some materials that have been helpful to us that I share in a Bible study *Balancing the Active Life* and a separate organizational planner called *Get It Together*. Both are listed under *Special Needs Resources* on our website and can be purchased there as well.

We've both worked very hard on managing the time God has given us. To be able to accomplish daily what He places before us, we studied what God's word says about the use of our time and have diligently desired to apply the principles. We have learned to prioritize our individual relationships with God, strengthening our marriage, devoting quality time to each child, spending time with extended family and friends, working hard in business and ministry, learning to rest, and recognizing when time was wasted or taken from us and when we weren't being good stewards of the time God had given us.

Here are a few things we learned that helped us manage our time:

✓ Do the most difficult thing of the day early (or first).

✓ Do the most important thing of the day early (or first).

✓ Do one thing you like, then one thing you don't like as you go about the day.

✓ Find the prime time of the day for you and make the most of it.

✓ Learn to say yes to the best and no to the rest.

✓ Learn who drains us (discourages) and who fills us (encourages)—and be encouraged!

✓ Ask the tough questions and answer them honestly.

✓ Using the gifts and talents we have is what should motivate us. (Example: those who enjoy serving will thrive serving others, but will likely not enjoy being asked to sing in the choir, unless that is their gift. It's the "bloom where you are planted" idea. We will enjoy and accomplish more when using the gifts we've been given.)

✓ If what we choose to do hinders instead of helps our marriage and family, we should not do it.

✓ Determine the motivation behind wanting to say yes.

✓ Put things away as soon as possible to reduce clutter.

✓ Always reevaluate to see whether what you are doing works for you.

✓ Teach others in your home to help. (Show them how, help them do it, watch them do it, release them to do it on their own, and show your appreciation often.)

✓ Reprioritize as often as needed because things change often.

✓ If you can't or don't want to do certain things because care giving is so time consuming, examine your budget and consider hiring someone to clean the home or do yard work.

✓ Dismiss the idea that only you can do it. Be satisfied with the way others help.

....

- Any organizational material I can get my hands on, I use. It may not be written for my specific needs, but I try to adapt it creatively to my needs.

- I have different projects throughout the house that I can work on. When the one I care for needs to be in different places throughout the house, I have something to work on in each place. I'm never at a loss for something to do!

- Our household is very structured and scheduled. We tried to treat our son with special needs like everyone else in the family. We expected him to help with chores, have the same bedtime as the other children, and follow the same rules for behavior.

Toileting and other Personal Issues

Caregivers who care for an adult of the opposite sex often find themselves in the dilemma of where to take her or him to use a public restroom. We are so thankful for the public venues that have public family bathrooms. While Joey can wipe himself after a bowel movement, he is not usually thoroughly clean because he does not have the motor skills to do so. He is able to blow his nose but may not notice or even feel if there is something left in or on his nose. He knows he should wash his hands after each of these personal tasks but almost always forgets. Being able to take him into a place where his needs can be taken care of is a wonderful thing!

- Family bathrooms in public places are the best!

- Changing diapers on an infant or toddler is much different than on an adolescent or adult. Having a place in public to take care of this is wonderful.

- Transferring from a wheelchair to a toilet or into a bath tub is often impossible alone and without some type of apparatus to transfer the person, thus very time consuming and very physically taxing on the one lifting and helping.

- When my father-in-law was dying, he was in diapers. It was very hard to lift him to change him. We were so thankful for nurses who could help us learn how to do it.

Sensory Issues

People with various brain disorders or abnormalities may have sensory issues ranging from an inability to touch some things like certain fabrics to sexually stimulating themselves to banging their heads on the wall constantly. Some sensory issues can be worked through, but some will never change.

When Joey was a toddler, we put him on the grass on his belly. Instantly, he flailed his arms and legs upward like Superman! Then came crying and screaming, which we've not seen Superman to do! To this day, he won't walk barefoot on grass because it's "too much" for him to take in. He won't even walk on the deck unless he has his socks on! When he was a little older and able to open gifts, he would gag just touching the paper. It took years of practicing touching crinkled paper, tearing paper, and opening gifts to eventually master that skill without almost vomiting.

One area that continues to challenge Joey despite many efforts and years of teaching is his reaction to sounds, particularly loud and surprising sounds. When Joey was an infant, loud and unexpected noises startled him and made him cry. Cindi's sneeze is a burst of noise followed by three to thirteen sneezes. When she can, she announces it; otherwise, Joey will be startled and start yelling, hitting, or pinching. At least he doesn't cry anymore.

With most of these types of sensory issues, avoid overreacting. Whenever possible, it's best to redirect the person's attention to stop the misbehavior or reactions.

- Children with autism have so many sensory issues. Loud and sudden noises, quick movements around them, touching certain textures, too vivid colors—these stimulate them in different ways that can initiate behavior problems.

- My friends don't understand, and often say unkind things about how hard it is for my daughter to be with other children because she can't handle their fast movements and loud talking. I'd like for my friends to take her for a few days to see what I have to deal with every single day.

Sleep

Glorious sleep! Not something a caregiver can plan on—ever! Joey finally slept through the night consistently at age five. We did all the things we were taught—from foods to eat or not eat right before bed to massage therapy, music, changing our tone of voice, letting him cry, a warm bath before bed. As an adult, he goes to bed easily and enjoys listening to soft music. That took years. While getting him to bed has settled into a good routine, we never know when he'll get up. Some mornings (4:00 a.m.) we'll hear him getting up to play computer games on the TV. Sometimes he'll come up to our room and say it's time to get up, long before the alarm is due to awaken us! Other times, we'll hear him get up, use the bathroom, and actually go back to bed. OK, that's happened maybe five times, but it's happened!

- Sleep deprivation and fatigue are my biggest enemies. (MANY gave this response.)

- If someone wanted to know what they could do for me… I would say, "Stay overnight with me sometime and take care of my child who will awaken me with seizures at least 6 times a night."

- If I could afford to hire someone to stay overnight so I could sleep just one full night a week, I would do it! I'm sure it would make me into a different (better) person!

Social Life

Any social life a person with special needs has will likely be arranged by the caregiver. In addition to making the calls, the activity often becomes part of their social life, too. Coordinating the effort can be a bit of a challenge.

Joey's social life throughout his school years was good. At each of his schools there were groups of kids who helped organize things for the special needs students. Some schools have Student Council for Exceptional Children, engaged in activities with the special needs classes. How nice it was to see kids "high five" the special needs kids in the hallway, sign up to help with field trips, and spend time with them during the school day! Now that he is out of school, more effort is required to create a social life for him. We know of several people who have put together their own groups for monthly outings. Sometimes we're not available when an activity is planned but a wonderful opportunity for those who can make it. We have enjoyed the times we've been able to join them.

Joey doesn't have much of a social life beyond work unless we provide it for him. We enjoy family occasions like birthdays and Christmas. We have on occasion made arrangements with one particular friend from his work to include him in our plans. Joey doesn't initiate conversation with him on these outings, but days later he'll say how nice it was to spend time with that friend. Including any friend usually means providing transportation as well as planning the time or event.

What about the social life of the caregivers? We'll talk about that in Chapter 11.

Speech: What We Say and How We Say It

Colossians 4:2-6, "Persevere in prayer, with mind awake and thankful heart; and include a prayer for us, that God may give us an opening for preaching, to tell the secret of Christ; that indeed is why I am now in prison. Pray that I may make the secret plain, as it is my duty to do. Behave wisely toward those outside your own number; use the present opportunity to the full. Let your conversation be always gracious, and never insipid; study how best to talk with each person you meet." (New English Bible)

Colossians 3:12-14, "And so, as those who have been chosen of God, holy and beloved, put on a heart of compassion, kindness, humility, gentleness, and patience; bearing with one another, and forgiving each other whoever has a complaint against any one; just as the Lord forgave you, so also should you. And beyond all these things put on love, which is the perfect bond of unity."

There's a lot packed into these verses. We are not talking about speech therapy here. We are talking about how we respond by what we say. (We'll be covering things others say in a moment!) When other people say things that ruffle our feathers, we need to decide ahead of time whether we will *react*, saying things that will be hurtful but get our point across quickly or whether we will *respond* graciously. It's OK to *react* in our mind, but we need to learn to develop the skill of *responding* appropriately. No, it's not easy. After a long day (and after many years) of doing what we do (caring for a special or ill child or caring for a parent in decline), we sometimes just want to say, "WHY DON'T YOU GET IT?" to others who say things that rattle our cages. But unless they enter into our lives, they probably won't get it—ever. And then when they do, we will need to listen to them as if it's the first time we've ever heard of how difficult life can be. And that's why we need to be gracious.

Over all these years of caring for Joey and after the years we helped care for aging parents, we now find ourselves in the midst of others we know well, going through some of what we've experienced. They are seeing their own children bear children with special needs, or their children have gone into a profession teaching those with special needs or are caring for and burying their parents after years of care. What we learned earlier in our lives, our friends and others we know are now experiencing and realizing all that is involved in the care and provision of one with special needs. They now know the exhaustion, demands, time commitment, and financial burdens. This is our opportunity to help them and their children or parents by loving, helping, and praying them through this tough time! Let's not miss this golden opportunity! No matter whether or not people took time to listen or help us, we need to be available to listen and care for them. Second Corinthians 1:3-5 should be our response: "Blessed be the God and Father of our Lord Jesus Christ, the Father of mercies and God of all comfort who comforts us in all our affliction, so that we may be able to comfort those who are in any affliction with the comfort with which we ourselves are comforted by God. For just as the sufferings of Christ are ours in abundance, so also our comfort is abundant through Christ."

In the next section about **Words** we hope to give examples that will help us all respond properly when we are challenged with the issue of what people say or how they say it, when it's clear they don't "get" what we're going through. May we be in God's word daily, praying to Him for us to respond with the right responses, so it will come naturally to us to bless and help others going through what we have experienced. Will we slip? Sure. Will we have regrets over things we say? Sure. But the more we read and pray and saturate our minds and hearts with His word, the easier it will be to respond properly. Doing so doesn't come naturally but will become more a part of us the more we practice it!

Words Others Say and How We Respond

Those closest to us hurt us the most. Maybe it's because they say foolish things in an effort to protect us or because they know us so well, they know what "button" to push to hurt us, or feel the freedom to speak too freely! Those in our outer circles, whom we don't know well, may randomly hurt us for the moment with their actions or words, but we can more easily brush that off because we don't have the same level of closeness to them as to our close friends and family. In this section we will share things that have been said to us. In most, if not all, we don't believe these were ill-intentioned comments. Communication is talking **and** listening, and both need to be done well in order to achieve positive results. These comments were very likely meant for good; however, sometimes we neither say clearly what we desire nor hear accurately! If we are able to recall how we handled each comment, we'll share with transparency. We aren't perfect; we're still in the growing process, both in what we say and how we receive it. We all need to watch what and how we say things because sometimes we aren't even aware of hurting another.

When Joey was initially diagnosed, a patient of Joe's, a fellow Christian, sent us a card having learned of Joey's disabilities. Psalm 27:14 was written in her note, "Wait for the Lord; be strong, and let your heart take courage; Yes, wait for the Lord." It was truly a sweet encouragement with a personal and kind note about how special it was that the Lord placed Joey with us. What was hurtful was that some years later, she made a comment to us about the miscarriage of her grandchild. She said, "I know my daughter is having a hard time going through this miscarriage, but God probably took the baby because it might have had all kinds of problems. That would have meant a lifetime of troubles for them." That comment left us feeling like a child with problems was disposable. Besides, what happened to "wait upon the Lord?" We said nothing.

When we had moved from our first home, a ranch, to a colonial, someone actually asked us, "Did you win a lawsuit to buy this house?" Fortunately, we burst out laughing and said, "No, we saved for it like everyone else." They have not been invited to our third home.

Hosting a Bible study in our home and inviting a couple for dinner before each study, we would have thought they'd have noticed that our seven-year-old Joey couldn't talk. The couple was having a hard time financially and had a small child. The four of us parents and three children had dinner around the table with Joe's parents, who then babysat the children as their ministry and labor of love. Some months into our knowing one another, the young mom said to me (Cindi), "You have everything I want." I was taken by surprise. As I was dropping her off at her tiny apartment, I sensed she probably meant she wanted the material things I had, and knowing a bit more about her marriage, I thought perhaps she also meant that as well. Just a guess. I wasn't angry. I actually felt sorry for her. I felt my response needed to be concise, so I responded instantly, "Well, if you mean **everything**, I guess you'd want a retarded son, too. We would sell everything we own to have a son as healthy as your daughter." She gasped! She had no idea that Joey was retarded. As I briefly shared his disabilities and health issues, she was shocked. She had not even recognized Joey's lack of abilities at the kitchen table. My response to her was meant to show her that the "grass isn't always greener on the other side."

The one you've all been waiting for—"God gave you this child because He knew *you* could handle it. I could never deal with what you are going through." Hold us back! Honestly, we have never felt that we were special in any way. Ever! Not because we have been given Joey or challenges in caring for aging parents, or our own health problems. We don't know of anyone who likes that comment, either! Our response has been, "No, we're not special. God just needed to teach us something we could only learn this way." You might be wondering what could be said to someone who seems to be handling a challenge well. Here are a few options to consider and work from:

✓ "I can't imagine (unless you have a similar situation) what you must do on a daily basis. I appreciate (if you mean it) the heart of compassion I see in you. Your child is blessed to have such care."

✓ "You seem to really have it together, but I imagine your life has many challenges. What do you do for yourself that you really enjoy? What does your child enjoy?"

✓ "Your child is beautiful!" (Yes, you can say that even if the child isn't the kind of beautiful we're accustomed to seeing in magazines because to parents their child is beautiful. We are accustomed to what our child looks like even if he is different in some way. We don't see our child as different from anyone else even if that's hard for others to grasp.) Then qualify your statement with something definite like "Her eyes are so blue!" or "His hair is so dark and curly!" or "WOW! She has such a cute personality!" Although we don't compliment on "looks" over character qualities, we feel this is one area where that is needed. People with special needs won't get puffed up with pride. Your compliment will be endearing!

- At a high school reunion a group of former fellow classmates circled around one gal who was talking about her rather difficult life; some by choice, some by chance. She was saying, "Yeah, you know how it is. Life stinks." She then looked at us and said, "Well, *you* wouldn't know about that." The pregnant pause of silence took everyone including us by surprise. A few in the circle knew our situation (and so did she). We simply said, "Unfortunately, everyone knows life stinks sometimes. Our problems are just different than yours." We didn't need to give examples. She may never come to realize the hurtful impact of her words, but it was no time for us to tell our story. Truthfully, her life had been hard, and we knew that. We felt sorry for her in some ways. In others, we realize, most of life is what you make of it. We've tried to make the best of it, and hope that others will see that. And when/if they do, we want to point them to Jesus.

- When my brother (he was one of two of my siblings with special needs) died, some people said, "You must be so happy."

- I was in a large meeting with my paraplegic friend and we were discussing a deadline that he had missed. One of the managers said, "You're really dragging your feet on this project." The room went completely silent. Apologies followed but the damage was done.

- I literally turned my retirement years upside down to care for my father. After about five years of doing so without much help from anyone else, I really wanted to talk about it with a good friend of mine. I didn't get two sentences out, and she said, "Don't be a martyr." A conversation that I really needed to have was abruptly over, and I never tried to discuss my situation with her again.

Unpleasantness often occurs when people try to make unlikely comparisons. If we share something about Joey (having a temper tantrum at age twenty-five) and others follow up about their normally developing children doing the same thing, but at age two, it doesn't fit! We can't put our six-foot three-inch adult in a time out! It's funny just thinking about it. It's comparing apples to oranges.

A woman shopping near us said this to us about her three-year-old girl, "She talks non-stop! I just can't get her to shut up!" First of all, that wasn't nice to say, and secondly, we would have given anything for Joey to speak at age three! When she looked at Joey, we wonder what her thoughts were about her own little girl.

Relatives, friends, and acquaintances have said this to us and sometimes in front of Joey, "I feel like such a retard!" We can't imagine that they didn't catch themselves. We wished they had apologized. We let it go and don't hold a grudge, but do they honestly think we didn't hear them? Do they honestly not think about Joey when they say that? Or do they think we'll forget they said it? Although we doubt that Joey understands that he is retarded, we still feel it's an unkind remark to make in his presence, as well as an unkind remark to make in general.

None of us is exempt from saying things that hurt or miss the mark of what we're trying to communicate.

Before we share ideas to encourage others verbally, let us humbly admit that we have probably done all of the above sometime in our life. None of us is exempt from saying things that hurt or miss the mark of what we're trying to communicate. Now that we've lived through the hurt of these types of comments, we know better ways to say some things; and after we share ideas below, we will all be accountable to using our words carefully and to not hurt those who can't care for themselves, their caregivers, and their families! May we be the first to practice kind and caring words.

Words That Encourage

Here are a few tips to help us all to communicate in positive ways. The more we practice these ideas, the better we'll be at saying what will encourage instead of discourage others and the easier words of encouragement will roll off our tongues.

For caregivers and people with special needs who are communicative:

✓ Be ready to bless others with a kind word.

✓ Forgive others when they say things that are hurtful or unkind, realizing they most likely did not mean it intentionally. Give them the benefit of the doubt.

✓ Give grace to others who seem uncomfortable or say things that are unusual or unkind. Let's try to make them feel comfortable by including them.

✓ Be transparent in a loving way so others can learn to understand "where" you're at in the challenges of everyday living. Be as positive as you are able because the person who constantly whines and carries on is soon to be tuned out.

✓ Don't keep silent if you are able to lovingly correct an unkind or incorrect statement regarding the person you care for. Make sure your word is a "word in season."

✓ When someone is mean spirited and intentionally insulting or ridiculing a special needs person, you will need discernment whether or not to "call them on it" and risk further problems. It's rare that this type of person will be humbled by their actions. We need to be the one to take the high road. (Proverbs 15:1, "A gentle answer turns away wrath, but a harsh word stirs up anger.")

For those who come in contact with people with special needs in your family, in your friends' families, or out in society:

✓ Be kind. If you don't know what to say, just be kind. Say something nice.

✓ Give the person a blessing. Say, "God bless you." You can't go wrong with that one!

✓ Ask appropriate "non-prying" questions. Observe the situation and the caregiver for clues to how you should act and behave.

✓ If you have a kind thought or word, share it. If you can't say it, send it in a note.

✓ Remember Proverbs 15:23, "A man has joy in an apt answer, and how delightful is a timely word!" Your encouragement might make the difference between a person quitting or moving forward.

- Talk to me about your typical kids because I really do want to hear about it. Please don't forget to ask about my kids—even the one with special needs.

Walk a Mile

If we truly walked a mile in other people's shoes, we'd quickly understand what they have to deal with. We'd become aware of the hot button issues that tick people off, and we'd become sensitive to what makes them tick. We wouldn't have all the answers. We wished we could have had people to talk to when our son was small. The people we reached out to were probably not equipped to mentor or help us. Today, we desire to mentor couples with young children, to listen to their challenges, to cry with them, and to encourage them. Sometimes listening to them is difficult because we relive in our minds the complexities of our early years. The positive outcome is that with the help of the Lord, we make it work; and we can give them hope to make it, too.

Every time we feel as if we want to quit, we remember that we are called to this purpose and that God did not make a mistake. Remember that we can help others who are a few steps behind us. We need to restate our purpose and responsibility, balance relationships, rules, and reality, check our attitudes, and ask for God to help us. He's never failed to keep us on the right track.

- I finally was able to express my fear and disappointment regarding our handicapped child. As a man I cannot easily share my heart, but I did so through my tears, only to hear the cutting words of a sibling: "I thought you were tougher than that." That was the last time I shared anything about my child with that person or anyone else.

Humorous Story

I (Cindi) decided to have some fun with Joey at the license bureau. He needed a state ID after 9-11 because he often travels with us, and had no ID except for a birth certificate. He needed something with a picture. We went into the appropriate lines for getting IDs, but others waiting in line didn't know if he was getting an ID or his license renewed. It was hilarious. People were trying to figure out what he was doing. I had to lead him to the seat, guide him to the place to have his picture taken, and I was talking to him about driving, and where he was going to take me. He joined me in the silly conversation; he's good at make-believe! The workers at our BMV don't tend to smile, let alone laugh; but I think they enjoyed watching the people in line as they watched Joey. What we were doing was not meant to hurt or make fun of Joey, only to be playful. When we got to the car, I asked Joey, "Do you want to drive home?" He laughed and said, "Mom, that's silly!"

In our learning to communicate with Joey, we moved from charades to sign language to telling stories. One day Joey was getting in the shower and said, "This is not too hot, not too cold. Just right—like Goldilocks!"

- I have learned the importance of laughing, having fun, and enjoying my child's unique personality.

- I find it "odd" and humorous that the armed services call to enlist my handicapped brother!

- Our child has missing fingers. Our other child said, "Mommy, is he going to grow more fingers?" I think she thought they were like teeth and would eventually grow in!

- I lead worship and have a person with special needs who prays that I lose my job. (I think *he* wants it.) He has offered to buy one of the worship "teams" so he could be the owner.

Your Story

Look back over all the issues listed. Pick the top five that trouble you most and list them below. Then, tell a story about why each is an "issue" for you. If you're doing this in a group, perhaps choose one of the five to share.

1. _____

_____

_____

_____

2. _____

_____

_____

_____

3. _____

_____

_____

_____

4. _____

_____

_____

_____

5. _____

_____

_____

_____

Perhaps there are issues we did not discuss in this chapter that are issues for you. Write them below and find someone to share it with who will be a good listener.

_____

_____

_____

Share whether you are a caregiver, person needing specialized care, or one who is reading this to learn more. Then share your perspective on some of the things you read about in this chapter. Perhaps tell how you might see things differently as you begin to understand the many things caregivers are required to do to make another's life better.

_____

_____

_____

_____

_____

_____

Finishing Well

All of us have a platform from which to share our faith and from which to serve. Dentist, teacher, parent, caregiver—all have special opportunities. Sometimes we just have to figure out exactly where our niche is. We all want to finish well. We can. But we need to ask ourselves whether we are using the platform we've been given as God intended: for His glory.

One good thing about living day to day in the Lord is that we have the opportunity to be renewed daily. When we feel that we've messed up, we know we need to ask forgiveness of the person we've wronged, and then ask forgiveness from God, showing we understand our limitations and weaknesses. The more we practice doing that, the better individuals we become, and the better the chances we'll have to finish well. People who hold grudges, hold onto bitterness, and stay inside their little shell have a slim chance of making *life* count for something.

OUR STORY

Even as a young couple, our desire, no matter where *life* took us, was to end well. When we were contemplating marriage, our prayer was this: "Lord, we desire to be married, but if You can use us better individually than together, then we will end this relationship. If You can use us better together, then we desire to *go the distance* as a married couple, no matter where You take us. We desire to finish well." Because that was our desire all along, we have always had the mindset that we will continue to pursue that which we believe is from God and keep moving forward. When we were challenged with Joey's retardation, cerebral palsy, seizures, and health issues; our parents' cancer, Alzheimer's and dementia; and people trying to run us off the road, we knew our only choice was to do what He called us to that day and move forward so that at the end of the journey, we would know we finished well.

For any of us to tell whether we're doing a good job is difficult if we choose any one day; but what we've done consistently over the course of a lifetime tells the story of whether or not we've finished well. Our story is not yet completely told; neither is yours. Let's consider where we are and be sure we can finish well when we take that glance back over our lives. After all, we're here to tell you that the last chapters of life come more quickly than we expect!

OTHERS' STORIES

- I daily desire to walk with the Lord and to someday hear Him say, "Well done, my good and faithful servant." The problem is I know I fail sometimes, and that really frustrates me. Sometimes I just want to *get to do* what I *want to do* and that is seldom an option!

- I've not always made the best choices, but when my husband presented me with the choice of putting our child in an institution or living without him, I believe I made the only (and best) choice by letting him leave. My ultimate desire was for him to stay and work at caring for our child together, but that was not what he wanted.

- I often hear "For better or worse" ringing in my ears as I daily care for my husband who can do nothing for himself from his wheelchair.

YOUR STORY

How are you working toward ending well in life as you care for another?

_____

_____

_____

_____

_____

_____

CHAPTER NINE

One Way:
Ministry Opportunities

Kellie and Sandra are roommates at a Christian college, both majoring in special education. They love their course of study, but they most enjoy the children with special needs at their church. They have organized a small class for this group of individuals and have initiated a "Parents' Time Out" once a month. They have a number of volunteers who make the parents and the kids very happy, and many enjoy the blessing of working with these young women.

⋯⋯⋯⋯⋯⋯⋯⋯⋯⋯⋯⋯⋯⋯⋯⋯⋯⋯⋯⋯⋯⋯⋯⋯⋯⋯⋯⋯⋯⋯⋯

Kyle is a single parent of a special needs son. He has difficulty getting to church and enjoying worship because the church offers no programs for his son, who communicates only by making noises. Some parishioners are intolerant of his presence.

⋯⋯⋯⋯⋯⋯⋯⋯⋯⋯⋯⋯⋯⋯⋯⋯⋯⋯⋯⋯⋯⋯⋯⋯⋯⋯⋯⋯⋯⋯⋯

Whitney is an adult, caring for her elderly mother's numerous health and mobility issues. She has become housebound because taking her mom with her on outings is now impossible. Her own need caused her to initiate a ministry of "helps" to others in similar situations. She volunteers to care for the parents of others in similar situations, and in turn other families help her out. They keep a tally of how often each person cares for another and make sure that they are all helping and being helped.

⋯⋯⋯⋯⋯⋯⋯⋯⋯⋯⋯⋯⋯⋯⋯⋯⋯⋯⋯⋯⋯⋯⋯⋯⋯⋯⋯⋯⋯⋯⋯

Paul, an adult with Down syndrome, takes a glass of cold water to his pastor before he goes up to preach every Sunday. This is one of Paul's ministries at the church. He blesses the whole congregation by his act of kindness.

⋯⋯⋯⋯⋯⋯⋯⋯⋯⋯⋯⋯⋯⋯⋯⋯⋯⋯⋯⋯⋯⋯⋯⋯⋯⋯⋯⋯⋯⋯⋯

OUR STORY

Pain and Suffering Have a Purpose

We are often asked why a good God would allow pain and suffering. Pain and suffering always have a purpose: to help others or to be helped by others.

When suffering captures our attention, we question life in such a way that points us to the Creator. Job 2:10 says, "Shall we indeed accept good from God and not accept adversity?" Adversity points our feet in the right direction. We recognize the need for *something or someone* beyond ourselves to help us. We reach out for answers and He supplies Himself.

If we allow ourselves to come to an understanding of suffering in our lives, we know that God will use it to shape us to be more Christlike. Suffering is the instrument God often uses to mold our character. Romans 5:3-5 says, "And not only this but we also exult in our tribulations, knowing that tribulation brings about perseverance, and perseverance, proven character; and proven character, hope; and hope does not disappoint because the love of God has been poured out within our hearts through the Holy Spirit who was given to us."

When we meet people in their pain and suffering, we often make lasting friendships because too few will risk entering into the pain of another. Pain brings us together with others. We learn we need one another and relationships; and then we learn to meet those needs. We can do as Romans 12:15 teaches, "Rejoice with those who rejoice, and weep with those who weep."

We believe that *ministry* is serving, giving, and sacrificing and that it is multifaceted. Facet 1 entails our seeing a need and providing for that need by helping in some way, that is, ministering to others. Facet 2 involves others ministering to us. They must be able to see a need and then act upon that need and provide for it. Facet 3 concerns helping others see how and where they can serve. Some people can be selfish, seeing that their needs are met comfortably or oblivious to others because they remain in their small circle of family and very close friends. Some close their eyes to the needs around them because they really don't want to get *that* involved or worse yet purposely avoid ministry opportunities. We must realize that we are all a small (or big) part of some puzzle. We all need to figure out where we fit in. Maybe we'll be in the border of the puzzle, showing others where they fit; or perhaps we're one of the many pieces in the body of the picture, any of which would indeed be missed if not placed where needed.

Ministry will look different for each of us, but the basic principles are universal. Opportunity for ministry occurs when someone is hurting emotionally, is in physical pain, or has some unmet need—physical, mental, emotional, or spiritual—and someone seeks to meet that need.

We may easily perceive the needs of those with visible disabilities like Down syndrome or someone in a wheelchair; but what about the needs of those with disabilities more difficult to spot? People with hidden disabilities (serious emotional, behavioral, developmental, or neurological disorders with no outwardly apparent symptoms) often find themselves isolated in our churches and in our culture. What response does the family of a child with a hidden disability experience? Will they call attention to their needs when they're unsure of the way they might be received by the church? And who invites these families to their church? If you've ever had such a need and no one has come to your aid, no one has called you, no one has prayed with you—you know what we're talking about. It's hurtful. Key Ministry Foundation (www.keyministry.org) works to resolve this need.

Facet 1 entails ministering to others. We see a need and provide for that need by helping in some way. Some people are "called" to serve; accepting the call is a gift that comes naturally to the one who is gifted. But as Christians we are all compelled to serve when we see need even if service is not our spiritual gift. We can serve through our churches, our first layer of opportunity and provision after the immediate family. In addition, giving, serving, and ministering bring us some of the greatest joys we will experience as Christians. We see how much Jesus did for us; thus we are privileged to serve others in His name. When we serve where we are called, God generally has us extend ourselves beyond the "usual, customary, and reasonable," which is exactly where we find great joy, satisfaction, and fulfillment. Jesus said in John 13:34-35, "A new commandment I give to you, that you love one another, even as I have loved you, that you also love one another. By this all men will know that you are My disciples if you have love for one another." If we want others to know what Christ can do for them, we need to show and tell them what He has done for us. Serving paints the perfect word picture.

In our church bulletin we have a listing of the pastors and ministry leaders, indicating their primary job. At the end of that list appears the notation: "All believers—full-time ministry." Perhaps that means different things to different people, but to us it says we should always be ready to say "yes" to the Lord in whatever way He might be summoning us to serve. Are you ready? Are you ready to serve at work, in church, at home, at the grocery store, helping the child with autism, the neighbor with paralysis, or the family member with Alzheimer's? David Jeremiah has said, "We only reap *if* we sow. We only reap what we sow. We always get *greater than* what we sow. And we always get *after/later* than when we sow."

Those of us already caring for someone with special needs give and serve daily, even moment to moment in many cases. As people watch us doing the tedious and the mundane, they see repeated giving, which shows God as our source of strength, patience, and love. We can be such a great example to point others to the Lord, and when we go outside the circle of the ones for whom we regularly care and offer care to others, people *really* take notice!

We need to remember that although we might have a full plate caring for someone, opportunities to serve others may also arise. Different stages and ages come with varying levels of availability, but we always want to be sure to serve others beyond our own four walls and family. Holding a pity party to let everyone know about our hardship would have been so easy—letting everyone know that we sometimes felt like quitting, putting our giftedness on a shelf and saying we'll serve others when this or that situation is over, making excuses for withholding service. Even in our weakness we can be a blessing, give openly, and be an encouragement. We didn't want life to happen *to* us but *through* us, so we look for people to whom we can *give*. We didn't want to miss opportunities to bless others. As we have faced difficulties, we need to help others through theirs. II Corinthians 1:3-4 says, "Blessed be the God and Father of our Lord Jesus Christ, the Father of mercies and God of all comfort; who comforts us in all our affliction so that we may be able to comfort those who are in any affliction with the comfort with which we ourselves are comforted by God." As we seek the Lord, He shows us needs for which to provide; and when we live biblically, we make choices that others don't always understand. We can give because He has given to us.

How We Can Make This Facet of Ministry Happen

- ✓ **Luke 14:12-14**, "When you give a luncheon or a dinner, do not invite your friends or your brothers or your relatives or rich neighbors, lest they also invite you in return, and repayment come to you. But when you give a reception, invite the poor, the crippled, the lame, the blind, and you will be blessed, since they do not have the means to repay you; for you

> *As we make plans to move out of our comfort zone, we'll see that meeting the needs of others, even in our own needy place, is quite refreshing!*

  will be repaid at the resurrection of the righteous.'" Be hospitable and helpful to those who need it and can't necessarily reciprocate.

- ✓ A relationship with God must be our top priority. Devotions in God's word and times of prayer will keep us spiritually nourished and open our ears to Him. When we are spiritually malnourished, we don't have the reserves from which to give to others.

- ✓ As we make plans to move out of our comfort zone, we'll see that meeting the needs of others, even in our own needy place, is quite refreshing!

✓ We can pray for others as we empty the dishwasher, drive to work, hear sirens, as we shower or mow the lawn. We need to put away our technology and spend time talking to the Lord. We will respond to the needs we're praying for as we hear from Him during those uncluttered moments of quiet.

✓ When we see people sad, crying, or depressed, we can go up to them and ask them if they'd like to talk with us or have us pray with them. Expect sobbing. Expect anger. Expect that they don't know what to say or do. Just pray for them out of love, and they will appreciate it. If you suspect they could hurt themselves or someone else, get help. Take a step in faith and God will show you the next step. That step of friendship can dispel loneliness and show compassion that will give them hope.

✓ A friend and I (Cindi) once coordinated our efforts and helped out a young mom at our church. She had just delivered a newborn by C-section and her back had gone out! I took piles of laundry home to do. My friend, a sweet and merciful gal, would not have wanted to do the laundry but instead gave of her time to talk with this new mom and did some housework. What we learned is that we all have our own areas of giftedness and abilities. I am better if I keep moving, so doing the laundry and having it all done by day's end was right up my alley. But what my friend did was perfect for her. We hoped we met all the needs of this mom because we were doing tasks God created us for!

✓ Visit a nursing home and deliver glasses of water to residents. Our guess is that you'll visit only a few rooms. You'll be delivering more than just a glass of water as you listen to residents' hearts, talk with them, and pray with them. If ever we feel bored, this is one of the first things on our list to do. Having been in almost ten nursing homes with our four parents' various rehabilitations, recoveries, and stays, we saw firsthand the difficulties the aides faced in meeting the never-ending needs of each patient. Someone just providing drinks of water would be helpful to the aides and to the patients.

✓ Look for ways to help. If we hear of a death or tragedy, we know someone has an immediate need, but what about the family member who day after day cares for someone with special needs *and* washes windows *and* does grocery shopping *and* goes to the doctors and tries to keep it all together?

✓ Ask to help. If the person can't give an answer, be observant and see whether you can be creative and come up with a helpful idea. (Can you do some dusting or light housework? Might windows need washing? Does yard work need doing? Can you provide transportation to give the caregiver a break?)

✓ Don't ignore the people facing a particular situation. Acknowledge the death, tragedy, or situation, and be willing to listen. Saying things like "I'm thinking of you," "I care," "This must be very difficult," "I'd be willing to listen" are all great ways of letting someone know we care and are there. We don't have all the answers, and often we have none of the answers. (One time someone asked us something about Joey. After a few minutes of sharing, the person said to her spouse, "They probably don't want to talk about this any longer." Personally, we felt maybe *they* wanted to be done listening. So we said, "Actually, people seldom ask us about Joey, so it's refreshing to think someone would really want to listen." We shared another moment or two and changed the subject. End of conversation.) The ability to listen is such a wonderful gift. It requires only time and attention. Let them tell their story over and over if they need to. Focus on their needs, not yours (but don't act as if you never have a struggle). Romans 12:15, "Rejoice with those who rejoice, and weep with those who weep."

✓ Share a word of encouragement. A card, a note, or a quick phone call can say, "I care" in the midst of a really bad day. A voice that shares hope is so uplifting!

✓ Keep in touch as often as you are able. Once is nice, but repeatedly is usually appreciated. Remember that caring for another can be lonely, stressful, and exhausting. Visits are often restorative. (Don't over do it. If you sense you've overstayed your welcome, give it a few days before you call or stop by the next time. If the caregiver or special needs person seems agitated, ask when would be best to stop by again. If it's two weeks, mark your calendar.)

✓ Focus on Christ's example and love when talking to someone in need.

✓ Give an appropriate hug or touch the individual's hand to be physically present in his or her situation.

✓ Give people time to readjust to life after something challenging occurs. Life is not normal for them, and they have to reach a new normal before they can shift gears from reverse to drive.

✓ An invitation to go out for a cup of coffee or lunch can be such a "pick me up" in the sequence of daily tedious and mundane tasks that happen. Arrange for someone who is able, capable, and willing to stay with the person with special needs while you take the caregiver out for a treat.

✓ Offer to help at a certain time for a specified length of time. When our own time to help is limited, we can at least offer our availability and see whether the person would like our help. We should consider our gifts and talents and make offers accordingly yet be willing leave our comfort zone to help in other ways that might be asked of us (I Peter 4:10).

✓ The key word is "practical." Most people in this situation aren't expecting grand things. They just need to have normal everyday needs met.

✓ Mentor someone younger who is traveling the same road as you and who would be greatly encouraged by what you've been through and experienced.

All of these things are simple ways to make the difference between a person's carrying on or giving up. When in the middle of a major challenge, many of these things are not within the ability of the caregiver even to think about.

Facet 2 involves people ministering to us. They have to be able to see a need and then act upon that need and provide for it. When we are on the receiving end, we have to be willing receivers.

When I (Cindi) was pregnant with Joey, I had planned a freezer full of meals for Joe and myself because I wanted to be prepared for whatever curves mother-hood might throw me. Fortunately, I had lots of meals, which came in handy recovering from a C-section. Unfortunately, a few people offered to bring a meal, but I did not accept their offers because I already had so many (which I explained). Looking back, I feel I took a blessing away from them as well as taking a blessing away from myself. If I were to do that over again and knowing how much I personally enjoy being able to give a meal to others, I would gra-ciously accept the meal offered and save the ones I had made for "one of those days," which we all wind up having! Live and learn.

A short time later when a kind single man named Tom, who is our age, offered to watch Joey in the church toddler class so we could attend church together (we had to divide and conquer for years), we said yes to him. Did he notice we were always ten minutes late for church or absent? Did he see how we struggled to keep Joey quiet in our little church because we had nowhere for him to go and participate? Did he instinctively recognize that Joey would frustrate and exhaust the Sunday School teacher because he couldn't handle all the stimulus of noise and commotion and would need far more help and attention than any teacher could give, thus adding pressure to that teacher? Somehow this kind man determined from what he observed that we needed help if we were to learn or participate. In those early years Joey could not handle the noise or the fast movement of the other children—it was all too much for. We don't remember how long Tom helped, but it was a blessing to know his compassionate heart.

Families struggle with these issues on a daily basis and long to be a part of church and community but often simply can't. The struggle to get out the door and the expectation that they will participate are beyond the realm of possibility.

Many outsiders don't see that struggle because it's seldom expressed. When it is articulated, the possible solutions are often very unrealistic. Outsiders seldom understand the struggles unless they have shared the experience. Except for family in the early years, few took the time to help us and even fewer understood just how difficult life could be.

When Joey was in elementary school, we were asked to teach the class for children with special needs at our church. Most times we're asked to do things, we pray about it and make a decision, but this time we knew our response had to be a quick and resounding "NO." Because we were in the midst of many medical issues, uncontrolled seizures, and behavioral issues, we needed all we had just to deal with Joey. We needed time off; we could not afford the time to plan lessons and spend more time with a classroom of the youngsters with special needs we'd be in charge of handling. We needed others to minister to us and others like us.

Consider the Samaritan man, so quick to respond to the badly beaten man he found on the road (Luke 10:30-35). What hardships must he have experienced to motivate him to meet so immediately the need of a man he didn't even know? Probably plenty. Those who initially heard this story despised people from Samaria. That's why this story is so poignant. The man who made a snap decision to get involved could very likely have been spit at by the injured man.

How much did it mean to him to be interrupted in his daily plans and allow for this divine appointment? Just when we think we have our plans set for the day, Jesus inserts an intrusion or interruption into our schedule. How will we respond? Will we have compassion or dismiss the idea, thinking someone else can meet the need? Will we stop to care or move on? Do we allow Him to change our course? "Trust in the Lord with all you heart, and do not lean on your own understanding. In all yours ways acknowledge Him, and He will make your paths straight" (Proverbs 3:5-6).

This Good Samaritan chose to help (Luke 10:25-37). Allowing the interruption and accepting his assignment, he also seems to have realized his limitations, hiring others to help in the care of this injured man. He went about his business yet did not neglect following up on this man. He ministered in the midst of life, seeing the interruption as a way to serve, as an opportunity to show the Lord's love. Perhaps he saw it as a divine appointment.

How We Can Make This Facet of Ministry Happen

✓ (Cindi) I lovingly call Marvel, a woman at our church, the "Lasagna Lady." The day before Joe's dad passed away, Marvel showed up at our door with a huge pan of lasagna and, if I remember correctly, her famous "cinnamon sticky buns." Because we had learned (the hard way) not to take a blessing from someone who had offered meals after Joey's birth, we gratefully welcomed the meal and thanked her. After Marvel left I said to Joe: "That was so nice of Marvel, but I feel guilty because we don't really *need* a meal right now. We'll still enjoy it, but I wonder whether someone else should have received it!" In the middle of that very night, however, Joe's mom called to say his dad had gone to be with the Lord. With all the preparations that needed to take place immediately, the meal we questioned was perfectly timed!

✓ The day after Cindi's father's death, which was just five days after her mom's death, a woman we barely knew from church, a restaurant owner, showed up at our door with three huge tins of various foods. She had heard of their deaths, looked up our address in the church directory, and delivered food enough for the next few days. Again, a perfectly timed blessing from someone we barely knew but whose kindness will never be forgotten.

✓ A male friend plays "Santa" for little children—and Joey. He is *so* excited to see Santa, and watching the two of them is precious. We've even had family stay later on Christmas Eve to watch the interaction from the balcony. Santa has brought his own family members to watch, too. Joey's innocence will allow him to be a child forever. No matter who watches, Joey is concentrating only on Santa! The visit takes on such a special tone, and we're not sure who is most blessed.

✓ We have several friends whose children are grown and gone and have offered to help with Joey's work transportation when we speak out of town. They consider it their way of helping our ministry. Because of what they are willing to do, we feel they are a very important part of our ministry to others.

✓ Some personal friends take a young man with special needs from our church each summer to a baseball game downtown.

✓ A neighbor has recently begun helping in the special needs ministry and has become quite attached to the group! He started helping in Sunday school and branched out to help at "Parents' Night Out."

✓ A relative offered to come and help with our friends' special needs children while they prepared their home for a move. They could not have done it without her.

✓ Be honest and transparent about our needs if we are able. We need to be able to share our heart. Sometimes people just need to know that we *have* a need. Others might assume extended family members are stepping in to help or someone else in the church is helping. Verbalizing what is needed is helpful.

✓ Don't let pride get in the way. Be humble, be gracious, and thank the person who is willing to help. Those who are more "giving" find accepting help somewhat difficult because they'd rather be giving than receiving.

✓ Someone from church sent our special needs son a note saying, "It was a pleasure to get to meet you personally. I appreciate your sharing your dad's time to give me direction. I really felt welcomed when you allowed me to be a part of your evening prayer time." He printed his message further showing he thought out that cursive might have been too difficult for Joey to read.

✓ Recently, we had a water problem. We were scheduled to meet some friends for dinner, and we simply couldn't leave the situation the way it was and had to cancel our plans. A bit later, our friends who have two children with special needs had planned to stop over for a visit. We had to tell them honestly that we couldn't have them over because we had spent several hours dealing with the water clean up and were exhausted. With all they have to deal with, they said, "Would you like us just to stop and help you clean?" We couldn't believe it. We knew their day consists of feeding tubes, changing, and caring for these two children, and we were just amazed. No one would miss the love of the Lord shining through this couple! They went way beyond their needs and were thinking of someone else! By the time they called, the work was done, but we so appreciated their asking whether they could help us.

✓ Offer to do something that is hard for someone else—shoveling a driveway, planting the garden in summer, cutting grass, helping clean house.

✓ Put actions behind your words, and instead of asking, "What can I do?" show up with a meal or for a visit.

Facet 3 concerns helping others see how and where they can serve. Some people choose not to serve because they like to be comfortable and don't want their routine disrupted. Some are selfish and figure someone else will do it. Some are afraid to care or help because they know doing so will cost them time and energy; they realize that they might actually have to become involved, and they recognize how difficult involvement would be. Some don't have a clue how to serve because they never had anyone serve as an example to them. Everyone must learn that we are all here to serve, not to be served. *When possible* we must move from observing and receiving to participating and serving.

Our church provides a Friendship Class (organized by our church through Friendship Ministries) for two different age groups. Group members value each individual for who they are and how they were created, helping them discover their gifts and strengths. They create an environment of love and understanding with opportunities to learn and grow in God's word. They also have a wonderful ministry called "Parents' Night Out" for those who have children with special needs. Because we have had the great fortune (to this point) of having some-one to watch Joey when we needed to go out, we have not been a part of this ministry. Those who have taken part have truly benefited. Those who have been asked to serve have said caring for those with special needs is one the greatest blessings they personally receive and they are always appreciated by the parents because for some of them, this is their *only* time away.

Mike Buus, president of D.O.O.R. (Deaf Opportunity Outreach) International said in an article entitled "Signs to Another World" in the July 2008 issue of *Focus on the Family*: "Less than 1% of deaf people in the Western world are in an evangelical church on Sunday morning. Outside the Western world, less than a quarter of 1% have been presented with the Gospel in a way they can un-derstand, [and] 90% of parents with deaf children in the US and Canada do not learn enough sign language to have a conversation with their child. Deafness is not much about disability; it's almost all about communication." In this case, serv-ing must begin in families; and the more opportunities we can provide within our churches, the better.

> *"Less than 1% of deaf people in the Western world are in an evangelical church on Sunday morning... [and] 90% of parents with deaf children in the US and Canada do not learn enough sign language to have a conversation with their child."*

But let us share with you a reality. When someone needs total care, no matter how much time the primary caregiver gets away from the situation, no matter how much she or he appreciates the help and chance to be removed temporarily from the responsibilities, it never is enough. We know that sounds unapprecia-tive, cold, and rude. But it is true. This is so because when they are out, they are thinking, "I hope everything is OK. I hope they remember to give the meds. I hope they remember the breathing treatment is at 4:00 for twenty minutes." So when the caregiver returns to the situation, it's as if they never left. Picking up where the helper left off, the caregiver may not have help again for another two weeks or longer.

Let us share some ways people have entered our lives and the lives of some oth-ers we know. We've figuratively entered their names under the heading "You'll Never Be Forgotten." Perhaps as you read the list below, you will realize that any of us can do some, if not all, of these things to learn how simple serving others really is.

✓ A friend called one day after having heard one of our "Joey stories". She saw things differently from how she had previously, and offered several options to us, one of which was making dinner at their place and then coming to our home to have a nice evening together. She and her husband recognized how challenging it was for us to pick up and go out, so they made a meal at their home, came to our house to serve the meal, and enjoyed dessert over a game of scrabble. It was such a special treat!

✓ Think about how *you* like to be treated and treat everyone else that way.

✓ Invite people with handicaps, disabilities, and special needs to join you in something you are doing. Think through what your plans are before you ask them to do something they can't participate in. If you're not sure, ask them what *they* would enjoy doing.

How We Can Make This Facet of Ministry Happen

✓ We've heard it said that "we can go a lot further together than we can go alone." With that thought in mind, helping others will give them the extra push, the incentive, the encouragement to continue.

✓ Rise to the occasion. It might not be easy—it often isn't—but taking the opportunity to help in some way will bless the helper beyond measure.

✓ Rely on God. What you lack He will supply. What you fear He will help you through. Show up and He'll work through you.

✓ Helping another will show love in action. I John 3:18 says, "Little children, let us not love with word or with tongue but in deed and truth."

✓ Do what you can with what you have.

✓ Pray about what opportunities might be available to you.

✓ Don't wait to do what God is prompting you to do. Ecclesiastes 11:4, "He who watches the wind will not sow and he who looks at the clouds will not reap." If we wait for perfect conditions, we won't do what we should.

✓ Consider what you might do as a ministry instead of a task. II Corinthians 9:6-8, "Now this I say, he who sow sparingly shall also reap sparingly; and he who sows bountifully shall also reap bountifully. Let each one do just as he has purposed in his heart; not grudgingly or under compulsion; for God love a cheerful giver."

✓ Ask God to "enlarge [your] understanding" of what another is experiencing.

Stop Making Excuses

Those of us caring for others sometimes want to opt out of life. When we're in a situation for the long haul, excuses can come easily. Of course, at different times and in different circumstances, excuses will be valid. When a loved one is in the hospital, we will not likely make a meal for the neighbor in need of one. It's all we can do to get one on the table for our own family unless someone provides it. But we have found that, in times of disruption, frustration, change, and challenge, we've had to stop making excuses and ask, "What would you have me to do, Lord?"

"I'm too busy," "I don't have time," "I'm too tired," "I have no one to help me"—we may say these things as our way of holding our "issue" over the heads of others in an attempt to get sympathy. That attitude gets old fast, yet we have seen the opposite to be true most of the time. Most people who have the responsibility of caring for those who can't care for themselves are the ones who do more for others than those who have no one but themselves to worry about.

So many people talk about purposelessness, boredom, having nothing to do, or not having the desire do anything and then wondering why they feel hopeless. We heard Ravi Zaccharias say in a message, "Hopelessness does not come from growing weary of pain and suffering. Hopelessness comes from growing weary of pleasure." When we help and bless others, we are blessed. Proverbs 11:25 says, "A generous man will be prosperous, and he who waters will himself be watered."

When we stand next to Joey in church and watch him freely worship, hands toward heaven, eyes closed and unaware of who's watching him, we realize that he may have a greater impact in ministry than we can even imagine. He makes no excuses for his freedom in worship, and although he can't share the gospel, he's sharing it through his worship. He's not worried about how long he will sit there, nor does he judge others who haven't talked to him or helped him. His intentions seem pure and simple. Many have told us what a blessing it is to watch him, and we agree. I guess we all have a lesson to learn. If he is able to share his faith in his actions and limited abilities, how might we?

Missed Opportunity

Let's return for a moment to an incident we shared earlier. In a meeting with several other Christians, we shared the hardships, exhaustion, and frustration we experienced; baring our souls was difficult because over the years, we had not shared much regarding our tough times and challenges with Joey, let alone everything else with extended family. We didn't want friends to tire of listening to the same old struggles, which were ours day after day after day for so many years. We didn't want to sound like a broken record. When our friends closed our time together with a prayer, we realized this was the first time anyone had stopped to pray *with* us. Many said they were praying *for* us, but this was the first time anyone prayed *with* us. After our friends briefly prayed, they quickly got up and left. We realized that just when *real* ministry could begin they walked out, closing the door behind them. We felt abandoned and awkward, but did they also feel awkward? Did they feel it was best to leave us alone with our sorrows and challenges? Did they wonder what to do? Did they talk out in the hall or go on their way, thinking they had done their Christian duty? Did they not want to get involved? Did they not care? Before you think we're being negative toward them, let us tell you what went through our minds.

We sat stunned and numb. We felt as if they had missed a golden opportunity to meet our needs. They might have asked if we wanted to talk further, if we needed any help, or if they could get assistance for us during this stressful time. Our meeting hadn't been convened to discuss our trials, so we came expecting nothing; but we were wounded to be left weeping and in shock when they moved on as if they were checking the meeting off their list.

As time cleared the fog we were in, we asked ourselves whether we had been all we could be to others when *they* needed an ear or help during a trying time. Were we sensitive to the needs of others? Had we taken that extra step? Do we say to each other, "That's too bad about 'so and so' and then go about our business?" Or do we care enough to *get involved*? It's foolish to think that anyone can fill another's every need. But we *must* seek the Lord and discern where and how He would ask us to help others when we so visibly see the need.

The bottom line? Will we be moved to action? We can't wait for hurting people to ask. They may not have the energy to do so; actually they may not even *know* what they need. And if they've been in a tough place for a long while, they're getting from point A to point B one baby step at a time; and they don't even know whether they'll make it that far. We have to go for it.

If you've been through a tough time, think about what would have helped get you through it—a note, a call, a meal, a prayer, taking the kids for a day, an errand taken care of, an ear to listen. Believe us! The hurting person or couple on the receiving end of any of these will be forever grateful. You may relieve some pressure that was about to make them burst!

OTHERS' STORIES

- My advice to people visiting who are near death would be to come and listen, not lecture, visit with a heart to hear what the dying or grieving person wants to say, and if he or she has nothing to say, sit quietly, or ask if he or she would like to hear scripture read or quiet music.

- When I was stuck at home caring for a parent and small children, I cherished notes of encouragement. I know we live at a time when sending an e-mail is easier and stamps are getting more expensive, but those handwritten notes brought me joy over and over again as I reread them throughout my day.

- I sent a note on nice stationery to someone I do business with to encourage her. The note was posted on a wall near her workstation. An email message likely would have been deleted. She lets me know that note keeps her going. I had no idea it meant so much to her. I now try to write notes for others when the situation calls for them.

- As one who has a disability, I enjoy singing the chorus to the song "Use Me" by Dewitt Jones: "If You can use anything, Lord, You can use me. If You can use anything, Lord, You can use me. Take my hands, Lord, and my feet. Touch my heart, Lord. Speak through me. If You can use anything Lord, you can use me." However I can be used by Him, I am willing.

- I feel hurt when people from church are insensitive to our feelings and concerns, for example, when others quote a scripture to put a Band-Aid of disregard on what we deal with everyday.

- Through all our trials we continued to serve God 110%. You'd think the Christian family would be supportive and encouraging, but after living this experience for over twenty-nine years, I can't honestly say I feel that's true. We obtain so much more support from local people who understand special needs. Churches need to be more responsive to those less fortunate and extend their support. Their failure to do so seems to be the invisible handicap, like my son, who appears normal physically but has the mentality of a four-year-old, gets ignored, and doesn't fit in anywhere. There are ads for respite outlets for seniors and normal children, but getting assistance for my son is very expensive and difficult. Although we have raised our son in a Christian atmosphere, it has been that very circle that has embarrassed us, shunned us, and even hurt us through the years. I want my son to maintain his Christian roots and beliefs (however limited that might be for his mentality), but finding a source of strength after we are gone might be impossible. I've made subtle comments hoping to get help. No responses.

- We were fortunate to have support from our church. Our pastor's wife and another friend took our daughter to her afternoon school once a week until she was old enough for public school (because I worked). When she lived at home, we were grateful when someone offered to take her for even an hour or two to give us a break. We felt doubly blessed if someone offered without "being asked."

- Several people surveyed mentioned that their special needs loved ones served in the church as greeters and communion servers. All God's children have work to do regardless of their age or ability.

- I work in a special needs ministry, and I pray that people will pray and think outside the box when it comes to sharing the love of Christ with people with disabilities. I think people immediately assume because they do not have training, they can't help or talk to people with disabilities. A heart for Jesus is all it takes. Imagine for a moment how it feels when someone looks directly at you without acknowledging you. Because of their disability some folks face this type of reaction from people daily. What a terribly lonely feeling that must be! Is that what Jesus would have us do?

- Some people treat animals better than those with special needs. What does that say?

- How can I authentically encourage the caregiver in my friend's life in a meaningful and long-lasting, consistent way? [Authors' note: Be sure to read this book, and thank you so much for asking with such sincerity!]

- When our child was going to have a second surgery, his cousin (age ten) told his parents that if he could take his cousin's place, he would do it!)

- During the acute times of our son's illness, we were so blessed by people who love us in practical ways, bringing meals, providing childcare, mowing the lawn, shoveling snow, praying, and encouraging us. At that time we were too "spent" even to be able to focus enough to pray anything more than, "Lord, please help." We so depended on, and appreciated people praying for us during those times.

- I hope someday to minister to others, but right now I'm pretty involved with our family and several special needs challenges.

- Practice forgiving others. Do it often and make it ongoing.

- As a parent of a special needs child, I can't really minister besides what I do at home. I can pray for and write letters of encouragement to those incarcerated or unable to leave home. Perhaps someday I will be able to branch out of my home.

- Honestly, I haven't offered to help others because I'm too selfish about my time.

- My twin sister, who suffered severe brain damage from an accident, has been the person who has most greatly influenced me.

- You can serve only if you make the time to do so.

- I am not afraid to ask for help and have had friends and family fold laundry or watch one of the children; some have cried with me. I have great friends.

- It seems the people who have the closest relationships with God have more of a heart to help others than those who do not.

- I spend weeks at a time at my mother's house helping her with all her health issues. We live many miles from one another, so the travel, the task, etc. is not easy. Medicines have made her tired and weak, so I need to be there as often as possible. I hope I am encouraging others to really keep a watchful eye on what's happening with their own parents when that time comes for them to travel this road.

- We have dear friends who have said to us, "If you would allow us, we'd like to be the ones who would care for your child(ren) with special needs should anything happen to the both of you. I would be our privilege."

- I wish people would be more interested in how they can help than seeking information on how our challenge happened, why it happened, and when and where it happened.

YOUR STORY

Consider what things you do for yourself that pursue "self-interest, self-riches, self-generosity." How much of it lasts for eternity?

_____

_____

_____

Now consider what way you can serve, give of yourself, and help someone who has need.

_____

_____

_____

Do you think you can teach more with your life situation than with your lips? Explain.

_____

_____

_____

Are you all that you say you are (caring, compassionate, helpful, kind)? Are you willing to prove what you say in action rather than in word?

_____

_____

Do you invest intentionally in ministry if you are able-minded and able-bodied? Where?

_____

_____

Do you allow others to minister to you if you are having trouble or are caring for one who has special needs?

_____

_____

Ask yourself, "How can I bless _____ today?" Take a few moments and write down some ways you feel you can help.

_____

_____

Who needs to hear from you? Will you write, call, or visit?

_____

_____

What do you want your legacy to be? Talk it out, and then walk it out.

_____

_____

CHAPTER TEN

Merging Traffic:
Relying on Relationships

Carissa, the mother of a teenager with special needs, is never happy with what the teachers and aides do. She criticizes how they do things, questions why they do things, and seldom has a kind word for those working with her daughter. She wonders why teachers, aides, and administrators avoid her.

Josh, who has cerebral palsy, is able to take public transportation around town and to and from work on his own. He lives in a government-funded housing facility by himself. In speech that is difficult to understand he says, "I'd rather live alone. When I've had roommates, they sometimes don't talk to me because they can't talk, and that's no company for me at all."

At age sixteen Carolyn helps care for her mom, who has multiple sclerosis. She manages her mom's finances, cooks, makes plans for daily nursing care in their home, and takes her mom to doctors' offices when needed. Everyone loves Carolyn and her mom because they both have great attitudes. Helping beyond the limits of their job description, all the workers say that they want to accompany Carolyn and her mother as they travel the long road and help them overcome the many challenges they are sure to face along the way.

OUR STORY

Caring for others is arguably one of the hardest tasks any of us will ever be asked or called to do. Others will never know the difficulties involved until they face it themselves. Perhaps one of the things we regret most is not speaking up more when we really needed help. Sometimes we needed someone just to listen or someone to take a child for a few hours. We should have asked, but often we didn't. When someone offered, we seldom turned down the help; but asking was difficult for us.

Was it pride, embarrassment, fear of rejection, or utter exhaustion that kept us from making our needs known? We're not sure, but none of these are good excuses. As the Lord guided us through our own mistakes and failings, He helped us to see how we needed to handle the relationships in our life in a way that we could all experience win–win situations.

We learn from the paralytic man in scripture: Luke 5:18-19, "And behold, some men were carrying on a bed a man who was paralyzed; and they were trying to bring him in and to set him down in front of Him [Jesus]. And not finding any way to bring him in because of the crowd, they went up on the roof and let him down through the tiles with his stretcher, right in the center, in front of Jesus." At the end of this story Jesus saw *their* faith and healed the paralytic. Then the man stood up and walked out carrying his mat and glorifying God.

At times we felt we were caught in a relationship drought, and at other times we felt great blessing when others embraced us with caring support. Having family and friends to support us, just like those of the paralytic, is very important. He could go nowhere without the help of his friends, dependent upon those who served. We can learn a lesson in working together, trust, love, dependence, and appreciation; and it goes both ways.

How Do You Do It?

A question we silently asked of those whose lives showed dedication and devotion to someone with special needs is "How *do* you do it?" How *do* they deal with the responsibility? How *do* they do it with a smile on their face? How *do* they do it day after day after day? How *do* they deal with the drooling and the diapers and the difficulties they didn't ask for? Perhaps we should have asked out loud and learned some of the lessons we had to figure out the hard way!

We didn't know how to respond to those with special needs as we do now. And we're still learning. Having Joey has opened our hearts and home to a world we didn't know existed. It was like snorkeling for the first time! The new adventure took our breath away. The new view, the depth, the scenery all looked so different from what we were accustomed to, and we had nothing to grab onto for support. The more we swam in the water, looked around, and grew familiar with the surrounding, the more comfortable we became. Such is all of life when change and the unknown occur!

So how do we do it? Just as we need common food staples in our pantries to be able to prepare dinners daily, we needed to incorporate into our lives a few staples that we need day after day. Of greatest importance is the need to have a daily time in the Word of God as well as prayer to give us the strength we need. It's the fuel that gets us going and keeps us going. In the Word we find direction

(Matthew 6:33), counsel (James 1:5), and a place to cast our burdens (Matthew 11:28-30). We desire our relationship with God to be what defines us—not religion, not our marriage, job, ministries, or relationships with our children, friends, and family—yet we fully acknowledge that we need strength from each of those to make it in this journey. With God all things are possible (Matthew 19:26). We know we can't get from others what only Jesus can provide: peace, contentment, and satisfaction. We are thankful to Him for providing those very things that form the basis for how we do it.

Help! I Need Somebody! What About Needing Others?

Giant redwoods have very shallow root systems, which would seem to indicate that they could not grow that tall without being blown over by strong rain and wind. They are able to grow to 150 to 300 feet tall because the shallow root system of each tree entangles with neighboring trees for stability and strength. They don't stand alone.

If any of us tried to stand alone through the storms of life without the strength of others who entangle their lives in ours as we entangle ours in theirs, we don't think we could stand either. We need others to help us make it through life. I Corinthians 12:12-27 provides a beautiful example of how we need each part of our physical bodies to function properly. Verses 25-27 relate to all believers in the body of Christ: "there should be no division in the body; [instead] the members should have the same care for one another. And if one member suffers, all the members suffer with it; if one member is honored, all the members rejoice with it. Now you are Christ's body and individually members of it." We need to be available to *help* carry one another's burdens (Galatians 6:2) and to "weep with those who weep and rejoice with those who rejoice" (Romans 12:15).

So at a time when a doctor tells a young couple that their own family and close friends might avoid them because they must care for someone with special needs, how do we establish relationships that have depth and meaning without making them feel the sense of obligation that we ourselves must carry?

We Need One Another

We *need* one another in many ways: practically, spiritually, emotionally and physically. We can't do everything ourselves. We can try, but we will fail. We know because we've been there. When the tasks we need to perform take longer than the day we've been given, we need to ask for help. Let's see how to go about doing so!

Paul gives us a picture of the way he tried to include others in his journey to carry the important message of the gospel to others. II Timothy 4:9-11, 16-17

319

says, "Make every effort to come to me soon; for Demas, having loved this present world, has deserted me and gone to Thessalonica; Crescens has gone to Galatia, Titus to Dalmatia. Only Luke is with me. Pick up Mark and bring him with you, for he is useful to me for service. At my first defense no one supported me, but all deserted me; may it not be counted against them. But the Lord stood with me and strengthened me in order that through me the proclamation might be fully accomplished and that all the Gentiles might hear." He understood the reality that not everyone was going to help him even if they shared the same goal. Some might stay with him, but others would be sent in different directions by the Lord or would choose to go elsewhere. Paul recognized that God stood with him and kept him strong to accomplish his purpose, keeping his focus no matter who went with him.

Like Paul we must learn to discern who will walk with us in this journey, who will be of help, and who will not and yet never expect everyone to take up our cause. We, too, must stay focused and accomplish God's will for our lives. By following this example we are able to *build* bridges rather than *burn* them.

Building Bridges

"Two are better than one because they have a good return for their labor. For if either of them falls, the one will lift up his companion. But woe to the one who falls when there is not another to lift him up" (Ecclesiastes 4:9-10). As we reach out to help others and nourish relationships, we eventually see the cream rise to the top; and those people are the ones who will likely be of greatest help to us because they are about serving and relationships are established. Often easier said than done!

Nurturing and establishing relationships occur in a natural progression over time. When we rush the process, we often get disconnected.

Nurturing and establishing relationships occur in a natural progression over time. When we rush the process, we often get disconnected. Sometimes it takes years to blend our lives into the lives of others, listen well, and serve well; and then realize we have exhausted our emotional and physical resources on people who drain us instead of energize us. We're not saying only to spend time with people who serve us, help us, meet our needs, or do things our way. We are saying, however, that we must have a balance of types of people in our lives. The progression of relationship building is relatively simple but time-consuming. For what we're about to share in chart form, go to our website or read it in *Balancing the Active Life*, also available on our website.

Casual Relationships

One type of relationship is the *Casual Relationship*, which involves the greatest number of people in our lives. This relationship operates on a very nonintrusive level. We share intellectual, factual, familiar, and casual information with one another on a fairly superficial level. We know these people casually and see them occasionally, usually unplanned. We learn about them through initial introductions and conversations, and we ask and answer unobtrusive questions opening with "who, what, where, when and how" as we try to get to know each other. This relationship will not go any further if people are uninterested or unwilling to answer those simple questions designed to "get to know you." The person who maintains only casual relationships wants to keep life light and comfy but doesn't want to make commitments of any kind.

Let's put some faces on the people in this group: They look like the people you shake hands with in church, those you serve with on committees at school or in the community, those who stop to say hello and talk about the weather or a recent game, or the kids who give you a "high five" as a quick hello!

If those involved in a casual relationship are willing and interested, the relationship develops; and we naturally move into the next level of friendship, involving varying degrees of cultivation.

Cultivated Relationships

Along that continuum are relationships characterized by varying degrees of cultivation, the next level of involvement being Cultivated Relationships. Few relationships make it through the cultivation stage because the nature of the process at this level is emotional. Sharing on an emotional level makes some people very uncomfortable. Those people will not participate in this process. Cultivation of a relationship can take place only when similar interests are shared and enjoyed; those working on cultivating their relationship will plan activities to enjoy together. They will sense that they "click." When the parties spend time with each other, they come to know each other better and more deeply. They are able to "dig" more deeply into the relationship, cultivating growth by asking and answering the "why" questions in life. They have moved from the simple everyday questions and answers to ones that reveal more about a person. Each discovers "why" they like their job, "why" they're having a hard time serving on a committee, "why" they go to church.

Putting a face on this group, we'll find the person we occasionally invite to dinner or a sporting event or the one we see weekly at a class and realize we have similar interests and concerns. We keep current and connected with these people. They might even be the people who are a step ahead of us on the journey we're taking. We respect such people and can talk to them about all that is happening in our life, and they will relate to us easily and lend ideas and suggestions.

If they are *willing* to answer the "why" questions, and we reciprocate, then this relationship has a chance to move to the committed relationship.

Committed Relationships

Only a very few relationships qualify as committed relationships. What is required in this type of relationship may be a little too heavy for most people. A committed relationship extends to a deeper level, one that is often seen as spiritual. Those who reach this level of relationship are faithful and committed to each other, no matter the cost. They discover each other's strengths and weaknesses and are open and transparent in their communication with each other. They have the freedom to speak, listen, and act upon what they hear yet are committed to confidentiality. They are able to encourage, correct, confront, and help each other reach goals and fulfill dreams; each is willing to be inconvenienced to help or console the other, and doing so is freely reciprocated. One person cannot make a committed relationship: It takes two people willing to invest their time, talents, and treasures in each other. They are available whenever they are needed, not merely when convenient.

Each stage of a relationship will require us to forgive and ask forgiveness, but the committed relationship will provide us with the best opportunities to extend and offer forgiveness because we know each other more intimately, having more opportunities to experience hurt. Of people with whom we share committed relationships, we might be left to think, "Oh, they know me, they'll understand if I don't ask for forgiveness. They know I didn't mean it the way it sounded." That is not true. Anytime we feel we might have offended someone, we need to go to that person, say what we did, and ask forgiveness. (Hebrews 12:14 and I Thessalonians 5:13). Owning up to our sin and mistakes strengthens the committed relationship.

Let's put some faces on the people in this group: They look like friend who tells you to call at 3:00 a.m. when you need to talk, the person who will pray with you when you're down and out, the one who will bring you a meal without asking, "Let me know if I can help." It's the people who will call when they think they've said or done something hurtful or offensive, and call you right away to apologize. It's the person who in able to read between the lines of what the other is *not* saying, and persists in asking the tough questions until there is an answer or resolve. These people know and love the real you, you love the real them, and you love each other in spite of it!

Who Are These People in My Life?

Let's take a little quiz. Put a number in front of each example and see if you can pick up where each relationship belongs.

1 = Casual Relationship
2 = Cultivated Relationship
3 = Committed Relationship

_____ Sandy makes it a point to ask John how his sports team did last week.

_____ David always stops to ask Kevin how work is going.

_____ James asked Anthony directions to the party in math class.

_____ Max takes Justin to the game and makes sure they have time to talk at lunch.

_____ Josh is enjoying getting to know Cassie in the dance class they take together.

_____ Alanna enjoys several of her fellow church friends when they study the Bible.

_____ Shawn is having a Bible study with Tim to develop their character.

_____ Desiree told Susan that she did not handle a situation properly.

_____ Sarah listened closely as Jessica shared some future hopes with her.

Relationships include friendships of varying degrees. We have relationships with our family members and people at church, in our community, in school, and in the organizations to which we belong. All relationships start out casual in nature. We get in trouble, however, when we try to jump directly from the casual relationship into a committed one without cultivating it first. If we don't know how to nourish and cultivate a friendship or a relationship, it is often doomed to fail. Each step in the process of cultivation takes time and can't be rushed. Each person may be on a different time schedule in the process of development; furthermore, we simply can't carry on numerous committed relationships. Doing so would take too much work. The committed relationship must accommodate a give-and-take rapport.

So, let's get back to the quiz. If you marked the first three with #1, the second three with #2, the last three with #3, you are correct. How did you do?

Let's Get Practical: The Caregiver

As caregivers, we are already busy, but being busy doesn't exempt any of us from serving beyond our comfort level. We're not trying to send anyone on a guilt trip, but when others see that we can serve when we have so many limitations already caring for one (or more) with needs, they see what sacrifice and service are all about. Quite honestly, simply meeting our own family's needs is far easier than stretching ourselves to reach out and serve others. Because we desired deep relationships with others we pursued others even though sometimes we knew that they or we would be hurt in the process. Hurt feelings aren't easy to overcome, but if we never take a risk, we never have the wonderful opportunity to find a friend willing to stick with us through thick and thin. Finding those chosen few is a wonderful blessing.

In general, we desire to build all relationships by treating others graciously and kindly. We want others to sense from us that we are willing to work together, not just have things our way. We want our participation in a relationship to be "life-giving," not "life-draining." In our desire to balance those fragile areas of relationships, we want to love like Jesus and not be indifferent to others. Sometimes that means protecting ourselves and our family, and other times it means giving above and beyond what we think we are able. In both instances we seek the Lord and depend upon Him for guidance and direction.

Here are some of the ways we have reached out to develop relationships (in our families, at church, in school):

- ✓ Helped in Joey's art and computer class in elementary school (and brought the girls when they were old enough to help and not interrupt what was going on)
- ✓ Invited teachers to our home for dinner to get to know them
- ✓ Chaperoned field trips when additional help was needed
- ✓ Answered calls and notes promptly so people knew we were caring individuals
- ✓ Wrote notes of encouragement to others in challenging places in life
- ✓ Thanked people who helped us at church as well as family members who reached out at various times showing concern and/or compassion
- ✓ Tried never to make people feel as if they should help us
- ✓ Allowed others to help us
- ✓ Asked for help when needed (We're still learning this one!)
- ✓ Tried to stay connected to those we love in our lives
- ✓ Shared our joys and struggles only with those willing to listen
- ✓ Desired to be transparent in our struggles so that others didn't think we had it all together
- ✓ Did not take advantage of others' help

- ✓ Took chances in building relationships by learning with whom we could share, what we could share, and with whom we could cry or not
- ✓ Prayed with and for others, including doctors, teachers, family and friends
- ✓ Provided meals for others as we were able
- ✓ Watched others' children when needed
- ✓ Helped others in practical ways when needed
- ✓ **Idea: Form a Casserole Club.** Find four women who will prepare four of the same casserole. Meet the first Tuesday (or day of your choice) of each month for six months or a year, and exchange casseroles. You will make one mess for your casserole, but get three new ones in return. It was great to freeze them and pull them out for Sundays that were always a bit hectic when the children were small.
- ✓ **Idea: Form a babysitting (or adult day care) group.** Find two or three families with a few kids (or an adult) each that you trust and enjoy and take turns watching each others' children (adult). You may watch a larger group of kids one time and get two or more times out! No one pays for a sitter, but everyone gets time away!

Here are some ways we accepted the help of others in various relationships:

- ✓ We accepted advice and counsel from our parents, friends, doctors, teachers, aides, and even our children.
- ✓ When someone offered some service, we'd write down their name so we could ask them for help when we had need. That list came in handy a number of times.
- ✓ We accepted meals with gratitude and always wrote a note of thanks.
- ✓ We tried to show appreciation without criticism, expectation, whining, or complaining about how those who helped did things differently from us.

Let's Get Practical: How We Can Help Those Willing To Help Us

If we could change one thing about how we handled the challenges with our son and our parents, we would have been more vocal. We would have expressed to others exactly what was happening to our loved ones and to us as we cared for them. As our friends had grandchildren with special needs and cared for their aging parents, we discovered that they were shocked to know we had gone through the same things they were going through. We did not want to sound like a broken record (or CD!) and get stuck in the groove of saying the same thing over and over and over for those twelve years we were in that sad and lonely place. Some friends were good listeners, but in looking back, we can see that we tried not to overdo it and perhaps "underdid" it!

Others will not understand what we are going through unless we tell them. Sadly, when even close friends are shocked that we still shower and shave Joey as a grown man, that he can't stay home alone, that he continues to have severe behavioral issues from time to time, and that we still experience times of great frustration in trying to deal with him in a positive and Christ-honoring way, we realize we should express ourselves more clearly and thoroughly and probably should have and should continue to reach out to ask for help. And when others offer to help, we need to be honest and practical in allowing them the privilege.

We should be open to hearing what others might share but only after they've taken the time to understand what life is really like on the path we travel daily.

When others tell us how we should do things, or ask us why we aren't doing certain things, we might ask them to come alongside us and do what we do on a daily basis for a week or so to help us find better ways to organize our time and conserve energy. Perhaps we've overlooked better ways to care for our loved one. We should be open to hearing what others might share but only after they've taken the time to understand what life is really like on the path we travel daily.

So if we actually have people who offer to help, we must realize we can't just dump information on them and expect them to remember it. We must help them learn by training them and then release them to do what they have learned. Whether it's a family member, friend, someone you hire, or help provided by a county or local organization, here is some information we found helpful in assisting those who are willing to assist us.

Make a Manual

Having one place to keep directions, instructions, and contacts (doctors, hospitals, and family members) is very helpful for those who offer to help. It will allow the helper to feel secure when you leave them on their own with your loved one!

Writing down all the things we've learned along the way takes time, but doing so helps the one who is helping you. Using list form is more helpful than written paragraphs. Lists help the caregiver see quickly what is expected.

Set Boundaries

You know the care your special needs person requires. Listing in writing what you expect is very helpful for substitute caregivers. If notes are available, the caregivers can look back at them to review what is permitted and what is not. As you work with others and find you've left something off your "help" list, be sure to write it down immediately. The more help you offer others, the better their experience will be and the more likely they will be successful. That helps you in the long run!

If caregivers don't observe the boundaries you've set, you'll have to determine whether their help is needed or not. Having to undo what has been done negates what we had hoped to accomplish by having someone in to help us. So for those who are helpers, make sure to be a good listener and one who follows the family's guidelines.

Some **boundaries** to consider:

- ✓ How long is the caregiver expected to be there? Setting a starting and end time helps the caregiver/helper mentally budget how long they'll be helping. Then be home on time (your boundary), so they aren't frustrated. If they've not performed caregiving responsibilities daily they will not likely have your stamina level, so start them with smaller time frames at first.

- ✓ Be sure they know what you expect of them as they interact physically with the person with special needs (feeding, toileting, bathing, etc.).

- ✓ Be sure they know what you expect of them as they interact verbally with the one needing care.

- ✓ How should the caregiver respond if the one needing care cannot make her or his needs known to the caregiver? Call you? Can the caregiver make the decision about what is needed?

- ✓ What foods is the person requiring care permitted to have? When? How much? (And be sure to have food for the caregiver, as well.)

- ✓ How does the person requiring care best fall asleep? What is their usual night-time or nap-time routine?

Specific Instructions for Care to Include in the Manual

We made a form for all caregivers (paid or unpaid) that includes the following:

- ✓ Home phone number and full address in case the helper needs to call 911

✓ Where we can be reached: cell phone, hotel, meeting, etc.

✓ Health forms of the one being cared for

✓ Health issues and procedures on how to handle them

✓ Hospital, doctors' offices, emergency telephone numbers and addresses

✓ How to handle specific medical issues or emergencies, how to handle the person if she or he has an epileptic seizure, how to handle the feeding tube (or any medical equipment), and what constitutes an emergency and how it should be handled

✓ School and work plans and schedules, especially if a plan must be followed when the regular caregiver is to be out of town

✓ Others who can be called to help and what they are willing to do to help

✓ Duties to be performed and rules to be followed (e.g., when and how to give medicines, whether or not the helper needs to make dinner, clean up dishes, do laundry)

✓ Toys or activities the person being cared for likes, dislikes, or can/can't handle

✓ Ways to calm or correct the person that have worked for you as well as what doesn't work

✓ Names of other family members who will be present in the home and whether or not they are able or permitted to help and if so, how

✓ Instructions on the use of communication devices, boards, or other methods the person with special needs uses to express herself or himself that the caregiver needs to understand or learn

✓ Give a tour of the home so the helper knows where everything they need is located

Some of these items may not make sense to those who have never cared for one with special needs or an adult whose mental or physical capabilities are failing. We can't assume that a person's chronological age automatically indicates what a person should be able to do. For example, Joey could not hold his head up when he should have been able to. Helpers needed to know they should hold his head as they would a newborn's. As an adult, Joey still can't chew gum or eat cherries. He'd swallow the gum and the cherry pits. As our parents' health declined, they couldn't eat solid foods. These wreaked havoc on their intestinal tracks and bowel movements at one stage, and later they simply couldn't swallow things that needed good chewing. At that point their food needed to be pureed. Caregivers need to know these details and follow what they are told.

For duties and chores like laundry and food preparation, first consider the caregiver's job description. If his or her responsibility is to care for the person with special needs, then hire someone else to do other work. On a day-to-day basis we might be able to "do it all" because we have developed a routine and system that works for us, but we have to be careful not to burn out those who are stepping in to help.

As we would put the manual into practice, we could see it needed changing from time to time. Every six months or so, we'd update whatever was needed so that we (and our helpers) kept current with what was needed and expected based upon what was working or not.

The better the training we can give others, whether professional caregivers or dear family and friends, the more success they will have and the happier everyone will be. Having a supportive team of helpers in place is necessary. Waiting until an emergency to ask people for help is frustrating and sometimes impossible for all involved. We must also be aware that not everyone will work out well. Not all personalities "mesh," no matter who the people are—special needs or not. Humbling ourselves to allow others to help is difficult at times, but doing so is a great exercise in working with and appreciating others.

Specific Relationships

The Professionals:

The relationships we develop with professionals in caring for someone with special needs are very important to all involved. We must act in a professional manner when dealing with them so that we are taken seriously in our efforts to provide the best care we can for our loved one. Although we need the expertise of the professionals, we generally know our child, parent, or loved one better than anyone else; and so we must be bold enough to say what needs to be said when professionalism isn't accomplishing what is needed. We all want to work with the professional who is an able communicator, well educated, compassionate, and caring. Finding such an individual and then learning to handle the relationship professionally requires a fine balance.

Doctors need copious information to diagnose illnesses, diseases, and injuries before prescribing tests, medicines, and other treatments. The doctor usually welcomes as much written information as possible during an appointment; such information will reduce the amount of time we have to spend with him or her. Writing down what the doctor says is also very helpful. Having a second person along to help ask questions and take notes eliminates forgetting important details in the midst of a rough situation. We recommend asking whatever questions you have even if you think they might sound foolish.

Unfortunately, sometimes we may have no choice in the doctor we see because of the specialization involved or an insurance situation; however, when we have choices, we should look for a doctor who is trustworthy, caring, and compassionate, one who will listen to our thoughts. If physicians are uninterested in the thoughts of the one who knows the patient best, we wonder how interested they really are in the patient.

Ask your doctors where they went to school and inquire about their credentials. Are they specialized in what you need? Have they been published? This gives you an indication where their skills and interests are. All doctors have traveled a long road to get to the place they are; but not every doctor will suit your needs. If you and the physician are on the same road, you will get what you need in a timely fashion, and often times is the essential element in helping the person for whom you care.

We have, over the course of our years of caring for Joey and our parents, learned that sometimes we need to leave a doctor. We finally needed to leave the pediatrician who kept Joey as a patient until he was well over eighteen! We'd still have him as Joey's doctor because he knew Joey and us so well, but we needed to move him to someone who could help with Joey as an adult. We've also left doctors for other reasons. We left one because of the length of time we'd wait in his office and because of an attitude we didn't appreciate. Our time is just as valuable as the doctor's, and we are no less worthy; so we moved on. Having another doctor in place before moving on is a good move. Remember to build bridges; don't burn them. Telling a doctor why you're leaving is not easy, and sometimes it's unnecessary; yet sometimes letting a doctor know why you're disappointed or frustrated is helpful because you might be one of many who have left for the same reason. Figuring out how to handle each situation is a lesson in discernment.

Lawyers can be very helpful in seeking legal counsel on issues such as malpractice, trusts, wills, and power of attorney. Remember that the moment you sit down in their office, you are paying them. They keep track of their time with you, the time they work on your documents, and the time they email you or talk to you on the phone. The bottom line is to be prepared so that we are not wasting their time and our money.

Social workers and caseworkers serve as the bridge to many organizations and outside help as well as Social Security, disability information, Medicare, Medicaid, government assistance. Joey had an occupational therapist at our city hospital in the early 80s; we met up with her some twenty years later at a talk we were doing for a school. Yolanda came up to us and asked if we remembered her. Of course, we did. When you see someone week after week for years, you get to know her. What a surprise for all of us! We were able to catch up and thank her for the good start she gave Joey back in the days we never thought we'd see him walk or talk.

In the process of writing this book, we saw some wonderful opportunities unfold for a couple we mentor and with whom we've become friends. Their early intervention specialist, who was assigned to them through our County Board of Mental Retardation, saw the great needs of this couple and could foresee the needs they would have in the future caring for their two daughters with extreme special needs (at the time of this writing toddlers who need total care.) This wonderful woman wrote letters to find a way to secure better housing for the family. Their tiny Cleveland bungalow would not accommodate wheelchairs or showering aids for their girls now, let alone when they grew and need larger equipment. She contacted a family-run company in town, explaining what she was trying to do; and when they returned her call, she was excited to think they might donate the paper products she'd need to get things started for a fundraiser for this couple. To her surprise and joy, the company representative called to say that the company would build a house for this couple! It was to be totally handicapped accessible with tracking in the ceiling so they could move the girls from one room to the next. The relationship has blossomed into a trusting friendship with members of the whole community involved!

We need to be intentional about getting to know our school contacts, community, county, and state organizations representing the disability or health issues with which we are dealing. We need to ask questions, make phone calls, talk to others, and do it over and over until we get the answers we need to help on our unexpected journey. We can't stop and we can't quit.

Teachers are a wealth of knowledge, help, and guidance. Starting off on a good note is vital for the future of any small child but especially for the child with special needs who can't communicate.

We had the most wonderful experiences with all of Joey's teachers. Each year we offered to help in the classroom, mostly art and computer classes that were simple and adaptive to special needs. We didn't have to know much, which was a good thing! The teachers and aides just needed extra hands to help, and they guided us to help the kids. We never went in with our own agenda or thoughts. We yielded to their authority and did whatever they asked in a win–win situation for all of us. The teachers got our help, we got to know them, the kids had the help they needed, and it was fun!

We had always heard that one should inquire where our children's teachers went to school and ask whether they had specialized in the particular area of the child's need and what their credentials and qualifications are. All that is extremely important, especially making sure they are qualified; but observing them as you help in the classroom or during meetings to assess how compassionate and caring they are is far more important. Certified but without compassion does not make a good teacher.

Other service professionals continue to be a part of our lives. Nearing his senior year of school and his twenty-second birthday, Joey was ready to "graduate." Caseworkers, teachers, and counselors helped us to locate work for him at this time. They were able to find placement for him through United Cerebral Palsy at a plumbing manufacturing company on the outskirts of the city. The company wins awards every year for being one of the top ten companies to work for in Cleveland. And guess what? Just as we prayed for each and every teacher, we prayed for a wonderful supervisor. Karen isn't just a supervisor; she is a gift from God. Joey was able to enter the workforce under the direction of someone who loves the Lord, understands Joey, and goes out of her way to teach Joey in the workplace. The pattern continues!

Some lend their professional services in ways we don't always think about. We have seen in our area a barber on wheels. He makes appointments for house calls for those who aren't able to leave home. Joe used to do the same for people recovering from cancer and for people with special needs in nursing homes. Examinations and simple cleanings could be done "on the road" but for more intensive work patients would need to be transported. Check the Yellow Pages (on or offline) to see what types of service professionals can help you in your area of need. If you have special skills, you might think "outside the box" about how you can be of help to others who cannot leave their homes, or have special needs.

We recommend networking with people in situations similar to yours to find out what has worked for them, how they have found and contacted various service people. *High School Musical* says it all: "We're all in this together," and when we work together, we can do so much better than going it alone.

Help from Paraprofessionals and Family Members

Teachers' aides, who are trained but not necessarily studied in special education; nursing home aides, who may not have been schooled to prepare them to care for others; and family and friends are all important pieces in the puzzle of life that God sets before us. Every person in Joey's life has been placed there purposefully. It was our responsibility to grow those relationships. Let us briefly tell you about some of the other relationships and how they became a piece of the puzzle that is Joey's life.

Family—Grandpas and Grandmas Ferrini and Chmelik—helped care for Joey with such love and devotion. They were ones who had our manual memorized!

Aunt Sue and Aunt Mary Jo each have made wonderful contributions to Joey's life as well as to our parents' lives in their declining years. As a family we worked together to make each of our lives work. Our "We're all in this together" attitude made us more than family—we're friends, too.

Interestingly, as the grandparents left us one by one and the list of helpers dwindled, a list grew with the names of friends who offered to help in many different ways. Some offered rides. Some have offered to watch Joey if we needed to get out for a meeting or other commitment. We have maintained a list of names form which to draw when we have need. Too many to recognize by name have left their marks by stopping over to play a video game with Joey, bringing over a favorite toy (like plastic swords), driving up on a motorcycle to let Joey sit on it, lugging over a big screen (make that GIANT screen) to play bigger-than-life Playstation, playing Santa and Mrs. Claus, vacationing with us, providing transportation, going out of their way to give him some OSU item or asking how the game went—all in ways that allow Joey to connect with them. It takes effort on their part because Joey isn't very expressive. He can't tell them how much he appreciates it, but we can see that he does! We wish each of those people could see how excited Joey gets when he knows one of his "buddies" will be wherever he's going. And often his "buddies" are the conversational bait that gets him into the car to go!

Help doesn't just come from friends our own age! One little friend years ago heard me say to her mom, "Joey will probably never get married." She came up to me to tell me she'd marry Joey someday. We've forgiven her for finding the man of her dreams and starting a family but know that those kinds of words came from a heart of compassion like we have experienced from so many people.

Many have generously shared their lives with us. When we needed to look outside the family for help for Joey (once all the grandparents were gone and both daughters were grown and gone), God uniquely provided for us a close friend who was already trained and certified to provide help for people who qualify for a "Level 1 Waiver." (Under the Level 1 Waiver people with mental retardation or other developmental disabilities can receive supports from the county in their home.) Certified to provide care for her brother-in-law and able and willing to help us as well, our dear friend was all

Although no two people think or do things the same way, we must be mindful to appreciate when others help, and never expect everyone to join our team.

ready and set to go when we needed her! Interestingly, she has a grandson with special needs, too. We couldn't ask for a better helper! We share these memories and stories to let our readers know that God has placed others in our life in special relationships. Each person bridges a different gap. And some people bridge the gap just for a given time. As caregivers, we must be very careful not to expect, demand, or be highly critical of those who are kind enough to help us and those who do not. Although no two people think or do things the same way, we must be mindful to appreciate when others help, and never expect everyone to join our team. When we get stuck feeling sorry for ourselves because we've done something for someone who's never reciprocated or when we feel lonely or left out, we need to look back as we just did and see the faithfulness of God in the past. Doing so will help us to trust that He will be faithful to us in the future and put others in the lives of our special needs person when we are no longer there for them.

The FamilyLife Weekend to Remember

We met two sweet young couples at a conference where we spoke. They approached us saying, "We have some friends who have a son who sounds just like your Joey but younger. We wished they could have been here to hear your story." We said to them, "The reason they aren't here is that they will never be able to leave their son alone unless they have someone they can trust. Do you think you could be that someone? If the four of you ask the parents to teach you how to care for the child, you could send them next year to this conference. In fact, we think that the four of you could probably handle for a weekend what the two of them do every single day. We challenge you to do that this year. You will make a friend forever, and they will forever consider you heroes!"

Joey's Graduation Party

Knowing Joey would never marry, we decided to throw him the best graduation party we could. We themed it *Happy Days* and asked everyone to dress accordingly. Joe wore jeans and a t-shirt with the sleeves rolled up. Cindi and the girls wore 50s skirts, and Joey was dressed as a soda-jerk with a white shirt, bow tie, apron, and cap. All his special needs friends came with wheelchairs, walkers, and their families and danced to the tunes of the DJ. Teachers came dressed like Mr. and Mrs. Cunningham. Bus drivers, aides, therapists, friends, and family all came dressed for fun! We rented the converted rocket car from Euclid Beach Park that was a popular ride in the 50s, and everyone got to ride around in it through town. Even the kids in wheelchairs were lifted into the rocket car to get a ride. It was truly a celebration!

As each person entered the room, a memory was recalled and new one made. Kristina read a "thank you" story that we had written and asked each person mentioned to stand to be recognized as she read. There were few dry eyes in the place as one by one each person was honored for the part they played in Joey's growth and development. It's a night etched in our memory and a vivid reminder that God is bigger than whatever our biggest challenge.

Let us introduce to you twenty-two years of therapists, teachers, and others who invested in relationships with Joey and our family. In tribute to these terrific people, we have used their real names.

....

The Good the Bad and the—Well, You Know!

I, Joey Ferrini, was going to read this before dinner. I decided to let Kristina read it for me because I think most of you came pretty hungry. Dad and Mom hope you did because if you don't eat a lot, we will have to take home leftovers, and we still have leftovers from Kristina's graduation party! So thanks, Kristina, for reading this for me!

Over the years I've had a lot of different people in my life. Well, I say different because I have had a lot of people involved in my life. But mostly they have been different because they have been so special.

For instance, in my life I have had family and friends, doctors and nurses, physical, occupational and speech therapists. Come to think of it, my parents went to a therapist to talk about raising me. After three visits he told them they didn't have to come back anymore. There are others, too, the teachers and aides, transportation people, neighbors in three different neighborhoods, people from Dad's work, and people from my work. People I've met as I've visited throughout the county for a lot of different things like guardianship, United Cerebral Palsy (UCP), SSI, VGS, JVS, PDC, ABC, and YMCA—Oh! That's a song we'll dance to later! One county place I never visited was the jail! But it was closed the last time I tried to run away! The last time I tried, Mom's policeman friend met me right in the driveway! I didn't know he came to drop off reunion information. I sat absolutely still while they talked because I thought I was busted! There are so many people, but I want to mention a few that are here tonight to celebrate this special day with me!

I'm glad some of my classmates and their families could come tonight (please raise your hands). Now they are a **different** group! Some have wheelchairs, some have walkers, some have machines, some are tall (OK! That would be ME!), some are short, some talk a lot, some little, and some not at all—but their eyes **always** have something to say! Some graduated last year, some still have to do their time, I mean, finish school. Some walk fast, some slow, some not at all. Some like Ashley, I played baseball with. I loved that Grandpa Ferrini helped coach that team. Our team **always** won. Funny thing—the other team always won, too. I don't know how that happened, but we all went home REALLY happy! Then there's Brian. We go way back. Our moms carpooled back when we were three! We have a lot of history together. I remember the short time that Brian walked, but we also had fun checking out each of the new "wheels" Brian got over the years. His legs slowed him down, but with one finger he can move that wheelchair in and out of any parallel parking space! And Elena—the bus ride home wouldn't have been as much fun if YOU weren't there! Every one of my friends is different, and they have so many different things to offer. I have never met so many special—very special people all in one place. They are THE BEST!

We have some really **brave** people here tonight! Those would be my former teachers and aides. I've had a lot of different types of teachers—young ones, old ones, tall ones, short ones, ones who are still working today, and ones who took the early retirement plan after having me in their class! After early intervention therapies and my special preschool for three years, my first public school years were spent at Memorial Elementary in Brunswick because Strongsville didn't have classes for kids like me. Mrs. Gates was the product of my parents' diligent prayer of over a year. God knew I would need a very patient, loving, understanding, and tolerant teacher for those years of experiencing bad allergies, severe seizures, turbulent behaviors, and trying different medications. At first I wondered if I'd get her to leave teaching special education, but I guess when you get "prayed into" a job, it's pretty hard to get out! I had Mrs. Saucier for 4 years! It took her that long to help me learn to write my name and address! The really wonderful thing about these two teachers is they knew the Lord and helped me to get through those years by pointing me to Him. Next was Mrs. Flick in Strongsville. I REALLY put her to the test! She and Mom even had someone named PhD from the county come to talk about behavior modification. They tried to figure out why I was so competitive with Frank. Hey—it was nothing! It was just MY way of keeping Mrs. Flick on her toes! Mrs. Bull helped out in that class. She was very patient. She already knew about challenges—her sweet daughter with special needs helped teach her at home so she knew just how to handle me! At that same school I had Miss Chmelik [Joey's aunt]for music! This was a VERY different situation! What was different with Miss Chmelik was that I KNEW she knew my home telephone number! I acted differently for her than for my classroom teachers! I could never decide if I liked her better as Miss Chmelik or Aunt Sue. She was, and is, good at both! Mrs. Lillis was in that mix, too! She had so much patience. But even more than patience, she was a wonderful encourager! I don't think I ever heard her raise her voice—and don't think I didn't try!

Funny thing about Mrs. Lillis—she followed me to Jr. High! There was NO WAY I was going to get away with ANYTHING with that practically "fresh out of college" Miss Thomas! Mom really liked her because she talked about her class being a class of "geniuses"! I don't know who she taught before, but Mom was going around telling people that "Joey was in a gifted class" now! Mom loved hearing all of Miss Thomas' wedding plans and prayed she wouldn't leave town! My favorite memory of the new Mrs. Kempf was when she showed the new teacher how to use the EPIPEN, only to realize that it wasn't a DEMO but an expired full injection! I never saw anyone walk and talk so fast in my life!!! Except the day I had a seizure outside on the track. I think EMS wondered about her and me with all the trips they made to our school that year! Mrs. Buckley was an aide in that class, too. She is a **perfect** Mom for Robert (whom she and her husband adopted and later learned had special needs), but she would **never** have worked out as a mom for me. With her tiny stature, I would have put her in a neck brace in no time! Even though she was assigned to care for Brian, she cared for me, too. Then she followed me to the high school. Is there a pattern here?

Somewhere in there, I had Mrs. Stineman as an occupational therapist. I don't think she ever saw an IEP with "he will learn to tie his shoes" for as many years as she saw that one on mine! The year we took it off the IEP I think I saw pom poms in her school bag. She was very polite and didn't cheer or anything, but I knew she was glad to get that shoe-tying thing off my IEP!!

At the high school I had some different, I mean, great teachers! Mrs. Johnson was my speech therapist! I spent so much time with Mrs. Bittner in junior high, trying to get two or three words together that Mrs. Johnson's job had to be a cinch. All she had to do was ask me about the Indians, and I would talk with thirteen-word run-on sentences. She didn't even have to tell me to "speak up"! Then there was Mrs. Vazac. She has a great sense of humor and seemed to appreciate mine! Like the time—OK, times— I would run away carrying my book bag and coat. Mom really liked when Mrs. Vazac would tell her all of my "hide and seek stories" That's what I called that "running away" stuff! And of course, there was Miss Sgro, now Mrs. Halvorson! How Mrs. Halvorson could **ever** think of going to, or watching another Indians game is beyond me! She heard me share EVERY trade, score, and play for the last five years! Every once in a while I would talk about the BROWNS just to keep her from going crazy! Then there was Mrs. Rhein. She wasn't officially my teacher, but she was always in our room. The Board of Education has her teaching another class, but I think the REAL reason she was always there was to help Mrs. Halvorson keep her wits about her! Talk about wits—that Mrs. Cifranic is one witty lady! I got to know her pretty good these past two years, and so did Mom when they roomed together as chaperones for the New York City trip. Mom got to see first-hand just how much fun she is! Mrs. Pettit was the other aide in my class. She couldn't be here tonight because she had other plans—like REST after having me in class all year!

Mr. DiAngelo and Mr. Kelly couldn't be here tonight. I think they are at Polaris finishing the dishes I didn't get to! Mrs. Shuler and Mrs. Kostur are friends of ours from church but also aides at Polaris Vocational School. I personally think Dad and Mom sent them to Polaris as spies. I figured out they probably knew some things about me that they just prayed about because they gave nothing but glowing reports about me to my folks. Of course THAT was the answer to MY prayers! And we can't forget Mrs. Laskey, who was not a classroom teacher but a "transition coordinator"! She went anywhere I went, and even when Mom and Dad were out of town one time, she put on goggles and funny shoes JUST to check up on me at a manufacturing job assessment. She looked funny, but she sure is nice. I think her special little Mary gave her some good practice before going to heaven. Little Mary is one of the reasons Mrs. Laskey is so, well, SPECIAL!

And then there were the transportation people. This group cannot be called bus drivers and aides. In my case I like to call them personal chauffeurs. No matter where I lived, they would pick me up **right** at the end of my driveway. My personal chauffeurs would have the daily sports page for me—kind of like a fine hotel! Sometimes we'd arrange for extra cars or lawn maintenance vehicles to park in the cul-de-sac just to see if they could REALLY drive that bus—but it NEVER fazed them. They were a wonderful and special group!

Try as we might, and you'll see what we mean once the music starts, we can't forget friends! Friends of my parents, friends of my sisters, and friends of mine have been very special. Some are from work; some are neighbors, and some we just met a few minutes ago outside! (Or at least that's what we'll tell you if we have to introduce them to anybody!) Mom and Dad said they can't talk about all of them. They say the ways they've been here for me (and them) are too many to tell. They just say, "If you want to know a really special group—that's them." They've listened, they've laughed, they've helped in tough times and many of them have done a LOT of praying. It says a lot when some of those friends have stuck around since **they** were in high school—and you know that's a LONG time!

And last but not least is family. Some couldn't be here because they are with Jesus. But I have a feeling they are watching—just getting ready for a polka! The thing that's special about this group is they are all the other groups rolled into one. They have prayed, watched me, encouraged me, and helped me to read, to fish, to walk, to talk. They have disciplined me, showered me, nursed me back to health, sat with me through hour-long seizures one after another, gotten mad at me, laughed with me; and some of them have even gotten beaten by me in Nintendo! And they all say that life just wouldn't be the same without me. I know I have taught them a lot.

I've taught my immediate family a lot, too. Kristina has gotten really good at helping me keep my routine when Mom and Dad are gone. She knows how to use psychology and make funny voices to get me moving. Kathleen has really come a long way. She hardly ever cries anymore when I "blame" her. She just rolls her eyes and says, "I know, I know, I did it, it's my fault." Someday she will really laugh about this. I think she is RIGHT NOW! And then there are my parents. Talk about **different**. They always say they don't like when people say, "You must be special for God to give you a special child." They say, "NO! GOD GAVE US A SPECIAL CHILD BECAUSE WE HAD SO MUCH **MORE** TO LEARN!" I'm glad they are learning, but I'm more glad that it's God who's teaching them. After all, without them, I would not know how very special I was created and that I'm God's handiwork. My parents said that I have been created to give glory to God—to give glory means to rejoice proudly! So I rejoice that I **know** Him and that He **created** me just the way He wanted me to be!

This day is special for me, but there is only one thing that would make this day more special than having you all here. It would be to know that you know Him—Jesus—and will be in heaven someday! After all, that's where I'll be someday. Only I will be very different than I am now. **And that is one party you won't want to miss!** Thanks for being here and sharing my day. You have made it very special!

Love, Joey

We share this story of relationships with you for several reasons. First, it wasn't always easy to cultivate relationships, but we intentionally did so to stay connected with others. Second, we continue to have contact with each of these people through Christmas greetings, emails, and occasional visits. Third, because we know these people fairly well, we know we could go to them if needed for help, encouragement, or guidance, for Joey then and now. Intentional moves in the direction of relationship building and endurance are vital in growing and keeping those friendships fresh and active. As a result of keeping these people in our life to one degree of another, we know they know that we could call upon their area of expertise to help us at any time.

Just the other day we crossed paths with one of Joey's former bus drivers. We stopped to chat, and she remembered to ask about each of our family members and we about hers. It was like seeing an old friend from a time past. When you see these people every day year after year, it makes for golden opportunities to build relationships; but it seldom happens unless you put for the time and effort. When you do, it's worth it.

OTHERS' STORIES

- At some point during the last year Dad was at home, he would start coughing shortly after eating. I foolishly kept giving him Robitussin because I thought he had a cough. Apparently, he was already having trouble swallowing and this was the sign. It is a miracle he didn't get food in his lungs and develop pneumonia. Someone told me it happened to her dad numerous times as well. Sharing these kinds of things with each other helps us learn, develop helpful relationships, and when we discover what the problem is, can help caregivers know what to watch for when taking our place to give care. We all help each other.

- Unless you're a very close friend or family member who is a part of our life and helping in our challenges, please don't tell us to *look* for the silver lining in the challenge we have. And don't *tell* us what that silver lining is if you think you see it. Let us find it out on our own. It might be different than what you see.

- It is very hard for me to listen to another person's struggles, hurt, and pain when they are unavailable, distracted, or disinterested when I try to share mine.

- For the first time in almost thirty years, someone invited my husband, our handicapped son, and me to join them out in public for dinner.

- When our child was born, the doctor told us, "You'll lose family and friends because they won't understand how different life is for you. They will be uncomfortable and want to stay away." He was right. I wish he would have been able to tell us *how* to deal with people like this. We were lonely and needed support emotionally and physically. We eventually found friendship, support, and help through other families dealing with special needs who understood what our lives were like. It's a shame some families stay away. It has been quite hurtful.

- I've had to make many phone calls to find things like free at-home nursing care, but all the time was worth it when I found something to help us. Talking to others to get names of organizations in our area was a great resource. Those of us in the same boat can really help each other out. We have to stick together.

- Wanting to keep my parents in their home as long as possible, I looked for organizations that provided home health aides to assist with bathing, dressing, meals, shopping, medication reminders, and errands. Searching the Internet for home health care is where I started.

- We have organized and held periodic social activities (e.g., games, miniature golf) for special needs adults. Participation in *Special Olympics* provides many opportunities for relationships for the special needs person and their caregiver(s). I think it is the greatest organization in the world.

- A neighbor asked me about "my story," and the next week I found a sweet note in my mailbox telling me she thought I was incredible. It made my week. No, my year! This is how friendships can start!

- As a teacher I try to have a close enough relationship with parents that we can work well together but not so close that I feel "obligated" to them to meet their every need for their child. I want to provide appropriate level of intervention, education, and ultimately independence for their child.

- Special needs students who are mainstreamed don't always receive all they should. Parents need to stay close to their child's teacher and listen to their objective suggestions, which, more often than not, are in the best interest of the child.

- Having someone to support me in prayer was strengthening.

- I appreciate when people reach out in relationship, not just because of their feeling of responsibility or sympathy but friendship. Most have moved on to their own activities, but I am thankful for those that remain.

> *I appreciate when people reach out in relationship, not just because of their feeling of responsibility or sympathy but friendship.*

- I need relationships, but so does the one I care for (husband). As he has been able to do and talk less, we have had fewer visitors.

- It's fun to watch the face of the special needs person we know, when he sees us. He loves people who make an effort to build a relationship with him. (Aren't we all like this?)

- I was at the high school picking up my son when a special needs young man walked by the lunchroom, and a friend of my son's said, "See that kid? He is so awesome." My son followed by saying, "That's my cousin."

- In first grade a student with special needs was in our gym class. He participated with us, but he was a slow runner; so I stayed back to run his pace.

- I have been involved with Easter Seals as a board member and have helped with the children. Relationships are not deep, but certainly meaningful.

- I am thankful to have worked with children and adults with special needs but always got to walk away and go home for a rest. I felt for people deeply, wanting to make things better for them and had sweet relationships with many of them.

- As a specialist, I encouraged parents to communicate well to their child's team and ask lots of questions. They need to be open and honest about their feelings, expectations, and frustrations. Most people on the team care about your child and want the best for them. There is no right plan. It's so individual, but there are right ways to establish a good working relationship.

- Don't expect pastors and friends and even family to understand all you deal with.

- I don't have the time to nurture girlfriend relationships.

- Regular social interaction is necessary for everyone.

- As a teacher I want to encourage parents to get involved. Build relationships with your child's teachers, aides, helpers, and bus drivers, so you know what's going on.

- When our child graduated and walked across the stage, he received the loudest cheering from the graduating class. I believe he was a classmate others liked and respected. [Several shared similar stories.] It made me happy to know others knew him and several [through a helping group] got to know him even better.

- Our son's disability has kept shallow and selfish people away from us. Only those who see the courage, loyalty, and love his cerebral palsy has developed in us step closer into our lives and hearts. Those are the kind of relationships we need.

- My husband and I met a family with a special needs child while on vacation. Because we also have a child with special needs, we immediately bonded. We had planned to talk to each other after vacation and made a plan, but had not heard from them. We called them only to find out their child had just died. We loaded up the car, made a 6 hour trip to their home, and participated in the funeral as though we had known them for years— which is how it felt.

- When I've felt I don't have the support of family and friends, I remember that even Jesus' three closest disciples weren't supportive in His darkest hour.

- It is wonderful to have friends who validate our journey.

- We're grateful for our Special Needs Sunday school and Special Olympics which provide friendships and support that family and even close friends haven't provided.

YOUR STORY

Read Luke 10:30-37. Are you challenged to respond to the needs of others?

_____

_____

_____

How will you respond to those He puts in your path?

_____

_____

_____

Can you see, spot, or seek to meet a need in someone? Put yourself in another's shoes and describe what you see from her or his perspective.

_____

_____

_____

Choose several relationships in your life and describe the current stage of the relationship (casual, cultivated, or committed):

1. _____

_____

2. _____

_____

3. _____

_____

Then describe what you will need to do to move yourself to the next stage:

1. _____

_____

2. _____

_____

3. _____

_____

Are you willing to move to the next stage to deepen the friendship?

_____

_____

_____

If you are not willing, what is keeping you from doing so? Are you saying, "I can't do it" or "I won't do it." There is a difference.

_____

_____

_____

_____

_____

CHAPTER ELEVEN

NEXT
REST STOP
34
MILES

Next Rest Stop 34 Miles:
Stressed? ... Rest!

By age twenty-seven Betsy had already taken care of her ailing father for six years. He was now in a nursing home, but she continued to visit him daily; and the stress and strain of all this caregiving took a toll on her own health. Suffering from panic attacks and depression, she knew she needed to talk to a health-care professional long before these symptoms appeared but simply couldn't take the time.

Max's health problems have mounted since his mother-in-law moved in with him and his wife. His wife is caring for her mom, but Max finds it so stressful on all of them that he has extreme problems regulating his blood pressure. He knows his wife is pulled in too many directions, but neither know what to do. They are Christians and say they are the ones who need to be the caregivers.

Louis has severe special needs. Noises and sudden movements make him very nervous and he squeals and cries in response. Try as they might his parents have difficulty consoling him. They then become nervous and stressed and have stopped going out in public because they know others don't understand what Louis is doing.

OUR STORY

We've heard it said that a gem can't be polished without friction, nor can we be perfected without trial. So here's the question: Are we shiny enough yet? I Peter 1:6-7 says, "In this you greatly rejoice, even though now for a little while, if necessary, you have been distressed by various trials, that the proof of your faith, being more precious than gold, which is perishable, even though tested by fire, may be found to result in praise and glory and honor at the revelation of Jesus Christ." A friend of ours once said, "If this [trial] is what it takes to be refined like gold, I wonder if I can tell Him I'll settle for silver?" Can you relate?

Stress can be both good and bad when it comes to gems and life lessons. The outward characteristics can be beautiful, but a state of crisis or friction was needed to produce it. Crossing a fine line tips us "over the edge" from a minor frustration to full-blown stress. It's so fine that we don't see it, and it varies from person to person. Like the tension on a piece of elastic, we can handle a lot of tension and frustration for a long time; but at some point something has to give. Even a perfect-looking piece of marble has stress points, and if that point is touched, a masterpiece in the making can be shattered.

Many times we felt as if we were ready to crack. How much can we do before the pressure overtakes us? We'd handle things well for what seemed a long time under immense pressure, and then all of a sudden the dam would break. It was too late to plug the little hole that was once in the dyke. The dyke suddenly needed major repair.

Like the tension on a piece of elastic, we can handle a lot of tension and frustration for a long time; but at some point something has to give.

Adjustments to any challenge are difficult, especially when it is both physically and emotionally draining. An initial diagnosis that is life-changing puts the attention on the problems and issues of the person needing care, and often the caregiver's needs are overlooked or at best put aside temporarily. Unfortunately, we don't always know whether this care we give is for a season or a lifetime. By the time we figure out that God has presented us with a challenge that will last a lifetime, the caregiver is already well into a routine that others think is going pretty smoothly. A Walgreen's ad put it best: "If only caregivers had caregivers." Yes, the caregivers—supportive, sensitive, caring, available, loving, and tired.

The Road to Weary

Sometimes we think caregivers drive the road to weary, but the person who requires care deals with stress as well. All that we'll share in this chapter pertains to anyone dealing with stress. Because caregiving can be and often is a full-time job, we need to understand that although great satisfaction can come from caring for a loved one, some very negatives outcomes can put the caregiver at great risk as well.

Stress involves feeling responsible for what we cannot control or putting pressure or strain on something. Stress can be good, for example, when preparing to go to college or planning a wonderful wedding, activities that make us feel alive and excited; stress can also be bad as when dealing with difficult in-laws, money problems, divorce, or trying to accomplish too much in a day. Sometimes we get rolling, and we don't know when whatever we are doing becomes too much or when the good stress turns bad, much like driving the highway without realizing we've gone from 60 to 80 mph when all of a sudden we see the police car on the side of the road! We may have been cruising for a while at 80 mph, but we suddenly realize we'd better slow down. Just as we grew accustomed to driving the highway at a high speed, we adjust to cruising life at unsafe speeds and become comfortable there. What we are doing works for us and might even feel comfortable, but at some point we will run out of gas! We know what to do but often believe we can't slow down or simply fail to see the need until something stops us.

What might stop us is, for example, a marital relationship falling apart at the seams or our kids showing signs of rebellion because we aren't taking care of the relationships properly. What stopped me (Cindi) was having my back go out and spending weeks in bed and also losing huge clumps of hair, leaving a bald spot the size of a tennis ball. In our minds we may think we've got it under control, but our bodies may start falling apart, unable to take the pressure we're putting on them—emotionally or physically.

Many drive the road to weary without even knowing we were headed there. Stressors like protecting the person we care for, the many choices we must make, life-threatening procedures or surgeries, financial burdens, guilt, dealing with the perceptions others have of our situation, disagreements on treatments, sibling resentment or extended-family squabbles, and finding competent medical doctors, therapists, and teachers all add up to pressure. Sometimes we put the stress on ourselves, and sometimes others try to put it on us. Establishing boundaries with people and maintaining them is one way to balance the many stresses that come our way, but what about those stressors over which we have no control like illness or emergencies?

We have been better able to relieve stress caused by uncontrollable situations when we purpose not to over schedule every area of our life (having no wiggle room to experience an emergency) and when we see that stress can be God's way of drawing us closer to Him. When Joe owned his dental practice, he budgeted into each day a "buffer" time, a half-hour before or after lunch scheduled to allow for emergencies. Around lunchtime he could see a patient who called about a tooth she or he had chipped that day. If no emergencies arose, then the office staff enjoyed a longer lunch break. The patient was happy to get an appointment, and the staff was happy because they didn't have to stay late or add more procedures into an already full day.

The advantage to this buffer time was planned pressure. The staff knew they'd have to accommodate a need. Wouldn't it be nice if we could schedule life like that? Little Johnny, you can skin your knee at 12:35 because we can take care of that emergency at that time; however, life doesn't allow for this kind of scheduling. If we have so much to do in a day that we can't be inconvenienced by this type of emergency, we are likely too busy; and we'll snap because we can't take any more in our day.

On the flip side to this kind of stress, we have the kind of emergency (like Grandma having a massive stroke or a child requiring emergency hospitalization) when life stops suddenly and we realize we actually have all the time we need to deal with it. We will never avoid stress altogether, but we can try to reduce it. God allows some stress in our lives because it causes us to need Him and be drawn to Him. Great stress can develop in us a great faith, which points others to God and allows them to see His grace. Some stress we put on ourselves and some others put on us. We need to distinguish between the stress God has given us to make us look up to Him in need and the stress we allow others or ourselves to put on us to bring us down. When left unattended over time, both can cause us to experience situations that become warning signs telling us to stop and get rest.

Warning Signs

Although each of us will succumb to stress after varying lengths of time, we all respond to some degree or another in the following ways:

- ✓ Depleted or lack of energy
- ✓ Stop caring about things, people, life
- ✓ Isolate from people (lacking desire to pursue relationships)
- ✓ Lack interest or strength to encourage others
- ✓ Strain in marriage (and other relationships, too)
- ✓ Apathy, can't focus, can't listen
- ✓ Frustration
- ✓ Fatigue and exhaustion
- ✓ Forgetfulness
- ✓ Gaining or losing weight unintentionally
- ✓ Depression
- ✓ Chaos, confusion; feeling overloaded and overwhelmed
- ✓ Tension, headaches, backaches, jaw pain, etc.
- ✓ Irritability, nervousness
- ✓ Easily angered, having a short fuse

- ✓ Arguing
- ✓ Cry easily, frequent crying spells
- ✓ Emotionally out of control
- ✓ Lack emotion, compassion, or patience
- ✓ Denial
- ✓ Desire or need to escape
- ✓ Neglecting the one being cared for and/or self
- ✓ Bitterness toward others; resentfulness
- ✓ Lacking sleep
- ✓ Feeling exaggerated sense of guilt
- ✓ Thoughts of suicide
- ✓ Physical signs of sickness, aches, pains
- ✓ Substance abuse: drinking, drugs, overeating, pornography (anesthesia of choice to numb the pain felt emotionally or physically); lack of discipline
- ✓ Fear or panic
- ✓ Driving recklessly or uncontrollably; road rage
- ✓ Health problems
- ✓ Difficulty making decisions
- ✓ Feeling stuck without options
- ✓ Making nasty and demeaning remarks to the one you care for and/or others
- ✓ Wanting to or using physical force to move, quiet, or redirect the one you care for
- ✓ Leaving your loved one alone longer than she or he should be
- ✓ Not answering, not responding to the one you care for

What might start as simple physical and mental exhaustion can lead to doubt, failure, helplessness, and a crisis.

Internal, External, Physical Stressors

Look at the above list and see which would be categorized as internal (of the mind) stress. Thoughts of perceived, assumed, or expected situations can cause internal stress. We ask ourselves, "What did I do wrong" or "What am I doing wrong?" Internal stress may also manifest itself by our desire to *look* or be perceived a certain way, and it's not happening. Negative emotions can weigh us down.

External stressors result from dealings with extended family, friends, neighbors, teachers, and doctors and managing those relationships and behaviors. Planning doctor visits and organizational situations like arranging car pools can cause external stress.

Physical stressors require exceptional amounts of energy. These may include the lifting that is involved in caring for our loved one or the amount of time and energy we must spend each day seeing to it that our special needs person is taken care of physically, emotionally, and spiritually.

These stressors can affect our digestive, circulatory, urinary, nervous, glandular, and immune systems. We can experience inflammation in our joints and muscles, causing pain. Some stress can lead to infection, skin diseases, and—we've read—cancer.

Once we understand the warning signs triggering our stress (and they are different for each of us), we can explore the purpose of rest, look for ways to get rest, and then see what true rest really looks and feels like.

The Purpose of Rest

In music composition a rest represents a moment of quiet reflection. In life, rest has a purpose and should not be considered sinful.

In life the purpose of rest is to refresh us. Rest happens when we learn to cope with the feelings, frustrations, and exhaustion that will prevent us from the "burnout" we so often experience or watch others experience. We need rest to replenish our energy and feelings of well-being. After creating the universe, God took time to rest. Scripture (Ex. 31:17; 20:8-10; 23:12) actually says God Himself was *refreshed* after He rested.

HOW to Get Rest to Avoid the "Warning Signs" on the Stress List

None of us can escape the need to have our batteries recharged. We would never purposely leave our car lights on and say, "Oh, when the battery dies, I'll just recharge it." We turn everything off so the battery isn't used up. If we let the battery die, we have to go through all the extra work and effort to figure out how and where to get it recharged. That preventative step of shutting the car down and letting it rest is necessary for it to start the next time. Anyone who's accidentally left headlights on knows the inconvenience of finding the car unable to run.

We must also shut our bodies down and give them proper rest in order to allow them to keep going. When I (Cindi) was seeing a doctor for severe back problems (herniated discs, etc.) the first thing I was asked was, "How much sleep to you get? Not added together in a night, but uninterrupted sleep." I was hard pressed to say much more than perhaps three or four hours. The doctor told me that our bodies need rest in order to recuperate, and that 7-8 hours of sleep in a row is what is needed. I had to put into practice some new concepts in order to allow my body to repair. Some of those same things have been very helpful to both of us when we have arrived at a place where we are stressed out, exhausted, and frustrated when caring for people and their special needs.

Seeking the Lord to determine just what is necessary to get refreshed is tops on the list. Sometimes we've sensed we needed to get away; other times we just needed to say no to a few requests until we felt we were recharged.

Realize and recognize when we do or don't have control of different people or situations. We need to control our reactions and responses, not people. We need to practice responding calmly, precisely, and honestly instead of reacting in anger, retaliation, or by shutting down. We learn to do this by thinking first, not reacting first.

Intentional and proactive decisions and actions need to be made. We discovered long ago that no one will come to us and say, "Perhaps I can come to your house today so you can catch up on the rest you need or all the paperwork that is left undone." Sure, some people will see the need and step up to the plate with offers to help, but we can't expect it, demand it, or wish for it. We need to plan it. If that means saying no to people or asking to be released from previous commitments (by going to the person in authority), then that is what we must do. It's like taking a shaken pop can and purposely setting it down until you know you can open it without it spraying all over the place. We need to take charge of what is going on so that we don't explode.

When we are fatigued and someone asks us to do something, we need to practice saying "no." Capability is not the same as availability.

Discipline is needed in order to be intentional and proactive. If we are tossed by the winds of others' demands and expectations on us, we will never say no and always be in need of rest. When caring for those with special needs, we must put aside time for ourselves. That will take discipline in a world where most people don't realize that what we do for ourselves we are also doing for another. We are left exhausted and depleted if we don't stop and recharge.

Barter with others and **delegate** to others for help. If you can provide a service for someone who can provide another service for you, make the trade. When our children were young, we had a relative who helped clean while Cindi did some sewing for her. Neither paid the other in currency, but each did what she enjoyed and both got what she needed. Sometimes we must look for a creative solution to the problem in order to get sufficient rest. When we do what we enjoy, we expend much less effort and experience far more enjoyment, so we are less exhausted. Time is required to find someone who can fill the gaps of what you need and whose gaps you can help fill, but the time and effort eventually pay off for both of you. Delegating means putting someone in charge of what you've asked them to do without necessarily returning the favor.

Procrastinating can get us every time. When we put off what we know we must do, we keep putting today's list into tomorrow's, and before we know it we have a list too long to bother with. We get overwhelmed.

Practical Tips below provide us with ways to refresh our bodies and minds to avoid or reduce stress. Not everyone will be able to do all these things all the time. You will need creativity to alter them to suit your own needs. Remember, solutions are not the same for everyone; we must learn to do what works for us in our specific situation. When we sense the stressful warning signs in our lives, try the following:

- ✓ Listen to slow, soothing music, not fast or loud music.
- ✓ Pray. Isaiah 40:31, "Those who wait upon the Lord shall renew their strength."
- ✓ Schedule "buffer" times when we can put our feet up for a few moments.
- ✓ Get exercise—walk, run, stretch, kick box, swim.
- ✓ Sit and stand in comfortable positions with good posture, so we don't put stress on our back and neck. Keep this in mind at work, home, and at play.
- ✓ LAUGH! Take the stressors of the day and pretend we're in a sitcom. This doesn't work all the time (when things are serious or critical), but sometimes we just have to laugh or we'll wind up always in tears.
- ✓ Rest. Take a daily short nap, a weekly day off, and a yearly vacation, if possible.
- ✓ Work to get seven to eight consecutive hours of sleep a night.
- ✓ Walk outside and take a few deep breaths of fresh air.
- ✓ Organize the desk, purse, junk drawer, or closet (start somewhere).
- ✓ Women: Check the calendar to see if PMS is an added emotional issue.

✓ Stay away from people who know how to "push our buttons."

✓ Avoid negative thinkers.

✓ Delegate things that need to get done.

✓ Call someone who will encourage us, make us laugh.

✓ Discover a hobby to enjoy.

✓ Find someone who will hold you accountable if we feel you are "losing it"—a mentor or advisor to listen and help guide.

✓ Plan dinner the night before or very early in the morning so it's not always a last-minute stressor.

✓ Correct situations that need improving, but don't manipulate to get our way.

✓ Express thankfulness often—to God, to family, to friends.

✓ List priorities. Are we doing what we say is important?

✓ Expect interruptions every day. Don't expect to watch an entire movie or television show, or have lengthy phone conversations.

✓ Don't answer any phone calls if in the middle of a stressful situation.

✓ Limit email responses to once daily. Keep messages brief.

✓ Limit email reading to a convenient time of your day. Delete messages that require sending attachments to ten people. Delete message that contain urban legends.

✓ Learn to say no to people and projects that weigh down and discourage. (Yes, this is an ongoing struggle.)

✓ Learn to accept our limitations in the situation—in all resources of time, money, energy, talents, gifts, and abilities.

✓ Learn to let go of what we can't control.

✓ Allow time for the person you are caring for to respond if their response time is not typically normal.

✓ Consider all the steps we need to go through and plan for them (e.g., showering or bathing the person needing care); explaining the activity to them, writing it out for them to view if that is helpful. Anything that helps them understand makes our job easier and smoother.

✓ Rephrase what and how we say things. Use a different tone of voice so others respond better to us.

✓ Don't respond sharply to someone who is stressed out (Proverbs 15:1).

✓ Turn off the television or radio.

- ✓ Learn relaxation techniques (deep breathing, quiet music).
- ✓ Slow down the pace of life (Mark 6:30-32) by surrendering tasks (Matthew 11:28-30) in the day that are not priorities.
- ✓ Learn when to leave a tense situation and have a place to go. If thoughts arise of harming the person with special needs or ourselves, have someone to call so we do not become abusive in any way—verbally, physically, or mentally.
- ✓ Plan a day away or a vacation, if possible. Taking along a special needs person does not always constitute a true day away or vacation because we are doing nothing different from the normal routine, not resting or being refreshed.
- ✓ Prepare for holidays, parties, and company weeks and days ahead, not the day before.
- ✓ Stop procrastinating and start something that needs to be done.
- ✓ Put an activity on our list we know we'd really enjoy doing.
- ✓ Eat well, not on the run. Sit down and relax.
- ✓ Learn time management techniques to make better use of the time we have.
- ✓ See a doctor for yearly check ups and share our stress level with her or him.
- ✓ Serve someone who has a need. Doing so will help us keep our situation in perspective.
- ✓ Cry.
- ✓ Smile more.
- ✓ Take simple trips often to get a cup of coffee, see a movie, and enjoy ice cream.
- ✓ Read.
- ✓ Enjoy a Jacuzzi or bubble bath.
- ✓ Watch a movie.
- ✓ Play a game.
- ✓ Go to www.cindiferrini.com or www.joeferrini.com and print the *Questions to Help Balance the Active Life.*
- ✓ "Let go" of people's stares, people's comments, the lack of help received. (Yes, we're still learning this one, too!)
- ✓ Say yes to help.

✓ Don't let the one we are caring for always be the center of attention.

✓ Try to look at daily struggles as daily blessings whenever possible. Doing so facilitates a positive attitude.

✓ Grieve the things that are lost to us, but begin to dream about the future and positive things that can happen as that future unfolds.

✓ Seek support from support groups or others in a similar situation.

If we are stressed, too busy, upset, and frazzled, we will be unproductive, unable to care for the special needs person in our life or our own well-being. Stress and lack of rest result in a distorted perspective on most things. If we aren't healthy, how can we expect to care for our loved one(s)? When we eliminate the stress others cause us and the stress we cause ourselves, we are left with the stress God has allowed. From there we learn, live, develop, and grow.

Stress and lack of rest result in a distorted perspective on most things.

When going through the practical ways to avoid and reduce stress, we need to ask ourselves which ones will be most helpful and meaningful to us personally. Walking may be good for one, but not necessarily for another. One might actually find walking stressful. The idea is to choose ways that help you and your situation.

If We're Rested, What Will Rest Actually Look Like?

When we are physically rested and filled with the Holy Spirit, we will feel refreshed and sense restoration in all areas of our life (mentally, physically, spiritually, and emotionally). We'll resemble Jesus quietly meeting the needs of the woman at the well (John 4:6), be able to sleep through the fierce gales of wind and waves crashing over the boat (Mark 4:38), and be able to discern when to find quiet and when to minister to others (Mark 6:16-47).

Being rested, refresh, and restored will look like this:

✓ New and renewed love for God, others in our life, and the one we care for

✓ We'll enjoy the platform from which to share our life with others because we have endured and grown

✓ Zeal for life

✓ Passion to do whatever God has called us to do

✓ Realistic expectations, that is, figuring out personally what that looks like

- ✓ Acceptance of the reality of our purpose and that of the one for whom we care
- ✓ Acceptance of our own limitations and willingness to ask for help
- ✓ Marking boundaries for healthy balances in our life, for example, getting out verses staying home, dismissing wrong comments verses confronting in love when needed
- ✓ Good time management and goal setting in the midst of much caring
- ✓ The development of good problem solving skills and seeking and knowing how we can improve our situation
- ✓ Working well with the support system of professionals, paraprofessionals, family, and friends
- ✓ Making mistakes and willingly admitting them
- ✓ Honesty in admitting sin and humility in confessing it
- ✓ Flexibility during the day-to-day and moment-to-moment inconveniences, irritations, frustrations so that others see patience, wisdom, and understanding yet realizing we'll never be perfect
- ✓ Controlling our own behavior (Galatians 5:22-23)
- ✓ Controlling our expectations, wishes, desires—yielding to God's plan
- ✓ Asking for help when necessary and needed
- ✓ Making recreation and exercise a part of our day
- ✓ Recognizing our limitations *and* God's unlimited resources
- ✓ A sense of refreshment, rejuvenation, happiness, joy, and energy that might be described as inner peace and outer contentment
- ✓ Moving from victim to advocate by changing our mindset from what is happening to us in this challenge to what we can do for the one under our care

And in this process, we will be a good example to others who are in the midst of their most challenging times. Pressure on coal is necessary to produce a diamond; and the irritation of a grain of sand in any oyster, to produce a pearl. We all want to be the sparkling gem, the pearl, the marble masterpiece or the refined gold, but are we willing to go through the process to get us there? Even in the midst of great hardship, struggle, and stress, we can thank God for the trials that strengthen our faith. (Psalm 73:26, "My flesh and heart may fail; but God is the strength of my heart and my portion forever.") We don't make muscles without working them. It is the pain and suffering, the pressure and the irritations that allow us to experience growth and endurance as we develop to be all God wants us to be!

Evaluate

We'd like to think that by implementing the practical tips noted above we'd reap the benefits of a life that allows rest, restoration, and refreshment. Although this is true to an extent, we should be realistic and understand that our human nature will require us to evaluate the decisions we make to be sure we are rested, restored, and refreshed. Sometimes—OK, we'll speak for ourselves—we get off track again and find ourselves in need of rest because stress has crept back into our life. Instead of feeling as if we're "in the game," we find ourselves two steps behind where we want to be and can't quite catch up; we may have bad attitudes or are frustrated. So what do we do? We stop, reevaluate, ask ourselves what is working and what is not. We ask according to James 1:2-8 for the wisdom we lack in a given situation, trusting that God will provide it. We ask for creativity to see a problem from a different perspective, find a new approach to a continuous problem, or a new method to accomplish a goal in a new way. That may come from God through our minds or through the help of people in our lives.

If we sense failure, we need to reevaluate (gathering as much information as we can) to see where we need to pray, get help, or move on. If our difficulties are a matter of unfulfilled expectations, then we need to find hope. If we feel we can't move from where we are, we need to get professional psychological help. Sometimes others can see things so much more clearly and get us on a right path quickly. Don't waste precious time wondering and waiting.

We can't fool God, and if we're honest, we don't fool others or ourselves either. We need to reflect honestly, redefine, refocus, renew, respond, and reenter life! We fine-tune passions, talents, experiences, motivations, and gifts to blend with what God already has for us. The journey can be exciting.

Coping While Caring

The *Practical Tips* can put us on the road to rest, but most times we must be the ones giving ourselves permission to see them through. We can't expect others to provide them for us. We need to be realistic and realize that others either can't or won't help. We might desire free time to exercise or pay bills, but have difficulty in finding it because caregiving responsibilities are so time-consuming. So how do we handle that?

For us to cope while caring for our loved ones, we made it a point to have something to do to fill those moments of free time, making the most of any free moments we had. Having a few minutes to do things we enjoyed helped us to make the best of a challenging situation, giving us some time to divert our attention from the situation at hand to something we could enjoy for a short time for ourselves. Depending on whether we were in our own home or out, our list may have had some of the following to choose from:

- ✓ Read—catching up on articles, books, devotions, mail, magazines that we'd put aside for a quiet moment
- ✓ Exercise
- ✓ Make phone calls
- ✓ Write letters or notes to encourage or keep in touch with others
- ✓ Cook
- ✓ Do a handcraft
- ✓ Listen to music
- ✓ Take a nap while they slept

Keeping a list of tasks and chores we *needed* to do as well as things we *wanted* to do helped us to accomplish things along the way. Doing so, we felt a sense of satisfaction.

We continue to find laughter a great way to cope. At age twenty-seven, Josh Blue won *Last Comic Standing* by the vote of the public by laughing at his own disability (cerebral palsy), describing his humor as "spastic and energizing." We need to laugh at ourselves. People like him help us do that.

When a Caregiver Helps or Is Employed in the Home

Having additional people in our homes for extended periods of time can be very stressful, whether they are family or those hired to help. Having people in our home for Joey's or Mom Ferrini's therapies, Dad Chmelik's overnight caregiver, or the company (friends, visitors) they receive while under our care causes interruptions in our schedule accompanied by comments, advice, or ideas they want to share; and that boils down to additional relationships to manage within the home.

We need to go back to learning to handle relationships, knowing how to set boundaries, and expressing thanks for their help. We need to situate our minds and our day to accept help and/or visitors and then set out to use the time wisely to get things done that we need to, or to get the rest we need when our loved ones are under the care of others. There may be a time period where we feel we can't give ourselves permission to rest or do something we want to do, but the sooner we get over that guilt trip, the better. Others can help, and we should allow them. By doing so, it allow us to take care of ourselves and stay healthy. Psalm 127:2 gives us the permission we need: "It is vain for you to rise up early, to retire late, to eat the bread of painful labors; for He gives to His beloved even in his sleep."

- We have a daytime nurse to help with our two special needs children. She takes care of the children so I can write checks and pay bills and make administrative phone calls (many are required and most last thirty minutes) as we seek care for our children. I needed some time to feel free to do other things while the nurse worked. For a while I felt as if I were a bad mom if I didn't stay with her and help meet the needs of my children right along with her. I had to get over that.

- The life-threatening accident and subsequent health issues that gripped my husband permanently finally got us to restore our values, get our minds and hearts on what is important, and learn how to weather the storms and stresses of life. Our trials brought us closer to the Lord and His perfect peace.

Having some mentors and people to advise me as I learn to "go the distance" has been a great stress-relieving help!

- My husband I take advantage of every moment of quality time we can fit into our schedules. When our son is at his workshop or a planned supervised activity, my husband and I spend time with each other. We are both employed full time (just to keep above financial disaster), and time is short.

- I don't have much personal life because there is very rarely time for ME.

- Having some mentors and people to advise me as I learn to "go the distance" has been a great stress-relieving help!

- Relief is not just a spa day away. I need consistent times away for refreshment, alone (by myself), with my husband or with girlfriends sometimes.

- I let technology help me. I let the answering machine take messages and I answer when I have a convenient moment. I try to keep phone calls to about 15 minutes so the day is not consumed with phone conversation.

- Because I am constantly in the caregiving mode, I make sure I close my eyes and nap whenever my loved one is sleeping. I may not get the laundry completed all in one day, but I stay refreshed and feel good. When I feel good, I'm more pleasant and better able to end the day on a happy note.

YOUR STORY

On a scale of 1-10 (10 being the highest) rate your STRESS level: _____

On a scale of 1-10 (10 being the highest) rate your REST level: _____

If you are observing someone ready to implode or explode, what one thing could you say to her or him or do to provide encouragement?

_____

_____

Where are you on the road to weary?

_____

_____

What warning signs are you experiencing? Are they internal, external, and/or physical stressors?

_____

_____

_____

Can you say you are rested? Why or why not?

_____

_____

_____

Review the Practical Tips for refreshing yourself. What three or four would most help you?

_____

_____

_____

_____

How can God be the source of both stress and rest?

_____

_____

Do you think finding yourself at a point of weakness is necessary in order to experience God's strength?

_____

_____

How do you typically respond to stress? How has God helped you over that?

_____

_____

Are you holding onto anything that adds pressure to your life?

_____

_____

Read Psalm 94:19 and put it into your own words:

_____

_____

Describe what a healthy routine would look like for you:

_____

_____

Real peace is not just a matter of positive thinking alone. What other things have you learned that will help you go from stressed to rested?

_____

_____

_____

CHAPTER TWELVE

Fork in the Road:
Who Knows What is Good or Bad?

Living in Fraser, a suburb of Detroit, Michigan, I (Cindi) remember our family enjoying a close relationship with the family next door. Just a year older than me, their son Mark was different from anyone I had known. All the neighborhood kids played softball in the empty lot across the street. Mark would hit the ball fine, but running seemed to be quite an effort. Even as a kid I noticed that he loved sports. We eventually moved away, but I remember my folks always telling me of his continued love for sports and his desire to go into that field in some capacity. It never occurred to me as it had to my parents that it would be challenging for a Little Person to make it in the sports industry.

I don't recall ever seeing the words *sports* and *Little Person* used in print in the same sentence, unless of course the author was writing about Mark Andrews. Mark might have been short, but what he lacked in height he made up in perseverance, character, stamina, and humor. When I think of Mark, I recall his good nature and humor before his stature. I actually thought little of his stature, no pun intended, because he was big hearted, fun-loving, and kind! He had said, "I'm not unusual, but I guess I am different. Being a dwarf (born to normal-sized parents) has never bothered me. In fact, I truly believe that if I had been of normal size, I wouldn't be where I am today." His journey took him from hard-working push-up king of his junior high school (with a record seventy push-ups) to radio disc jockey and newscaster to the public address announcer for the Lions, Pistons, Michigan Stags, and Panthers and finally from his off-camera jobs to TV sports announcer and motivational speaker. He always said, "If I can do it, you can do it" (Tom Greenwood, "Being Short is No Big Deal," *Detroit News*, September 4, 1991).

I recall his visit to our home in the Cleveland area, bringing along his good friend, a seven-foot player for the Pistons, and his great sense of humor. He said, "When he and I hang around together, people can't help but look at us. I wonder if they think we're in the circus." His humor was trumped only by his work ethic. "My message is always the same: With hard work you can be as big

362

as you want to be."

Mark lost his battle to cancer some years ago, but he's never lost his place in our hearts— a great example of motivation, a wonderful father of two, and someone whose legacy continues.

OUR STORY

We've enjoyed hearing a story told about a farmer and his horse via radio and the Internet. Join us in the Internet version to get a feel for where we're going with this chapter!

> *Once there was a farmer whose horse ran away. His neighbor came over to tell him he felt sorry for him, only to be told in return: "Who knows what is good or bad?" It was true. The next day the horse returned, bringing with it eleven wild horses it had met during its adventurous escape. The neighbor came over again, this time to congratulate the farmer on his good fortune. Only to be told once again "Who knows what is good or bad? True this time too; the next day the farmer's son tried to tame one of the wild horses and fell off, breaking his leg. His neighbor came back again one more time to express how bad he felt; but for the third time all the farmer had to say was: "Who knows what is good or bad?" And once again the farmer was correct, for this time, the king of that land had started a war and the following day soldiers came by to draft young men into the army, but because of his injury the son was not taken.*

Well! Life isn't fair, or is it? We have so much to lose, yet so much to gain. This little story certainly puts a new spin on our thinking, doesn't it?

Having a special needs son who has needed full time care all his life and parents who needed help for a short time in their declining years had us asking ourselves questions like these:

✓ Is this fair? (To us, to him, to them?)

✓ Is what we're dealing with ever going to amount to anything good?

✓ Should we continue to pray for Joey to be healed?

✓ Should we pray for anyone to be healed?

✓ What in the world is God trying to show us here?

✓ When will this journey end? It seems never-ending.

Helping Joey put a worm on his hook to fish at my father-in-law's pond; I (Joe) was thinking about how helpless my little boy was and how unfair it all seemed.

Dad Chmelik's words pierced my heart as I thought he heard me say those thoughts out loud, "Joe, someday your son will be a blessing to you." My immediate response was "But right now I don't see it that way." Today I do. The years have blended together like the beautiful colors on a watercolor painting. Time has us in a place where the scene is just as Dad Chmelik said it would be.

Like the farmer in the story above, we see things from a perspective today that we did not have for a long time. We have come to see God's faithfulness in many ways. Our journey has allowed us to observe things from a perspective different from the one we might have had otherwise. We gained a good perspective as we learned to see things God's way. We've learned to embrace life as we never thought we would or could.

Initially, we were afraid, frightened, worried, frustrated, and sometimes angry about our son's day-to-day care and future. We wanted a son who was normal, who could play sports, do well in school, know and serve God, play an instrument, and have a great job someday. We had parents whose health was declining rapidly before our eyes, and we felt the same emotions and frustrations with them as we did with our son. Watching God work in Joey's life and ours, we knew He would work in the life of our parents as well. We simply needed to trust that God would give us only what we could handle and that He would show us how to get through it. He gave us the faith to believe and trust Him in it. (Hebrews 11:1, "Now faith is the assurance of things hoped for, the conviction of things not seen.") Once we trusted, we saw Him as trustworthy. That grew our faith. As our faith grew, we were better able to obey Him instantly in handling the most difficult situations and in making some of the most challenging decisions. His faithfulness has shaken us out of what might have been a life of complacency. Crisis will do that. Crisis initiates change.

In James 1:2-4, 12 we find the positive and negative of trials and triumphs in our lives, "Consider it all joy, my brethren, when you encounter various trials, knowing that the testing of your faith produces endurance. And let endurance have its perfect result, that you may be perfect and complete, lacking in nothing. Blessed is a man who perseveres under trial; for once he has been approved, he will receive the crown of life, which the Lord has promised to those who love Him." If we believe Psalm 138:8a—"The Lord will accomplish what concerns me"—then we must also believe that what concerns us will have a perfect result in our lives. He will use those trials that seem so negative and tragic to make us more like Him, to make us need and depend upon Him, and in the process lead others to Him. As we anticipate seeing

His faithfulness has shaken us out of what might have been a life of complacency. Crisis will do that. Crisis initiates change.

the vast Grand Canyon, we can anticipate that God will use the vastness of our difficulties and trials and travel the road with us. "For it is God who is at work in you, both to will and to work for His good pleasure" (Philippians 2:13).

So how do we do it? How will you do it? What will we do with what He has given us? We embrace it. Like the farmer we embrace whatever comes our way. We embrace it all! After all, who knows what is good or bad?

EMBRACE

The unfamiliar became familiar as we embraced it; we learned to rejoice in the little things, embrace them; and we actually lived long enough to help others learn to do the same thing! We embraced the challenges and difficulties early in our lives because we had to. It was a matter of survival. Today we embrace things because we have the privilege of doing so and the privilege of thanking God for bringing us through those challenges and difficulties. Are we done? Are there no more difficulties? No, we still have them every day. We're just learning better how to handle them, embrace them.

Embrace Special Moments

As we look at life from our rearview mirror, our Joey ended up playing sports after all! He played on a team with fifteen other special needs kids. Yes, they were a team of fifteen. They ran (by foot or wheelchair) the bases when the coaches told them to and were able to steal bases because the outfield took a lot of time getting the ball back to the playing field. Every game ended in a tie. They kids never understood that one, and as parents, we just had such joy watching those kids play and have fun. They could have never competed unless they were with others who had special needs. No one made fun of the kid in the wheelchair, and everyone cheered the kid who could hit the ball but then had to be given his walker to get to first base. Playing at those games was just like playing in a big stadium to those kids. Who knows what is good or bad?

Our Joey indeed graduated from high school *and* a vocational school. Although his certificate looks different from the ones our girls received, we figure he's graduated with a double major. He was also named the Polaris Vocational School Top Student in his class. Did we ever think something like that would happen? As his dad said, "He has faithfully used the capabilities, abilities, and availabilities God gave him to do the very best he could. Not everyone can say that." He serves God without the ability to say a word. Watch him worship, and you know there is a God. He was allowed to play the tambourine in middle school because the teacher said she wanted someone to do it who could keep a beat! The high school kids had it figured out, so he was out of a job there; but after high school he got a "cream of the crop" job that keeps him busy with people he enjoys and gets paid to do it. Who knows what is good or bad?

As a twelve-year-old our elder daughter said she'd take her brother some day and has never wavered from that commitment. She even married a wonderful young man who agreed to have Joey live with them someday. Where does that character come from? Who knows what is good or bad?

And what about our other little girl who has grown from one who was easily frustrated by Joey to the young woman who will let him kiss her on her cheek or hug her in *public*? When did that transformation take place? Who knows what is good or bad?

Embrace the Waiting Room of Life

This life offers us so much to taste, experience, and enjoy. And with so much at our fingertips many do it all at an unhealthy pace. In the waiting room of life, we tend to experience situations differently from the way others may; for example, speeding things up with people who are challenged is impossible. We wait for them to use the bathroom, to put their shoes on, to finish their temper tantrum for the fifth time that day at age thirty-five. If we aren't waiting for them, they are waiting for us to meet their needs. Joey will put his shoes on and wait 20 minutes for us to remember to come and tie them. They may be easily distracted, which is good when you want them to stop something but bad when you don't want them to stray. Yes, they slow us down. All that waiting actually gives us time to figure out that life involves more than our own needs, what we want to experience, what we want to do or say or feel. How negative is that? Some people take a lifetime to learn that lesson; some never do. And for the record, we have met some of the nicest people in our waiting room of life: the person (whose daughter had special needs) who opened up a spot for Joey (in his wheelchair) to fit in a close spot to see the Disney fireworks display; the one who recommended reading material to help us care for our parents when they had special needs. These people are faces without names but we are thankful for each of them. Who knows what is good or bad?

Embrace the Moment

Teaching Joey how to choose clothing and how to put it on took years. He still doesn't get it right. Instead of feeling frustration with having to turn a shirt around for the eight thousandth time (this is not an exaggeration—do the math) we embrace the moment and laugh. Hearing Joey call us to help him tie his shoes, wipe himself, or clean his nose is not tops on our list of fun things to do; but we have learned to embrace the moment and thank God that he can put his shoes on by himself, walk to the toilet and sit until we help him, and he can reach for a Kleenex by himself. Others are not so fortunate. We are. Who knows what is good or bad?

We watched Joey blowing air out of his mouth for years, only to enjoy his first whistle at age 21 hearing him say, "Just like Grandpa Ferrini – Joey whistled!" What twenty five year old loves watching Lawrence Welk and dances around the family room with his mom, and both enjoy it? What twenty year old lights up to see a commercial for Care Bears and remembers having one as a kid, and asks for it again?! What young man is as excited to see us pick him up after work as he is to greet us after being gone for 3 days? They are all moments to embrace, and who knows what is good or bad?

When we tuck Joey in at night, we know he's going to stay there. He won't be out until 3:00 a.m., making us wonder where he is and whether he'll arrive home safely. He's right where we left him. Who knows what is good or bad?

When he kisses us goodnight, initiates a family group hug (and will include you if you're with us), asks to have help to leave a *nice* note for Dad, tells us to "Speak up good" at conferences, gets excited to see us when we walk in the door, all like a five-year-old, who knows what is good or bad?

When we'd fight our frustrations helping our parents eat because they were messy and drooling, we learned to treasure those moments knowing there were to be fewer and fewer of them. Embrace each moment.

Embrace a Perspective

We'll take Joey talking to Raggedy Ann and Andy because we've not had to deal with a rebellious teen. We'll take wiping Joey's face and bottom over wiping our own tears over a wayward son. We'll take his occasional outbursts over a disrespectful child who talks back; doing so willfully and defiantly. We'll appreciate that Joey's needs are simple and seldom asks for things over a child who expects everything handed to him or her. We appreciate that his lack of verbal skills keeps him from gossiping or criticizing others, and his lack of mental skills keeps him from analyzing everyone and everything as we do. We'll always have Christmas in our home because one of us will always believe in Santa—after all, he makes a personal visit! He loves Spiderman, the Power Rangers, and all super heroes and likely always will. We'll embrace the fact we have to drive him 13,000 miles to work every year, thankful that he has work and the self-worth that comes with it. Who knows what is good or bad?

We have enjoyed watching our daughters care for their brother to allow us to go out, seeing them minister to others in their areas of giftedness because they have learned to serve. Who knows what is good or bad?

Embrace a Personal Faith, Prayer, and Our Creator

We'll treasure fond memories seeing Joey on his knees in his bedroom with the door closed, looking up at our interruption, opening his eyes, and saying, "I was on my knees praying and worshipping God."

At age seven Joey kept touching his head as we tucked him into bed. We were unsure what was wrong. He'd say, "Nonnie's nap." After a while we figured it out with Grandma's help: He was telling us that Nonnie (Grandma) would wash his face before his nap so it was clean for the angels to kiss it.

Sitting in church, Joey heard many times the invitation to be baptized. We never mentioned it to him because he did not like going under water. But at age twenty-one, he tapped us on the shoulder and said, "Me do that." Joey completely cooperated as our pastor helped him into the water. He allowed Pastor Jonathan to lay him back getting everything but his face wet! Then with a plastic pitcher, Pastor poured water over Joey's head to seal the deal. Joey to this day will say, "I already did that," showing us he understood he only needed to do that one time. He shows us over and over what it is to have the childlike faith the bible tells us we should have.

We suppose he has treasures beyond what we could possibly know. Matthew 6:21, "For where your treasure is, there will your heart be also." Luke 18:16, "Permit the children to come to Me, and stop hindering them, for the kingdom of God belongs to such as these." Clearly, spiritual life of someone special is indeed special. Who knows what is good or bad?

Embrace Humorous Moments

Laughter and fun diminish the negatives that result from everyday frustrations with people and their attitudes. Sometimes we have such a serious crisis that we can't laugh or we might laugh quite inappropriately to release the pressure that builds during those difficult times. Onlookers catching us laughing at inappropriate times need to understand the pressure and give grace in the moment. At all times we should avoid inappropriate actions and responses because we can hurt others, surprise them in a negative way, or cause questions as to our intent. It happens, but all parties involved must learn to extend grace.

In Chapter Five we told you how Joey had difficulty dressing himself properly. Well, just the other day, we went to check to see how he was getting along after his shower. His undershirt was on inside out. His pajamas bottoms were on backwards, and he was trying his best to get his head to fit into the sleeve of his pajama shirt. This has not changed all these years. Should we express anger or frustration or try to hurry him along? Sometimes we just have to laugh.

Dropping Joey off at work one day, we asked him what the handicapped sticker was for in our car. He quickly responded, "For Daddy!"

After high school graduation Joey informed us he would like to go to Ohio State to become a coach. Visiting Columbus that summer, we took a side trip with him to the stadium. We told him we could leave him there if he was ready to get to work. After taking one look at The Horseshoe stadium, he was quick to let us know he had changed his mind!

Joey asked me (Cindi) to do something he was able to do, "Mom, you do this for me?" I said, "What do you think I am?" Without missing a beat he said, "A maid!" (How many times had he heard *me* say that?)

A bunch of us sat around the table at my (Cindi's) folks' house. Dad was at a point where we needed to assist him in eating. Everyone was eating popcorn. He dropped a piece or two but said nothing. I had dropped a few kernels, too, but he wasn't saying anything about himself or me. Normally he would have. He had always been a neat and polite person and dropping food would have been embarrassing. So I started dropping kernels on purpose. Everyone noticed and was watching Dad observing but not saying a word. As I wheeled him from the table, he looked at everyone around the table and said, "And don't you think all those on the floor are mine. Most of those are Cindi's!" We all had a good laugh, and I think Dad did, too!

Joey said, "MOM, BRUCE (a friend from work) GOT A NEW CAR!" OK, actually, his *driver* got a new car. Joey was truly happy for him!

When we have a good laugh and can see the humor in a situation, who knows if it's good or bad?

Look For Benefits

Embracing life allows us to look for the benefits in what we are experiencing. Doing so allows us to look for ways to appreciate all aspects of life. The following are benefits we've enjoyed over the years of caring for a son with special needs and parents who required our help:

- ✓ Relied on God, not ourselves, in our challenging situations
- ✓ Strengthened our love and devotion to God (Psalm 116)
- ✓ Watched all three of our children come to a saving knowledge of Jesus Christ
- ✓ Learned our weaknesses and who we were in the midst of them
- ✓ Discovered our strength was in the Lord and saw we were to become

more like Him as long as we surrendered to His will

✓ Determined what was realistic about life, what was important, and what to let go—coming to recognize the privilege of serving our loved one

✓ Enjoyed what bound us together—prayer, love, family and friends

✓ Learned discipline helping Joey, our folks, and our family develop routines to deal with constant and unending challenges

✓ Developed flexibility in our attitudes and in daily adjustments, making quick changes often

✓ No pain? No gain and life would be mundane!

✓ Learned to use time wisely because we seldom had free time; no room to waste time

✓ Gained a perspective of appreciation, thankfulness for the little things regarding people, places, and things as well as Joey's accomplishments, taking nothing for granted (Philippians 4:12)

✓ Realized early in our marriage that a personalized character-building opportunity had presented itself to us, our children, and our extended family—moment to moment, day to day and watched God equip us in our weakness

✓ Watched Joey overcome obstacles that our girls found very simple

✓ Welcomed guests to our home and extended hospitality; a few years in a row we topped a thousand visitors to our home for meetings, meals, dessert, fellowship; tired but blessed and fulfilled to have company

✓ Watched Joey and our parents learning to live in the moment and learned to do the same—not a day in the past, not a moment into the future

✓ Made some great friends—perhaps you're one of them! Our life is so full and blessed with people who have embraced us that it's becoming easier to brush off unkind words of those who are unkind or uncaring.

✓ Developed the ability to give unconditional love to one who can't always give us what we need or want and truly understand the privilege we have to serve

✓ See the value in every life, not the length or quality of life but its value

✓ Discovered that being *dis*abled with special needs does not mean a person is *un*able. Individuals might do things more slowly or need a lot of help, but they can do some things, even if just a simple smile.

Yes, caring for another certainly makes our life different from that of others, but when we see where God has been faithful and carried us through, we can reflect on the past and contemplate with assurance what the future will be like.

- ✓ **Romans 5:3-4**, "And not only this, but we also exult in our tribulations, knowing that tribulation brings about perseverance, and perseverance, proven character; and proven character, hope; and hope does not disappoint, because the love of God has been poured out within or hearts through the Holy Spirit who was given to us."

- ✓ **James 1:17**, "Every good thing and every perfect gift is from above, coming down from the Father of lights."

- ✓ **Isaiah 35:5-6**, "Then the eyes of the blind will be opened, and the ears of the deaf will be unstopped. Then the lame will leap like a deer, and the tongue of the dumb will shout for joy."

- ✓ **Jeremiah 29:11-13**, "'For I know the plans that I have for you,' declares the Lord, 'plans for welfare and not for calamity to give you a future and a hope. Then you will call upon Me and come and pray to Me and I will listen to you. And you will seek Me and find Me when you search for Me with all your heart.'"

- ✓ David wrote in Psalm 119:71, "It is good for me that I was afflicted that I may learn Thy statutes."

- ✓ Perhaps God has a plan that is preparing us for something we don't know about. Who knows what is good or bad?

OTHERS' STORIES

- "Blessed Be Your Name," a song by Matt Redman says it all for me. "Blessed be Your name when the sun's shining down on me, when the world's all as it should be, blessed be Your name. Blessed be Your name on the road marked with suffering. Though there's pain in the offering, blessed be Your name. Every blessing You pour out I'll turn back to praise. When the darkness closes in, Lord, still I will say, 'Blessed be Your name.'" No matter what He sends, we will bless His name for it.

- Joni Eareckson Tada of Joni and Friends Ministry was interviewed for the winter 1996 issue of *Leadership Magazine* in an article entitled "Thriving with Limitations" about the paralysis she suffered from a diving accident as a teen. She said, "But for me, life is always difficult. These are issues I must face every single morning. (Dave, would you give me a sip of my coffee?) The woman who helps me each morning is going through some difficult times. When she tells me her struggles, I could say, 'Snap out of it. I've been paralyzed for twenty-eight years. You only think you've got problems.' But I need to look at her needs rather than my own. How can I bless her today? Now, many years later, it's not a bed of affliction anymore. It's become an altar of praise. This physical enforcement of stillness causes something in my life that wouldn't have happened if I were on my feet running around. I'm forced to lean on God whether I like it or not. My choices are limited" (p. 62).

- Our son (who has learning disabilities) has made some negative choices with addictions, broken relationships, and attempted suicide; but one always has hope with the Lord. We see glimpses of good.

- Therapies are so exhausting: Having to go out, meet people, learn things you never cared about or wanted to know and now have to, coming home and repeating the therapy over and over until my son's brain "gets it." All that work and then months later—the joy of seeing him learning what we were teaching!

- All the time and work we put in when our daughter was little was exhausting. She currently lives in a group home with full-time staffing and is very happy with a busy schedule. Letting her go as she says "to have her own life" was a huge challenge. She is doing well. All the work was worth it.

During an EEG for our adult son, the technician showed us the change in his brain waves when we sang hymns to him. He has very little ability to respond, but now there is proof he does.

- During an EEG for our adult son, the technician showed us the change in his brain waves when we sang hymns to him. He has very little ability to respond, but now there is proof he does.

- My friend with special needs always makes me feel good, and he is such a blessing to watch worship. He has a special relationship with the Lord because of his childlike knowledge of Him. There are no barriers to understanding God's love.

- He may have special needs, but he never holds a grudge or exhibits self-pity. He does not display jealousy, is always happy for others, and said to us one day, "I have had a hard time with this, but I know it's not my fault that I'm so slow."

- If we know Jesus, we're all perfect in His eyes. He just gives us all different strengths and weaknesses.

- I am concerned that manipulation of genes or killing atypical fetuses in the womb would mean robbing us of the lives of these very special individuals who help us see life and accomplishment in a very different way. (The same was said about mercy killing – taking the life of those aging with severe needs and those born with special needs.)

- My son has Down syndrome and volunteers at a place that gives him a free lunch. He is happy with that and his other little job. We should all have such positive attitude and gratitude.

- In my new (and empty) home I had but one table. It had just been delivered fresh from the furniture store when my dear friend and her child with special needs stopped over. The child hopped on the table, the buckle of her shiny shoe scratching a long line across the whole table. I never had it fixed so I would remember to pray for this mom and child each time I dusted or looked at it.

- I wish people would understand how my daily caretaking differs from what other moms do. The sheer number of medical appointments, therapy sessions, and time spent on the phone makes a big difference. I don't like to complain about these things, but they are the things people don't see. I also wish people knew the absolute joy that is mine in caring for my child. My child is amazing, God is amazing, and I wouldn't change a thing—except maybe more sleep!

- We've traveled a long road, but I can see that I was spared from many things, too.

- Life has been a blessing and a trial because we have been able to reach out to many in a similar situation, but we've also been kept from doing other things we might have enjoyed.

- Working with special needs adults (my son being one of them) in Special Olympics allows me many learning opportunities. I was paired in a cycling event with one young man with special needs and because we were slower than the rest of our group, we lagged behind. My partner seemed confident in each turn he told me to take, however, 30 miles and 5 towns later I realized he had no idea where he was taking me and I had no idea where we were! My mind did not fully reason that even though he was in great shape for cycling, he did not have the same level of ability to remember directions!

- I watch all the workers with special needs walk out of the workplace when I pick up my son. They all have the same gait. When we talk, they all have the same sound in their difficult speech. When I talk with them they all have the same simplicity about them. Honestly, sometimes I envy it. They truly are special.

- I never would have expected this to happen, but now I know how blessed we are NEVER to take anything for granted (even a smile). Even though I can't see our future, the Lord has taught me a lot through this and has given me a joy that only He can provide.

- Patrick Henry Hughes is a multi-handicapped individual who has captured the hearts of many telling others that we all must see the potential in others not their obstacles. Look him up on the Internet and enjoy his achievements.

- No sleep, no vacations, no nights out, no money—but our child is our absolute joy that few understand. I trust God as I never have before!

- Someone has said, "Experience is what you get when you don't get what you want."

- I get really excited about the next motor skill my child will learn even though the road is long to get there.

- When it comes to understanding what life has been, I say, "There are two sides to every coin." We can't always see both sides to every situation, but there are!

YOUR STORY

Read Ecclesiastes 3:1-8. If there is a time for everything, how do you put into perspective where you are in life right now?

_____

_____

_____

What are you able to embrace with the challenges you face daily?

_____

_____

_____

What is good and/or bad about what you are going through?

_____

_____

_____

What things are you learning that you can see as a benefit?

_____

_____

_____

Reread James 1:17 and discuss what "Father of lights" means to you.

_____

_____

_____

_____

EMERGENCY
STOPPING
ONLY

The Rest of the Story

CHAPTER THIRTEEN

Emergency Stopping Only: Never Quit!

A story is told of a 1976 Special Olympics track and field event that occurred in Spokane, Washington. One contestant took a tumble, and several others stopped their mission to run and win, turning around to help the fallen one; crossing the finish line together. This tender story reminds us that what truly matters in this life is helping others win, even if it means slowing down and changing our course.

OUR STORY

Honestly, we could have quit many times. Tough times bring pain and sorrow, weariness and discouragement. Giving up and quitting would be easy! If we had a dotted line on which to sign, we would have resigned long ago! Sometimes we'd fall and no one was there to help us up, but we knew we had to keep going. Sure, God is always with us, but sometimes we need a person to join us when the tough times come. The longer we have continued on this journey, the more people have come alongside us to help us finish this race. Well, it's not a race. We don't get to win anything, and we certainly don't feel we deserve any awards or honors. We want to finish well to be able to say we did it. At the 1968 Olympics, an hour after the marathon's winner crossed the finish line, Tanzania's John Stephen Akhwari limped across the finish line, injured in a fall early in the race. Asked why he didn't quit, he said, "My country did not send me 7,000 miles to start this race. My country sent me to finish." We could say the same. God has a plan for us, and He wants us to finish well. We hope somewhere along the way we will have inspired others to want to finish well, too.

Waving our little white flag of life and surrendering is not what God wants. He wants us to surrender to Him because that place of brokenness and humility is where He can best use us. But He doesn't want us to check out and quit. Where he has us takes incredible courage to continue. We win the war by winning small (and big) battles along the way. We can't know the victory until the war is over, and from where we sit and from where you sit, the war may be far from over. We can do it. Colossians 1:29 encourages us, "For this purpose also I strive according to His power, which mightily works within me." If He energizes us and gives us the power to go on, how can we possibly quit? He doesn't want us to resign or retire. He wants us to re-fire!

The Best Day of Your Life

As a young girl, Kathleen said to us, "I hear people say all the time, 'This was the best day of my life!' How do they know that is the best day of their life? How will I know the best day of my life?" We told her none of us can predict our best (or for that matter our worst) day(s). We need to live each day as though each one is our last because we never know when that day will be. As we live each day, we are privileged to look back to see the good, the bad, and the ones that fell in between. We can learn to be excited about what the future will bring because we have experienced the faithfulness of the Lord in the past.

Today Was Such a Long Day

Caring for others makes for some long days. Now and then we wish we could pick up and go somewhere without having to think about caring for someone else. What a luxury that would be for us, and yet if we had it today, we know we would be longing for someone missing from our life. It's happened to us before, and the void left by a loved one's departure is devastating.

Some care requires only our temporary involvement. The finish line is closer than we know; it's just not in view. I Peter 1:6-7 tells us, "In this you greatly rejoice, even though now for a little while, if necessary, you have been distressed by various trials, that the proof of your faith, being more precious than gold which is perishable, even though tested by fire, may be found to result in praise and glory and honor at the revelation of Jesus Christ." What a way to finish!

Some care will require us to be involved for many years. We did some simple math to calculate the number of showers or baths we've actually given and how many days we've actually spent in hospitals and nursing homes for various loved ones, but what happened was interesting. The estimated number didn't overwhelm us as we'd imagined it would. Instead we were grateful—grateful to have good health and the ability to help, to serve the Lord by serving others, and to be able to see that this situation, in light of all eternity, was still really only temporary!

When the day is long sometimes we don't feel like doing all the caregiving. Sometimes we don't feel like making dinner or going to work either, but we just do it. It's part of our responsibility and we just do it. We're not heroes. We're not special. We've just been called to do a job and desire to complete it with excellence.

Would You Like God to Heal the Person with Special Needs in Your Life?

If we had been asked as younger parents whether we wanted a cure for Joey, we would have said "yes" in a second! Today, we're not so sure.

Driving the hard road we've traveled so long has allowed us to enjoy parts of the journey we would have otherwise missed had we not taken the trip. We would not trade the way Joey kisses our hands and tells us he loves us even though he is a grown man. We would not trade the family group hug he initiates from the kindness of his heart. We would miss our six-foot-three-inch toddler climbing into bed with us during a thunderstorm—OK, we're exaggerating with that one! That gets a little tight, but even so, it's cute for the first ten minutes.

Healing would have meant missing the outstanding achievement award Joey received in high school. It would have meant not hearing him say out loud at a solo Kathleen did, "WOW! She hit the note!" (He knew the time she practiced, and he did not withhold his awe!) It would have meant missing all the lessons of growth we personally experienced.

By Not Quitting We—

- ✓ Learned that God is indeed faithful. Lamentations 3:22-23, "The Lord's loving- kindnesses indeed never cease, for His compassions never fail. They are new every morning; great is Thy faithfulness."

- ✓ Continue to learn that He never leaves us alone to conquer our trials. "Deuteronomy 31:6, "Be strong and courageous, do not be afraid or tremble at them, for the Lord your God is the one who goes with you. He will not fail you or forsake you." That is quite a promise!

- ✓ Look to the future with hope. Lamentations 3:25, "The Lord is good to those who wait for Him, to the person who seeks Him."

- ✓ Saw Him take us from trials to triumph. Lamentations 3:32, "For if He causes grief, then He will have compassion according to His abundant loving kindness."

- ✓ Learned the joy of doing not what was easy, comfortable, and fun, but what was right and good; and it is worth it.

- ✓ Followed His hand until our heart was able to catch up.
- ✓ Are learning that this adventure is more like a marathon than a sprint, more like a Tour de France than a walk in the park, and certainly more like a full-length novel than a short story or chapter in a book.
- ✓ Know we have honored and valued life by caring for our parents and our son in the best ways we could.
- ✓ Are still learning to depend on God and His reliability.
- ✓ Have learned to serve in ways others will never see and may never experience themselves.
- ✓ Had the opportunity to perform our daily and often menial tasks with an overall vision and sense of purpose, knowing God had a plan just for us.
- ✓ Have learned to keep our eyes on Jesus. Hebrews 12:1, "Let us also lay aside every encumbrance, and the sin which so easily entangles us, and let us run with endurance the race that is set before us, fixing our eyes on Jesus."
- ✓ Give Him all the credit for bringing us to this point in our lives. Galatians 6:14, "But may it never be that I should boast, except in the cross of our Lord Jesus Christ."
- ✓ Drew upon His strength instead of our own. Philippians 4:13, "I can do all things through Christ who strengthens me."
- ✓ Hope others will be encouraged to go the long haul.
- ✓ Had the privilege of writing this book to tell our story and let you tell yours!

Be Prepared for the Rest of the Ride

We can't ever expect things to be perfect. Ecclesiastes 11:4-6, "He who watches the wind will not sow and he who looks at the clouds will not reap. Just as you do not know the path of the wind and how bones are formed in the womb of the pregnant woman, so you do not know the activity of God who makes all things. Sow your seed in the morning, and do not be idle in the evening, for you do not know whether morning or evening sowing will succeed, or whether both of them alike will be good." We have to make plans; we can't wait for the conditions to be perfect for us to get moving. We have a loved one to care for, and we need to make the best of each day.

We keep praying. We know He hears our prayers and has answered them all but not always as we expected. We asked for an instant healing, which never happened in any of our caregiving situations; but we've recognized that He's always stood with us throughout the trials and challenges. He's sent the most compassionate and incredible people to us along the way. He has never left us stranded.

We all have a story that's in process and yet to be told. We have choices to make that will have a ripple effect many generations into the future. It's not about just today.

When Joey was about twenty, we decided to go through the courts to provide him guardianship. According to the law, he was able to make decisions on his own at eighteen. That was a scary thought! A woman was sent to our home to interview Joey toward the end of the process. I (Cindi) was permitted to sit in the room, but I intentionally resisted the temptation to answer for him and let the woman see that Joey indeed needed help in making decisions. The last question she asked Joey was, "Is there anyone besides your mom that you would like to have to watch over you as your guardian?" He looked at me for an answer. I told him, "Please tell the lady what you are thinking. You can tell her if there is someone you'd want to watch over you besides me."

I clearly expected him to say Aunt Susie or one of the grandparents. He looked her straight in the eye and said, "Only Jesus."

She wrote that in her notes, and it was part of the court hearing. On the day of the hearing, the magistrate said to us, "I see that Joey has another choice of guardian. I'd like to make it a part of the court documents that his first choice was Jesus; and his second choice, you, Mrs. Ferrini." I was pleased. I also wondered how many others (lawyers, court recorders, filing clerks) might have read those words. In Joey's own way, he was sharing his faith.

It may take twenty years for us to hear our loved one say something like that, and we may never hear it. But that day, his words melted away the thoughts of wanting him healed. Today, we wouldn't want Joey any other way than how God gave him to us. Joey has been a gift. Healing for Joey will be in heaven. He will be made whole, speak with clarity, walk with confidence, and probably run a few cities.

God has used the trials and challenges of caring for Joey and our parents to learn that we've had the most privileged job assignment. It's not what we signed up for, but it's the place God wanted us and the place we needed to be. We wouldn't trade it. We pray we will finish well. Matthew 25:21, "His master said to him, 'Well done, good and faithful slave, you were faithful with a few things, I will put you in charge of many things, enter into the joy of your master.'"

End of Route: When the Journey Ends

Cindi:

Although my sisters, mom, and I had worked hard together to care for my dad, it was clear that he would never improve. Mom really wanted to celebrate their fiftieth anniversary, which they did by exchanging new wedding rings. Mom inscribed in Dad's "Love all ways." They surpassed that milestone by a year and a half. About the time Dad was ready to receive hospice care, Mom asked to be alone to talk with him. We don't know what conversation ensued, but we have a feeling it went something like this: "Spark (his nickname), I'm tired. I have a feeling my heart is giving out. I'm having pain, I'm tired and want to stop going to doctors. I don't know how much longer you have, but I've cared for you the best I can. We know your time is short, and I'm thinking my time is, too. Whoever goes first, the other can follow soon after, OK?"

We might not be prepared for the journey to end, but when we have completed the task to which we were called, we will have satisfaction, no regrets, and the assurance that God was with us through it.

When Mom suffered her massive heart attack, Dad mumbled his insistence to see her. Sue lifted Dad from his own hospital bed at home to his wheelchair and rolled him out to the wheelchair lift in the van. The whole family met in the ICU for what we knew would be our last goodbyes to Mom. Dad was so confused he really didn't know where he was and Mom was nonresponsive. The picture etched in my mind is one of Sue lovingly placing Mom's hand in Dad's and watching him sob.

Mom's death came the fifth day after she collapsed. Dad's came five days later on the day I had the privilege of caring for him. I'm not sure we can ever be prepared for when the journey ends. "I love you" were the last words we said to each of our parents. The end came without regret.

We might not be prepared for the journey to end, but when we have completed the task to which we were called, we will have satisfaction, no regrets, and the assurance that God was with us through it. Psalm 84:10-12, "For a day in Thy courts is better than a thousand outside. I would rather stand at the threshold of the house of my God, than dwell in the tents of wickedness. For the Lord God is a sun and shield. The Lord gives grace and glory; no good thing does He withhold from those who walk uprightly. O Lord of hosts, how blessed is the man who trusts in Thee."

- I'm thankful to rest in knowing that my daughter, who had special needs, is with the Lord. I can recite and even embrace the verses that assure me she is eating at the banquet table, that she was spared suffering and so were we, but that's all theology. I am numb, hurting, expected to get over this quickly, and I'm learning all over again who I am and what my purpose is.

- Going to church after the death of my special child was strange. I used to get looks and stares as I wheeled her into the sanctuary. Now no one looks, and I wonder if anyone knows how empty I feel. I see another mom with her handicapped son and feel like I don't belong anymore—as if I got voted off the island. Even though it was a hard island to be on, I was familiar with it and miss it now. I am redefining myself, and doing so is hard.

- After my child's death, my biggest adjustment was being able to "choose" what to do. His needs dominated everything I did throughout the day and the thought of vacationing without him and all the gear he needed is amazing to me in exciting and frightening ways.

- The Lord sent us our daughter not because we are special parents but because He wanted to make us into the right parents for her.

- People who feel sorry for me get on my nerves. My child is the biggest blessing!

- The person I care for looks at me with the most loving and caring eyes, and I truly know unconditional love. What a great example of God's love!

- I know if our child died, we would be free of the physical things we do in caring, but we would never be free emotionally.

- The special needs person is like our missionaries in a far off land, sometimes out of sight and out of mind. Both need support to do well, whether it's daily communication, prayer, care packages, a helpful hand or encouragement on their journey.

- We have had challenges and worries but the joys far outweigh them.

- I see a special needs individual who takes great joy in wiping tables, taking a dish or mug from people when they're done, and sweeping the crumbs others have left. That made such an impact on me because there he was— the one with the handicap—and he was serving all of us. But do we serve him? Or would we? We all need to ask ourselves that question.

YOUR STORY

What makes you think you want to quit?

_____

_____

_____

Have you surrendered and quit or surrendered and yielded to God?

_____

_____

_____

Where do you see your finish line in this race?

_____

_____

_____

What has kept you from quitting? If someone has been an encouragement to you, be sure to tell them. Write an email or card. They will read it over and over.

_____

_____

_____

What have you learned by not quitting?

_____

_____

_____

Your story is not yet complete. How to you hope to see it end?

_____

_____

_____

_____

_____

Conclusion

MY STORY

Well, it's about time I get a chance to tell you things from my perspective and share my story. As you know, there are always three sides to every story. You've heard from my parents, and you'll hear from me now, but also be ready to hear from God. He's the one who'll tell you all you need to know in your own situation.

All this time my parents were writing, they never quite told you what my diagnosis is. Would you like to know? We if you do, read the next 3 paragraphs from a website that tells you about me. For years my parents didn't want to look this up because they said they liked me just like I am. But then I think curiosity got the best of them and they just *had* to get the details. I think it tells a lot about my brain, but not a lot about who I really am.

Pachygyria with mental retardation and seizures is a rare neurological disorder that is characterized by mental retardation, delays in the acquisition of skills requiring the coordination of physical and mental activities (psychomotor retardation), and/or sudden episodes of uncontrolled electrical activity in the brain (epilepsy). Several different types of epileptic seizures may occur in the same affected individual. Associated symptoms and findings are believed to result from abnormal development of the outer portion of the brain (cerebral cortex) during embryonic growth (neuronal dysmigration). In pachygyria with mental retardation and seizures, it is believed that there is a reduced number of folds in the cerebral cortex that are larger than normal (pachygria) or deep folds that are abnormally numerous and small (polymicrogyria). In some cases, the neuronal dysmigration may be the result of an underlying genetic abnormality that may be transmitted as an autosomal recessive trait.

DEFINITION: pachygyria (macrogyria)

A condition in which there are few broad gyri (hills) with shallow sulci (valleys and ridges). This anomaly is more common than lissencephaly (smooth, rather than convoluted, brain structure), and the insult producing it can occur later in gestation. The clinical picture includes severe to profound mental retardation with seizures; many people with pachygyria also have spasticity (increased muscle tone). Most cases are sporadic; however, when found with lissencephaly, pachygyria can be familial. Pachygyria can be visualized on a magnetic resonance imaging (MRI) scan.

(Lissencephaly is a birth defect that occurs during brain development in the first or second trimester of prenatal development. Basically, a gene spontaneously mutated and disrupted the normal migration of cells to form all the little ridges and valleys of my brain. The front of the brain looks pretty good, but the back and sides are either smooth (agyria) or only have large folds (pachygyria).

OK, enough of that science stuff! I'm back to telling you about myself. I have always heard I am special. I know that from listening to my parents, our family, and many friends. Since Webster defines *special* as unique, noteworthy, or particularly favored, I find that quite compliment! And indeed, that is how God created me. I'm unique in many ways—like how I walk and talk and even how I think. I know I'm different from a lot of you because sometimes I can see it in your eyes when you're tired of waiting for me to say something or want me to move faster. When someone meets me, I know I make an impression, so I guess I'm noteworthy. Most of the time people treat me pretty good, so I guess I'm particularly favored! My sisters call me the "free magnet." Wherever I go, people give me things. At county fairs I win stuffed animals all the time. The people running the games at fairs call me to come over and tell my dad I can just do it. I don't even pay to play! People try all day to win what I did in just one toss of a ring. And I love sports (Cleveland teams and The Ohio State Buckeyes). I have a collection of hats, bobblehead dolls, backpacks, signed jerseys, and all kinds of things that people have given me. My parents have saved a bundle by others' generosity! I think that's good, though, because I've watched them writing checks to doctors I've seen, therapists I've gone to, and medicines I need every day. But in God's economy I think he works out the details and has a way of equaling everything out somewhere.

You can see being special has a lot of advantages; but sometimes I see things that are a disadvantage. For instance, sometimes I think people look at special needs people as if they are contagious or something. They're afraid to touch us, hug us, and shake our hands. But those of us who have disabilities aren't contagious unless we have a cold or something. What *is* contagious is what happens when people get to know us! People start to see the world differently. Those who take care of us all catch something that makes them want to find the answers on how to better care for us. They get a super hero's dose of strength and endurance. They figure out how to get things for us that they wouldn't have ever asked for before, but because we need it, they have the guts to ask for it. They also have the guts to say things they wouldn't have said before, ask others to help that they don't even know, and find the endurance to stay awake and alert for days in a row like few others. They know that without help from others we couldn't survive. It is amazing to me how all the caregivers seem to have similar characteristics.

I think God gave my parents some doses of strength, endurance, and guts even before I was born; otherwise, He wouldn't have given me to them. From the time that student asked my mom, "If you knew your baby was going to have problems, wouldn't you have an abortion?" I knew I was being sent to the right place. I never had another worry. If she was willing to keep me safe and let me live, even after sensing that something might be wrong, I knew I'd have it made. Those nights I was up having seizure after seizure, I was so glad God gave my parents what they needed. I saw them cry sometimes, but I wasn't able to respond. I don't think they needed me to, but I saw it. I remember being in the hospital one time, and it was great that I was never left alone. I even remember Mom sleeping on some cot. I know with her bad back that wasn't easy, but she did it, and I don't think she complained. Maybe to dad, but not to me. I remember those nurses coming in to check me, and Mom would open one eye and watch everything they did, pretending to be asleep. If something would have been wrong, I know she would have popped up like a popcorn kernel! She might have fooled them, but she didn't fool me. I really enjoyed the time my folks spent with me because I knew they didn't want to be anywhere else.

I wish people knew how much I love everyone. Dad and Mom often say what a blessing it is that I never say anything wrong about anyone, except when I'm mad when "the other team" is winning! I really don't ask for much either. Really, what more could anyone want when you have all the bobbleheads and sports stuff I have—and lots of video games! When my parents got me that, the kid at the store said, "Wow, your kid is lucky. You're buying him the 'full meal deal!' I hope he knows how lucky he is!" He does! I also know how lucky I am to have a Dad who plays it for hours with me. He gets me to the next step almost all the time!

Sometimes I get really mad. I don't know why, either. It just comes out of nowhere. Sometimes I think it's because I can't express what I want to say. Sometimes it's because I'm tired, and I don't think to go to sleep. Sometimes I'm just crabby and wish I were allowed to be! Sometimes other people are grumpy, and they're allowed! I heard Mom say something about how I'm always with people and never get a break just to be alone without a parent, caregiver or supervisor. I think I've gotten a little nicer since they try to leave me alone when they go for walks or if they visit a nearby friend. They taught me how to use the redial button on the phone, so I can easily call them and not have to remember all the numbers *and* push the right buttons. And I call them a lot. I make sure they know the score of the game I'm watching. I make sure they know most of the plays. I don't think their friends mind. I really appreciate that my parents let me have some time alone.

As mad as I can get, I am quite affectionate. I often kiss Mom's hand and tell her I love her. Sometimes when I see a scratch on Dad or Mom, I'll want to kiss it. I feel bad if they are hurting. I like to hug my sisters and my brother-in-law Cos. Mostly they don't mind. If I try to give kisses on the cheek, sometimes my sister doesn't like it. I know not to give kisses to others. It's not appropriate. I shake hands and say "How are you?" to others. I finally said "How are you" on my own without anyone telling me to when I was 26. I say it very clearly and quite regularly now.

When it comes to things like clothes, I really don't need much. I like having a certain number of pants for work and a few for church. I appreciate that my family lets me wear sports shirts all the time. Everyone at work knows how much I love my sports. I've almost lost my job because of it, too. I get so excited and really don't like one particular football team, which shall remain nameless. My coworker is from that city.

Mom and Dad let me wear what I want mostly. I like that I can wear black if I'm in the Batman mode, or red, green, or white if I'm in my Power Ranger mode. When I'm watching *Joseph and the Technicolor Dreamcoat*, I have a perfect sweater Mom helps me put on. I know all the words to all the songs of most musicals I listen to. I know I'm hard to understand, but I know you can hear them if you listen carefully. Speaking of singing, I love singing in church. Sometimes people turn around. I'm not too loud, but I think people wonder where that heavenly harmony is coming from.

Things are pretty simple for me. Work all week, come home and play video games, watch movies, listen to music, go to church on Sunday, and be with my parents—that's really what I like. I liked having a Raggedy Andy, but since he left (something about a dry cleaner accident), I like having Raggedy Ann in my room. She and all my action figures (Power Rangers, Disney and Narnia characters) keep me company.

Perhaps I didn't know it so much when I was little, but I know it now. I have it made. I have parents who are dedicated to me, who drive me every day to and from work. If they didn't have me, they could have their own job! But now, I'm the only full-time worker in my house, so I think it's good they want to drive me! It keeps them busy.

Saying "I love you and like you just the way God made you" is my favorite thing to hear from Dad and Mom. I like them just how God made them, too.

Dad's my best buddy. I have lots of buddies but none like him. Mom is my only girlfriend. She told me so! I stay with her when everyone else goes for a ride or does something she is afraid of—like the helicopter ride over Niagara Falls. No way was she going to ride that! That's what she said, but I am suspicious that she caught on how afraid I was!

I've heard people say things to my parents like, "Wow, I would love a car like that," "I wish I had your house," "Wish I could have that vacation," or "I'd love to have a daughter like your girls." Funny thing, but only a very few times have I heard someone say they wished they had me. I imagine sometimes life would be so much easier if my parents and sisters didn't have me; but I hope they won't remember the heavy load they carried with me and my grandparents but that they'll remember some of the nice views on our journey along the way.

I've also heard people say to Dad and Mom, "You must be special parents to have a special child and taken care of parents who had so many problems." They usually say, "No, we're not special. We just needed more refining, and this is how God wanted to make it happen." I really think they are special. They've given up a lot to take care of me and my grandparents, but they also recognize how much God has given them. God has given them His grace to get through all kinds of situations. He's worked through and in them to make them who they are becoming. God let them see things in me that framed me like a piece of artwork, and I learned and grew. Then they learned and grew. They learned that sometimes making biblical choices others don't understand cost friendships and positions, but if God is honored and glorified, that's all that matters. It's been an exciting journey for all of us.

We are all a work in progress. Sometimes we impose handicaps on ourselves that we don't need to. I sometimes watch people stress about things that don't really matter, and their worry won't change anything. Plus I know that suffering and challenges can teach us what we can't learn any other way. I've seen it in my own life with my grandparents and in my own family.

Oh, you want to know if I want God to heal me of my disabilities? You're funny. I've been asking Him to heal you! I really don't think I have as many special needs as some others do. I definitely want people to be healed of how they treat people like me! Don't hurry past people like me. You're missing out. We have a lot to teach you and a lot to offer if you just slow down to take some time to get to know someone special. My grandpa and grandma got to be special before they died. I think they loved me so much they wanted to be like me. I don't think it was the same for them as it is for me, but they needed special attention just like I do. Actually, at some point they needed more help than I did. I miss so many people who have died, but I know that I'll see them again. When I think of them, I say them in order of their deaths and say, "But I'll see them in heaven."

No need to cry because I know what God's word says. I am so glad that Cos and Kristina will let me live with them when Dad and Mom die. I probably won't cry then either. I'll just be happy with my new home. I think I'll visit Kathleen a lot, too!

When I hear the word *handicapped* I ask myself, "So who has the special need? Who's really handicapped?" We all are. People can build ramps and special elevators for those who need them, and we can pass all kinds of laws to make life better in school and out in the world, but what really needs to happen is that all people need to have a heart for those with special needs. We all need to be healed of different things. Some need to be healed of pride and come to know Jesus. Some need to be healed of attitude problems that keep them from walking closely with the Lord and their families. Some need to be healed of prejudice and hate. If we know Jesus, He will heal us when we ask. I know I will see Him. I said to my Mom one day, "I can't wait to see Him face to face someday." When Mom asked, "What do you think that will be like?" I knew just what it would be like. I said, "I'll touch His robe and I'll freak out!" I can't imagine how freaked out I'll be to be able to talk and walk and sing and dance and run and think—for all eternity. I know that I Corinthians 13:12 is true: "For now we see in a mirror dimly, but then face to face; now I know in part but then I shall know fully just as I also have been fully known." What a day that will be! What an eternity that will be. I hope to see you there!

YOUR STORY

You have read the same story and messages from the same messengers, yet each reader will have a different response. What will it be for you?

_____

_____

_____

_____

_____

_____

_____

_____

_____

....

Psalm 73:21-26, *"When my heart was embittered, and I was pierced within, then I was senseless and ignorant; I was like a beast before Thee. Nevertheless I am continually with Thee; Thou hast taken hold of my right hand. With Thy counsel Thou wilt guide me, and afterward receive me to glory. Whom have I in heaven but Thee? And besides Thee, I desire nothing on earth. My flesh and my heart may fail; but God is the strength of my heart and my portion forever."*

....

Please take time to visit with Joe and Cindi Ferrini at their websites:

www.joeferrini.com

www.cindiferrini.com

where you will find helpful resources, other materials, photos, contact information and a list of upcoming speaking engagements.